The Con.~~~~~~~~~~uide

THE CARIBBEAN
VOLUME 1

Dominica
Martinique
St. Lucia
St. Vincent and the Grenadines
Grenada and Carriacou
Tobago
Barbados

Colleen Ryan and Brian Savage

Text: Island background sections by Chris Doyle. All other text by Colleen Ryan.

Graphics: Brian Savage

Photographs: Brian Savage except where indicated otherwise. *Bianca C* and St. Pierre photographers unknown.

Design and Production: Roxanne Thoeny, Compass Publishing Ltd.

Editing: Sally Erdle, Compass Publishing Ltd.

Publisher's Notes

The information in this guide was correct to the best of our knowledge at the time of going to press. No warranty, expressed or implied, is made by the publishers for any errors or omissions in this publication.

Scuba diving is an inherently hazardous activity and it is the responsibility of each individual to determine the suitability of any dive for their experience level and physical condition. Where dive site conditions have been described in this book they are relevant only to the particular wind, sea state, and visibility pertaining to that specific occasion and it should be borne in mind that different conditions may significantly alter the nature of the dive.

Maps in this book are only schematic representations and all distances and depths are only approximate. No maps in this book should be used for navigation nor any depths given either on charts or in the text be used to plan the dive profile.

Distribution

USA and Worldwide:
Complete Dive Guide Publications
Maplewood Road
P.O. Box 471, Corinth, VT 05039-0471
Telephone: (802) 439-5252
E-mail: vtwdmag@sover.net
Also available through Cruising Guide Publications 1-800-330-9542

Published by:
Complete Dive Guide Publications
ISBN number 0-944428-42-8

Acknowledgements

We offer our sincere thanks to all of the dive operators on the islands covered by this book. They gave us time, information, encouragement and some terrific diving. In producing this book, we could only reflect what we saw; so thank you to the operators who showed us their diving and allowed us to experience and describe what divers to this area can expect to find.

A personal expression of thanks is due to Nicole and Michel of Aquanaut Diving in Sharm El Sheikh. They not only taught us to dive but also to appreciate the marine life, a lesson which has grown into an absorbing and rewarding interest.

About the Authors

Colleen Ryan and Brian Savage are both from England. They are both PADI dive instructors with extensive experience of diving in the Red Sea and the Caribbean. Having sailed their yacht, *Theta Volantis,* to the Caribbean, they now live aboard, carrying out research and writing about the marine environment. They combine Colleen's interest in marine life with Brian's interest in underwater photography to produce diving and sailing articles about the region.

Chris Doyle also lives aboard his yacht, *Helos,* in the Caribbean. He spends his time sailing up and down the island chain, updating his cruising guides which cover Anguilla to Venezuela. Chris is a keen diver and enthusiastic naturalist.

5

Contents

Introduction 7
　Diving Options 10
　Diving Independently 14
　Marine Life 19
　Photography 25
　Key to Symbols and Matrices 28
Dominica 33
　Dive Sites 44
　Dive Facilities 66
Martinique 75
　Dive Sites 84
　Dive Facilities 107
St. Lucia 119
　Dive Sites 128
　Dive Facilities 148
St. Vincent and the Grenadines 155
　St. Vincent 159
　　Dive Sites 164
　　Dive Facilities 179
　Bequia 181
　　Dive Sites 184
　　Dive Facilities 197
　Mustique 200
　　Dive Sites 202
　　Dive Facilities 207
　Canouan 208
　　Dive Sites 210
　　Dive Facilities 215
　Southern Grenadines 216
　　Dive Sites 218
　　Dive Facilities 229
Grenada and Carriacou 233
　Carriacou 233
　　Dive Sites 238
　　Dive Facilities 252
　Grenada 254
　　Dive Sites 262
　　Dive Facilities 280
Tobago 287
　Dive Sites 296
　Dive Facilities 327
Barbados 339
　Dive Sites 352
　Dive Facilities 377
Glossary 388
Bibliography 390
Accident and Emergency Information . . . . . Inside back cover

Getting to Know the Sidebars

Identifying marine life after a dive is fun, but to know what you are looking at while you are looking at it, to understand the behaviour you are observing and to know why something is the way it is, is even more rewarding. The sidebars have been designed to provide relevant background information about the marine life you are likely to encounter, as well as some historical information about wrecks.

Coral Reefs

Awash with Sponges 21

Plantlife on the Reef (Algae) 41

Coral—Shaping up to Its Environment 144

Red, Green, White—It's All Black Coral 173

Sunset on the Reef 190

The Pecking Order of Coral 247

Coral—Where Has All the Colour Gone 309

A Fringe, a Barrier, or a Bank? (Reef Types) 346

Fish

Frogfish—The Fish That Fishes 59

Parrots Are Not Just Found in Trees 88

Inflatable Fish—The Pufferfish Family 138

Schools Parade 195

Jaws Revisited—Sharks in the Caribbean 220

Trumpetfish—Masters of Disguise 242

Personal Valet Surface—Cleaning Symbiosis 271

Manta Rays—The Gentle Giants 300

In Defence of the Misunderstood Eel 325

Invertebrates and Reptiles

Worms That Live in the Sea 56

A Family of Fifth Cousins—The Echinoderms 105

Octopus—Not Just a Lot of Legs 133

Turtles—The Caribbean's Only Sea Water Reptile 358

Diving into St. Pierre's History 91

The Ship with Nine Lives—The *Bianca C* 276

Dry Diving in Barbados (Recompression Chamber) 351

Introduction

When we arrived in the Caribbean, expecting to do some diving, we had almost no preconception of what the diving would be like.

Two things happened quite quickly. First in St. Lucia, we dived on the stunningly beautiful Anse Chastanet Reef which succeeded in setting our expectations of Caribbean diving. Not only was the reef every bit as colourful as those in the world's premier dive areas but it had its own range of marine life, much of which was quite different from what we had seen before. The sponges in particular were a new treat for us.

Second, realising the potential for diving in the area, we went in search of a good diving guide, so that we would not miss any of the region's diving highlights.

No guide we found gave us detailed and comprehensive information for every island in the Caribbean chain. We are fortunately able to spend a few years here, getting to know the diving on each island. But had we been planning a vacation, no guide would have given us the information to choose wisely between the islands or dive stores. Also, we like to have some idea about the underwater terrain and what we are likely to see. It not only helps when choosing which sites to visit, but also enhances the anticipation and pleasure of the dive if we know what to expect.

Purpose of the Guide

In the absence of a guide that met our needs, we decided to write our own. Its purpose is to describe the diving on each of the islands, to paint a picture of the underwater environment and the onshore facilities, to detail any relevant rules and regulations, and to raise awareness of the conservation and marine life issues pertinent to the region. In summary our goal is to provide you with the information required to enable you to choose where, when, and how to dive.

Coverage

The book covers the southern half of the Eastern Caribbean Island chain, sometimes referred to as the Windward Islands, and includes the islands of Tobago and Barbados. We have organised the book geographically, from north to south; each country has a separate chapter. Where several islands make up one country, we have dealt with each island separately, but within the same chapter.

Onshore Facilities

The proportion of your time that you spend under the water will be small compared to your land time, so we have also provided information about each island in terms of other activities and attractions. In addition, you will also find information about accommodation, though it was not our intention to create a hotel guide. Where dive operators are part of a resort or operating within a hotel complex, there is usually some information in the text, especially if dive packages are offered. For detailed information about hotels and other accommodation, contact the relevant tourist office, the dive operator of your choice or your travel agent. Tourist office addresses are given in the contact information section for each country.

Climate

The Eastern Caribbean Islands are located south of the Tropic of Cancer, and offer all the benefits of a tropical climate with few of the negatives. The climate is neither uncomfortably humid nor excessively wet. While the occasional rain shower is heavy or prolonged, rainfall is generally fairly light, producing, on average, less than 6 inches per month. The last half of the year receives more rain than the comparatively drier months from January to May.

The days are relatively short, 6 a.m. to 6 p.m. during the winter months and 5 a.m. to 7 p.m. during the summer, but delightfully sunny. Night dives can be undertaken early enough to be back in time for dinner and the evening's entertainment. Suntan cream and sunglasses are needed all year round.

The trade winds provide cool breezes, keeping the temperature at a pleasingly bearable level. The temperature range is between 78° F and 85° F, with very little variation between the winter and summer months.

As scenes of hurricane damage tend to get broadcast around the world, perhaps making you wonder if this is a sensible place to visit, the hurricane season warrants some special comments.

Hurricanes form in only a narrow band around the world. The Caribbean lies precisely within this narrow band, where all the requirements for hurricane formation are met.

Although there is an official hurricane season extending from June to October, the probability of a hit does not rise significantly except during August and September. Most years, most islands will not be hit by a tropical storm of hurricane strength. Apart from 1995, which was the worst on record, the most recent hurricane that caused significant damage in the Caribbean was Hugo, in 1989. And, these days, forecasting information is reliable, giving plenty of warning and offering visitors the chance to leave, long before the wind starts to shriek.

Even though hurricanes can hit anywhere along the island chain, the northern islands (the Leeward and the Virgin Islands) are more frequent victims than the southern islands. Grenada and Tobago, for example, are generally considered to be too far south to be in the hurricane belt. The only way to be absolutely certain of avoiding a bit of unplanned excitement is to time your trip outside the hurricane season. Any time between December and May is fine, although in reality you would be very unlucky to experience a storm if you were to stretch that to include November and June. Prices are often more competitive at the beginning and end of 'high season' and resorts are not generally as busy.

One of the concerns many divers have is that the underwater environment will suffer the same destruction as the land. Fortunately, this is rarely the case. The reefs generally seem to survive remarkably well. Wave action does destroy coral, but it is often the faster growing varieties and, in any case, these areas of rubble provide a substratum for other organisms to settle and begin to grow. Another problem is silting, causing damage to both coral and sponges. If these organisms become covered in sand stirred up by the wave action during a hurricane, they are unable to feed properly.

Fortunately, they are extremely efficient self-cleaners. Starlet coral, for example, can rid itself of surface silt in as little as 30 seconds, but this is only achievable with small amounts of debris. These animals soon become choked when large quantities of sand become water-borne.

After the hurricanes have subsided, many of the dive operators inspect the reefs and have developed techniques for helping corals and sponges to rid themselves of the sand. The result is that, even after the fiercesome hurricanes of 1995, there is surprisingly little long term serious damage.

Sea Conditions

The sea temperature matches the tropical warmth of these islands, rarely falling below 78°F. Where the dive sites are located on the leeward (west) side of an island, the sea state will typically be quite calm. Dive sites that are further offshore or on the exposed windward side will have waves in the 3 to 6 feet range when the trade winds are moderate, increasing as the wind strengthens.

Although the water is warm on entry, after 45 minutes or so it can start to feel quite chilly. Most people find that a thin wet suit or a lycra body suit is necessary. Sometimes the plankton in the water can irritate sensitive skin, making some kind of cover advisable, especially for night diving.

Visibility varies by dive site, of course, and can be affected by wave action and land run-off after heavy rain. A range of between 30 and 80 feet can be expected in most areas, with over 100 feet on occasions. Visibility is better in the dry season, though there is very little variation for most of the islands. But take into consideration that Tobago and the southernmost islands are affected by the fresh water of the Orinoco River rushing in to the Gulf of Paria during the summer months. Apart from turning the water a rather lurid green, visibility can be significantly reduced.

Diving Options

Divers come in many types and so, thankfully, do the options for diving in the Caribbean. The range of accommodation and dive stores is such that everyone should be able to find the right combination to suit their needs.

Considering the options available to you, it becomes obvious that some will satisfy your needs better than others. So what are the options? There are five different types of diving holiday available in the Caribbean:

- Liveaboard dive boats

- All-inclusive resorts offering diving

- Hotels, guest houses or apartments, with diving arranged through the hotel dive store or an outside operator

- Cruise ships

- Charter yachts - bareboat or crewed

Liveaboard Dive Boats

This is a good choice if everyone in the party dives and you want to do mainly diving and not much else. Generally, it is possible to do three or more dives a day, and they often have other water sports equipment on board. At the time of writing, there are no liveaboards operating in the area covered by this book. There are quite a number operating in the Virgin Islands and the Leeward Islands, so, if this is your preferred option, you might be better to consider that area.

All-inclusive Resorts

These resorts generally specialise, serving either couples only or family groups. One of their key attractions is knowing that what you pay for your stay includes everything, so you can dive as often as you want, without incurring extra costs. Usually, though, you will be charged for any training courses that you take. All-inclusive resorts are a good choice if not everyone in the party wants to dive, as a wide variety of other activities are on offer.

The demand for diving sometimes exceeds the boat and staff capacity, making it worth checking before booking whether there will be sufficient space on the boat for you to dive every day, and whether you can dive more than once a day. Club Med in Martinique, for example, limits you to one dive a day regardless of the boat's capacity.

Hotels, Guest Houses and Apartments

This group covers everything from large multinational hotel chains to small local guest houses. The larger hotels will sometimes have a resident dive store, which usually, but not always, operates as an independent store within the hotel. It is common for dive and accommodation packages to be offered if you make the arrangements in advance.

All the islands have apartments and self-catering cottages for rent. The dive operators know of local accommodation and can make arrangements for you. This gives you the advantage of being able to choose an operator that suits you best, and then to choose suitable accommodation. Check whether the operator will pick you up from your accommodation, as the cost of taxis on the islands can be very high.

Cruise Ships

For those who like variety, a cruise ship allows you to sample the diving on several islands. Some cruise ships are equipped to offer diving using the ship's own dive boat and instructor, whereas others have arrangements with local stores. Although, in an ideal world, you should be able to experience the best of the diving on each island, beware of being taken to over-used sites or those which are nearest to the ship's anchorage, but which are not necessarily the best sites.

Before you arrive somewhere, read the relevant chapter and be specific about with whom you want to dive and where you want to dive. If you are only going to do one or two dives on each island, you want to be sure you see the best sites.

Charter Yachts

Charter yachts are available either with or without professional crew, catering for both experienced sailors who want to captain their own boat and those who are inexperienced or who simply enjoy the luxury of being looked after.

Bareboats will not have dive gear on board and you will need to rent any equipment that you do not already own. They will not be equipped with a dive compressor, requiring you to get tanks filled at dive stores along your route. Compressors are available for rent (see Carriacou and Martinique operators) but remember they will be slow—at least 30 minutes per tank—and noisy. The information matrix for each island tells you where tanks can be filled and equipment rented.

Crewed charter boats are often equipped with diving gear.

Diving from the authors' yacht, Theta Volantis. *Dive operators bring their boat alongside to pick up divers and take them straight to the dive sites.*

Your charter broker will be able to tell you exactly what is on board. Recent changes in insurance rules have meant that some yachts will not allow you to use their equipment to dive from the yacht. Instead, they require you to use a rendezvous dive facility, i.e. a local dive operator comes to the yacht to pick you up.

Choosing a Dive Operator... As a Beginner

Dive operators will only permit certified divers to dive. So, if you are not already certified, you will need to take a basic course. A number of organisations exist which offer training courses leading to certification. Those that you will find in the Caribbean include PADI, NAUI, SSI and French Federation whose training programmes are graded as CMAS levels (CMAS one star, two star, etc.)

Most commonly offered, the PADI basic training course (leading to the 'open water' certification) consists of 5 modules of academic teaching and confined water training, followed by 4 open water dives. Confined water means calm water shallow enough to stand up in, for example either a swimming pool or a sheltered beach. Usually this training takes 2 or 3 days.

After this section of the training there are four open water dives, i.e. in the sea. The same skills as have been learned so far are practised in real diving conditions. These dives are conducted over 2 days, so by the end of 4 or 5 days you become a qualified open water diver.

One option worth considering is to do the confined water training in a swimming pool near your home. That way you have only to spend the first couple of days at your dive destination completing your open water training dives, and the rest of your time you are free to enjoy diving as a certified diver. This is called the PADI referral system. The instructor who teaches you for the first half of the course gives you a referral form to verify which parts of the training you have completed.

Although the NAUI and SSI courses differ slightly, the principles are the same. When deciding where and with whom to learn, make sure you elicit the following information before you enrol:

How many people will there be in the class?

The fewer there are the better it will be for you. Though for a bit of moral support, it is good to learn with one or two other people. You are going to need some personal attention sometime during the course and an instructor has his or her hands full with more than six student divers, especially during in-water training. So try to avoid classes of more than six.

Will the instructor's time will be devoted entirely to the class?

Sometimes instructors also have to act as divemasters on the boat, i.e. supervising other divers. If so, you are not going to receive as much attention as you deserve and will find that you spend a lot of time hanging around waiting for other activities to be organised.

How long will the course last?

If it is fewer than 4 days, you are not going to be taught well.

Classroom work may not be your idea of a holiday. Why not do this part of the course near your home and finish off the course in the Caribbean?

Is the instructor someone you can get along with?

If you are making the arrangements locally, ask to meet the instructor. You are planning to spend an intense and occasionally stressful few days together, so someone you respect and with whom you can get along is a must.

What does the fee include?

Inevitably costs vary from place to place, so check what is included in the fee when comparing prices. For the course, you will need to rent all the scuba equipment required to dive, including tanks. You will need to buy a training manual, a log book, a set of dive tables, and a certification form. Some quoted prices include only some of these items.

If you are not sure if you want to do a full training course or do not have time, it is possible to do an introductory half-day course which will allow you to dive providing that you are accompanied by an instructor. The depth at which you can dive is carefully controlled by the instructor, and if you want to dive again after a period of time has elapsed, you will have to repeat the training.

Choosing a Dive Operator... As an Experienced Diver

Personal taste is much more the determining factor for experienced divers, and Caribbean dive operators cover a wide range of styles. There are small one-person owner operated dive stores as well as large scale, highly organised operations.

Some people will prefer to dive with the latter, knowing that there are regular boat dives at set times each day, employing fast comfortable boats. Others might want to find a local dive operator who will also be able to offer information about the life and culture of the island. Some dive stores have particular areas of specialisation, e.g. photography, conservation or wreck diving. See the diving facilities section and information matrix in the relevant island chapter for information about the operators.

There are a few additional factors you may want to consider to help you make your choice. For example, the Caribbean is blessed with sunny weather all year round so some shade on the dive boat is advisable for anyone with fair skin, and especially where the dive sites are some distance away.

Some operators have large purpose-built dive boats and while this may mean diving with a large number of other divers, entry and exits are usually easy. Other operators use local fishing boats or other types of small boats not designed as dive boats. This results in a smaller, more intimate, dive group but can demand feats of athleticism to re-enter after a dive.

Whatever your personal taste, the general standard of diving operations is good, and you are unlikely to be disappointed if you make your selection based on what is important to you.

Diving Independently

If you are planning to do your diving from a yacht, you will probably want to experience a mixture of independent diving and local operator-led dives. There are many sites where it is only possible to dive safely with a dive operator, and you will enjoy the benefits of local knowledge. Most good divemasters know exactly where to find a seahorse or a tame eel to amuse you.

NOTE: By diving independently, we mean diving without the services of a professional dive operator. We DO NOT mean diving alone. NEVER dive without another certified diver as a buddy.

Many divers also enjoy planning and organising their own dives, and by exercising proper care this can be a rewarding way to dive, enabling you to explore the site at your own pace. We find that we see a great deal more when there are not large numbers of divers in the water at the same time.

Our intention is to give you a few tips that will make diving independently safer and more enjoyable. But this is not a substitute for proper training, nor do we suggest that any site is suitable for independent diving regardless of conditions. You are responsible for determining the safety of each dive you make independently. Many people feel more comfortable leaving that decision in the hands of a professionally trained and licensed local dive operator. A good compromise is to ask the dive leader if you and your buddy can do the dive apart from the rest of the dive group. Some operators allow this when they have checked out your diving skills.

Independent Diving Regulations

First check whether independent diving is allowed. Currently it is not permitted in Dominica and the Soufriere Marine Management Area (SMMA) of St. Lucia. There are plans for marine parks in other islands that may result in restrictions being placed on independent diving. It is possible that you will need to buy a permit to dive in a marine park, but often it means that buoys have been installed making independent diving easier.

Training

Most people who dive independently are trained up to the level of a PADI rescue diver or equivalent. An open water (novice) certification will not have provided you with sufficient training in underwater navigation, dive planning and search and rescue techniques. If you do not have a current first aid qualification you will also not be sufficiently familiar with resuscitation techniques. A rescue diver course fills in these gaps.

Of course, experience counts for a great deal, but if you have always dived with a divemaster-led group then your navigation skills may not be adequate. It seems so easy when the divemaster gets you back to the boat with precisely the right amount of air remaining that you could be forgiven for believing that some universal rule is at work. Well, it is not; nor is there any luck involved. Instead, it is well-trained divemasters drawing on their skills to ensure that it is a safe and comfortable dive for all concerned.

Equipment

If you are going to dive independently, you will need either to rent or provide your own equipment. Our information matrices for each island list the operators who have equipment for rent. If you are using your own equipment make sure it has been serviced recently and that tanks have current test dates. Operators will not fill out-of-date tanks. Visual inspections can generally be arranged on the islands, but hydrostatic tests cannot always be organised locally and may take some time.

It is sensible to carry a comprehensive first aid kit and you should check that the yacht you are diving from has one. It is unlikely, however, that the yacht will carry oxygen so you should make sure you know where the nearest supply can be located. Most dive stores will have an oxygen kit as, of course, will hospitals. Speed is vitally important in dive related injuries and fast access to oxygen is essential.

There are very few shore dives in the area covered by this book. Therefore, if you want to dive independently, you will need to dive from a dinghy. Small yacht dinghies do not take seas well, so do not be over-ambitious about the distance you can cover to a dive site. Remember if the dive site is down wind, you will have a very different ride on the return journey, and either sea or wind may have strengthened. The reliability, or otherwise, of the dinghy's outboard motor is another consideration.

Bareboat dinghies tend not to be designed with diving in mind, and the outboards suffer from having a different user each week. In our experience, bareboat charterers enjoy diving more with dive operators, free of the stress of having to locate and safely organise the dive for themselves. And, with some imaginative dive packages around, it can be as cheap as renting equipment and getting tanks filled.

> ## EQUIPPING THE DINGHY
>
> The dive site may not be far from your yacht but it will almost certainly be beyond shouting distance, so we suggest you use our dinghy equipment checklist:
>
> - **Hand held VHF radio**
> - **Flares**
> - **Spares for dive equipment (O-rings, fin/mask strap, extra weight)**
> - **Tools for outboard**
> - **Adequate mooring line and dinghy anchor**
> - **Drinking water**
> - **Suntan cream and a T-shirt or towel**
> - **Basic first aid kit**
> - **Dive flag and surface marker float for drift dives**

Anchoring the Dinghy

In some areas, buoys are provided, and it is a simple task to attach the dinghy securely to the buoy. Others may arrive to share the buoy while you are diving, so do not tie the line to the buoy too short.

Where it is necessary to anchor, please do not anchor on the coral. Find a sand area, even if it will involve a short swim to the reef. Alternatively, dive down and tie a line to a rock. Most of the anchor-related damage to reefs is caused by the chain or rope so, even if you anchor in sand, make sure the rope/chain will not scrape across the reef as the dinghy swings. Use as short a scope as possible, whether anchored or tied to a rock, or put a float on the line to keep it off the bottom.

Underwater Navigation

It is not our intention to provide training in underwater navigation in this section. We want only to refresh your memory about some of the key issues and to reiterate the importance of carefully monitoring your location underwater.

In terms of equipment, a compass is essential and, if you have a poor memory or are likely to become absorbed in an examination of the marine life, take a slate on which you can jot down key markers and compass bearings.

Your eyes are, of course, your most important pieces of equipment, so get in to the habit of noticing special features which will help you to retrace your route. Make a mental note of which way sea fans are bending or the direction the fish are facing. Both are good indicators of the direction of current.

Be especially vigilant for currents. These can change direction and strength dramatically while you are diving or approaching underwater features such as headlands. If you are caught in current remember it is likely (but not always) to be stronger at the surface. The bottom causes drag and you will find less current there. Do not swim into current, swim across it, towards the shore.

Practice swimming along a reciprocal course and get used to how many fin kicks you normally make in a given distance. Do not wait until you need to use these skills in earnest. As with any diving skills, practice removes the stress when you need to tackle underwater problems.

Drift Dives

Often currents make a drift dive the only viable option. If you have had proper training, these are safe and easy to organise, providing that you use a surface marker buoy and brief your top cover properly. Without a surface marker buoy there is no way that the top cover boat can be certain to be there when you surface. Dinghies drift at a different speed from divers, and currents at depth can be not only a different speed but a different direction from those on the surface.

Even with a surface marker, be very careful when diving around headlands. Local fishermen have very fast and powerful boats and know exactly how close they can cut in to the rocks. On numerous occasions we have had fishing boats zoom over us while diving. So do not surface on a headland; start and finish the dive around the corner. If you have to surface, become as visible as possible as quickly as possible by fully inflating your BCD and staying close to other divers.

Locating Dive Sites

To some extent this depends upon your idea of 'good'. If you mean the most popular sites on the island, then all that is necessary is to watch where the dive boats go. We have indicated where there are recognised sites suitable for independent diving along with enough information for you to locate them. Check the list of dive sites for each island, on which we have used this dinghy symbol to indicate the dives that are suitable to do from a yacht's dinghy. See the description of the dive in the main text for further information about the dive profile and how to locate the site.

Cost

Some crewed charter yachts are fully equipped for diving, but remember that if neither you nor the yacht carries equipment and compressor, the cost of hiring equipment (on average $35 per day) plus tank fills ($5 per tank) will not work out any cheaper than paying an operator to take you for a dive.

Rules, Regulations & Preservation

Each island differs somewhat in the specificity of its conservation rules, but there are many common elements. Taking lobster and spearfishing on reefs that are dived are either illegal or seriously frowned upon. What is the point of admiring it in the morning and killing it in the afternoon?

Independent of any specific laws laid down by each island, there is a universal acceptance of the unwritten rules governing the protection of the coral reefs. In many ways, the reefs are admirably resilient. But coral is very sensitive to factors such as water temperature and salinity. There is usually little we can do about these, but man-made pollution is our responsibility.

Pollution puts nutrients into the water, promoting the growth of algae on the coral, eventually causing it to die. Algae takes hold on damaged areas of coral, and damage can be caused by something as apparently insignificant as you placing your hand on it. Where your fingers have touched, the coral's protective covering of mucus will be destroyed and the polyps probably killed. Just the sort of spot that algae can alight upon and begin to grow. Soon the algae will spread across the coral, blocking access to light and food. The brain coral you admired today may be dead when you visit the site next year; please do not be the person responsible for its demise.

You will find that not just dive operators and marine park officials have opinions about how you should behave toward the underwater environment. Many recreational divers are now very aware and protective of the needs of the coral reefs. Careless finning, wearing excessive weights, and handling the marine life are all considered bad diving practices. You will not be a popular dive buddy if you do not show due respect to the reef community.

To protect the reef, your reputation and your conscience, we suggest the following:

Do not wear gloves. You will feel more vulnerable but you will be less likely to touch and you will improve your buoyancy skills by learning to control your position without hanging on to things.

Improve your buoyancy. Many stores offer specialist courses in buoyancy control. The course usually takes only a day or two, and many operators make it good fun by having you swim through hoops and play various buoyancy control games.

Be properly weighted. Being too heavy makes it difficult to swim horizontally, increasing the likelihood of kicking the reef below you. As a side benefit, you will also use less air if you are properly weighted.

Become fin aware. Know where your fins are at all times, ensuring they are not making contact with the reef. Keep them away from the bottom so that you do not stir up sediment.

Tidy yourself up. Loose hoses, dangling slates and sound devices drag along the reef leaving a trail of destruction behind you.

You will not only be seen to be a better diver but there will still be a reef for your children to see.

The marine life in the Caribbean is as lush and varied as the flora and fauna of the islands. Growing awareness of the need for conservation means that most reefs are still in good condition, with an abundance of fish. However, reefs close to shore tend to suffer from over-fishing, reducing the number of large species.

Marine Life

Coral

There are around 70 different coral species in the Caribbean, but only a handful accounts for over 90 percent of what you will see. Both elkhorn and staghorn coral will be found, the latter being more typical on the sheltered leeward side of the reefs. These, along with star coral, are important reef builders. Several types of brain coral occur, often up to several feet across. Tobago has the second largest recorded brain coral in the world. But we like the majestic pillar coral, which grow up to 10 feet high. Unlike most other stony corals, the polyps are often extended during the day, giving a furry look to the pillars.

Pencil and finger coral are common, often in wide expanses, glowing yellow in the reflected sunlight. Patches of flower coral perch like flowers frozen to stone. Boulder coral will be found around all the islands. And, look out for the fire coral which occurs in both the branching and encrusting varieties, and will cause a burn-like sting if touched.

A Word on 'Soft' Corals

The Caribbean does not have true soft corals, and anyone who has dived in the Indo-Pacific region, where soft corals are abundant, may be confused by hearing a divemaster brief you about how good the site is for soft corals. You will not find any. But you will see octocorals and antipatharians (black coral) instead. Octocorals take the form of sea fans, gangly whips, plumes like ostrich feathers, and bushy sea rods. Their polyps, extended even during the day, create a soft furry covering on a flexible skeleton, which has attracted the term 'soft' corals. They

Tiny fish flit among gangly sea rods and deepwater sea fans, common octocorals on Caribbean reefs.

more than make up for the absence of the delicate pastel blooms of the Indo-Pacific reefs.

The descriptor 'soft corals' is so widely used in the area that we have adopted the local terminology for the purpose of this book.

Sponges

If you are new to Caribbean diving, you may not at first realise that a lot of what you are looking at on the reef is not coral, but sponge. Often it is the sponges that contribute most of the colour on the reef. Some seem to be almost luminescent. The azure vase sponges are perhaps the most obvious and eye-catching of the varieties you will see.

Sponges occur across the whole region, as they thrive in a wide range of conditions: where there is current and where there is not, in dark recesses as well as on the light part of the reef, shallow and deep.

Apart from their intrinsic interest for divers, they also play host to many other reef invertebrates and fish, as careful inspection will reveal.

Fish

The reef fish species are too numerous to discuss in any general way, so we mention here just a few that we have not seen before in other parts of the world or which captured our imaginations.

Look out for spotted drums under overhangs. These are quite large (6" to 12"), black and white, half spotted and half striped like a cross between a zebra and a dalmatian. The whole spectacle is then finished off with a Mohawk style dorsal fin. You will know one if you see one.

Porcupinefish will be found in similar nooks and are the largest pufferfish we have ever come across, growing up to 3 feet in length. They have large cow-like eyes, through which they peer at you, hoping you have not spotted them. You will invariably see trunkfish when diving or snorkelling anywhere in the area. They share the same large eyes, but add to these comical puckered lips and tiny rapidly moving fins that seem not to have kept pace with the growth of the body.

Frogfish and seahorses are the main favourites with Caribbean divers. Although increasingly rare, they are still present. We saw both in Dominica, St. Lucia, and the Grenadines.

Around some of the islands you will find turtles. Hawksbill and green turtles are the most common varieties. Historically they have been caught for their meat and their shell, but many islands are outlawing the practice. Turtle watching during the breeding season (May to September) is popular and helps to communicate the importance of preserving the breeding sites. Dive stores can advise you or arrange trips to watch the eggs being laid or hatching; but be prepared to sit up all night, quietly and with no camera flashes to disturb the process. Underwater, turtles will not necessarily swim away if you hover close by and do not move towards them.

Awash with Sponges

Between 1840 and 1940 a substantial sponging industry operated in the Bahamas, employing 500 ships and 2000 open boats, until a mysterious fungal infection halted this trade. Sponges have since recovered and synthetic substitutes have removed the human demand. But generally, sponges seem quite good at repelling predators. They taste and smell so bad that, with the exception of angelfish and butterflyfish, reef fish will not eat them. A few sponges will irritate human skin if you come into contact with them.

Sponges bridge the gap between colonies of one celled animals (having no internal systems, such as digestive or circulatory systems) and multi-celled animals having systems serving the whole organism. They have the least amount of cellular organisation of any multi-cellular organism known to man yet, they are more than a colony of independent creatures. They do act as one single organism. To prove the point, one gory experiment involved macerating a sponge in a blender. Within a few days the sponge had reconstructed itself, in the same shape. Not bad for a creature with no brain.

Sponges are not soft and pliant as people expect. Calcium carbonate or silica spicules give them a rigid structure. Water moves through the sponge through tiny openings (incurrent pores). Plankton is removed and the water expelled through one large or several smaller exhaust holes (excurrent openings). To gain one ounce in body weight, a sponge will pass one ton of water through its cells.

In the absence of a digestive system, ameboid cells travel through the sponge, transferring food,

Three foot tall yellow tube sponges sit on the reef top like chimney stacks.

removing waste and building spicules. Unlike coral, sponges do not have zooxanthellae so are not light dependent and can grow in caves and under overhangs as well as much deeper than divers venture.

On the reef, sponges compete with coral for space and food. Some bore into coral, eventually killing it. A more beneficial relationship exists with star boulder coral as the sponge grows underneath the flattened plate of the coral, protecting it from boring sponges and other damaging organisms.

Sponges make many positive contributions to reef life. Decorator crabs place sponges on their back, providing a convincing camouflage. Worms, shrimps, gobies and brittle stars make their home in sponges. Scientists have discovered eight antibiotics in fire sponge. Two are currently widely used in western medicine.

The most dramatic of the Caribbean sponges are the giant vases. Despite growing only about an inch a year they can grow to the size of a diver. They also come in a variety of other forms including tubes, balls, rope, and encrusting species.

Large rays, including eagle rays, electric rays, stingrays and the lovely mantas, occur throughout the region. If mantas are a high priority for you, then Tobago is the place to find them. Eagle rays are generally shy, allowing you to catch a glimpse rather than close inspection. If many divers enter the water together, they will usually fly away before you have time to see them. So, if you are first in the water, look down from the surface and you may get lucky. Stingrays lie in the sand and will not move if you approach them quietly.

The Caribbean has sharks. The most common sighting will be a nurse shark. They are often seen sleeping during the day under an overhang, tail protruding. Found mostly in the southern islands, they are particularly common in the Grenadines.

Whales pass through the islands from November to April. Dominica particularly seems to attract them. We have seen sperm whales off Bequia, St. Lucia and St. Vincent, but whale watching trips here are not on such an organised footing as in Dominica.

Critters

Most of the lobsters you will see are Caribbean spiny lobsters. They do not have large claws, having long conical antennae instead. Find out what the local regulations are before you go hunting. The open season is generally November to April, and there are often size restrictions or rules concerning the use of scuba gear and spearguns. Slipper lobsters are also reasonably common, along with one or two smaller varieties such as the red banded lobster. Other common crustaceans include the delicate arrow crabs and cleaner shrimps.

If your dive takes you across a sand area, you may see trails leading to the Caribbean's jumbo snails, Queen conch, up to a foot across. Though not as polished when attached to their owners as the shells you will see for sale ashore, these are impressive looking creatures. Approach with care and you will easily spot the

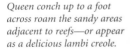

Queen conch up to a foot across roam the sandy areas adjacent to reefs—or appear as a delicious lambi creole.

protruding eye stalks and extended proboscis. Conch, generally called lambi on restaurant menus, is an important source of food on the islands. It is delicious curried or in a Creole sauce. If you buy raw conch, it must be beaten and cooked without salt initially or it will be too tough to eat.

Worms are another frequently seen form of marine life in the area, though they bear very little resemblance to the brown wriggly things from your garden at home. These worms have become sessile, living inside a tube buried in coral. The most delightful variety is the aptly named Christmas tree worms. They decorate the already lovely coral and do not disappear back into their calcareous tubes as long as you approach slowly. You will also see some of the wriggly varieties, although dressed in brighter colours than garden worms and often with bristles. One such variety is the poisonous fireworm.

Wrecks

In addition to the natural marine life, there are a number of wrecks around the Caribbean, including some which have been sunk recently. The wrecks range from a 30 year old 600-foot cruise liner in Grenada to a dozen century-old ships sunk off St. Pierre, Martinique, when Mount Pelée erupted at the beginning of this century. The island with most wrecks is Barbados. Many of Barbados' wrecks have been deliberately sunk as dive sites, and can be safely penetrated. St. Lucia, Tobago and St. Vincent have all sunk ships recently to extend their range of dive sites.

Dangerous Marine Life

Many marine plants and animals have defence mechanisms, most of which are quite harmless to humans, leaving the underwater world a safe place for divers. There are painful exceptions to the rule, though divers who are well informed are still unlikely to be hurt. Dangerous marine life is not lurking behind a coral head waiting to spring on an unsuspecting diver and adherence to a 'do not touch' rule will avoid all problems.

Touching coral or sponges will almost always harm the organism more than you. A small amount of damage to the surface of these creatures is enough to allow algae to take hold and can eventually lead to the death of the organism.

There are, in addition, a few sponges that will irritate skin if you come into contact with them. These include the varieties known as Brown Volcano, Touch Me Not, and Fire Sponge. If you experience irritation apply vinegar but, better still, avoid touching them. Fire coral occurs in both the branching and encrusting varieties and will cause a painful burn-like sting if touched.

Stinging jelly fish are fairly rare in the Caribbean. The highly toxic Portuguese man-of-war is found on the surface, although we have not seen one in all the time we have been here. There is also a stinging cauliflower (yes, it looks like one) which is also uncommon, fortunately, as it is highly toxic, and the slightly more com-

This fireworm's bristles may look purely decorative but they deliver a painful sting.

mon upsidedown jelly fish which is toxic but only very mildly so.

The one to guard against is the 3 to 4 inch-long sea wasp. These are highly toxic and victims should be treated for shock. Medical attention should be sought if the symptoms are severe. They are only a problem to divers at night, as they swim near the surface at this time and are attracted to the diver's light. A wetsuit should provide adequate protection.

You may see fireworms crawling on the reef. Pretty bristles along the length of the worm are very painful and difficult to remove. More obviously threatening are spiny sea urchins. No one is left in any doubt that the long sharp spines will inflict an unpleasant wound. They are easy to avoid with good buoyancy control, but take particular care in shallow water, especially if there is any surge.

Some fish, most notably scorpionfish, can be a hazard to careless divers. They look like a piece of encrusted rock, but carry highly toxic spines along their back. Placing your hand carelessly on a 'rock' could have serious consequences. The other well-disguised fish that can inflict a serious wound is the stingray. They have a habit of half burying themselves in the sand, and while they will always flee if given a chance, if a diver inadvertently stands on one it will lash out with its tail. As well as a painful sting, the ray's spine can cause a deep wound.

There are many views on how to treat such injuries but soaking the wound in hot water for 30 minutes or more is widely advised. Victims should be kept under observation and, in the case of stingray wounds, medical assistance should be sought.

There are sharks and barracuda around the reefs but neither pose a real threat to divers. The sharks are generally nurse sharks (round nose, grey, from 5 to 10 feet) or reef sharks (pointed nose, silvery, 5 to 8 feet). Neither will cause you any problems unless you are spearfishing or you pick a fight with them.

There are more injuries to divers caused by their own care-lessness on boats than are ever experienced from the marine environment. Tanks dropped on toes and damaged backs from lifting equipment are far greater hazards. So take care. Sit down when the boat is moving, ask for help with lifting, assist your buddy and do not leave your gear littered around as a trap for other divers or the boat's crew.

For further information about coral reefs and marine life, check the list of sidebars shown at the beginning of this chapter. The sidebars describe the habitat and behaviour of various members of the reef community.

Underwater Photography

When we first learned to dive, mastering the diving skills was all we could manage. However, we soon wanted to retain some of our experiences and bring them back to the surface, so photography was an obvious next step for us. We quickly learned that there was much more to this than taking a few snaps as you do on the surface. Firstly, most subjects on the surface are reasonably controllable; you can ask them to move to the left a bit or easily change your position to get a good shot. Also, by and large, the ground does not move while you are taking the shot. Our first attempts were a bit like trying to get a shot of a moving yo-yo while bouncing on a trampoline.

Quite soon a number of things changed. Our buoyancy control improved dramatically, taking care of the trampoline side of the equation. Secondly, we learned that trying to get a good picture 'like you see in the magazines' was almost impossible without some serious investment in equipment.

Nowadays there are a number of options available to the budding underwater photographer. A number of dive stores rent underwater housings that hold a disposable camera. This is a great start for little initial investment. You can snap away without wasting huge sums of money on equipment you hardly ever use. Alternatively, some stores rent purpose-built underwater cameras, giving you the opportunity to try it out before you make the big investment.

A few tips when using a camera underwater:

Make sure you get a camera with a flash. Below 5 to 10 feet the light changes dramatically, the spectrum disappears from the red end as you go deeper. A flash is required to replace the red end of the spectrum, otherwise all your shots will be composed of only shades of blue.

Let the fish come to you rather than the other way round. We would put money on your first film being composed of blank frames, or fish tails. The first instinct on seeing a fish you want to photograph is to move towards it. Aggressive behaviour from a big object will cause the fish to swim away. Hang in the water and let the fish swim around until it comes near enough to photograph.

Agree some simple signals with your buddy. Before you dive, agree on a signal for 'move closer to that object', and so on.

Get as close to subjects as you can. Particles in the water will bounce back light from the flash, giving your shots a speckled look. Proximity reduces the number of particles.

Getting near to objects raises one of the biggest issues regarding underwater photography. Some dive operators will not allow photographers unless they have seen them dive first. Why? Because having a camera seems to take over a person's mind. They focus only on the shot they want and not on what is happening to them or the environment around them. Breath control is important to stop you bouncing up and down, and breath holding tends to make you rise, with well-known results and problems. Better to use very long shallow breaths while composing the shot.

Much more important is that you may have managed to get the definitive shot of a lizardfish, but you also managed to trash 10 square feet of reef with your fins, knees and elbows. Hence dive stores do not like photographers, at least bad ones. Become a reef friendly photographer by following these guidelines:

No shot is worth damaging the reef. If the shot you want requires you to get close to the reef, be honest with yourself about whether your buoyancy skills are up to it, especially as you will be distracted while taking the shot.

Check out the area where your fins, knees and elbows will be. Make sure no part of your body or equipment will touch the reef.

Use your buddy to watch where your body is. Make sure you have a prearranged 'stop' signal if he or she notices you are about to cause damage.

Do not move a live object. The desire to get a better shot is not an excuse for interfering with the marine life.

Use buoyancy control to get clear of the reef. You have the shot you wanted, you did not damage the reef, but you have to get away from the reef. Use breathing and buoyancy rather than fins to elevate yourself until you are clear.

Note which objects will be OK to touch. If you need to steady yourself during the shot, before you get into position, look for bare rock or sand. If you need more than a light touch from a single finger, you need to practice your buoyancy more.

Finally, tell the dive store when you make the booking that you want to take photographs. Because photographers want to move slower and cover less ground, they are generally incompatible with a mixed dive group. If the store will permit it, make your own dive plan. Many stores in the Caribbean will not allow you to dive away from the main group without a dive leader, so you need to prearrange this. Most of the larger stores have told us they would prefer to assign a dive leader to a photographer, so ask if this would be possible. You will get much better shots.

Information About the Dive Sites

This guide includes a description of almost all the acknowledged dive sites of each island. Space neither allowed us to write about each dive in detail nor provide a site plan for every dive. Instead, we chose a representative sample for each island to describe in detail, and have produced summarised descriptions for the remainder. On the island maps and the list of all the dives, we have colour coded in green those sites we have reviewed in detail. Our choices were determined by what the local operators considered were either the best dives or those which represented a cross section of the diving of that island. We did most of the dives with local operators; a few we did independently from our yacht's dinghy.

Although we have dived some sites many times, many of the sites we visited only once. Consequently, our description of the dive is based on the conditions on that particular occasion. Bear in mind that a gentle dive can turn into a rip roaring drift under the influence of currents and tides. When we knew that we were diving in exceptional circumstances, we have commented to that effect in the text, stating whether visibility, current or sea life was different from the norm.

Clearly, we do not expect you to find the same grouper in the same hole, or the same turtle posing for photographs under the same overhang, as we found. Our purpose in describing the marine life is to illustrate the type of life you might see, and to convey the atmosphere of the dive site. This should help photographers to make decisions about which lens to take, those interested in sea life to bone up on the relevant type, and we hope it will help raise your awareness of and pleasure in the marine environment.

All the dives described can be dived within PADI recreational dive limits. There are dives described in this book which are sometimes dived using decompression tables. We have quoted technical diving operations who carry out this type of diving, where relevant. Please note, when we describe a wall dive as starting at 15 feet and dropping to 1,500 feet, we do not intend that you or anyone should dive it to that depth! It is intended only to provide you with interesting background information.

We have not rated the dives in terms of their quality. Our experience of this type of rating in other areas was that what makes a 5-star dive to one diver may equate to boredom for another. We hope that by describing our experience of the dive, you can decide whether it is the type of site that will appeal to you. And, taking the descriptions of the sites for the island as a whole, you should be able to get a feel for the type of diving you can expect.

Symbols

For those dives where we have given a detailed dive profile, we have indicated the difficulty of the dive using 1, 2 or 3 tanks. The number of tanks relates to the difficulty of the dive under normal circumstances. By this we mean in the typical wind and sea conditions and visibility that are generally found at that site. In determining the ratings we have taken into account the following: depth, current, surface conditions, descent and ascent procedures and underwater terrain.

A dive that is required to be done as a drift is not classified as

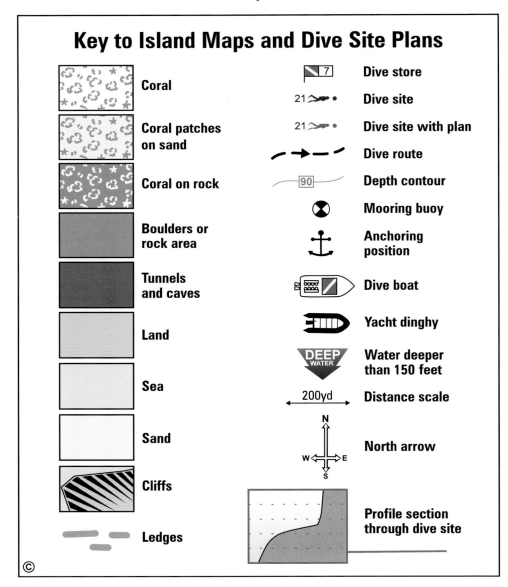

difficult unless other circumstances require it, e.g. speed of current, surface conditions, etc. If you have not done a drift dive before, we advise you to inform the divemaster so that he or she can ensure you are properly briefed.

 Single tank: a straightforward dive, suitable for all divers, including those recently qualified or who have not dived for some time.

 Two tanks: a more difficult site, suitable for those who have experience of that type of dive. You should be quite confident, have reasonable buoyancy and air consumption, and consider yourself a fairly competent diver. Operators may require you to be an advanced diver, so have log book evidence of your experience and/or do a check-out dive first.

 Three tanks: a complex or technical dive, requiring special training and/or proof of experience, e.g. wreck penetration, decompression diving. You should be a confident diver, have good buoyancy control and air consumption and be a competent diver. There are only three such dives in this guide; all are wreck dives. They are the *Bianca C* in Grenada, the *SS Stavronikita* in Barbados and some of the wrecks in St. Pierre. All of these dives can be made as non-decompression dives, although in the case of the *Bianca C* and St. Pierre parts of the wrecks are beyond the maximum depth of non-decompression tables.

If you are using an underwater camera with interchangeable lens, you will need to choose which lens to use before you descend. We have indicated which lens we would select on the assumption of normal conditions. Of course, what you actually see on the day will dictate whether it was the right choice. Please do not blame us if you take down a macro lens and see a hammerhead. Think creatively—what a great shot that close up of its eye will be!

 C = close up or macro

 W = wide angle or standard

Each chapter has a section on diving facilities that includes information about the dive operators. Every dive operator we have described was visited by us. We did not rely upon hearsay or brochures. Our visits enabled us to see how the store was managed, sense the atmosphere, talk to employees and chat to people who were diving with the store. Often we visited the store on more than one occasion. In most cases we dived with the store at least once.

Information About the Dive Stores

In writing about each store, we have endeavoured to be objective and scrupulously fair. The more the store told us, the fuller we were able to make our description of their operation. And, we have tried to bring out the particular positive aspects of each store, both quantitative and qualitative. Having said that, inevitably different operations will suit different types of people, so we have not made personal recommendations. Instead, we hope we have provided you with the type of information that will enable you to decide which operator is most likely to meet your requirements.

Remember that we have described the stores as we found them. A change in ownership can markedly effect both the level and tone of the service. We welcome comments based on your own experiences, which we will take into account for the next update.

As the diving market in the Caribbean matures, dive stores have to compete by differentiating themselves. Some have the benefits of an advantageous location, others invest in expensive boats, attractive deals and packages are offered, and many operators are trying to offer a higher level of service. One increasingly common manifestation of this is stores that not only carry your equipment but also put it together for you. We were always very grateful to anyone prepared to take some of the hard work out of diving, but we do have a reservation about this practice that warrants airing.

If you are renting equipment, it will not be very familiar to you. If, in addition, someone puts it together for you, you have missed an opportunity to familiarise yourself with it. We witnessed at least one occasion when a diver underwater was unfamiliar with the operation of their BCD, turning a minor incident into a near accident. Of course, all equipment works in much the same way, but when a problem occurs underwater it is too late to start working out the nuances of that particular item. Mistaking the inflator button for the deflation button can endanger you and other divers. If your equipment has been put together for you, spend some time going over it before entering the water, and check with the divemaster if you are in any doubt how it works.

Reading the Operators' Matrix

The matrix is intended to be a convenient summary of the key information relating to all the dive operators on an island. It was current at the time of writing; a copy was sent to each dive store immediately before going to press with a request that they verify the information and notify us of any changes.

Nevertheless, some changes will have taken place since printing, so we suggest that you check with the dive store before making any firm decisions based on this information. In particular you should take into account the following:

Instructors/Divemasters: Stores hire and fire all the time, so the number of instructors/divemasters may change. But, a store normally employing two instructors is unlikely to change to one with ten and vice versa. Thus the matrix should give you a reliable idea of the rough size of the operation.

Languages: Many operators have a sprinkling of several languages but the matrix only shows those languages in which the store can offer tuition, both oral and written. Some operators have instruction manuals in several languages though they can only teach in English. Very often the availability of a language is dependent upon the presence of one instructor. If that instructor leaves, they are not necessarily replaced with someone with the same languages. If it is essential that tuition is available in other than English, check with the dive store before making a booking.

Staff

A definition of the categories in the Operators' Matrix, found at the end of each chapter.

STAFF	**Instructors**	Number of certified instructors
	Divemasters	Number of certified divemasters in addition to the number of dive instructors
	Diving Associations	**C** = CMAS; **N** = NAUI; **P** = PADI; **S** = SSI
	Languages	**D** = Danish; **E** = English; **F** = French; **G** = German; **I** = Italian; **S** = Spanish;
BOATS	**Dive Boats**	Number of boats available to take out divers
	Shaded Boats	Number of (above) boats with shade
	Max. Divers per Boat	Maximum number of divers
	Time to Dive Sites	Time in minutes to nearest and farthest site
	Dives per Day	Normal number of dives per day, excluding night dives; **OD** = on demand
	Pick Up by Boat from	**C** = Cruise ship; **R** = Resort or hotel; **Y** = Yacht
EQUIPMENT	**Equipment Sets**	Maximum number of full sets, i.e. BCD, regulator etc.
	Dive Equip. for Sale	**1** = Few items; **2** = Modest range of equipment; **3** = Wide range of equipment
	Dive Equip. for Rent	● = Willing to rent to independent divers
	Photo Equip. for Rent	● = Camera, housing and/or video for rent
	Tank Fills	● = For tanks with in date inspection
	Equipment Servicing	● = Willing to service customer's own equipment
	O₂ on Boat	● = Oxygen carried on dive boat
	VHF on Boat	● = VHF radio carried on dive boat
MISC.	**Owned by Resort**	● = Wholly owned by resort or hotel
	Other Water Sports	● = Can arrange other watersports e.g. kayaks, windsurfers, water skiing
	Pers. Liab. Insurance	● = Has professional or commercial liability insurance

Boats

Dive Boats: Almost every dive store 'has a new boat coming'. Well, we only included the ones we could see. The number of divers per boat refers to the number of divers the operator considers the maximum for comfort. Often, the boat is insured for more than that number, so you could find yourself on the boat with rather more people than we have quoted. However, we never saw the maximum numbers we were quoted exceeded.

Equipment

Dive Equip. for Rent: This refers to equipment which can be rented by people not diving with the operator. For example, people on charter boats who wish to have dive equipment on board. All stores rent equipment to divers who are diving with the store.

Photo Equipment for Rent: Included in this category are those stores that have underwater housings and those with underwater cameras such as Nikonos and Sea & Sea systems. As the housing is the most common offer, we have mentioned in the narrative about each store when full underwater camera or video equipment is available.

Tank Fills: Stores that offer this service will want to see that the tank's inspection record is up to date. You will not be able to get out-of-date tanks filled.

Equipment Servicing: Many stores are willing to service your equipment, but getting spares is a problem. If you have the same make as the dive store, you should be OK. Where a particular make is prevalent, we have mentioned this in the 'Diving Facilities' section for that island. Many basic spares such as O-rings will fit several makes, but anything more complex could be a problem. We advise you to have your equipment serviced before arriving in the Caribbean.

Misc.

Owned by Resort: Although many stores operate on the premises of resorts, they are independent of them. If a store appears in this column then it is a wholly owned part of the resort. This does not mean it is necessarily an all-inclusive resort. See the narrative about each store for clarification.

The list of dive operators given alongside the island map indicates when a store is located in an hotel or resort. Those marked * are wholly owned by the resort, the remainder being independent stores operating on the property of an hotel. Where no resort is indicated, the store is located on independent premises.

Insurance: Included here are professional liability insurance and commercial insurance, e.g. a resort's general liability policy. We have taken the store's word for whether they have insurance. We did not check the insurance policy, so if this information is important to you, it is essential that you check before making a booking.

Dominica

Wild, exotic and with only a dash of tourism, Dominica is known as the "Nature Island of the Caribbean" for good reason. Towering mountains rise to over 4,000 feet, attracting a plentiful supply of rain on the island's rich volcanic soil. Greenery bursts forth from every corner, climbing, spreading and even tumbling over cliff faces like a lush emerald waterfall. Against the green backdrop, there are brightly coloured flowers, lots of birds, tree frogs and butterflies.

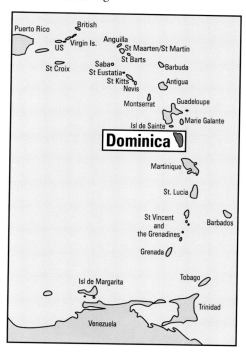

The ample rain that falls on Dominica's pristine rainforests makes its way to the sea by way of sparkling rivers and waterfalls. At even higher elevations, crater lakes and enchanting cloud forest reign. Other natural wonders include hot waterfalls and the second biggest boiling lake in the world.

It is difficult to believe that this magnificent island is a mere 25 miles long and 10 wide. But do not let the dimensions fool you; it takes some hours to drive from one end to the other.

With all this beauty you might wonder why Dominica is not a hotbed of tourism. The answer is written in the sand. The image most tourists have of the Caribbean is of long pale-gold beaches backed by swaying palm trees. Dominica does have beaches, and a couple contain a fair proportion of whitish sand, but they do not compare in quantity or quality with those of many other islands. You will also experience more rain showers here. Those that can stand some rain will be rewarded by the brilliance of the bursts of sunshine that follow.

The lack of tourism means you will be welcomed by the local people. The main industry is agriculture and you will see produce coming down from the hills on donkeys and in ancient pick-ups, some held together with baling wire and hope. Instead of tourism, Dominica has concentrated to some extent on processing its abundant agricultural produce and makes soaps, toiletries and a variety of canned foods.

When Columbus stumbled upon Dominica it was, like much of the southern Caribbean, inhabited by Carib Indians who had migrated from South America. These Caribs managed to repel European settlement for longer than most other islands because of Dominica's lofty and wild topography, and they later coexisted with the colonists. As a result, on the east coast of Dominica you can visit the only officially recognised Carib settlement in the Eastern Caribbean.

Dominica does get visitors, usually independent and adventurous individuals who have a particular interest in nature, above or below water. Recently, the island has encouraged cruise ships and some of them dock for a day while the passengers take a tour to the interior.

Two fairly large and pleasantly luxurious hotels have been built in Roseau over the last few years. They probably cater as much to visiting businessmen as those travelling for pleasure.

Otherwise, accommodation tends to be in a couple of dozen relatively small traditional hotels and guest lodges, some perched on the edge of the rainforest, others along the shore. There are hotels associated with most of the Dominica dive shops.

Divers will meet other divers in the bars near the diving establishments and evening entertainment will rarely go beyond dinner followed by bed. From time to time a hotel will bring in a local group or have some form of activity which will be as well attended by locals as visitors.

Dominica is from the pages of Somerset Maugham rather than Condé Nast's. Those whose idea of fun is shopping by day in glamorous boutiques and hopping by night to the latest dance music would probably prefer to visit the grave before Dominica. But those looking for an unspoiled island of outstanding natural beauty, who enjoy organising their own programme of entertainment and sightseeing will find it ideal.

Portsmouth and Calibishe

Portsmouth is the second largest town in Dominica, fairly small and poor on the surface but rich in a spirit of friendliness and good cheer. It lies in the huge Prince Rupert Bay, the best harbour in Dominica and one that is popular with visiting yachts. The north side of the harbour is protected by a knob of land made of two hills called The Cabrits. This is a national park with a fine example of dry forest and an historic fort and museum. There is a small cruise ship dock under the Cabrits and ships visit from time to time. The passengers all get whisked off for a day tour so the whole area has remained pretty free of tourist influences and has lots of unsophisticated charm.

Prince Rupert Bay has the best beach in Dominica, and even by Caribbean standards it is a fine stretch of white sand backed by seagrapes and palms. There are two small hotels and a guest house along the beach and one or two more dotted close to town or in the attractive village of Calibishe, a few miles away on the windward shore. There are about half a dozen small informal, inexpensive restaurants in the area. The local speciality is soup cooked with crayfish from the mountain streams.

Portsmouth is close to the northern mountain range which has splendid examples of protected rainforest and is where both of the endemic parrot species live.

A boat ride up the Indian River will take you through a dense curtain of swamp bloodwood trees. A leafy canopy covers the river and the dimly lit shore is a textured maze of the trees' sinuous snaking roots.

Diving in this area is good, but lacks the large variety of sites found at the south end of the island. A dive shop has just opened here which will expand the range of the diving.

Mero and Castaways

Mero and Castaways are about 7 miles north of the capital Roseau. While far from flat, this area lies between the two tallest mountain ranges and misses some of the showers that assail the higher ground. The coastline has low cliffs etched by the sea and is broken by pleasant beaches of darkish sand.

It is a fairly short bus or car ride to Roseau and it is not too far to the Carib settlement or the southern mountain range, with its wonderful hikes and waterfalls. There is also good gentle hiking close by, mainly through agricultural land up the Macoucheri River.

Two accommodations attract a modicum of visitors. Castaways is a pleasant quiet hotel right on the beach and the dining room and beach bar have a great view of the birds in the surrounding trees and the sea beyond. The Lauro Club Hotel is another agreeable establishment on a hillside a mile to the north, close to the Macoucheri River. Both places have dive shops, and there is good diving in the area.

Roseau

Roseau is the capital of Dominica. It is a picturesque city of traditional Caribbean wooden buildings, complete with balconies and overhangs. It has a slightly seedy well-lived in atmosphere that distinguishes it from many other Caribbean towns that have been prettified to make them more attractive to visitors. A little polish has now been applied to Roseau in the form of a new waterfront area which includes a cruise ship dock. Not far away are two smart new hotels. So far, this just adds a touch of class without spoiling the town's essential character.

There are wonderful hiking delights a short drive away. Trafalgar Falls tumble from high off the mountainside into lush rainforest. Two crater lakes lie high in the Morne Pitons National Park. Around them trees are stunted by mists and the coolness of the mountains, but it is enchanting to hike between the two lakes among ferns, small trees and shrubs which often are covered with epiphytes. For a longer hike, you can follow the 2-hour trail through the rain forest to Middleham Falls, Dominica's most secluded and beautiful waterfall. For the less energetic, the photogenic Emerald Pool is set amid tall forest trees with a dense canopy. You can get quite close by car, bus or taxi, and the hike is

JOHN DOUGLAS

*A green and fertile land,
never less than dramatic,
Dominica's streams plunge
from the heights as
impressive waterfalls.*

Scott's Head Village and Soufriere

short and easy.

The hardest and most unusual hike is to the boiling lake. A local guide is essential for this and, as it takes a whole day; you will have to forgo your daily dive. The path takes you through rainforest, over mountain peaks into the Valley of Desolation where steam bursts forth from bare earth coloured in unlikely hues of reds, browns, greens and yellows. The boiling lake shoots huge clouds of steam high into the air. In addition to this you can walk back into the hills anywhere in this area and find splendid scenery.

The only beaches near Roseau are made from large rounded stones. Despite this, Roseau and its surrounds have the largest number of hotels and guest houses. The two smartest hotels are right in town. Fort Young has been built out of an old fort and offers luxurious charm with a touch of history. The more modern Garroway is a multi-story building close by.

Another group of hotels are close to each other about a mile south of Roseau. Two of these, the Anchorage Hotel and Castle Comfort, are associated with two of Dominica's dive shops.

There are many charming restaurants to visit, with names like the Cartwheel Cafe, Evergreen and Robe Creole. Even a restaurant with the uninspired name of The World of Food turns out to be in a charming courtyard in what was originally the home of Jean Rhys.

These two small villages lie about a mile apart on a stony shore at the southern end of Dominica. The shoreline is the edge of an extinct volcano which sweeps round in a semicircle to Scott's Head: a hilly promontory that is attached to Dominica by a low spit of stones and sand. The view from the top of Scott's Head back into the mountains and cliffs is dramatic.

In the late afternoon, fishermen co-operate to pull their heavy wooden fishing boats up on the stones. Children yell, chat and splash in the water. As dusk turns to dark, cars become scarce and people plentiful on the pot-holed road. Most people will greet you if you stroll along the road past tiny restaurants and closely spaced rum shops. Just as the sound of one game of dominoes fades, you can pick up the clicking of another ahead.

This charming area is at the end of the road. A few yachts visit but, apart from this, tourism here is practically unknown. There is one guest house in Scott's Head Village called Gachette's or you may find a house to rent in the area. Gachette's has a restaurant and many of the local rum shops will cook a tasty local meal.

There is excellent diving here and there is a dive shop in Soufriere with a cottage to rent.

Language: English
Currency: Eastern Caribbean Dollar ($1.00 US = $2.66 EC)
Population: About 100,000
Telephone Code: Currently (809), changing to (767)

Après Dive

Dominica will appeal to nature lovers more than sophisticates. But for those who enjoy an active vacation, there is plenty to keep you busy when you are not diving.

Hiking

Hiking in Dominica is outstanding. We have outlined some of the better known destinations in our general section. Organised tours are a good option but for those who prefer to be on their own, rental cars are available or an inexpensive bus service covers much of the island. For those going it alone, two things will prove invaluable. One is a copy of the good survey map of Dominica, available from the Land and Surveys Department just outside Roseau on the road heading for Trafalgar. Another is a visit to the Forestry Department where they have maps of most of the marked trails along with information on wildlife.
Forestry Department, Botanical Gardens: (809) 448-2733
Tours:
Anchorage Tours: (809) 448-2638/9
Antours: (809) 448-6460
Coconut Beach Hotel, Portsmouth: (809) 445-5393
Maclean's Safari Tours, Portsmouth: (809) 445-5299
Trois Piton Tours: (809) 448-6977

Tennis and Squash

There is a squash court at the Anchorage Hotel and tennis is available at Castaway's Beach Hotel and Reigate Hall Hotel.

Water Sports

There are no yacht charter companies in Dominica. The Anchorage Hotel and Dive Dominica both run whale watching trips during the winter months when whales visit the area. Windsurfers and water-skiing are available at Castaways Beach Hotel. Deep sea fishing is available through the Anchorage Hotel.

Shopping

Dominica is strong on handicrafts. The Caribs produce many baskets and ornaments featuring hand-woven roots, screw pine leaves and grasses. They use traditional methods and designs, which date back before Columbus and are unique to the area.

If you visit the Carib settlement, you get not only to buy the handicraft, but to appreciate the way they are made and the lifestyle of the craftsmen.

Woven floor mats are another speciality throughout the island. They come in a variety of sizes and patterns ready to go, but they can also be made to order for whole rooms or houses. These get shipped to you some months later. Dominica processes some of its own agricultural produce and local jams, spices and soaps make a different kind of souvenir.

There are several handicraft shops dotted around Roseau and there is a craft market near the tourist office close to the new cruise ship dock.

Nightlife

Apart from eating well and enjoying the stars, you can have a lively evening on one night or another at many of the hotels. Try Reigate Waterfront Hotel on Wednesdays, Anchorage Hotel on Thursdays and the Evergreen or Fort Young on Fridays. Two discos, Aqua Cade and The Warehouse sometimes come to life on the weekends and holidays.

Aqua Cade: (809) 449-1489
The Warehouse: (809) 449-1303

Information on Accommodation

Tourist Board: (809) 448 2351/2186
USA: (212) 682-0435
UK: (171) 233-8382

Getting There

There are two airports in Dominica. The larger of the two, Melville Hall, is in the north of the island and takes the larger inter-island planes. Near Roseau, in the south, is Canefield airport which takes smaller aircraft.

Dominica has become much more accessible recently. In November 1996, American Eagle began offering a direct service from San Juan, Puerto Rico. There are currently ten flights per week. American Airlines connects from San Juan to most American cities.

From Europe, regular flights to Antigua, Barbados and St. Lucia (British Airways and charter flights) connect with inter-island hoppers to Dominica. Air France flies directly to Guadeloupe and Martinique, both adjacent to Dominica; L'Express ferry and inter-island flights serve these islands. The inter-island airlines serving Dominica are Cardinal, LIAT, Air Guadeloupe, and Winair.

The Diving

Evidence of Dominica's volcanic origins are to be found everywhere, including the underwater environment. A massive submerged crater off the southwest corner of the island gives rise to steep slopes on the outer face of the rim and true vertical walls inside. Lava plugs around the rim form underwater pinnacles and ferocious hot blasts have driven arches through the rim wall and scooped out caverns and crevices galore. And, we are not just observers of the aftermath of ancient historical activity. In places jets of hot water spurt from fissures in the rocks and bubbles trace escape routes to the surface like a mass evacuation from the too frenzied activity below the sea bed. This is truly an environmental drama, still being played out before our eyes.

Although Dominica's sand is the grubby shade of dark grey volcanic sand, the good news for divers is that, because the sand is relatively heavy, visibility is generally excellent, in the region of 80 feet or more on a good day. Rarely does visibility fall below 50 feet. Not only is the sand heavy but it also has a long way to fall. Sheer walls stand back while sediment plummets to 1,000 feet or more.

The colour of the sand affects the water colour, too. Though impeccably clear, the water is not the classic turquoise found off many of the islands, caused by the sun reflecting off the white sand on the sea bed. Instead it has a deep green tint, rather like looking through highly polished pebbled glass. The magnification effect of looking through water enhances this sensation. We thought it was more fun to imagine the incredible overcrowded green of the island's vegetation leaching out into the sea. But, then, this is an island where flights of fancy can be given free rein.

One of the real benefits of diving in Dominica is that it has not been over-dived. The reefs are in very good condition. Although divers are briefed not to touch anything, we were sorry to see that gloves were allowed and some dive leaders did not always hold back from hanging on to the coral or a vase sponge in their eager-

Scott's Head traces the rim of an ancient volcanic crater and provides some of Dominica's most dramatic diving.

SIMON WALSH

ness to point out interesting marine life. The role model message has not quite got through yet. Nevertheless, the marine life is healthy with as wide a variety of sponges as we have seen anywhere.

Initially, we were dismayed to find an unusually large amount of green and brown algae on the reefs, usually a warning that the water is polluted with land run-off and not a healthy sign for the reefs. Although we found algae on every reef we dived, it does not seem to be out of control nor does the reef seem to be suffering.

Big schools of fish are to be seen around all the reefs. Pelagics are not very common except that, at the other end of the scale, whales can be sighted regularly from November to March. We saw huge schools of dolphin several days running in Soufriere Bay when we were there in May. Whale watching boat trips are offered by most of the dive operators, but leave the dive gear at the hotel; you are not allowed to enter the water with the whales.

Dominica is one of the remaining islands where frogfish and seahorses are frequently spotted. We saw frogfish on 50 per cent of the dives we did in Dominica. Almost every dive has anemones to show and zoanthids thrive on many reefs.

There are no good wrecks off Dominica. Although a tug is a designated dive, hardly anyone is diving it. In the south, two wrecks near enough to each other to comprise one dive are visited occasionally. Instead of wrecks, almost every dive site has a tunnel or cave. From some, you emerge through the top of the reef, others run horizontally. All are packed with lobsters, soldierfish or sweepers.

Most but not all of the sites are buoyed. Local operators are working to improve some of the anchoring arrangements of the buoys to minimise reef damage. The Ministry of Fisheries is also involved in this process. Few dives are done as drifts. In those areas where currents are very strong, it is not usually advisable to dive when the current is running. We were regaled with tales of currents around Scott's Head strong enough to rip off a mask. Some operators do offer drift dives to expand the extent of the dive in milder currents.

The dive sites are clustered around two areas, the central west coast and the southwest corner. The central west coast has ten recognised sites, covering a range of dive types. There are a number of dives offering shallow caves and arches. The reefs are either extensions of the shoreline or are a few hundred yards offshore. One is a promontory extending seaward. The dives are either gentle or steep slopes and reef plateaux. Conditions are usually calm with little current, except for the northernmost sites.

Further south, most of the dives are clustered around the submerged crater which is the extension of Soufriere Bay. There are vertical wall dives as well as large pinnacles. In the relative shelter of the bay, conditions are generally calm whereas three dives further round on the south coast are exposed to the wind. This makes the sea state more vulnerable to weather conditions and the dives

Plantlife of the Reef

Although many divers think that gorgonians are plants, these soft corals are animals, despite their plant-like appearance. The only plantlife you will find on the reef is the algae. Tropical waters generally have little algae because the warm water is low in nutrients and algae are greedy plants which can overgrow a reef, choking the coral and causing it to die. Nutrient rich agricultural run-off is often the culprit where algae blooms occur.

But algae does make a positive contribution to the reef ecosystem. Without two vitally important roles played by algae, the reefs would struggle to survive. Red algae, rather like coral, generates hard calcium structures. It is called coralline algae. This function is put to good use on the reef as cement, holding the reef together. Many coral reefs would simply crumble away if it were not for the red algae. After storm damage, this role is crucial as the red algae is able to grow much faster than coral. To see coralline algae, look for reddish or purple smudges.

Tiny algae called zooxanthellae make an equally important contribution to the coral. The zooxanthellae live inside the coral using photosynthesis to assist in the processing of food. The coral would not be able to grow as fast without the zooxanthellae and would be not nearly as attractive, as it is the zooxanthellae that contribute the colour.

The green and brown algae growing on the reef look more like conventional plants and can be just as attractive. Elegant wine glass shapes grow on sand patches, others look like shaving brushes. Green grape algae looks just as it sounds and beautiful sea pearls can grow up to two inches across.

Green grape algae provide food for many species of nudibranchs.

Fan leaf alga has the appearance of delicate petals and Y branched algae display vivid blues and greens.

Although plant-like in appearance, they differ from land plants in having no roots. Rhizoids attach the algae to the substratum but are not used to absorb nutrients.

If algae growth gets out of balance on the reef, the coral is starved of light. But the many herbivorous grazers usually manage to keep things under control. Sea urchins roam the reef at night consuming all in their path while during the daytime surgeonfish, tangs, damselfish and a host of others act as effective harvesters.

Divers can help keep the algae under control by not wounding the coral or sponges. Even delicately touching these organisms can cause the death of a few polyps or damage the mucus coating, and algae may take hold before the coral can repair itself. Once it has a hold it could eventually smother the coral. Feeding the fish is another contributing factor as it means that they neglect their role as reef cleaners, allowing the algae to take over.

more prone to strong currents. Dive operators choose sites based on conditions. We were told that there would be at least an 80 percent chance of an experienced diver diving in the Atlantic off the south side of the island in the course of a one week stay.

We are aware that there is good diving in the north of the island. When we conducted the research for this book, there was no dive store in the area so we could not dive here (see regulations in this section). Since then, a dive operator has opened a store in Portsmouth and is diving the area.

Rules and Regulations

It is a requirement that you dive with a local dive operator in Dominica. All dives are accompanied but policies vary as to the amount of individual freedom permitted. Some operators require divers to stay in a loosely knit group, while others are willing to allow buddy pairs to follow their own profile.

No spearfishing is allowed in Dominica. The rule applies to locals and visitors alike. It is not permitted to take any marine organisms or to damage the reef in any way.

An outline plan is in existence for a marine reserve in the Scott's Head area. It is modelled most closely on the marine park in St. Lucia, the Soufriere Marine Management Area (SMMA), but it does not yet have the legal standing of the SMMA.

Plans and enthusiasm are not in short supply. The plans for the marine reserve include identifying separate fishing and diving areas and establishing fish nurseries. The water sports association is currently preparing proposals to prohibit the use of jet skis. A group of academics funded by a European Community grant are conducting a research project to form the basis of an ecotourism plan for the marine environment. The French Technical Mission are undertaking a reef monitoring programme. None of these plans or proposals will be executed until the project receives government approval and support. The marine reserve is not currently considered a priority issue with the government.

Independent Diving

If you want to dive in Dominica you must use a local operator. Some operators will allow you to do a beach dive unsupervised if you have booked a dive package with them.

Safety

Dominica has no recompression chamber nor any medical staff specifically trained in diving related injuries. Dr Sohraindo based in Roseau is a doctor who is also a diver and Dr. Moise is a partner in Nature Island Dive. All of the operators carry oxygen and are trained in its use.

In the case of serious accidents, the recompression chamber in Barbados is used. Although farther than the chambers in Martinique and Guadeloupe, language and documentation barriers make Barbados a simpler option when time is of the essence.

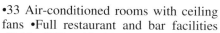 estled at the edge of a cliff overlooking the Caribbean Sea, cradled in the beauty of Dominica's mountainous landscape, is the Fort Young Hotel. The hotel lies within the walls of the original fort built in 1770.

Fort Young Hotel is as unique historically as the island it once defended. The concept in the design is intended to create a sympathetic blend of old and new in harmonious co-existence. In the same way the hotel blends the old with the new, so too are the atmosphere and services carefully put together to create an ambience that will delight both the business and recreational traveller.

•33 Air-conditioned rooms with ceiling fans •Full restaurant and bar facilities •Cable T.V. with 11 channels in every room •Swimming pool •Sea view rooms •Only 5 minutes walk from the city centre •Conference, seminar and private meeting facilities •Direct overseas dial telephones in every room •Typing, E-mail and facsimile services available •Day tours and car rentals.

 *Fort Young Hotel*

DIRECT RESERVATIONS & INFORMATION
Contact Fort Young Hotel
P.O. Box 519, Roseau, Dominica, West Indies
Telephone: (809) 448 5000 Fax: (809) 448 5006 E-mail:fortyoung@tod.dm

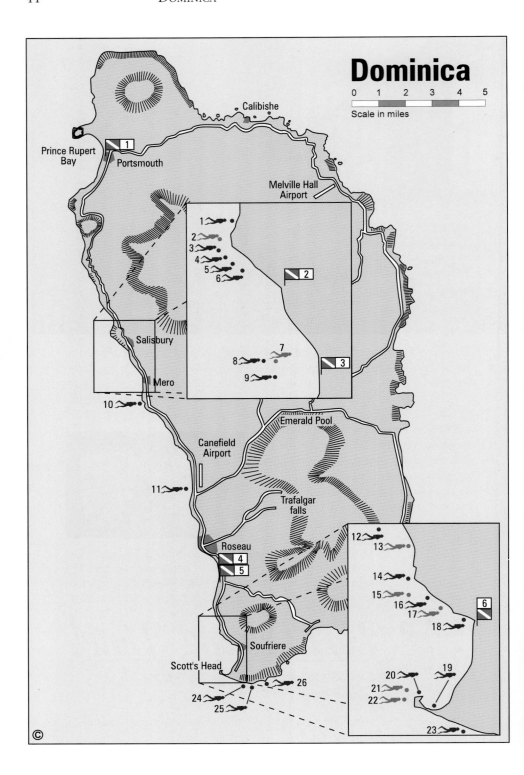

NO.	SITE NAME	DEPTH IN FEET
1	Coral Gardens North	30-105
2	Rina's Hole	30-50
3	Whale Shark	55-120
4	Nose Reef	40-55
5	Brain Coral	30-135
6	Salisbury Falls/Lauro Reef	35-120
7	Castaways	15-90
8	Berry's Dream	45-110
9	Maggi's Point	30-105
10	Rodney's Rock	10-60
11	The Tug	60-90
12	Wrecks	60-80
13	Champagne	5-100
14	Point Guignard	15-110
15	Dangleben's	30-120
16	Coral Gardens South	30-60
17	L'Abym Wall	20-1500 !
18	Soufriere Pinnacle	20-150
19	Scott's Head Drop-Off	20-120
20	Scott's Head Wall	30-130
21	Crater's Edge	30-150
22	Scott's Head Pinnacle	30-150
23	The Condo/Kai Bellou	15-70
24	The Village	40-180
25	The Suburbs	20-140
26	Des Fous	20-140

Dominica Dive Sites

NO.	OPERATOR	RESORT/HOTEL LOCATION
1	Cabrits Dive Centre	
2	East Carib Dive	
3	Dive Castaways*	Castaways Hotel
4	Anchorage Dive*	Anchorage Hotel
5	Dive Dominica*	Castle Comfort Hotel
6	Nature Island Dive	

*Owned by Hotel/Resort

Dive Operators

1 Coral Gardens North
30'-105'

This is a large reef which operators dive in three different areas. The boat's buoy line descends to 30 feet. A gentle slope extends from the shore to around 45 feet. Filefish and damselfish are always found on this ledge. At the end of the ledge a steep drop-off runs down to 105 feet where it flattens to sand. Snake eels are often observed and octopus and squid appear to frequent the site. Overhangs reveal spotted drums and porcupinefish.

2 Rina's Hole
30'-50'

  C

For those who love mooching among coral heads and under canopies, Rina's Hole is a delight. An exciting tunnel and more nooks and crannies than you have time to explore are packed with a bevy of sea creatures. But hang on to your hat because the tour can be a real roller-coaster ride as swift currents sweep across this area. Tucked down among the coral heads you hover in calm water then lift your head and you are back on the ride.

Unusual for Dominica, the sea floor at Rina's Hole is white limestone sand. The reflection off the sand makes the colours of the reef especially bright. A shallow dive with variable currents makes Rina's Hole suitable for different levels of divers, dependent upon the conditions.

Dive Profile

A buoy marks the southern edge of the reef in about 30 feet of water. If current is present you will be briefed to descend immediately to the anchor and to hang on to the line. A swim north takes you around the western edge of the reef in about 45 feet of water. We are struck by the colours which we have plenty of time to appreciate as we fin enthusiastically but achieve only a sea cucumber's pace, due to the current.

Schools of Creole wrasse, yellowtail snappers and blue chromis flash by, mocking our laborious attempts to stem the current. There are large numbers of energetic juvenile fish, giving great variety to the reef.

To the right, a vertical crevice opens up and we are out of the current. Inside the crevice there appears to be a canopy which turns out to be the entrance to a tunnel. Because the tunnel has a dog's leg turn, it is not immediately obvious from the outside that you can pass through.

Once inside, you can see the light source from the exit, providing just enough light to appreciate the sponges which adorn the walls like Neanderthal cave paintings. It is like entering an ancient sacred place; the costume of three spotted drums patrolling the inner recesses seems designed to ward of evil spirits. The long legs of spaghetti worms guard the entrance and brown tube sponges hang like stalactites, moving ominously in the current.

The tunnel is about 20 feet long, quite wide but low, requiring careful buoyancy control to avoid damaging the encrusted surfaces. Experienced photographers could capture on film some interesting varieties of sponge and invertebrates.

Back outside, big sea plumes stream in the current and yet more overhangs reveal a sculptured slipper lobster and numerous secretary blennies peering from their secure holes. Loggerhead sponges are everywhere, along with some truly excellent giant barrel sponges. Lobsters, both the Caribbean spiny and the spotted spiny species, hide in almost every crevice.

Follow the coral heads around first to the right and, as your remaining air demands, begin to head back toward the west. You can pass back through the tunnel or swim around the reef. Another large canopy on the outside of the reef is providing temporary accommodation to a stingray. Seeing us, it decides to fly away and heads toward the end of the canopy to launch its escape. From out of a small hole shoots the head of a spotted moray, causing the ray to do an emergency stop. It rather inelegantly bumps back into the rock before gathering its composure to carefully circumvent the territory of the moray.

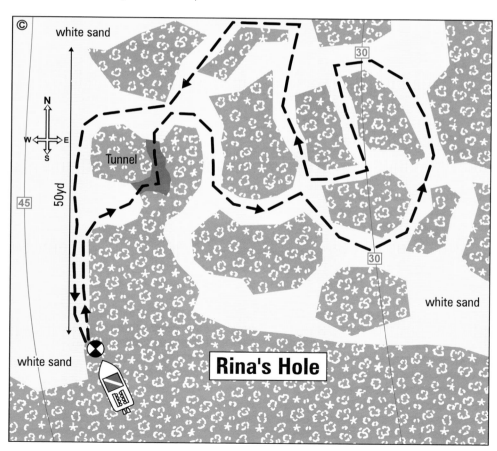

As we, too, emerge from the shelter of the reef, the current whisks us along in the direction of the boat. Catching hold of the anchor line was a highly desirable option, followed by a quick spurt to the back of the boat. There are not always fierce currents around this reef and while the roller-coaster ride is fun, there is a tremendous amount to explore. It would be an equally enjoyable dive to do on a quiet day, taking time to observe the marine life and take photographs.

Thanks to Kurt Nose of Dive Castaways.

3 Whale Shark
55'-120'

An offshore reef with contours giving way to a pleasing wall formation is the outermost dive site off the Grand Savanne bank. Bordering the depths of the ocean, pelagic fish and rays are often encountered.

The reef runs east and west with an attractive ledge on the east end in 55 feet. Eels and octopus make their home around the ledge and among the coral heads. The top of the ledge remains at 50 to 60 feet while the base drops away as you move west. The result is a wall formation incorporating many overhangs and crevices.

Approximately 50 yards to the south of the wall is a rock formation at 100 feet which warrants checking out. Barracuda and large rays, including eagle rays, linger nearby.

At the end of the dive, the area around the mooring buoy has a good variety of corals and marine life at 55 feet.

4 Nose Reef
40'-55'

An offshore reef with a beak-like overhang gives its name to this site. The dive is some distance from the shore, affording the opportunity to see pelagic fish. Barracuda often pay a visit and snappers are a common sight. The reef plateau at 40 feet is crowded with gorgonians. Giant barrel sponges nestle in the gorgonian forest, housing crabs and other sponge dwellers.

At 110 feet the overhanging nose is an interesting feature. Eels enjoy the protection of the overhang and butterflyfish flutter about tidying the reef. These pretty, delicate fish may look like they would do no more than pick over a salad for lunch, but do not be fooled. They are on the lookout for a meal of worms and other invertebrates.

5 Brain Coral
30'-135'

It will be no surprise to discover a proliferation of brain coral on this reef. Running from southeast to northwest, the reef edge is at 45 feet. From the edge, a steep slope falls to 135 feet. Grunts and jacks feed opportunistically off the reef while well protected scorpionfish wait patiently for the chance to feed.

A sheer bluff below the Lauro Club Hotel gives way to a reef platform. The western edge of the reef drops off as a steep slope. At 100 feet are two small caves where Ed, the resident moray, lives. The size of a man's thigh, Ed is quite a sight. Though no one guarantees he will be at home when you call, he is rumoured to be the stay-at-home type so your chances are pretty good.

**Salisbury Falls/ 6
Lauro Reef
35'-120'**

A large coral head is cast a few hundred yards offshore forming what is known as the Castaways dive site. There is little current in this quiet bay and algae thrive alongside a great variety of marine life. Crinoids abound, as do giant anemones, and tiny reef tunicates spot the coral. For photographers, Castaways is an interesting and co-operative subject for macro and close-up photography.

Castaways is adjacent to Berry's Dream. Because it is possible to swim around both reefs in one dive, we have shown them both on the site plan. Local operators tend to treat them as two separate sites, as each of them deserves independent exploration.

**Castaways 7
15'-90'**

  C

Local dive operators, East Carib Dive and Dive Castaways, have buoyed the reef. As you drop down the buoy line, sea rods and giant vases appear on the reef below. It is tempting to spend time here but head out to the main reef to the southwest and leave time to spend in this area at the end of the dive.

Swim across a sandy bottom at 50 feet and look out for rays. A large stingray lies almost covered by sand as we swim over it. Startled, it flees making a rather comical sight, having carelessly mislaid its tail (probably nipped off by a shark). Perhaps that is what it is looking for under the sand, muttering "I know that I had it around here somewhere."

The reef is covered in sponges and coral, forming a myriad of nooks and crannies that provide refuge for all sorts of creatures. The first area you approach houses half a dozen giant anemones with yellow and purple tips to their tentacles. Competing for space are long-spined urchins and golden crinoids, including the black and yellow variety.

Swim around the reef clockwise. Giant barrel sponges are scattered across the reef and at least half a dozen other varieties of sponges are growing. Tubes of yellow boring sponges proclaim their victory over their host. Ugly rough tube sponges vie with the scorpionfish for the Brute of the Reef Award. Azure vase sponges provide colour while brown tube sponges lurk like the tentacles of dormant sea monsters.

At around 90 feet at the back of the reef, you turn northeast and swim over the reef, back toward the buoy line. Across the top of the reef you will see large schools of wrasse and chromis. A school of boga flashes by, parting to clear the divers then recon-

Dive Profile

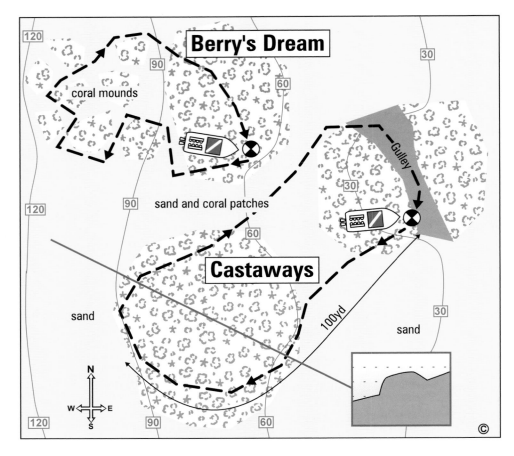

verging as though we had been a minor interruption to their purposeful activities. The reef top is a good place to spot eels, the golden spotted as well as the more common spotted variety.

As you pass over the barrel sponges, peer inside to find shrimps, balloonfish and, in one, we see a basket star curled into a boggling complexity of knots to wait out the daylight hours. The basket star feeds at night by extending its long limbs to filter plankton from the water. To look at this knotted bundle, one might think it would need most of the afternoon to untangle itself in preparation for its night time feast. And, it will most certainly have built up an appetite.

Back on the mound below the buoy line, arrow crabs pick their way across the reef, brave in the daylight hours. On the west side of the mound, an equally bold resident seahorse sometimes allows itself to be viewed. To spot these fish, you will need to look very carefully, as they are well disguised among the sea whips.

A popular night dive, the mound below the Castaways reef buoy offers a shallow and safe environment as the daytime

marine population changes places with the night time inhabitants. If you thought the reef was busy during the day, the level of night time activity will take you by surprise.
Thanks to Kevin King of East Carib Dive.

Berry's Dream 8
45'-110'

Three dive directions are described by local operators. Swimming south, the dive follows the reef round to the east. Going west takes divers to the deepest part of the reef ending in a sandy patch with blocks of coral-encrusted rock measuring 15 feet or more. The dive to the north gives depths on the reef between 45 and 60 feet.

This is a good dive for seeing lobster, crabs and conch. Eels and scorpionfish have plenty of places to hide and numerous types of wrasse make the reef home.

Maggi's Point 9
30'-105'

Beautiful pencil and finger coral adorn this gently sloping reef. A light covering of sargassum algae creates the effect of an underwater meadow. Balloonfish and porcupinefish seem to enjoy the habitat. Stingrays are common in the surrounding sandy area. Frogfish are also found by dive leaders who know this site well.

Rodney's Rock 10
10'-60'

The site is a rocky point running to the west, dropping off to a sandy bottom. One of Dominica's many submarine tunnels makes this a shallow but exciting dive. As well as the tunnel which it is possible to swim through, a small cave is also worth exploring. Tangs and surgeon fish keep the algae under control and a seahorse has been seen at this site.

The Tug 11
60'-90'

A 60-foot tug lies intact on a sandy bottom. In average visibility, it is possible to see the whole wreck. It is rarely dived but has developed well as an artificial reef. The problem is a local cement factory reducing visibility near the surface on working days. Weekends and holidays give clear water for the dive. Schools of fish visit more often than divers; snappers, jacks and mackerel are all common. Sunk 10 years ago, good sponge growth covers much of the hull. Wire coral gives the wreck a hairy appearance. Due to currents, the dive is for experienced divers.

Wrecks 12
60'-80'

Two wrecks, one a wooden shrimp boat, the other a steel inter-island freighter, lie to the west of Champagne. They are broken up as a result of the 1995 hurricanes. Encrusting sponges have taken a hold, and this is a good site for seeing rays.

13 Champagne
5'-100'

  W

When volcanic activity gave birth to Dominica, it unleashed an unruly and determined energy. And, that core energy has not fully dissipated, it has simply gone underground. Underwater you can see that force still venting its power through the sea bed.

This site gets its name from streams of bubbles of hot gas emitting from dozens of points on the sea floor. The bubbles are tiny, rather like the fizz of champagne, belying the hidden power below. The oily heat of water spurting through ruptures in the rocks gives a truer indication of the latent energy contained in the restless foundations of this wild island.

Dive Profile

The exhalations of the sea bed are close to the shore and in fairly shallow water so it is usual to explore the reef first and finish the dive among the bubbles. The reef is roughly round with many overhangs, deep crevices and caverns. Swim around the reef, anti-clockwise, toward the west, taking time to investigate the overhangs and coral heads on the west side. We found numerous spiny lobsters, including one hanging upside down from the roof of a cavern. Too much champagne, perhaps.

As you swim across the rock slope toward the reef, look to the sand on the right to see a 6-foot tall solitary sea plume. It looks as though it would be more at home in the foyer of a smart hotel. Peacock flounders and sea cucumbers make themselves available for inspection in the adjacent sandy area.

On the coral encrusted rocks many parrotfish and wrasse add splashes of colour as they move across the coral.

The shelter afforded by the overhangs and caverns makes this a crowded daytime retreat for squirrel fish, blackbar soldierfish and cardinals. We also see large schools of French grunt and an inquisitive king mackerel. The king mackerel is easily distinguished from the smaller Spanish mackerel by its distinctive silvery lateral line which first drops and then stops abruptly below the second dorsal fin. The lateral line is rather like the fish's ear, a sophisticated mechanism for detecting sound, vibration and, in some species, smell. Although less obvious on some fish than others, a lateral line is always present and can be easily spotted once you know what to look for. For example, the lateral line on a French grunt indicates a change in the pattern of the fish's markings; the yellow stripes are horizontal above the line and diagonal below it.

Both mat and sun zoanthids decorate the coral heads to the west of the reef. These pretty creatures are relatives of anemones and are often confused with coral, another close relative. The dominant corals on the reef are boulder and star coral.

As is typical of dives in Dominica, a wide variety of sponges have made the reef home. The many caverns and crevices mean that those species which prefer sheltered terrain can be seen. Tucked under overhangs are orange ball sponges and orange sieve encrusting sponges. The bright orange hues make the inside of the crevices glow with warm light like the aura of an open fire on a cold winter's night.

Once you reach the southern side of the reef, swim back through a canyon where the remains of a 17th century wreck rest. Two cannons can be made out and by brushing away the surface sand some of the hull and deck planking can be seen.

Finally, head northeast toward the shore to see the bubbling rocks and take a decadent champagne bath. The water is too warm for coral to grow but herbivorous fish nibble at the algae which has free rein to smother the warm rocks. The fish seem studiously oblivious to this strange phenomenon.

You can see where blistering hot water is forced through fissures in the rock. It is safe to put your hand near but not against these outlets: the water is hot but, after it has entered the ambient water, no longer scalding. And, it is a pleasant way to warm up if you are feeling cold at the end of the dive.

Thanks to Andrew Armour of Anchorage Divers.

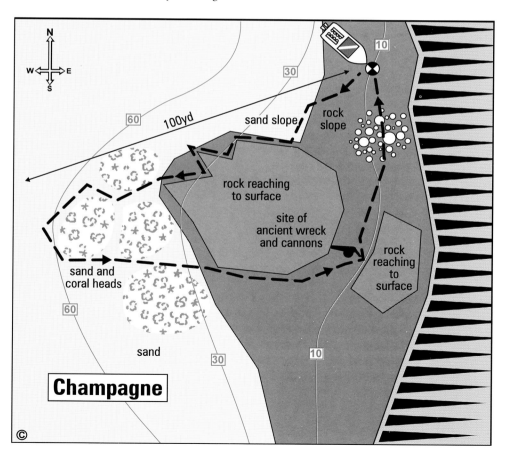

⓮ Point Guignard
15'-110'

Our enjoyment of this dive was seriously influenced by seeing a seahorse and a large orange longlure frogfish. An excellent cave can be penetrated safely for 20 feet with a good light. It was crowded with lobsters and a big school of glassy sweepers.

The point is a steep slope dropping to a sandy bottom. The slope is fractured with many deep crevices. Spotted drums inhabit the recesses and all sorts of invertebrates can be found, including sea stars.

⓯ Dangleben's
30'-120'

 C

Almost everyone we spoke to rated Dangleben's as one of their favourite dives in Dominica. It turned out to be our last dive in Dominica and, by then, it had received so much hype that we dreaded being disappointed.

We drop down on to a reef, pleasant enough but not exceptional by Dominican standards. The dive leader leads us around to the first pinnacle. Now we know why the dive is so highly rated. A riot of colour assaults our senses and, then, the sun comes out. The bright colours become brilliant and, taking a brief pause from scribbling notes, we just soak up the beauty of this dive.

Dive Profile

Dive operators do the dive a variety of ways, occasionally incorporating the dive site called Coral Gardens South. The way to dive Dangleben's is definitely to take it slowly.

We dive it as a drift, entering the water on the south side and swimming clockwise around the pinnacles. The entire surface is thickly veneered with colourful sponges but Dangleben's also has a healthy hard coral community. Boulder and brain coral are sprinkled around the pinnacle along with good examples of great star coral and the much sought after black coral.

As you move around to the west at around 100 feet, long strands of devil's sea whips trail into the blue, like the child who thinks the largest slice of the cake is always a little out of reach. As with all corals, they are filter feeders. But, unlike stony corals, each of their polyps has eight tentacles (instead of six) so, by one method or another, these whips make certain they capture their share of food.

A closer look at the reef as you pass around to the northwest, reveals many worms. Marine worms are not the brown featureless creatures we associate with gardens. In fact many are embedded in the coral, having found a feeding method not requiring them to squirm around.

Dangleben's has a good cross section of Caribbean marine worms. Bearded fireworms move openly as almost nothing can touch them without being badly stung. Humans, too, so beware. Brown fanworms are everywhere though they retract quickly in the presence of divers. Christmas tree worms crop up wherever

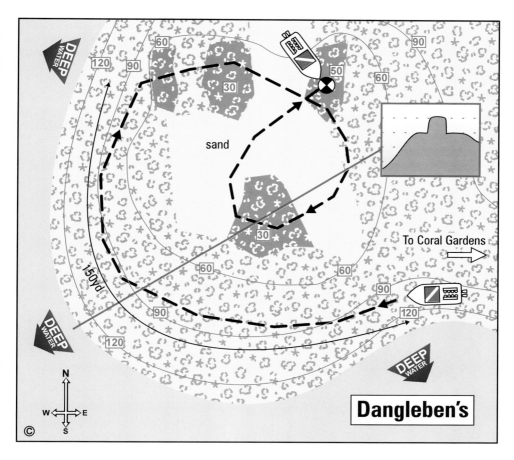

there is boulder coral, no matter what the season. They are so distinctly shaped that further descriptors are superfluous.

And worms are not the only creepy crawly creatures. Good dive leaders will track down lettuce sea slugs for you. These beautiful mollusks, only 2 inches long, look like pieces of frilly nylon.

On the second pinnacle you can find feather black coral, like a delicate green fern gently responding to a light breeze. Another filter feeder, golden crinoids, add yet more colour to the reef.

And for fish spotters, there are enough varieties of butterflyfish to keep you amused. Banded butterflyfish and foureyes are not at all coy and do not seem perturbed by the voyeuristic habits of the divers. Longsnout butterflyfish are more reticent about mingling but, even so, they rarely hide for long, being more interested in continuing their search for tasty invertebrates. Big schools of fish, including Creole wrasse, sweep the area.

This area sometimes suffers from current but it is possible to vary the route from the one shown. It is worth investigating the southernmost pinnacle which is topped with a lovely field of pencil coral. Being shallower on the top of the pinnacle, about 30 feet, the soft corn colours reflect the overhead sun. It is a good place to see eels and frogfish. The frogfish we see stares defiantly at us before shuffling round on its web-like feet to turn its back on us contemptuously.

Dangleben's offers an exciting deep dive and an astonishingly thick covering of sponges and corals. Whether it is this thickness or some other phenomena, the colours are very impressive. It is not over hyped.

Thanks to Cornelius Morris of Anchorage Dive.

Worms That Live in the Sea

Marine worms include a wide range of very different looking creatures. Some look like colourful versions of segmented land worms, others have more in common with the appearance of nudibranchs, and the strangest of all have formed hard tubes from which they spout feathery fans.

Worms which form a tube fall into two types. Feather duster worms build flexible parchment-like tubes while tube worms form a harder calcareous tube. Both are permanently attached to the reef, usually buried in boulder coral.

Looking like a flower arrangement, social feather duster worms display their radioles from parchment-like tubes.

Christmas tree worms (tube worms) could not be more aptly named. They grow in a delightful array of colours; two 'trees' close together are the worms' feeding mechanisms. The 'trees', known as radioles, filter food from the water and pass it down to the animal's body inside the tube. Other tube worms look like a butterfly's wings. Feather dusters are equally flamboyant and can grow to as much as 6 inches across the crown. Despite having no equivalent to an animal's eye, the eye spots on the radioles are so sensitive that the worm can respond 100 times faster than a human eye. When approached by a diver, the radioles will disappear inside the parchment tube faster than you can blink. Be patient and they will reappear, and you will be able to see the parchment tube protruding from the coral.

The main segmented worms on the reef are fireworms. They are very pretty but very toxic, and voracious feeders. They excrete enzymes on to their prey and then suck up the partially digested juices. Tiny worms live in sponges, becoming the same colour as the sponge on which they feed. Flat worms, although hard to see because of their preference for living under rocks, come in exotic colours and patterns. Bright purple with orange spots trimmed with a black and white spotted border might be considered a little gauche above the water but the leopard flatworm wears its colours with pride.

An area of sand and coral heads makes up the dive called Coral Gardens. A relatively flat shallow area, it is a good beginner's dive and is often used as a second dive or for night dives. The southern tip of the dive is at 60 feet. The area has a good cover of pencil and finger coral and seems to attract more than its share of octopuses.

Coral Gardens **16**
South
30'-60'

There are hardly any true walls in the Caribbean. Steep slopes, the occasional vertical section to an underwater structure, yes, but a real wall, no. Then we find the L'Abym wall. It is completely vertical, except where it becomes concave; it falls to over 1,500 feet (no, we did not check), and it is hardly broken by crevices.

L'Abym can be done as a deep first dive or a shallower second dive, as the wall is just as interesting at 50 feet as it is at 100+ feet. It is best dived as a drift in a northerly direction, although it is more of a fin than a drift as little current is usually present.

L'Abym Wall **17**
20'-1500'

 W

We start the dive at the southern end and swim north, the entry point being on a shelf which drops down to 30 feet. The approach to the edge of the wall is initially overgrown with algae but this soon clears when the wall becomes vertical. Thereafter, only those organisms which can cling to a vertical face survive. This excludes sedimentation which falls to the blue depths. Consequently, the wall is clean and bright.

Red, peach and orange encrusting sponges spread unfettered across the wall, leaving just enough space for anemones to snuggle into the odd weak spot. As well as giant anemones, we see a corkscrew anemone with an attendant cleaner shrimp.

After 30 yards, at 60 feet a large overhang is in use by a secretive porcupinefish. It tries the sympathy-winning cow-eyed look then gives up and decides to find another shelter. And, this is a smart porcupinefish because none of us are going to follow it down to 1,000 feet or more.

Sharing the overhang are branching tube sponges displaying all of their colour varieties: purple and green on a yellow background. Along the wall face, parrotfish nibble at the coral. Stoplight parrotfish predominate, a scaly reddish colour in their initial phase and bright shades of green and blue in the terminal phase.

A hundred yards along the wall brings you to a sand chute and two crevices. Fish shelter in these crevices, as the wall affords little protection. We see two huge dog snappers hiding in one. Vase sponges have basket stars draped around their rims like the fruits that decorate a cocktail glass.

Smart dive masters can find a frogfish at around 60 feet. These creatures are very territorial and, unless molested, can usually be found in the same place. We thought it was a pretty courageous

Dive Profile

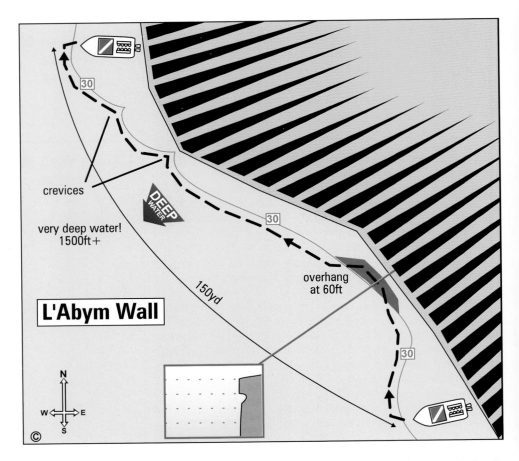

crevices

very deep water!
1500ft+

DEEP WATER

150yd

L'Abym Wall

overhang
at 60ft

N
W→E
S
©

frogfish to spend its life perched on a small shelf on a vertical wall, considering that they are not known for their swimming prowess.

The top of the wall flattens to a narrow shoreline ridge conveniently providing a playground for your safety stop. Once again, as the slope decreases, the amount of algae increases. Pretty fanleaf algae make the slope look like it has been sprinkled with green petals. We find an interesting algae-eating urchin ferreted away in a hole. Our find was a reef urchin. Long-spined urchins are a relatively common sight but the smaller reef urchins are fairly rare. It looks more benign than its long-spined relative but those stubby spikes still pack a punch. Other herbivores along the slope include blue tangs and surgeonfish.

Wall lovers will be seduced, sponge fans will be absorbed, and observant critter hunters will not be short of prey.

Thanks to Cornelius Morris of Anchorage Dive.

A hundred yards off the shoreline, tucked right into Soufriere Bay, the pinnacle rises to within 5 feet of the surface. It has a good cover of soft sponges and black corals offering both a shallow second dive and a deeper first dive. It is a good location when the weather is particularly poor, giving the Scott's Head area rough seas.

Soufriere 🔢
Pinnacle
20'-150'

Frogfish—The Fish That Fishes

Most people diving in the Caribbean have frogfish on their list of 'want to see'. Not that they are the prettiest of fish. On the contrary, they look like claymation models designed to a brief to make them as fat, ugly and blobbish as possible.

They look rather like the knobular sponges that they often use to provide camouflage. But, although they look like solid little lumps of sponge, they have a huge hollow stomach space, capable of holding a fish larger than themselves. A three and three-quarter inch frogfish was found with a four inch grunt inside it. No doubt a fair amount of grunting went on to achieve that. Nor are frogfish deterred by well protected creatures; a scorpionfish has been found inside one.

This healthy appetite requires some clever hunting to feed; a particular challenge if you are not a fast mover. The frogfish operates rather like a garden gnome with a fishing line. The 'line' leads from a fin on the top of the fish's head with a worm-like lure on the end. The frogfish moves the lure to attract prey, and the huge mouth (as wide as the body) sucks the fish in.

Frogfish are not very mobile. They shuffle along on web-like feet or can swim in short bursts by inhaling water and ejecting it through their gills. Making

This longlure frogfish waves its fishing line at the photographer. Surely this is too much of a challenge, even for this fish's stomach capacity.

up for their inability to out-swim predators, they are masters of disguise. Not only does their shape enable them to blend with sponges and coral, they also have the ability to change colour.

Because frogfish are sedentary, they make co-operative subjects for underwater photography. Once located, the frogfish will sit quietly, believing that its disguise has you fooled. They are only tolerant up to a point and you should not attempt to pick the fish up. We have no idea what effect the resultant stress has on these increasingly rare creatures. Please leave them be so that they will still be there for us to see.

19 Scott's Head Drop-Off
20'-120'

A shallow ledge along Scott's Head Point has a dramatic drop off on the northern face. This is a well protected dive site suitable for divers of all levels.

Pretty nudibranchs occur on the reef and you should keep an eye open for flying gurnards. Sponge growth is good and the drop-off attracts a wide range of reef fish.

20 Scott's Head Wall
30'-130'

An excellent first or second dive, the site has something interesting to offer at a range of depths. At 60 feet, several caverns punctuate the steep slope which is vertical in parts. The bottom of the slope is visible at 130 feet. Current is rare, giving ample time to explore what is a very colourful reef.

21 Crater's Edge
30'-150'

 W

We are hoping to do one of the Atlantic dives on the south side of the island but when we reach Scott's Head it is obvious from the sea state that the trade winds are blowing at full force, causing us to abandon our plan. Instead we dive Crater's Edge. As is so often the case, this unplanned dive turned out to be one of the most exciting of our dives in Dominica. It encapsulates everything that is special about diving off this island. Stunning underwater structures, a vertical wall, ridges, and a throng of tropical marine life.

Crater's Edge is the extension of the crater rim that runs west from Scott's Head. The crater's rim emerges as a ridge, giving some sense of proportion to this submarine structure. Deep crevices and towering pinnacles add to an impression of powerful forces having carved this dramatic arena.

Dive Profile

Dive boats take a buoy attached to the top of a pinnacle, at 30 feet. The dive begins with an anticlockwise circumnavigation of a large pinnacle. We descend to 90 feet and marvel at the mosaic of colourful sponges confronting us. Then, we look out to the blue where rainbow runners, yellowtail snappers and cottonmouth jacks move effortlessly through the light current.

Back to the pinnacle face to watch rock beauties munch on giant barrel sponges. Now our dive leader is pointing out two stingrays, one seemingly in hot pursuit of the other. We are going to get dizzy if this does not stop soon.

Back on the pinnacle wall we see brown bowl sponges like amplification horns for the hard of hearing. The bowls are 12 to 18 inches across. Octocorals have also claimed some of the substratum; colourful sea rods are sprinkled around much of the pinnacle. On the steepest face, tiers of gorgonians cascade down.

Another spin around to check the commotion behind us gives us a sight of schools of Creole wrasse and a crush of brown and blue chromis. It is getting crowded down here.

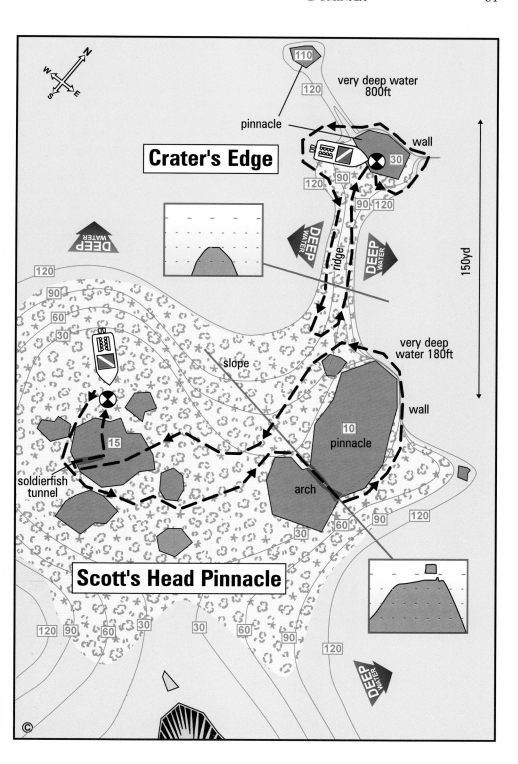

Crater's Edge

Scott's Head Pinnacle

We are now on the west face of the pinnacle and we cannot believe we have seen so much when, at 100 feet, we happen upon a flurry of activity, in a chute under an overhang. A group of black margates seems to be having some kind of synchronised swimming contest. They rush to the top of the crevice do a fluttering dance and then shoot back down through those who are ascending. The fish behaviour experts would no doubt ascribe this bizarre behaviour to some form of ritualised mating ceremony. We thought they were just having fun.

Out to the right, another ridge leads to a deeper pinnacle. The pinnacle marks the western outer limit of recreational diving around the crater rim.

Finishing the tour of the pinnacle we swim east along the main ridge, glad of the opportunity to recover our senses from the onslaught of the pinnacle, or so we think. Massive schools of sennets sweep across the ridge. Sennet have a perfect fusiform shape and they slide through the water, with only occasional spurts of energy. Immediately, their tail fins converge to reduce drag until they are needed again for the next spurt.

As we move along the ridge in 90 feet, rather less perfect examples of a fusiform shape and with considerably more drag, we are again focusing on the reef. Even the algae are attractive. Numerous bushes of variegated red algae are scattered along the ridge. Back to the buoy line for a safety stop, and a rest. There is only so much our eyes can take in and we have moved way beyond our brain's capacity to store and process the information. My note-taking slate looks as much of a mess as Brian's sketch map.

Back on the boat our dive leader, Simon Walsh, describes the orange ball corallimorphs which emerge on this reef at night, looking like miniature solar systems. It is hard to believe that this site has even more treats to offer.

Thanks to Simon Walsh of Nature Island Dive.

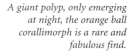

A giant polyp, only emerging at night, the orange ball corallimorph is a rare and fabulous find.

Perhaps the most famous of Dominica's dive sites, Scott's Head Pinnacle lives up to its reputation. A massive lava plug on the caldera of a submerged crater clings precipitously above the sheer wall of the inner rim which falls to over 200 feet. What we recall later that evening, as we sit watching the sun slithering below the horizon, is a vertical surface plastered with more colours, shapes and textures than even the most adventurous artist could imagine. It rolls by as we hang impotently in the current, so that afterwards it seems more like a dream than reality. And, it has nothing to do with the rum that is helping the sun down.

According to our divemaster, currents are variable. On the boat he had suggested we spend about 25 minutes on the wall—we wish. But there is much more to see than just the wall and, whatever the current, Scott's Head cannot fail to be an interesting dive.

The dive boat mooring buoy is in 30 feet of water, and over a small pinnacle reaching to within 15 feet of the surface. Immediately we drop down we see big schools of French grunt, initially obscuring the loveliness of the carpet of corals and sponges below us.

Following our dive guide, we weave around the small pinnacle and through a crevice. Delicate but potentially painful stinging bush hydroids flutter in the current. This is a mere taster for the variety of cnidarians (creatures with polyps or derivatives, such as corals, anemones and jelly fish) we are to see.

Greedy for space, daubs of orange elephant ear sponges enrobe the reef. Many small sea plumes jut up between the coral and sponge. All the usual night feeders shuffle together under the many overhangs. As well as cardinalfish and soldierfish, flamefish slip into protected recesses. Black margates and black durgons inhabit the area, adding a contrasting sombre tone to the scenery.

The route to the main pinnacle is to the east. As we approach the dramatic arch, a shadow overhead attracts our attention. Two very large barracuda hover above us like sentries at the entry to the arch. It is difficult to shake off the feeling that they are using this narrow crevice to take a good look at the traffic as it enters, deciding, perhaps, whether it is worth forming a welcoming party at the other end.

In 35 feet just before the arch is a substantial patch of sun anemones (another cnidarian). About 5 inches across, each disk is an independent creature. It looks like a distant crowd scene as their short stubby tentacles writhe when we pass our hand above them.

The arch is quite narrow, about 10 feet high and 30 feet long, and there is a strong current against us. The walls are frosted with white telesto, and the soldierfish are packed in so tightly that they seem reluctant to give way. We fin along the cobbled floor hoping to cheat the current as the crevice closes into an arch above us. A

Scott's Head Pinnacle

30'-150'

  W

Dive Profile

An arch at Scott's Head, an area riddled with tunnels and caves.

SIMON WALSH

large rock at the end of the tunnel forms a lip constricting the current into a stronger flow, making it quite hard to pass.

Through the arch and round to the left we find the wall. It is completely vertical, dropping to over 200 feet, and has sprouted a splendid array of gorgonians. They lie in layers down the wall face, just far enough away from each other to have access to light but close enough to form a lace curtain of fans as far as the eye can see.

We drop to 100 feet and watch as big fish cruise the wall. A cero does a close pass by to check us out and we see jacks and snooks eyeing us from the blue. Although we are quickly whisked past the wall, a brightly coloured area awaits us to explore for the rest of the dive. Fairy basslets, hamlets and harlequin bass give a lively feel to the reef. We see a number of corallimorphs (also a cnidarian), a mixture of blues and yellows, like soft furnishings complementing the stony corals.

Around the pinnacle where the dive boat moors, a number of tunnels are fun to swim through for those with good buoyancy control. One is completely packed with blackbar soldierfish. They clearly think that they have squatter's rights as they stay in tight military formation while you pass through their territory.

As a diver visiting Dominica, it would be hard to justify missing this dive but there are a number of dives clustered close together (see Crater's Edge map) and all are excellent dives.

Thanks to.Dive Dominica.

A massive rock (like a condominium!) runs east and west. The north face is riddled with crevices and caves. The swim-through tunnels, so typical of diving in Dominica, reveal a fascinating range of marine life. Lots of spotted cleaner shrimps are found here. Wire coral and tube sponges give the structures an interesting underwater profile. We see peacock flounders and a very disgruntled scorpionfish, glaring ominously at us.

Around the base of the rock is sand and another subterranean community. A crowd of brown garden eels peek out of the sand, disappearing in an instant if divers approach, as though they had been only an illusion.

The southern face, slightly deeper, drops to 70 feet and although it does not have the caves and tunnels of the northern face it is marked by big overhangs.

**The Condo/ 23
Kai Bellou
15'-70'**

A series of scattered rocks gives the appearance of a small settlement perched on a cliff top. The rocky shelf becomes heavily built up before the cliff calls an abrupt halt to the development. A wall falls away to over 200 feet. The wall is spectacular and intricate. It is not a flat surface, offering instead endless cracks and splits in the rock.

But, the biggest treat on this dive for us was the big bushy black coral trees. Mossy green and white trees grow out from the wall creating a hanging garden, as if an old building had become overgrown.

Located at the southern end of Dominica, the currents from Martinique bring the larger pelagic fish to this area. The currents make this a dive for experienced divers and is only viable for inexperienced divers on days when the winds are light or moderate.

**The Village 24
40'-180'**

Another exposed dive site, the Suburbs covers an area of large rock formations poised on a shelf at 50 feet. The outcrops of rock rise 20 to 30 feet then suddenly drop away into the channel. The surge can be very aggressive among these rocks.

It is well worth diving on a good day to see the enormous giant barrel sponges. Sea fans grow especially large in this area, enjoying the plankton-carrying currents. Black durgons are plentiful.

**The Suburbs 25
20'-140'**

The most challenging of the recognised dive sites, suitable for experienced divers only, it is one of the few areas where nurse sharks are regularly seen. If you are not lucky enough to see a shark, you can be certain of seeing plenty of other fish. Stingrays, snappers, Bermuda chub and margates all frequent this site.

The underwater features include a very large rock on a sandy bottom, joining a wall which continues down to 200 feet.

**Des Fous 26
20'-140'**

Dominica Diving Facilities

The number of tourists in Dominica is still relatively low and as a consequence only a small number of dive stores operate on the island. Most have been providing diving for quite a few years and have recently formed themselves into a water sports association. A voluntary and informal group, the association keeps abreast of developments on Dominica, studies development elsewhere in the Caribbean and is the voice of diving in negotiations with the Fisheries and Tourist Departments.

As is the case on most of the islands, all of the operators are on the west side. There was no store operating in the Portsmouth area when we visited Dominica but a new store had opened as we were going to press. All the other operators are located between Salisbury, about halfway down the coast, and Soufriere in the southwest.

The operators in the south tend to dive the sites around Scott's Head and Soufriere Bay. The two operators based about halfway down the island dive the area around Salisbury and Mero, most often. All of the operators tend to plan weekly trips outside of their normal diving area with the result that average boat times to the dive sites range between 5 minutes and 45 minutes.

Every dive operator has to be licensed by the Fisheries Department. The license includes clauses requiring the operator to hold personal liability insurance. We dived with all of the operators on Dominica and each had something different to offer. Our experiences were all good: friendly helpful dive leaders and boat crews, well maintained comfortable boats, and, of course, some tremendous diving.

Equipment

Most people who go to Dominica to dive are experienced divers and arrive with their own equipment. All of the operators can supply equipment but none carry more than 20 full sets. The largest operator has 70 tanks but finds he only needs to carry 14 full sets of equipment.

None of the operators sell equipment other than fins, masks and snorkels. Although they will have a go at repairing your equipment, do not expect them to carry many spares. They will only have spares for makes of equipment which they use. Sherwood was the most common make stocked.

The dive boats are either purpose-built or of an appropriate type, offering easy exits and entries. All have shade and somewhere to stow gear. There is no requirement to register dive boats with any regulatory body, but we found the boats well equipped and in good repair.

Because it is a requirement that you dive only with a local dive operator, none of the stores rent equipment or fill tanks if you are not diving with them. Nitrox is not yet available on the island although some of the operators are nitrox trained.

DIVE DOMINICA

With a staff of PADI and NAUI trained instructors and divemasters, three superb dedicated dive boats and an intimate knowledge of the reefs and waters surrounding the island, Dive Dominica offers the friendliest and most professional dive services found in the southeast Caribbean.

Join us on our whale and dolphin tours. Watch as these marine mammals break the surface of the water. Listen to the rhythmic sounds of the clicking communications as you relax on our fast hydrophone-equipped catamarans.

Castle Comfort Lodge is the epitome of the small, intimate dive resort. In this traditional style guest house, you instantly feel like a member of the family. The lodge rests directly on the edge of the ocean, and with only 15 rooms it is ideal for couples and small groups, desiring a quiet get away from it all lifestyle

Associations:	**NAUI Dream Resort** **PADI Dive Centre**
Associated Resorts:	**Castle Comfort Lodge** **Fort Young Hotel**
Languages:	**English**
Number of Instructors:	**3**

Contact:	**Ginette Perryman**
Address:	**Dive Dominica** **P.O. Box 2253** **Roseau** **Commonwealth of Dominica**
Telephone:	**(809) 448-2188**
Fax:	**(809) 448-6088**
US Agent:	**(800) 786-DIVE**
E-mail:	**dive@tod.dm**
Web Site:	**www/divedominica.com**

 # NATURE ISLAND DIVE

NATURE ISLAND DIVE is located in the heart of the marine reserve and is perfectly situated to take advantage of all that Dominica has to offer.

Dominica's top rated dive sites are only minutes away from our jetty. Enjoy our **quality diving** in a relaxed and comfortable atmosphere with small groups, friendly staff and personal service.

Kayaking around the marine reserve is a perfect way to reach secluded beaches and excellent snorkeling. There is also a chance of seeing dolphins frolicking in the bay and frigate birds diving for fish.

Snorkellers can explore 'Champagne' Dominica's famous underwater hot water spring, or snorkel on dramatic walls that disappear into the depths.

Our guided **mountain biking** trips are an excellent way to explore the island and can be tailored to suit your experience level. Spectacular views, swimming in rivers, relaxing in hot springs and hiking to waterfalls are all part of the experience.

Let the adventure begin!

Association:	PADI
Associated Resort:	Seaside Cottages For Rent
Languages:	English and French
Number of Instructors:	2

Address:	PO Box 2354 Soufriere, St Mark Commonwealth Of Dominca
Telephone:	(809) 449-8181
Fax:	(809) 449-8182
Web Site:	www.natureislanddive.dm

DOMINICA

Nature Island Dive

Cost

Compared to the more developed islands, diving in Dominica is relatively inexpensive. There is a small difference in prices between the operators so it is worth checking out what is included.

Single-tank dives cost between $35 and $45 and 2-tank dives are between $65 and $75. Many people who come to Dominica come solely for the diving so 10-tank/5-day packages are common, and work out more economical at just over $300. Operators associated with a hotel offer 1 week dive packages including accommodation, breakfast and dinner for $1,000 or less.

A PADI open water course costs between $300 and $400. NAUI, SSI, and CMAS courses are available for a comparable cost.

Operators

Because Dominica has not yet succumbed to the lure of mass tourism, visitors tend to be quite specific about their reasons for visiting. Most of the dive operators are offering focused packages for divers and are linked in some way to a hotel. Equally, there is not so much business that they can afford to turn any down, so all will happily accept divers from other hotels, apartments, cruise ships or yachts.

For those on a tight budget, some of the operators will find local apartments or guest house accommodation if their hotel is out of your price range.

The oldest dive operation is Dive Dominica **5**, located in Roseau. The owner and manager, Derek Perryman, also owns the Castle Comfort Hotel. Derek started the dive operation in 1983 and now promotes his hotel only to divers, giving a friendly clubby atmosphere to the place. The dive store is immediately in front of the hotel so you can watch your kit being carried down to the dive boat and set up while you hoover up your Caribbean breakfast.

In January 1997, Dive Dominica completed a new building for their dive store. It has a smart office, training room, and good storage for gear. The compressor is in its own room, minimising noise when tank filling.

A 2-tank dive leaving at 9 a.m. has you back at lunch time with the afternoon free to visit the parts of the island that are not submersed. And, if you are still not sated, there is a reasonable dive right in front of the hotel. We hesitate to call it a beach dive, as there is not any sand, but a giant stride off the end of the jetty puts you in deep water. It may not be on a par with the best of the dive sites but you can see flying gurnards and batfish cruising along the bottom.

Derek is a pioneer of Dominican diving and believes in selling the true Dominican experience. His policy of recruiting and training Dominican staff in the hotel and the dive store are evidence of his commitment to that goal. He is also committed to providing a high quality service to divers.

Dive Dominica has three boats, the smallest, 30-foot, takes ten divers, the next is 36-foot and takes up to 20 divers. The largest boat, a 47-footer, is used primarily for snorkelling tours and whale watching trips, unless one of the other two boats is out of commission. Although Dive Dominica has large dive boats, Derek will send two boats out when one could have coped, in order to keep down the numbers of divers per boat.

Dive Dominica provides diving to a number of the cruise ships which call at Dominica. As many as four ships a week visit Roseau's new cruise ship dock. Where Dive Dominica has a contractual arrangement to provide diving, they will collect passengers from the ship.

Right next door is Anchorage Dive **4**, part of Anchorage Hotel. Andrew Armour now owns the hotel that his father started, and he personally runs the dive store. Andrew sets a friendly tone to the dive operation, giving an animated briefing before the dive. Andrew is proud of the fact that all of his hotel staff are given the opportunity to become certified divers, putting them in a better position to understand and service the needs of divers. On average, about 50 percent of the hotel's guests are divers.

The hotel offers a full range of tours of the island. A pleasant bar and pool dining area gives a pleasing view across the bay and is a perfect place to relax after a dive. A squash court beckons the more energetic. Anchorage also has some 15-foot sailing dinghies for those who have not got wet enough diving.

Anchorage has two dive boats. One, a 39-foot motor cruiser taking up to 20 divers, is well equipped with heads and a fresh water shower. The second is a pirogue which can accommodate nine divers.

There are a few yacht moorings off the hotel. The modest fee which is charged covers 3 days' moorings and includes use of onshore facilities such as showers and garbage disposal. They have a great barbecue on Thursday evenings. It is a good location if you want to do a few days' diving as part of a charter boat holiday.

Nature Island Dive **6**, a partnership, run by Dr. Vivian Moise and two dive instructors, Simon Walsh and Ian Collombin, is situated in the centre of Soufriere, minutes away from the dive sites around the rim of the submerged crater which forms Soufriere Bay.

Simon Walsh exudes enthusiasm for the local diving and is well informed about the marine life. Two 22-foot custom built aluminium dive boats carry a maximum of ten divers each. The size of the boats and the dive group means that drift dives are easy to organise and many of Nature Island's dives are done as drifts. Simon claims to be the only operator regularly diving the two wrecks off Champagne.

Soufriere is a lovely town, quiet and friendly. The dive store is right on the waterfront. Because the dive sites within Soufriere Bay are all so near, Nature Island's boats return after each dive.

Nature Island Dive owns a cottage which is offered for rent as part of a total dive package for up to four people. This is an inexpensive but very pleasant option for those willing to self-cater. They provide diving for guests in several hotels, both in Soufriere and Roseau. The bus trip from Roseau takes about 25 minutes but costs only $2EC (less than $1US). Nature Island rents mountain bikes which, in Dominica, aptly describes the riding terrain.

Further north, two operators are based on the central west coast near Salisbury. East Carib Dive **2** is run by Gunther Glats and Kevin King who have been on the island for 6 years. They

Many relatives of coral inhabit Dominica's reefs such as these mat zoanthids. Look closely and you can see that some of the polyps are closed and some are open.

mainly provide diving services to the Lauro Club Hotel which sits on the headland overlooking Salisbury Bay. They will also make arrangements with local guest houses and apartments, for those looking for low budget accommodation.

East Carib Dive uses an efficient comfortable 22-foot custom-built aluminium dive boat. Gunther is recognised as something of an equipment specialist on the island. East Carib Dive is an authorised Bauer compressor repair clinic and a member of the Scuba Pro repair and educational association.

Located right on the beach, East Carib Dive has a good setting with a friendly local beach bar awaiting thirsty divers on their return. East Carib Dive is a small operation, allowing Gunther and Kevin to offer a personal service to their guests, most of whom are experienced European divers. Yachts can anchor in the bay and dinghy across to the shore to arrange diving.

A little further down the coast, in the next bay, is Dive Castaways **3** hotel and dive operation. Away from the bustle of Roseau, this hotel offers a peaceful picturesque setting overlooking a secluded bay.

The hotel is another family-run business while the dive operation, Dive Castaways, is managed by Kurt Nose, an American who has spent most of his life in the Caribbean. Kurt's background in education makes him a patient and proficient teacher.

The dive store, right on the sandy beach, has easy access to calm water for training dives. For certified divers, Dive Castaways' two dive boats can each take eight divers. A new jetty has just been completed, making access to the dive boat easy.

As well as diving, guests of the hotel have use of kayaks, water skis and sailing dinghies. Castaways Hotel beach gets swept away by hurricane swells periodically but miraculously recreates itself in a very short time. Yachts can anchor in the bay and dive with Dive Castaways.

As we were going to press, a new dive store opened in Portsmouth: Cabrits Dive Centre **1**. Although it was too late for us to visit the store, reports suggest that this appears to be a well stocked and professional facility. Clearly the presence of a store in Portsmouth will open up the diving in the north of the island, providing convenient diving for those staying in this area.

Contact Information

1	Cabrits Dive Centre	Michelle Springall	Tel: (809) 445-3010 Fax: (809) 445-3011
2	East Carib Dive	Gunther Glats	Tel: (809) 445 6575 Fax: (809) 445 6575
3	Dive Castaways	Kurt Nose	Tel: (809) 449 6244 Fax: (809) 449 6246
4	Anchorage Dive	Andrew Armour	Tel: (809) 448 2638 Fax: (809) 448 5680
5	Dive Dominica	Derek Perryman	Tel: (809) 448 2188 Fax: (809) 448 6088
6	Nature Island Dive	Vivian Moise	Tel: (809) 449 8181 Fax: (809) 449 8182

Dominica Dive Operators

		Cabrits Dive Centre (1)	East Carib Dive (2)	Dive Castaways (3)	Anchorge Dive (4)	Dive Dominica (5)	Nature Island Dive (6)
STAFF	Instructors	1	2	1	1	4	2
	Divemasters	1	0	1	2	3	4
	Diving Associations	P	CP	P	P	NPS	P
	Languages	EG	EG	E	E	E	EF
BOATS	Dive Boats	2	1	2	2	3	2
	Shaded Boats	0	1	2	2	3	2
	Max. Divers per Boat	10	10	8	8-14	10-30	10
	Time to Dive Sites	5-15	5-40	5-40	15-30	15-30	5-10
	Dives per Day	2	3	OD	2	2	2
	Pick Up by Boat from	CRY	CRY	CRY	CRY	CRY	CRY
EQUIPMENT	Equipment Sets	15	10	12	15	14	20
	Dive Equip. for Sale	2		1			
	Dive Equip. for Rent						
	Photo Equip. for Rent			•	•	•	
	Tank Fills						
	Equipment Servicing	•	•		•	•	•
	O₂ on Boat	•	•	•	•	•	•
	VHF on Boat		•	•	•	•	•
MISC.	Owned by Resort			•	•	•	
	Other Water Sports	•	•	•	•		•
	Pers. Liab. Insurance	•	•	•	•	•	•

Martinique

Unlike the other islands in the Windwards, which are small independent nations, Martinique is part of France. It is modern with many thriving small industries. Agriculture is also important and Martinique is a major producer of pineapples and rhum (the Gallic version of rum, with its own distinct flavour). Roads and hospitals are excellent, though it may be the only island in the group where you are likely to run into a traffic jam, mainly on the eastern road into Fort de France during rush hour. Martinique justifiably prides itself on being civilised, with good restaurants, fine wines and the latest Paris fashions.

The northern half of the island is lush and mountainous, covered in dense rainforest, most of which is protected. Martinique's volcano, Mount Pelée, rises to 4,000 feet and dominates the extreme north of the island. Attractive beaches can be found in the northern section, though most are of volcanic black sand.

The hiking is especially interesting in the north and there are spectacular views from the slopes of Mount Pelée. The Gorges de Falaises are dramatic waterfalls in a narrow canyon on the east side of Mount Pelée and you can cool off in the fresh water pool below. One of the most unusual hikes is along the Canal de Beauregard. In 1760 the rich farmers around St. Pierre wanted more water for their crops. So, with slave labour, a canal was built that runs for many miles, bringing water right around a mountainside. You walk along the outer canal wall which is about 18 inches wide and fairly level. There are no guard rails and the views are often dizzyingly precipitous.

The southern part of the island is less dramatic, with pleasantly rolling hills up to about 1,300 feet. Along the southern coastline are flawless white sand beaches.

Although Martinique is larger than the other islands—some 35 miles by 15—good roads enable you to get round it faster, except close to Fort de France where there can be traffic problems. Divers from the south often take a day trip to St. Pierre for a diving change of scene.

Small towns and villages adorn the countryside, with whitewashed churches and pleasant town squares, many so clean they look as if they have just been scrubbed. From the architecture to the smell of the coffee and the taste of the bread, everything is distinctly and delightfully French. It will captivate francophiles and those who like to take an hour or two to sit in cafés and watch life go by. For the independent traveller it is almost essential to be able to speak some French. Those who feel more at home in English may enjoy the famous Club Med which caters to at least as many Americans as Europeans and is completely bilingual.

The Northwest: St. Pierre to Carbet

This is the most dramatically beautiful area of Martinique. The coast is backed by steep mountains covered in lush green rainforest. It is wonderful for hiking and exploring and there are many beaches, mainly of darkish sand, though there is a pretty white sand beach near Carbet.

Until the beginning of this century, St. Pierre was one of the most important cities in the Caribbean. Known as the Paris of the West Indies, it had a population of 30,000, with fashionable shops, a beautiful theatre and many a sailor's bar. The surrounding agricultural land was unusually productive and had created at least a dozen millionaires. Early in 1902 Mount Pelée started rumbling and on May 8 a horrendous explosion blew out the southwestern face of the volcano. A giant fireball of superheated gas rolled down and engulfed the town. It has been calculated to have had several times the power of an atomic bomb. In just a few moments the town was reduced to smouldering ruins and an estimated 29,933 people perished. There were two survivors, both of whom were in cellars underground. Twelve ships sank in the bay, a thirteenth managed to limp away, though many on board died and those that survived suffered major burns.

Today St. Pierre has a particular quaint charm, especially for those interested in history. It is only a quarter of its pre-volcanic size and many ruins have been left intact. New buildings have been

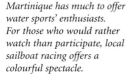

Martinique has much to offer water sports' enthusiasts. For those who would rather watch than participate, local sailboat racing offers a colourful spectacle.

added onto old so that every new structure seems to share at least one wall with the past. Several ruins have been preserved as monuments and are charmingly lit at night. There is a small museum depicting the tragedy and the splendour of St. Pierre's past.

St. Pierre has a good supermarket, pharmacy and bank, but for a large array of shops Fort de France is only an hour away and inexpensive communal taxis run throughout the day.

Carbet, spared by the volcano, is an attractive village a few miles to the south. There are a couple of hotels in Carbet and rental apartments are available in St. Pierre. This area is off the beaten track and, though not suitable for those who like socialising and nightlife, it is charming for people who like to hike and who enjoy a quiet rural atmosphere.

Just a couple of miles west of Fort de France, Schoelcher is a traditional holiday area with a beach and several hotels. Many people who work in Fort de France live here and you find some of the better restaurants and night-clubs. Being close to town it gets a fair amount of traffic. One of the larger hotels has a dive shop and it is not too far to some of the dive sites in the north.

Schoelcher and Fort de France

Fort de France is the capital of Martinique. While it has several good hotels, it is a little too far from the dive shops and sites for most serious divers.

Anse Mitan and Pointe du Bout lie on a small peninsula, 4 miles across the bay from Fort de France. They are well linked to the capital by a system of high speed ferries. Attractions include a pleasant quay-side marina and several beaches. This is Martinique's main tourist drag. There are large hotels, small hotels, pensions and rental apartments. Nearly everything caters to visitors, with many restaurants and pleasant cafés where you can sit and watch life unfold.

Anse Mitan

This area has the largest choice of dive shops, and while it is a fair way to the nearest dive sites, most have fast boats and some organise all-day trips which involve lunch and sightseeing on the way. This would be a good choice for those who like an active social scene, nightlife and a lively atmosphere.

Heading southwest from Anse Mitan the road winds up and down steep hills; the roads are often lined with pink flowering gliricidia trees. As you climb over one hill and tumble down into the next valley, you can see some peaceful bays backed by perfect white sand beaches. Anse L'Ane, Grande Anse D'Arlet and Petite Anse D'Arlet are small villages that lie in such bays.

The Southwest: Anse a L'Ane to Petite Anse D'Arlet

Anse a L'Ane has been a holiday area for many years. There is a smart hotel and many smaller apartment-style hotels, as well as inexpensive camp-style lodges. You could eat out every night for a week and not repeat restaurants.

Grande Anse D'Arlet and Petite Anse D'Arlet are charming little fishing villages which have turned of late to tourism. There are several restaurants in each and both have apartments for rent. This whole area will suit those who like a quiet rural atmosphere and perfect beaches in pleasant scenery.

The South: Le Diamant to St. Luce

The coast from Le Diamant to St. Luce is relatively low lying, with just gently rolling hills. Along the shoreline are several attractive beaches and one or two bays. Several hotels and rental apartments lie along this coast. They look out over Diamond Rock which is one of Martinique's best dive sites.

The Southeast: Ste. Anne

Towards the eastern end of the south coast, the land becomes more elevated and a hill slopes down to a large protected indentation called Cul-de-Sac Marin. This is the centre of yachting in Martinique, with a large marina and many charter companies.

Ste. Anne is a picturesque small waterfront town with a pleasant, laid back holiday atmosphere just outside the Cul-de-Sac. From here around to the southern shore perfect white sand beaches lie between low cliffy headlands. There are even more lovely beaches on the windward shore, a few miles hike over the hills.

Hotels and restaurants are spread along the coast, including a Club Med. Essentials are available in supermarkets and one or two souvenir shops will supply sunblock and hats. Not much happens here at night unless you are in one of the larger hotels which have their own evening activities.

Language: French
Currency: French Franc ($1.00 US = about 5 to 6 francs)
Population: About 250,000
Telephone Code: (596)

Après Dive

One of the advantages in staying on an island like Martinique with a well established tourist industry is that you can be sure of every entertainment and amenity.

Golf

The village of Trois Ilets, not far from Anse Mitan, has an excellent 18-hole golf course that takes you around rolling hills with views out over the water.

Golf Dept. Martinique, Trois Ilets: (596) 68 32 81

Hiking

There are excellent well-marked trails all over Martinique, which are maintained by the government. Several books with maps and colour photos have been written about these walks. They are available at nearly any shop catering to tourists. You can also walk into the Fort de France Tourist office and ask for a map and get them to mark the starting points of some of the trails for you. When you arrive at the starting point there is always a large notice board with a trail map showing distances. The easiest way to get to the beginnings of the trails is to rent a car.

Day excursions are big business in Martinique and are available through most hotels and travel offices.

Horse Riding

There are plenty of stables happy to take you riding. For the most part these are in the southern part of Martinique, from Anse Mitan round to St. Anne.

Centre de Tourism Equestre, Ste. Anne: (596) 76 80 75
La Cavale, Diamant: (596) 76 22 94
La Gourmette, Didier: (596) 64 20 16
Ranch Black Horse, Trois Ilets: (596) 68 37 80
Ranch Jack, Anses D'Arlet: (596) 68 37 69

Tennis and Squash

Most of the larger hotels have tennis courts. There are two squash and fitness clubs where you can rent facilities.

Espaces Loisirs, Anse Mitan: (596) 66 02 89
Squash Club Sport, Fort de France: (596) 63 00 34

Water Sports

Martinique is a major charter yacht centre. Marin is almost wall-to-wall charter yachts, available by the day or for longer and there are also a couple of charter companies in Anse Mitan. You can rent a bareboat or a boat with a skipper to sail around Martinique or to cruise the other Windward Islands. Smaller powerboats are available for day cruises or overnight camping.

The centre of the day-charter industry is Marina Pointe du Bout at Anse Mitan. You can stroll round the docks and peruse all the day-charter boats which hang out shingles advertising their trips. One or two include diving.

Every major hotel has windsurfers and sailing beachcraft. Most offer waterskiing. You can also rent gear from the beach in Anse Mitan and some of the beaches on the south and east coasts. The following is a selection of the many agencies offering sailing.

Bambou Yachting: (596) 74 78 05
Caraibes Yachting: (596) 74 95 76
Catana Antilles: (596) 74 88 87
France Caraibes Charter: (596) 66 16 87
Kiracoulis Antilles: (596) 74 86 51
Star Voyage: (596) 74 70 92
Stardust Marine: (596) 74 98 17
Sunsail: (596) 74 77 61
The Moorings: (596) 74 75 39

Shopping

Fort de France is the perfect place for shopping, whether you want Paris fashions, jewellery or souvenirs. There are two handicraft markets, one on La Savanne and the other on Rue de République near Rue Moreau de Jonnes. Fashionable clothing is available just about anywhere but you can see many of the best shops by walking down Rue Victor Hugo and back by Rue Blenac.

In addition, Anse Mitan has its own collection of boutiques and nearly every large hotel has a shop or two.

Nightlife

Martinique is large enough to support quite a number of entertainers who often do the circuit of all the hotels, so something different is going on every night. One group, called the Martinique Ballet, puts on dance shows in traditional costume, depicting life in the times of the big plantations and slavery.

For later night dancing, there are several discos around Fort de France, and many of the larger hotels have their own small discos. Except in all-inclusive hotels like Club Med, visitors can go to these for a cover charge. The Meridien in Anse Mitan has a small casino, for those feeling lucky.

Le Cheyenne, Schoelcher: (596) 61 04 33
New Hippo, Schoelcher: (596) 61 84 87
l'Alcatraz, Fort de France: (596) 71 90 43
Le Queens, Fort de France: (596) 61 49 49
Manhattan, Fort de France: (596) 60 46 69
Casino Meridien: (596) 66 00 30

Information on Accommodation

Regional Tourist Agency: (596) 61-61-77
Office du Tourisme de la Martinique: (596) 63-79-60
Paris: (033) 144 77-86-00

Getting There

There are regular flights from France to Martinique, as well as good connections with the USA and other Caribbean islands.

The Diving

Comparatively speaking, Martinique is a big island and just as there is variety in the landscape, from the peak of Mount Pelée in the north to the low rolling hills of the south, so is there variety in the seascape. Diving in the north tends to be on and around more rugged structures. The sand is mainly black, affecting the water colour, and the steep mountains can cause reduced visibility due to rainwater run-off.

In the south there is more hard plate coral, particularly below 65 feet, and the white sand gives a turquoise hue to the water. Ask them in the north who has the best diving and they will laugh, "We have, of course. Why else would the clubs in the south come up here once a week or more?" Good point, but to be fair they mainly go up to dive the famous St. Pierre wrecks. Most divers visiting Martinique have heard of them and do not want to miss the opportunity of visiting this submarine memorial to the destruction wrought by the Mount Pelée volcano at the beginning of the century. La Perle is the other big attraction, an offshore rock which attracts pelagic fish.

Speak to the operators in the south and you will get a different story. "We have better visibility, the coral is more interesting, and we have Diamond Rock" they counter. Moreover, many clubs are wary of the demands of regularly carrying out decompression diving on the deeper wrecks of St. Pierre. The southern operators have a wreck of their own, too. It was sunk in 1992 rather than 1902, but is a wreck nevertheless.

We are going to sit on the fence. Each area has something to offer, it depends what you enjoy. If you have the time, try both.

There are more pertinent issues relating to the marine environment of Martinique than its geography. Just as there is a large diving community there is also a large fishing community and with the large population of Martinique, they have a lot of mouths to feed. We had heard that Martinique had been over-fished and wondered what that had done to the reefs. Perhaps we did not have high expectations, but we were pleasantly surprised. Admittedly, some of the dive sites did have a paucity of fish but others were as well endowed as reefs on other islands. We did see some large snappers and groupers and a reasonable sprinkling of lobsters as well as all the usual reef fish on most dives.

Divers and fishermen generally have opposing needs and views, but in Martinique a truce is currently in place between the dive clubs and the fishing community. Like most truces, it came at the end of a war. In 1994 relations had got so bad that the fishermen were stopping the dive stores from operating normally, by harassing the dive boats and stopping them from putting divers in the water.

The problem was caused by divers interfering with the fishermen's traps, breaking them open to release fish, cutting the buoy lines and so on. Many of the dive boats now carry a sign, telling divers that they must not tamper with the traps. This seems fair, they have as much right to fish as we have to dive, but the use of too-small mesh sizes is very frustrating to see. Catching juveniles is not in the long term interest of the fishermen or the divers.

For their part, fishermen are supposed to leave alone buoys placed to mark dive sites so that the dive boats do not need to anchor on the reef. And, of course, to keep clear of the dive boat when there are divers in the water. In reality, few sites are buoyed and on most of the dives we did, the dive boat anchored. Ironically it is the artificial reefs (i.e. the wrecks) that are protected by buoys.

Other aspects of the marine life in Martinique worthy of comment are the abundance of sponges, common throughout the Caribbean but thriving particularly well here. Invertebrates are also present in large numbers. There are lots of echinoderms (see sidebar later in this chapter), anemones and all of the reef fish which feed on such creatures. It was also good to see black coral on several of the dives we did and very little of it for sale ashore.

Rules and Regulations

Martinique is very different from the other islands in this book in that it is the dive operators who are closely regulated. As a diver there are very few restrictions placed upon you. In the light of the truce between fishermen and dive stores, lobster should not be taken with scuba gear. They should be taken only by free diving, by hand and without the use of a light (i.e. not at night).

Independent Diving

This is permitted in Martinique, no permit is required and it is widely practised. We often saw private dinghies on the dive sites and we have dived here from our own dinghy. Several sites are accessible in a small boat. Please remember to respect the fishermen and their tackle; do not be responsible for starting the next war.

If you want to get tanks filled, they will need to have an up-to-date inspection stamp and you will need to show your certification card.

Safety

Martinique has its own recompression chamber housed in La Meynard near Fort de France. The hospital is 5 miles from the airport but there is a helicopter drop-off zone in front of the emergency check-in area. The chamber takes two people lying or eight sitting. In 1995 the chamber treated 40 divers, all from incidents in Martinique. This seemed to us a disturbingly high number. Half of the cases were local divers and half were tourists.

The medical technician whom we met when we visited the chamber blamed deep diving for most of the accidents. In his view, tourists arrive tired and out of condition and then dive the deep wrecks in St. Pierre, perhaps twice in a day. They may be strictly within the limits of the tables but these are only statistically calculated limits and do not allow for special circumstances, such as jet lag.

Local divers who experience DCS and lung expansion injuries are often pushing the limits or have an underwater problem causing them to surface without the required decompression stops. Aware of the potential problems of decompression diving, many of the dive operators in the south place a 130-foot limit on all diving, regardless of whether the diver has been trained for decompression diving.

The French system provides special training in decompression diving for advanced divers (CMAS level two). PADI, NAUI, and SSI certifications do not permit you to do decompression diving. Operators in Martinique will not allow you to do a dive requiring decompression stops without doing a crossover training programme to a minimum of CMAS level two.

Contact information for the recompression chamber:
Hospital: (596) 55 22 00 Service d'urgence hyperbare
or Medical Emergency unit: (596) 75 15 75
Contacts: Dr. Elisabeth or Dr. Medowie

Being able to speak a little French will enhance the pleasure of diving in Martinique. We have developed a list of vocabulary relevant to diving which will supplement your regular vocabulary.

Parlez Vous Français?

FRENCH VOCABULARY FOR DIVERS

General		
	bateau	boat
	club*/centre de plongée	dive store
	courant	current
	enseigner la faire plongée	learn to dive
	epave	wreck
	gonflage/gonfler	inflate/fill
	grotte	cave
	piscine	swimming pool
	profondeur	depth
	programme de plongée	dive schedule
	sable	sand
	tombant	wall or steep slope
Marine Life	*carangues*	jacks
	corail	coral
	eponges	sponges
	langouste	lobster
	merou	grouper
	poisson	fish
	poisson papillion	butterflyfish
	poisson-perroquets	parrotfish
	poissons de pleine eau	pelagic fish
	requin	shark
	sordes	snapper
	tortue	turtle
Equipment	*bloc*	tank
	combinaison neoprene	wetsuit
	couteau	knife
	detendeur	regulator
	ordinateur de plongée	dive computer
	lampe	torch/flashlight
	masque	mask
	palmes	fin
	stab/bouee de remontee	BCD
	tuba	snorkel

* In Martinique the words 'dive club' mean the same as a dive store.

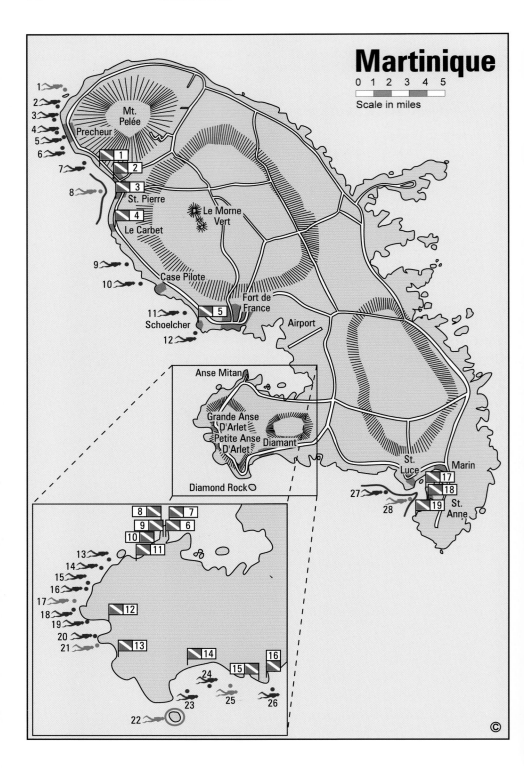

Martinique

0 1 2 3 4 5
Scale in miles

Mt. Pelée

Precheur

1
2
3
4
5
6

7

8

1

2

3

St. Pierre

4

Le Carbet

Le Morne Vert

9

10

Case Pilote

11

Schoelcher

5

Fort de France

12

Airport

Anse Mitan

Grande Anse D'Arlet

Petite Anse D'Arlet

Diamant

Diamond Rock

St. Luce

Marin

27

28

17

18

19

St. Anne

8

7

9

6

10

11

13

14

15

16

17

18

19

20

21

12

13

14

24

15

16

23

25

26

22

©

NO.	SITE NAME	DEPTH IN FEET
	THE NORTH	
1	La Perle	30-140
2	Le Sous Marin	25-70
3	Les Abymes	65-140
4	La Citadelle	20-140
5	Babody	50-140 ⊂
6	Pointe La Mare	35-140
7	Rivière Claire	10-80
8	The *Roraima* (St. Pierre)	35-165
9	Bellefontaine	10-50
10	Cap Enrage	20-65
11	Vetyvert	25-100
12	Wreck of the *Lady V*	20-50
	THE SOUTH	
13	Aquarium	20-35
14	Neptune	20-40
15	Pointe Dufour	30-100
16	Pointe de la Baleine	45-100
17	Wreck of the *Nahoon*	100-125
18	Cap Salomon	25-85 ⊂
19	Pointe Lezarde	15-100 ⊂
20	Grandes Jorasses	30-100
21	Pointe Burgos	25-140 ⊂
22	Diamond Rock	15-140
23	Le Tombant du Village	35-140
24	Fer a Cheval	35-85
25	L'Arche	30-80
26	Les Voutes de Trois Rivières	35-85
27	Pointe Borgnesse	20-140 ⊂
28	Red Buoy	20-70 ⊂

Martinique Dive Sites

Dive Operators

NO.	OPERATOR	RESORT/HOTEL LOCATION
1	UCPA*	UCPA
2	Bulles Passion	
3	Tropicasub	
4	Submaroubase*	Hotel Marouba
5	TropicasubAlize	Hotel Bataliere
6	Subchandlers	
7	Planete Bleue	
8	Centre Plongée Meridien	Hotel Meridien
9	Lycee Plongée	
10	Balaou Club	
11	Corail Club Caraibes	Hotel Frantour
12	Plongée Passion	
13	Cap Locations	
14	Okeanos	Hotel Calypso
15	Diamond Caraibes	Hotel Marine
16	Sub Diamond Rock	Hotel Novotel
17	Club Med*	Club Med
18	Histoires D'Eau	
19	Plongée Caritan	Hotel Caritan

*Owned by Hotel/Resort

The North

Although famous for the wrecks off St. Pierre, the north of the island also has good diving on fringing reefs and offshore rocks. The diving along the fringing reef is in sheltered water but as currents are common, much of it is done as drift dives.

1 La Perle

30'-140'

  W

Martinique has two gems of dive sites, a diamond in the south and a pearl in the north. La Perle is smaller than Diamond Rock and closer to shore. It is more vulnerable to weather conditions, though, as its size means it offers less shelter from the wind and waves.

You can dive right around the rock on one tank and it is the site where you are most likely to see sharks, turtles, barracuda and big schools of fish such as jacks. There are more parrotfish here than on many other sites in Martinique, too. It is subject to currents so the dive cannot always be done as planned but, if you get it right, there is very little finning required.

Dive Profile

The dive boat finds shelter in a small inlet in the rock, an area sometimes called the swimming pool. The dive will be done as a drift, going a little against the current to begin with and then allowing it to carry us back down the other side of the rock. The depth below the drop off point is 30 feet. Visibility is usually very good but nothing is ever guaranteed and in the wet months of summer it can get a bit murky.

La Perle is steep sided, at no more than 60 feet from the rock we are in 130 feet of water. This west side of the rock is almost a wall. Layers of hard corals and sponges cling to the cliff face as deepsea fans and black coral bushes extend out from the wall. We are reminded of the overgrown slopes of Mount Pelée above us.

This rugged terrain is polished clean by currents and wave action and unlike the quieter waters to the south there is no algae growing, no forests of sargassum. Groupers find other places to hide while they select their prey for lunch. Snappers and trigger-fish make up the rock's resident population and we look hopeful-ly for the distinctive shape of a turtle.

Around the east side of the rock the seascape is less rugged. It drops in a series of smooth ledges offering us lots of areas to explore in search of interesting life. A ray surprises us and allows us a few minutes to watch it before taking flight. The dive delivers

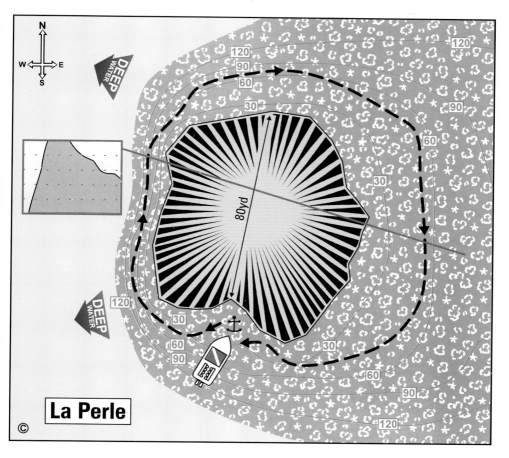

La Perle

©

Parrots Are Not Just Found in Trees

After a dive we often marvel at the unashamed mixture of the colours of the sponges and coral. But a significant contributor to this colour palette are the parrotfish. Not only does each species of parrotfish have its own specific costume, but most parrotfish will pass through three or more different colour phases.

Juvenile parrotfish have their own particular garb which then changes to their adult colours. Some species go through an intermediate phase along the way—why miss out on a new outfit? Adult parrotfish are generally the same colour whether male or female. Some of the adults will continue on to a terminal phase involving yet another suit of clothes. In this terminal phase they are called supermales, though they will not necessarily have been males in their adult phase. Many females become supermales and in some species all juveniles are female, allowing the reef population to settle on how many males and females are needed as the fish mature.

Stoplight parrotfish (initial phase), perhaps soon to swap this garb for the aquamarine livery of the terminal phase.

Parrotfish have a number of other behavioural quirks which suggest they are very well adapted to their environment. Experiments have shown that they have a finely tuned ability to navigate reasonably long distances using the sun. Some species, such as princess and midnight parrotfish, have the ability to wrap themselves in a mucus cocoon at night to contain their odour, thus protecting them while they sleep from fish which hunt using their well developed sense of smell.

For a fish which has a diet of algae, parrotfish seem to make quite hard work of it. They scrape coral and then extract the algae from it, excreting the coral as fine sand. It has been estimated that from one acre of reef, each year one ton of coral is excavated and converted to sand. The parrotfish's teeth are fused together to form a beak with which it scrapes the coral. But this beak is not used to grind it. Instead, they have a second set of teeth, deep in the throat, called a pharyngeal mill.

Of the 14 species of parrotfish found in the Caribbean, the largest are the rainbow, midnight and blue parrotfish which all grow to three feet or more. Smaller but very common on many of the reefs described in this book are stoplight and princess parrotfish. Both of these species go through dramatic colour changes. Stoplight parrotfish in their initial phase are a mottled red and burgundy, almost metallic looking. In their terminal phase they take on the classic turquoise with a dash of yellow, most associated with parrotfish. Young princess parrotfish have horizontal black and white stripes and also become bluey green as adults with a horizontal yellow flash as a reminder of their former striped livery.

Only a few islands still have native parrots in their rainforests but all have them on their reefs.

a cornucopia of marine life, interesting terrain, delightful colour combinations and an exciting adventure in offshore diving.

As we move shallower, the sun catches patches of orange elephant ear sponges like drops of honey smearing the rocks. We complete our circumnavigation of Martinique's pearl and hang in the water column surrounded by schools of chromis. A barracuda causes a flurry of activity but the chromis seem too inconsequential for it to bother with. Below the water, all is quiet and calm, belying the wild location of this site.

Whatever the partisan loyalties of the dive operators, we are all in agreement that this is one Martinique's best dives.

Le Sous Marin 2
25'-70'

This is the first dive site south of La Perle and is almost as popular with local operators and divers as La Perle. In this case the rock is all underwater and resembles a submarine, hence the name of the site.

The real joy of the terrain is the intricate mass of tunnels, arches and caverns which riddle the rocks. This complex architecture creates a fun route for divers and it also acts as a massive filing cabinet for a host of marine life. The larger crevices deliver turtles, the smaller ones a varied bag of crustaceans. Every hole and tunnel you peer into has antennae quivering in anticipation. It is probably worth taking a light to fully appreciate all the life.

Les Abymes 3
65'-140'

Half-way between La Perle and St. Pierre is the village of Precheur. Les Abymes is a reef just off the village. There is a coral plateau and, further out, a wall. It is a pleasant site, not subject to strong currents but often done as a drift nevertheless.

There is a good range of sponges and coral, providing yet more housing for a variety of shrimps and crabs. Some quite large fish pass by here, especially Spanish mackerel.

La Citadelle 4
20'-140'

Generally considered one of the best sites along this stretch of coast, La Citadelle is a luscious reef both in terms of the sessile life and fish. A gentle plateau at the top of the reef tips over into a near vertical wall at 50 feet, continuing down well into Neptune's cellars.

Again, sponges are very good here but so is the hard coral. Brain corals display their convoluted surface like a game of find your way out of the maze. Star coral, too, covers much of the terrain and gorgonians grow strong and healthy.

Reef fish, especially parrotfish, are abundant but look out for schools of snappers, jacks and barracuda. The wall is punctuated with crevices, concealing porcupinefish and lobsters.

5 Babody
50'-140'

It is surprising to find such a good dive so close to the beach. Apart from the pleasing marine life, the site offers an interesting cruise along a series of canyons lying side by side. These canyons descend to 200 feet.

Iridescent azure sponges light your way as you glide through the canyon and, as you move deeper, deepwater sea fans add their colours to the spectacle.

6 Pointe La Mare/ Tombant de Cocoune
35'-140'

Moving south, Pointe La Mare offers another small but near vertical wall, decorated with a mosaic of colourful sponges and coral.

The site has the advantage that the top of the reef is relatively shallow, allowing divers to extend their dive time by finishing the dive in this area. Garden eels will wave enticingly at you from the sand only to disappear the moment you move towards them. On the main part of the reef you will find moray eels and snake eels (which are eels not snakes despite their snake-like appearance).

7 Rivière Claire
10'-80'

Only a short boat ride from St. Pierre, a shallow generally current-free site makes this ideal for beginners. There is plenty to interest divers of any level on the reef top and along a small steep slope. Juvenile reef fish, especially wrasse and colourful parrotfish make up the fauna of the reef.

Wrecks of St. Pierre

These wrecks are dived by local dive stores every day. Although all very close to the shore, a steeply shelving sea bed demands a deep dive for all but one of the wrecks. The exception, the *Raisner* (K), south of the main harbour area, is in just 35 feet of water and can be seen from the surface. It is only 200 yards from the shore.

At the other extreme, the *Tamaya* (L) is at 285 feet and most people are content to see this by taking a trip on the submarine, *Mobilis*. A few locals are tempted to dive it each year, occasionally with dire consequences. The *Tamaya* is a huge three-master, lying on her starboard side on the edge of a sheer drop-off.

The most popular wrecks, because they can be dived within PADI and NAUI recreational diving depth limits, i.e. less than 140 feet, are the *Dahlia* (D) and the *Diamant* (E). Both wrecks are at around 100 feet, with the Barge (F) which the *Diamant* had in tow just a short distance away. Both wrecks can be seen during one dive. These wrecks are in reasonable condition and make an interesting site for those not wishing to do a deeper dive.

The *Roraima* (G) is the most popular wreck, however.

Diving into St. Pierre's History

On the morning of 8 May, 1902, stacks of barrels and cartons make the wharf almost unpassable, as a throng of people attempt to do their business. At least 12 ships fill the small bay. Ashore, the market stalls barely cope with the demand for fresh fruits from sailors too long at sea. Seamen and merchants fill the bars throughout the town, each to its own quarter. Deals are struck between merchants and local businessmen while sailors tell tall stories to local townspeople. The town exudes life and energy.

Then a massive explosion from Mount Pelée causes a fireball to descend upon the town of St. Pierre. At a stroke, all life is extinguished. Captaine Edward Freeman, commandant le *Roddam* arriving on the scene, declared: "We have arrived in hell; you can telegraph to the world that no one is left alive in Saint Pierre."

All of the ships in the harbour were sunk with horrendous loss of life. Almost nothing was left of the original town. Having conceded the role of commercial and administrative capital to Fort de France, it has been rebuilt as a small, quiet village. Only a few yachts and local fishing boats now occupy the harbour.

In the 1970s a combination of the evolution of modern scuba equipment and the curiosity of one man, Michel Metery, resulted in the first exploration of the harbour's sea bed. He and a team of friends, including Jacques Cousteau, discovered and identified a dozen wrecks.

A	Yacht Italien	80 feet
B	*Clementina*	160 feet
C	*Gabrielle*	100 feet
D	*Dahlia*	85 feet
E	*Diamant*	85 feet
F	*Diamant* Barge	85 feet
G	*Roraima*	165 feet
H	Broken up yacht	115 feet
I	Grand Voilier	115 feet
J	*Teresa Lo Vigo*	125 feet
K	*Raisinier*	35 feet
L	*Tamaya*	280 feet

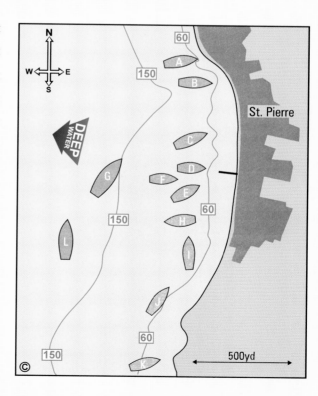

8 The *Roraima*

35'-165'

 or

 W

The *Roraima* (G) is generally rated as the best of St. Pierre's wreck dives. The top of the wreck only can be done as a no decompression dive. At 165 feet the bottom has to be done as a decompression dive. The dive operators in Martinique are all registered and controlled by the French authorities and French Federation. Their rules allow for decompression dives, i.e. diving to a depth which requires making a number of carefully timed decompression stops (N.B. this is different from the PADI safety stop). There are strict training and safety standards which have to be met. The local operators who were conducting decompression dives were meeting the requirements—providing extra tanks suspended at appropriate depths for decompression stops, for example.

PADI and NAUI divers who want to stay within their tables are taken on to the top section of the *Roraima* only. This is still an interesting way to do the dive as the light is good and the wreck is large enough to occupy you for the duration of your dive time.

Unlike the other ships in the harbour, the *Roraima* did not sink immediately. She burned for 3 days before finally joining the rest of the fleet on the sea bed. A Quebec Line steam ship, she carried half passengers and half freight. She sits still upright and pretty much intact, though evidence of the fire is everywhere. Twisted metal and distorted frames show the effects of the intense heat.

The bustling harbour of St. Pierre before the terrible events of 1902.

The *Roraima* is 400 feet long and 65 feet wide, a startling sight as you drop down through the blue. The top of the wreck is at 115 feet. Coral and sponge have encrusted the hull, but a combination of the effects of the fire, the covering of volcanic ash and the depth have inhibited growth to some extent. Sponges fare well as they do not need as much light as coral.

The bow is the most impressive sight as we drop down, pointing skywards wistfully, as if hopeful still of rescue, perhaps. Hanging from the bow, the anchor chain is so thickly encrusted that it is impossible to distinguish the links.

There is some damage to the port side forward section and the funnel is cut off to a level with the bridge. Various decks are visible, with access into the hull through a number of gaping holes. Passages have been cleared of dangerous cables and pipes, though wire coral sprouts from the superstructure, imitating the intestinal network of the ship's systems.

The engine room can be penetrated though there is little encrustation in these inner areas. You will need a light for a close inspection. Blackbar soldierfish have chosen these quarters as a safe sanctuary during the daylight hours and seem to be accustomed to curious divers.

The *Roraima* emits a powerful presence and diving such a large vessel at this depth is a sobering experience, like entering a grand church; appropriate when we remember that this is a memorial to the many sailors whose lives were extinguished by the wanton fiery breath of Mount Pelée.

Dive Profile

A large relatively shallow reef plateau extends from the town of Bellefontaine seawards. Consequently it is chosen by operators for beginners and families, where some will snorkel and some dive. The site will deliver much of interest with a small slope covered in corals and soft gorgonian sea plumes.

Bellefontaine 9
10'-50'

We like dives with lots of interesting rocks and caves, and that is exactly what Cap Enrage offers. Large boulders create small canyons and a shallow cave which echoes the sound of the swells above. This is a site subject to currents so dive operators will choose their time carefully to dive here. It will invariably be a drift dive. The current causes the beautiful array of gorgonians to ripple and stutter in the flow, like trees on a windy day.

Cap Enrage 10
20'-65'

This is another big coral reef with a gentle slope to a sandy bottom. Although there is quite a lot of hard coral, gorgonians are the notable species. Large plumes and sea rods shelter small reef fish.

Vetyvert 11
25'-100'

12 Wreck of the
Lady V
20'-50'

This 130-foot motor yacht, sunk in 1987, lies just off the beach in front of the Hotel Bataliere at Schoelcher. It tends to be dived only by the store based at the hotel. This in part due to its location. It is too far for the clubs in the north or those around Le Diamant and Ste. Anne. Clubs in the Anse Mitan area have a wide choice of dive sites along the coast to Anse D'Arlet which are all much closer than Schoelcher.

The South

The southern half of Martinique offers a good variety of diving, stretching right around the southwest and south coasts. The sites are mainly sloping reefs with some interesting underwater structures, adding interest to the terrain.

13 Aquarium
20'-35'

An easy beginner's dive tucked into the bay has a cave and a swim-through. At 35 feet a larger cave has a hole through the top, giving light and an interesting feature to explore.

14 Neptune
20'-40'

Again, an undemanding dive but with some very good brain coral at 30 feet. The site is a gentle slope strewn with large rocks and enough marine life to entertain you.

15 Pointe Dufour
30'-100'

A rocky plateau becomes a steep slope covered in rocks. It is described by local stores as being rich in flora and fauna. Being off a headland, it attracts schools of fish in the current and the presence of local fishermen as we passed by confirmed this.

16 Pointe de la
Baleine
45'-100'

Another steep slope littered with rocks, this is a charming dive and popular with the dive stores in Anse Mitan, as it is only a few minutes boat ride away. The water is very clear, giving the coral and sponges ample opportunity to show off their colours.

In the centre of the bay is a small wreck, at 35 feet. It was a sugar cargo boat and is very broken up. Nevertheless, it still attracts a lot of fish and makes a good night dive.

17 Wreck of the
Nahoon
100'-125'

  W

When people think of wreck diving in Martinique they think of the bay of St. Pierre in the north, but the south also has a wreck dive and one that we found very enjoyable.

The *Nahoon* is a 125-foot three-masted ship sunk intentionally as a dive site 3 years ago. She was sunk skilfully so that she sits upright, intact. Her hold and engine room have been made safe to enter; the engines are still in place. Two masts remain erect, the third lies alongside the boat. The *Nahoon* has a strange ghostly appearance, rather like a stage set. Bits of telesto and colourful sea rods hang in the rigging, reminding us of the decor of a cheap nightclub.

She is in fairly deep water at 100 feet on the top of the deck, dropping to 120 feet at the propellers, making it more appropriate for experienced divers.

The wreck is buoyed with a line attached to the bowsprit. Slipping down the line, the first sight which catches our eye is not the wreck but a school of boga boogying around the mast. The wreck attracts many fish including large yellowtail and dog snappers. A large Spanish mackerel had taken up station above the hull like a sea bird circling the rigging.

We swim across the foredeck and peer down through the deck into the hold in the centre of the ship. Dropping over the side we find the entry into the hold through a hole in the port side. Blackbar soldierfish hang in the water of the hold, swaying gently

Dive Profile

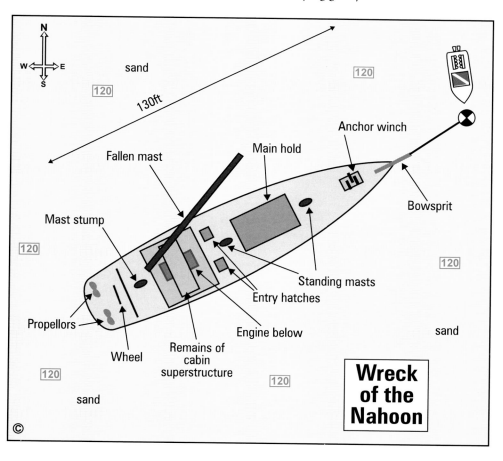

Wreck of the Nahoon

Not only is the hull of the Nahoon still intact, but also many of the hull and deck fittings have been left in place, giving the impression of a ghost ship.

with the water movement, like a mobile in a breeze.

On the outside of the wreck coneys, school masters, bi-colour damselfish and butterflyfish spray speckles of colour against the background of the ship's hull. While it is too early for much growth on the hull, there are features which compensate for this. The twin propellers are worth checking out and, best of all, the wheel is still in place. Like many who have come before us, we cannot resist posing for photographs holding the wheel. The stinging hydroids and fire coral reap their revenge for several days afterwards.

As you swim along the hull side, peer in through the portholes; hundreds of eyes will peer back at you. Nocturnal fish such as squirrelfish and blackbar soldierfish use the inside of the hull as daytime protection, their large eyes all the better to see at night. In the darker parts of the interior the eyes are all you can see, as the fish are red. Red is the first colour to be lost when the light diminishes, just what you need if you spend your life hunting at night.

Approaching the limit of our time at this depth, we follow our dive leader across the sand to the fringing reef in the bay where the dive boat has gone to anchor. We are able to finish the dive in 20 feet of water, drifting over large boulders. There are a mass of urchins, spaghetti worms, and sea cucumbers. It is also a good place for seeing stingrays. Watch out for the encrusting fire coral which spreads like caramel sauce across the tops of the boulders.

Thanks to Olivier Crozet of Corail Club Caraibes.

18 Cap Salomon
25'-85'

The dive is around the headland and dive stores drop you in different places, depending upon the currents. All around the headland the reef plateau is scattered with big rocks in a variety of colours, like a pile of children's building blocks. Encrusting sponges and fire corals create this colourful array. The variety of coral is impressive and includes pillar coral and flower coral.

Pointe Lezarde 19
15'-100'

Here is a site for both beginners and experienced divers. There are lots of things to amuse in the shallows. It is often described as a botanical garden.

The site is a coral slope covered in rocks and boulders, with small schools of fish darting in and out. This is a good site for photography. Although on occasions the current can carry you around the slope quite quickly, normally the current is quite light.

Grandes 20
Jorasses
30'-100'

For no apparent reason, a series of underwater steps occurs here. These ridges form both the Petit Jorasse and Grandes Jorasses sites. Although they are popular sites because of their natural beauty, currents can be very strong and operators select their timing carefully.

Pointe 21
Burgos
25'-140'

 C

This is one of those dive sites where the dive boat slows without any apparent reason and all those in the know start getting ready. We appear to be in the middle of nowhere. The fringing reef in this area does not begin to get deep until some distance offshore, about a quarter of a mile. It then becomes very deep.

Our dive leader informs us that we will be diving along a ledge which drops off steeply at 130 feet. Most stores set a maximum depth of 130 feet so the dive is along the ledge. Only those diving decompression profiles descend beyond the edge of the ledge.

The marine life on the ledge offers more than enough entertainment without any need to venture further down, where, in any case, poor light limits the opportunity to appreciate the scenery. It is curiosity that draws people to peer over the edge but, remember, curiosity killed the cat.

Dive Profile

The dive boat takes up station on the shallow top of the reef, in 30 feet of water. When we enter the water we are shocked to find not the usual animal life of corals and sponges but an extensive thick field of plants, sargassum algae. This plant looks like mistletoe, but it is difficult to take up the offer of a kiss with a regulator in your mouth. The things that look like the berries of mistletoe are air sacs which keep the plants upright. Sargassum is the warm water relative of kelp and it is the free-floating species of the plant which gives its name to the Sargasso Sea.

The Sargassum disappears at 45 feet and is replaced with coral heads and large sponges, bordered by sand the colour and texture of face powder. Azure sponges and orange ball sponges make this a colourful reef and fish of many types are plentiful. Some large snappers watch our progress and black margates engage in some odd swimming rituals. As we descend to 125 feet, deepwater sea fans appear along with straggly purple rope sponges.

The number of fish increase, if anything, with schools of Caesar grunts, surgeonfish and small groupers putting in an appearance. The reef has a good covering of hard corals; star coral, boulder coral and patches of flower coral add colour and texture to the seascape. Scorpionfish attempt, quite successfully, to look like lumps of coral, and worms pop out of the coral like sun umbrellas.

During our cruise across the reef we find three fish traps. Every one of them has trapped an eel, two in one case. They are spotted morays and one purple-mouth. It is sad to see both the eels and the small reef fish in the trap as they are of little or no use as a catch. If only larger net sizes were used, this unnecessary loss would be stopped, to the benefit of divers and fishermen. However, we leave the traps alone as a fragile truce exists between dive stores and the local fishing community.

We complete the dive in 40 to 50 feet of water, swimming slowly back toward the dive boat. White feather hydroids make a pretty sight. The stringy legs of spaghetti worms straddle the coral and we spot the twitching of a lobster's antennae. Tucked securely under a

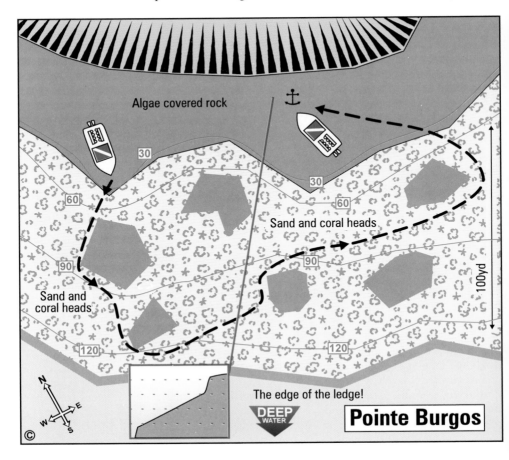

Algae covered rock

Sand and coral heads

Sand and coral heads

100yd

N
E
W
S

The edge of the ledge!

DEEP WATER

Pointe Burgos

ledge it tolerates our stares, ready to disappear deeper into its recess at the first sign of our passive observation becoming more active.

We return to the boat when our air consumption demands it to do a safety stop under the boat. Our dive leader has two tanks as a precaution against out-of-air emergencies and a further tank hangs from a line in case anyone needs air for their safety stop.

Thanks to Laurent Quaeybeur of Planete Bleue.

This craggy multi-faceted protrusion not only looks like a diamond but was once the jewel in the crown of the British fleet of war ships attempting to dominate the Caribbean islands. The British and the French fought over so many islands in the early nineteenth century that ships were sometimes in short supply. Only one ship, the 74-gun *Centaur* was assigned to blockade the ports of Martinique. By capturing a French ship they were able to double their defences but even this was poor cover because Martinique had two harbours, St. Pierre in the north and the bay which is now called Fort de France in the south.

Short of ships but not imagination, Commodore Sir Samuel Hood declared Diamond Rock a man-of-war and proceeded to equip her as one. Guns were hauled to the top of the rock and the passage between Martinique and Diamond Rock was secured. They even built a hospital in one of the caves on the rock. This was no temporary gesture; the rock remained in service for 2 years.

Thankfully, scuba equipment had not been invented or no doubt someone would have decided that the easiest way of unseating the British would be to send a crack team of navy divers to plant explosives under the rock, although the underwater terrain suggests that someone might have tried.

Diamond Rock

Diamond Rock

15'-140'

 W

When we arrive at the rock our dive leader decides to do the site known as La Faille, meaning a fault or breach in the rock. We anchor on the west side of the island, protected from the easterly wind and waves. The boats are able to anchor here on sand in 65 feet, on the top of a ledge. As we drop down the anchor line, we can see the edge of the ledge as it drops away steeply, and are tempted to explore. But, we had been briefed that a tunnel was fun to swim through so we follow our dive leader as he moves off anti-clockwise.

On the sand and the rocks a healthy crop of sargassum is growing but it soon clears and the scenery changes to a rainbow of sponges and coral. Lively shining crinoids wave their long arms medusa-wise. Towering clumps of encrusted rocks sprout anemones and a variety of hydroids. There are numerous trumpetfish well disguised by the sargassum.

A curtain of sea fans draws us through a small tunnel where yet

Dive Profile

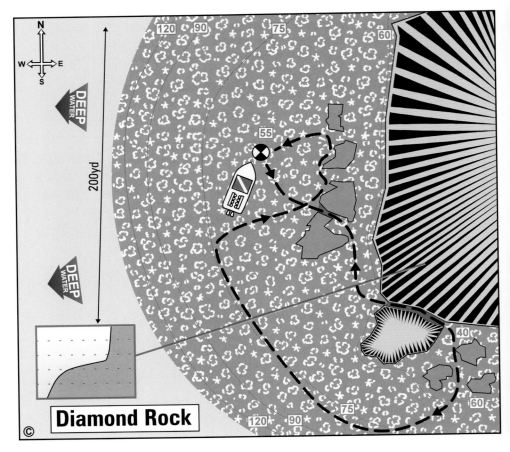

Diamond Rock

more crinoids hang from the walls and ceilings, filtering the water that passes through and stroking the divers like the outstretched arms of fans eager for contact with their idol. As we emerge from the tunnel a decorative display of hard corals greets us.

Thinking we had seen the tunnel mentioned in our briefing, we are unprepared for the arch ahead which, as we enter, opens up into a tunnel right under the rock. The noise is extraordinary as the sea forces itself through the tunnel, tugging at the very foundations of the rock. The surge lifts and discards us as if we are feathers or at least inconsequential compared to its battle with the cold hard material of Diamond Rock.

As we reluctantly leave the tunnel behind, we are greeted by sunny yellow tube sponges and a whole rock covered in mat gorgonians like a shag pile carpet. Turn and look back at the tunnel and you will see a rock formation like a ship's bowsprit, perhaps the rock's attempt to modify its morphology to fit its historical role.

After the tunnel, we turn right and return along a slope toward the anchored boat. There are good brain and flower corals here and elephant ear sponges like huge pieces of discarded orange peel. We see several sargassum triggerfish along this stretch of the slope. It is interesting terrain from 50 feet down to as deep as your dive profile and air will allow. Sergeant majors and damselfish will chase you off their patch and look out for spotted drums under the numerous ledges.

Back on the boat we gaze up at the rock, imagining the colourful life it had for a short spell in the early 1800s. It seems strange to think of the colourful life below the waterline going on then as it does now.

Thanks to Philip Callewaert of Subchandlers.

There are a number of different sites around Diamond Rock. One known as La Piscine is relatively shallow (15-25 feet) and suitable for novice divers. At one site there is an old French warship anchor at 35 feet. On the west side an English warship anchor has been found but, unfortunately, it is at 200 feet. Although the rock is on the south side of the island, hence exposed to the open sea, the dive stores are usually able to find a sheltered area for divers to kit up and the area can be dived almost everyday.

A long fringing reef parallel to the shore provides a number of dive sites along the south coast which the operators in Le Diamant frequent. Le Tombant du Village is at the western end of the town. It is an almost vertical slope starting at 35 feet and going down to a sandy bottom at 200 feet. It is a pretty dive with a thick covering of coral.

**Le Tombant du 23
Village
35'-140'**

Two coral formations create a horseshoe. An interesting cave is at 50 feet and it is always full of lobsters. More surprisingly, you will find a statue of Josephine De Beauharnais. It is obviously considered a bit of a novelty by the marine life too, as many fish seem to congregate here.

**Fer a Cheval 24
35'-85'**

We set out from the dive boat jetty on a sparkling Caribbean Sunday morning. The pirogue skims across the flat water scattering flying fish before its bow. It is a pity we have a journey of only 2 or 3 minutes; for once a long boat ride would be welcome.

The reef which runs parallel to the south coast offers some pretty diving in the vicinity of Grande Anse de Diamant. The site chosen for this morning's dive has the added attraction of a submersed arch, a good photo opportunity we think. Arches allow you to frame subjects, capturing the light in the background.

**L'Arche 25
30'-80'**

  C

Dive Profile

Our dive leader identifies the drop-off point, skilfully lining up transits on the land but not too proud to check it out by leaning over the side with a mask on. When he is satisfied with our position we anchor in 30 feet of water.

We drop down onto the reef and Jean-Luc leads us out to the edge where we expect to descend the reef slope. Instead he continues to swim out into the blue with us trailing, a little mystified. Ten yards from the reef he turns around and instructs us to do likewise. The reef face is not a wall but a hole, 20 feet high and 60 feet across. This is not an arch, it is a viaduct! Because of its size you need to be this distance off to take in the whole. It is obvious our photo ideas of framing an angelfish are inappropriate. You could frame a whale shark in this.

Swimming back to the arch, we begin our exploration at the base in 75 feet. The reef sits on a sandy bottom at this depth. The walls of the arch are painted pink and blue with an occasional splash of yellow or brown like faded wall paintings in an ancient temple. Vase sponges protrude, mimicking ornamental masonry,

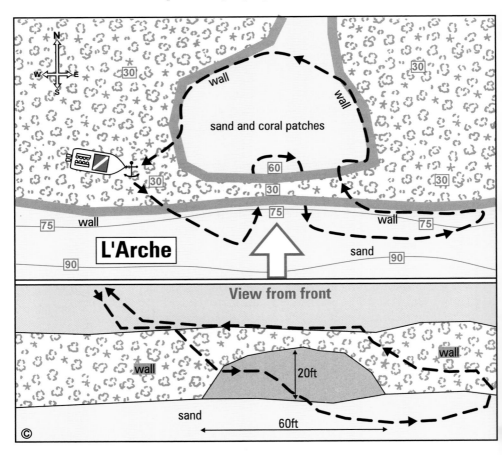

and purple fans like rotted drapes soften the outline of the walls and roof. Large black coral trees, hanging from the top of the arch, reveal a channel clinging crab tucked up inside the coral bush. Juvenile trumpetfish also seek shelter there. Fish swimming through the arch are dwarfed by its size and we, too, swim back out and follow the reef toward the east.

The reef is pretty much vertical along this stretch, with some good hard corals at 40 to 50 feet. Small fish move along the wall and we see the occasional rock hind tucked into a crevice. At half tank we retrace our route, swimming along the top of the reef this time. We surprise a striped burrfish but it chooses to flee rather than puff itself up.

We have plenty of air left by the time we reach the top of the arch so we investigate the semi-circular area behind it. There are many nooks and crannies here, revealing red heart urchins and a white variegated urchin. They look like prickly marshmallows.

One last swim through the arch and we surface to what continues to be a glorious Caribbean day.

Thanks to Jean-Luc Cecillon of Sub Diamond Rock.

Just off the town of Trois Rivieres is a coral canyon which offers a pleasant dive among both hard and soft corals. This is the last area dived along this stretch of coast and, although infrequently used, it provides variety for those diving from Le Diamant. The next dive area to the east is rarely visited by operators in Le Diamant, who prefer instead to go to the Anse D'Arlet area to add an extra dimension to their diving.

Les Voutes de **26**
Trois Rivière
35'-85'

Like all the dives along this fringing reef, the dive is down a slope starting at 20 feet. Off Pointe Borgnesse the reefs drops slightly deeper than it does on the other side of the Anse Marin channel, reaching sand at 140 feet. Those venturing to the base of the reef slope will be sure to see rays lurking in the sand, but anyone diving the upper portion of the reef will see plenty of other life. There is a pleasing display of sponges and coral and a healthy population of lobsters.

From Pointe Borgnesse a fringing reef parallels the coastline as it bends in towards Le Marin. On the other side of the bay a similar reef extends out and around Ste. Anne. The dive operators dive all the way along this reef. The sites being very similar, we have described just one—Red Buoy—in detail as being illustrative of this area.

Pointe **27**
Borgnesse
20'-140'

28 Red Buoy
20'-70'

  W

Whilst highly descriptive geographically (the dive begins next to a red navigation buoy) the name of this site hardly does justice to what we thought was a pleasant and interesting dive. There are no swooping walls or startling underwater structures but for those interested in marine life the dive will not be long enough. We were still finding new odd-looking creatures right up to the end of the dive.

The site is a gentle slope along the reef which opens out to form the entrance to the Anse Marin bay. It slopes to a sandy bottom at around 70 feet. There are dive sites all along the edge of this reef.

Dive Profile

The dive boat anchors on the shallow reef plateau in 20 feet. Patches of sand, rock and coral await us as we descend and begin to move deeper. Mounds of finger coral make a charming sight as blue chromis shimmy across the surface.

As on many of the reefs in Martinique, crinoids thrive well. The proliferation seems to have encouraged diversification of

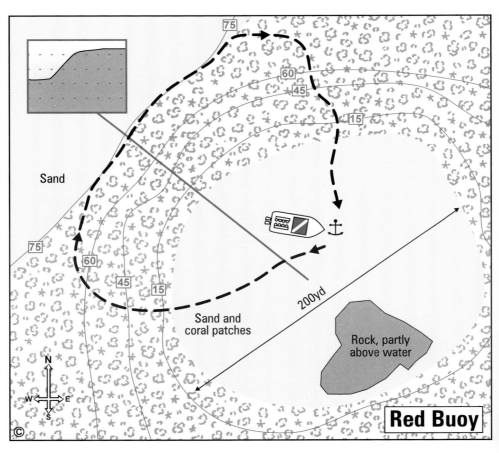

Sand

75
60
45
15

Sand and
coral patches

200yd

Rock, partly
above water

75
60
45
15

N
W   E
S

Red Buoy

A Family of Fifth Cousins— The Echinoderms

What does a sea star have in common with a sea cucumber? How about an urchin and a crinoid? A sand dollar and a brittle star?

Echinoderms are a very old family which has evolved into various forms in order to adapt to the world's changing oceans. What all of the forms have in common is a five-part body plan and a highly efficient internal hydraulic system. Originally the pentamerous body had a radial symmetry, a central disc divided into five parts. This is still true of all echinoderms except sea cucumbers which have evolved elongated bodies with a front and a back. The five body parts are still evident in the five muscles running the length of their bodies.

Sea cucumbers move along the sand ingesting sediment from which they extract food particles. It has been estimated that a sea cucumber processes 500 to 1,000 tons of sand annually. They not only expel sand but will expel their stomach and other organs if harassed by a predator. Its not clear whether the effect is to give the predator something to eat while the cucumber escapes or so disgust the predator that it changes its mind. Another bizarre practice is the five toothed cucumber's habit of housing a pearlfish in its anus. The pearlfish, up

The twitching spines of a long-spined urchin protrude from its daytime retreat.

to 6 inches long, leaves at night to feed and at dawn wriggles its way back into the sea cucumber.

The other common denominator is the ability of all echinoderms to pump water around a circular ring canal and then into radial canals leading to tube feet (podia), operating a powerful hydraulic system. These feet are used for locomotion and to pass food to the mouth. In the case of sea stars the podia are used to attach themselves to mollusks. Once the podia are retracted, it requires little or no energy to retain their grip on their prey. Some species of sea star simply eat their prey whole and spit out the shell later. Others force their stomach into a tiny gap in the bivalve's shell and by releasing enzymes they digest the contents in situ.

The five part body system of sea stars and brittle stars is generally obvious as most species have five arms. That is unless a predator grabs hold of one, in which case they simply abandon the arm. As with the sea cucumber, body parts can be regenerated. Crinoids may seem to have many more than five arms but there are five main arms which branch immediately forming ten to 20 arms, always a multiple of five.

So, what of urchins? Anyone who has seen a sand dollar will have seen the five segments of the disc and although you cannot see the test (shell) of a long-spined urchin, the same pattern is present. So, they are not such a miscellaneous bunch of relatives as it may at first appear.

colour and we saw as many shades here as we have seen anywhere. From bright yellow to deep bronze, green and white beaded species stretch out as many as 20 arms. Barrel sponges revealing brittle stars stall our progress again. Brittle stars are close relatives of the crinoids (also called feather stars); they look a little like them but are more mobile.

A more unlikely relative of the crinoids and sea stars, the sea cucumber, is also in abundance on this reef. These comparatively featureless giant slug-like creatures share with their more delicate leggy relatives a pentamerous sectioned body plan.

The cucumbers crawl around the sandy bottom at 55 feet, which is also where we see several lizardfish. The bottom of the reef slowly deepens to 70 feet and has a liberal scattering of black coral trees. They are big and bushy, clearly healthy and in both green and silver grey. Hamlets and baby trunkfish are taking cover in the coral trees.

A big school of yellowtail snappers is being stalked by two Spanish mackerel just off the edge of the reef. Suddenly a school of Creole wrasse sweeps in, mixing its purple and blues with the silver and yellow of the snappers like a psychedelic light show.

At half tank, we turn back and swim along the reef at 40 feet. The coral heads are adorned with many segmented worms, feather dusters and fanworms. Arrow crabs and cleaner shrimps are plentiful, so easy to spot.

Look more carefully and you will see many creatures which look like variations of anemones. Some of them *are* anemones. An anemone is a single polyp (just like the polyps that form corals but much bigger and with no hard skeleton) which attaches itself to the substratum. But, some of the things that look like anemones are zoanthids. You will find sun and mat zoanthids on this reef. They are smaller than anemones with fewer tentacles, found only around the edge of the disk.

We use up the rest of our air in shallow water under the boat, discovering clams, sea stars, urchins and yet more anemones. A spotted moray eel watches our progress, intrigued perhaps that we seem able to find so many creatures yet make no attempt to eat them. It probably thinks we have a most peculiarly fussy diet.

Thanks to Benoit Grondin of Plongée Caritan.

Martinique Diving Facilities

The size of Martinique's diving business creates both competition and choice. Each operation has its own style, strengths and weaknesses, and will appeal to different people. For non-French speakers, language will be an important consideration so as well as listing in which languages each operator can teach, we have commented further in the main text which follows.

The other thing to bear in mind when planning any diving in Martinique, if you are not French, is that the operators primarily teach and certify divers only within the French system (although recently one or two have been able to offer NAUI and PADI). Some of the operators do teach NAUI and PADI (see information matrix) and all will allow divers trained by other organisations to dive with them. They will want to see your log book and may want to do a check-out dive with you—certainly before tackling any of the deeper dives.

All the dive stores in Martinique have to be approved by the French authorities. There are very strict standards laid down covering things such as the number of instructors per diver, insurance, safety equipment and procedures. You will not be asked to sign a liability release as the authorities specifically hold the dive instructor responsible for your safety. If a store is found not to adhere to these standards it is closed. And, the authorities do check. They will even send divers down to check the instructor-to-diver ratio. Two-tank dives are not permitted so the usual schedule is one dive around 9 a.m. and a second dive at 2 or 3 p.m.

Many of Martinique's dive stores are based on the premises of hotels and resorts but most are independent (Club Med and UCPA are notable exceptions) and welcome divers from a variety of hotels, apartments, cruise ships and yachts. At the weekend and on public holidays you will also find many local divers sharing the dive boat with you.

Equipment

One of the positive aspects of the size of the diving market in Martinique is the presence of stores selling equipment. (The only other island in this volume large enough to sustain a retail sector is Barbados). There are two retail operations: one offers retail sales only, the other also offers diving. The latter, Subchandlers, is described in the operator section below.

The other retailer is Nautica Antilles, located near the airport at Lamentin. Nautica Antilles sells and rents equipment including photographic equipment and small portable compressors. They will also repair equipment and fill tanks. If you are on a yacht you can make purchases tax free by showing the ship's papers and your passport. See the end of this chapter for contact information.

The dive stores in Martinique use a range of equipment, mainly European manufacturers. Spiro, Scubapro, CressiSub and Omersub are commonly used, with one or two stores having some Dacor. If your equipment is US made you would be advised to ensure it is serviced before you arrive in Martinique.

All of the stores use steel tanks. The French authorities insist that aluminium tanks be thrown away after five years i.e. they cannot be hydrostatically tested and continue in use. You will either need no weights or significantly less than you are used to with aluminium tanks. Do a buoyancy check on the surface so that you are not overweighted for the dive as this would increase the likelihood of your damaging coral and cause you to use your air faster.

Cost

Competition has served to keep prices under control, with the average cost per dive being between $35 and $45. To learn to dive with the French system will take approximately 8 dives thus the cost to become certified is likely to be around $350.

Operators

In an earlier section we have described how the diving is separated into the northern area, which includes the St. Pierre wrecks, and the southern part of the island. The distances involved mean that those operators based in the north rarely venture south. The popularity of the St. Pierre wrecks does cause the clubs in the south to make excursions north.

The North

Based at the northern end of Martinique, within a few minutes of the St. Pierre wrecks, four dive operations are located. Two are independent and two are attached to sports resorts. The two independents are Bulles Passion and Tropicasub, both based on the waterfront in St. Pierre.

Bulles Passion **2** is owned and managed by French born Jacques-Yves Imbert. Jacques has over 15 years experience diving the wrecks in St. Pierre and, not surprisingly, considers himself something of an expert. A small selection of artefacts on a shelf in his office attests to his frequent exploration of the wrecks.

As with most of the operators, the *Roraima* is his favourite dive, though for those who prefer no decompression diving, he is equally animated about the *Diamant* and *Gabrielle*. His dive boat holds up to 10 divers and he is able to reach all of the northern dive sites in less than 25 minutes. Jacques speaks quite good English and is able to teach NAUI in addition to the French training system.

Tropicasub **3** is based on the beach at the southern end of the bay in St. Pierre. Lionel and, his wife, Françoise Lafont, own and run the dive store, drawing their business from local hotels. As with all the operators who dive these wrecks, safety is an important issue and Françoise described to us their procedures which include carrying out check-out dives with new clients, having a tank suspended at 15 feet and, of course, carrying oxygen on the boat despite the proximity to the dive sites.

Both Françoise and Lionel speak English. They are happy to take non-French trained divers diving, but, if you want to dive with them several times, Françoise suggests that it is easier to have the diver cross over to a CMAS approved level.

To the north of St. Pierre, UCPA **1** are a sports association offering diving as one of the activities available to members on holiday with them. The UCPA village is in the heart of good hiking country at the base of Mt. Pelée. Oliver Leblanc is responsible for diving and he welcomes divers from outside of UCPA.

Michel Metery, who first discovered the St. Pierre wrecks, is based at UCPA. His book, called *Tamaya*, describes the thrill of first finding and then identifying each hull. UCPA is a French association and there is little or no need for staff to be able to speak anything other than French.

Carbet, 3 miles south of St. Pierre, is the location of the Marouba Hotel and Submaroubamarine dive centre **4**. Rather like UCPA, a wide variety of sporting activities are on offer, including aerobics in the swimming pool. Right on the water's edge, the dive store supplies daily dives for the hotel's guests and happily accepts divers who are not staying at the hotel.

Laurent Teillet and his team provide a friendly and professional service, covering all of the dive sites at the northern end of the island. Only French is spoken by Laurent but at the time of writing he had a colleague who spoke a little English.

Moving further south, Schoelcher is perched on the headland just to the west of Fort de France. Located in the Hotel La Bataliere, a luxurious hotel right on the water's edge, is TropicasubAlizes **5**. Some, but not the majority, of its business comes from the hotel. Other customers come from nearby hotels and apartments—a mixture of tourists and local people.

The dive store is well equipped, the staff friendly and helpful and the boat is able to take up to 10 divers to both the north or south of the island without excessive travelling time. Eric Varlet, who runs the operation, speaks a little English but only when your French vocabulary fails you.

The South

The remaining operators are in the south of the island clustered around Anse Mitan, Anse D'Arlet, Ste. Anne and Le Diamant. The biggest centre is Anse Mitan which has half a dozen stores to chose from. Two of the larger operations are to be found in the Pointe du Bout Marina complex. Subchandlers **6** is a retail outlet which also offers diving. A retail store has been in operation since 1993 but Jean-Jacques Aleci has been joined recently by Philip, who now offers daily dives. Philip is an Australian, fluent in French, and Jean-Jacques has a good command of English. The store, open every day except Sunday, is well stocked with a comprehensive range of equipment for sale and rental. In addition to the store at Anse Mitan, Subchandlers also have a store in Marin. From this base they rent equipment to the large fleets of bareboats in this area. Portable diesel compressors are available in a variety of sizes.

In Anse Mitan, Subchandlers has a fast, 20-foot, purpose-built dive boat. The boat is well equipped including ample fresh water to rinse both your equipment and yourself. And, this is a fast boat, reaching Diamond Rock in just over 30 minutes. Philip promotes a friendly family atmosphere on the boat. Once a week Subchandlers make a dive excursion to La Perle in the north. The trips offers two dives with a lunch break in a restaurant ashore. The boat ride is about an hour but in flat water in the lee of the island.

This operation can offer both NAUI and French training and will organise a free medical examination prior to starting a course. Underwater camera rental is available and Subchandlers are happy to arrange accommodation in one of the many hotels or apartments surrounding the marina. Every effort is made to make guests feel at home, including serving a complimentary rum punch after diving. The French authorities have very strict safety-related rules about almost every aspect of diving, but have obviously recognised that they are not going to stop the French from having a drink after a dive.

Moored in the marina almost alongside Subchandler's boat are the two Planete Bleue **7** boats. For Planete Bleue, the boat is the store. There is a small office in the marina complex but pretty much everything else is on the boat. All the equipment is permanently stored here, even the compressor is on board. You just get on the boat and everything is taken care of on board. It works remarkably well, no hauling tanks, no forgotten pieces of equipment. It can clearly only be organised on a boat that is large enough. Planete Bleue's boat can take up to 40 divers, their smaller boat takes 20. The largest boat is a 45-foot twin engined catamaran. It has efficient tank racks, adequate dry storage and good shade.

With this capacity it is not surprising that Planete Bleue not only boasts being the first dive centre but also the largest. They do 1,300 dives per month in the height of the season. Their clients are drawn from hotels, cruise ships and local communities. Special deals are available for groups, including allocating a devoted boat to groups of 20 or more. They also cater for children with equipment to fit those 12 and up.

Laurent Quaeybeur who speaks some English is a PADI instructor so can provide PADI training, although the French Federation do not encourage this. You are likely to find yourself meeting the requirements of CMAS one star which is the equivalent of PADI open water.

Every week (twice in the high season) Planete Bleue goes to the north to dive the St. Pierre wrecks or La Perle. The trip includes two dives and lunch on board. This is a big, efficient operation which nevertheless manages to maintain a sense of personal service, one of the advantages perhaps of having strictly enforced diver-to-instructor ratios.

Centre de Plongée Meridien **8** has a booth in the hotel Meridien and a dive store on the beach at Anse Mitan. Owner Philippe Negrel is just as likely to be found in his handicraft store L'Hyppocampe in the marina complex. Two instructors Laurent and Pippi, who speaks a little English, run the day-to-day operations of the store. This store is also able to offer PADI training. The hotel pool is available for confined-water training. A variety of other water sports are available at the Meridien hotel.

At the time of writing Centre de Plongée Meridien is planning to obtain a second boat and will then offer trips to the north. Customers are for the most part drawn from the Meridien Hotel, Bakaua Hotel and the Carayou.

You will find Lycee Plongée **9** on the road from the marina. Thierry Poisard used to be a yacht charter skipper in the Grenadines before starting his dive store in Martinique. This is a relatively small operation servicing the Hotel Bambou just a little way along the beach.

Thierry speaks quite good English although almost all of his clients are French. He has two Sea and Sea underwater cameras for rent.

When we visited the Balaou Club **10** they had not yet completed their first season of operation. The store opened in March 1997, owned jointly by three friends who are all dive instructors. We met Philippe Denian whose background working on cruise ships has given him a service ethic which they hope will help set them apart.

They are offering cruise ships a special deal which involves a complete package. Passengers are met by a bilingual instructor who escorts them via the Anse Mitan shuttle to the dive store. The divers are taken for a dive and can relax afterwards on the beach in front of the dive store. Non-diving family or friends can enjoy the beach and other water sports while the divers enjoy their dive.

Balaou Club also offers budget accommodation in a self-catering bungalow for rent at 1,500 FF ($300US) per week for up to six people.

Just a little further along the coast from Anse Mitan is Anse a L'Ane and the Hotel Frantour. Located inside the hotel next to the pool is Corail Club Caraibes **11** which is an independent dive store owned by Elise Le Louarn and Olivier Crozet. The store has been on this site since 1993 when it was owned by Cyrill Boireau. Elise and Olivier used to run a dive store in the south of France before buying Corail Club Caraibes in 1996.

About 20 per cent of the store's business comes from the hotel. The remainder comes from local bungalows and studio apartments. People who dive with the store can use the hotel's pool, loungers, and beach.

Elise, who runs the office, speaks English well and although Olivier and Cyrill have only a little English, they create a friendly warm atmosphere on the boat and in the store in whatever language you are able to communicate. We found the atmosphere of the club warm and welcoming. For cruise ship passengers, there is a regular ferry which docks within 50 yards of the dive store.

You will board the dive boat from the beach, wearing your gear which is then lifted from you onto the boat.

On the western edge of the southwest peninsula of Martinique are two bays carrying the name Arlet. Grand Anse D'Arlet is home to Plongée Passion **12** a friendly club right on the beach catering for local divers and some tourists. In the high season the proportion of tourists to locals is higher than in the low season.

François Cavernes is an enthusiastic, safety conscious diver. He has been party to the formation of an association of dive stores (Syndicat des Centres de Plongée Professionels de la Martinique) aimed at raising diving standards. For example, they set standards for boats regarding their suitability for diving and state of repair.

Plongée Passion has some sites in the bay which other stores do not use, one has an anchor at 80 feet. A weekly trip to Diamond Rock is made. The store is conveniently located for divers on yachts anchored in Grand Anse D'Arlet bay. François speaks some English. Baby-sitting is offered at the dive store while you dive. The boat is boarded from the beach which is rarely a problem as the bay seems to get little surf.

Just around the headland is Petite Anse D'Arlet where Cap Locations **13** is based. The club is at the northern end of the bay, tucked back off the beach so is a little hard to find at first. If you walk across the bridge onto the beach then you have gone too far. Renaud has a reasonable command of English and attracts divers from local hotels and yachts as well as local divers. Renaud is from Brittany originally and has been living in Martinique for three years. He believes in offering good value to his guests who will typically find themselves diving in a small group as Renaud's boat takes a maximum of eight divers.

Le Diamant

The next diving area as you follow the coast round is Le Diamant where there are three dive stores. All of these dive stores are located in hotels but all take guests from outside. Okeanos **14** is owned by Michel Hager and his wife Michele. Located in the hotel Calypso just back from the sea front in Le Diamant, the famous Diamond Rock is in sight. Michel dives Diamond Rock every day. He uses five different entry points depending upon diver's experience level and sea state.

This is a relatively small operation offering a personal service. Customers come from nearby hotels and are predominantly French, Swiss and German. Michel and his wife have a very light sprinkling of spoken English.

Just outside the main town of Le Diamant is Pointe Chery. This small peninsula is almost entirely occupied by two hotels, each of which has a dive store. Joel Espinasse is the proprietor of Diamond Caraibes **15**, housed in the Marine Hotel. Joel has been in Martinique for 7 years and he started his dive store in 1994. Most of his divers are from the hotel though he attracts a number of local divers at the weekend. Joel uses a fast pirogue so can reach Diamond Rock in under 10 minutes. He is able to offer diving as far round as Petite Anse D'Arlet. The dive boat loads on a jetty just below the dive store.

The Marine Hotel is built on the cliff face leading down to the sea. The dive store's location is next to the pool overlooking the sea toward Diamond Rock and St. Lucia. It is a picturesque spot and divers gather on the club's balcony after the dive to enjoy a drink. Just save some energy for the walk back up the stairs to the hotel and car park.

On the other side of the peninsula is the Novotel and Sub Diamond Rock **16**. Jean-Luc Cecillon is the owner of this efficient pleasant store. The main office is well stocked with books and videos about local diving and history. The dive equipment store is clean and tidy, there is a warm shower and a pleasantly disinfected tub for soaking your kit. Your wet-suit may never have to smell again. All equipment is hosed off as you leave the boat then washed again in the tub.

Boarding the boat is via the store's own jetty, and the dive sites are all very close by. Jean-Luc can organise a souvenir video of your dive holiday, enabling you to relive it when you return home. Clients are drawn from many different hotels and apartments; about 45 per cent are French, the remainder being German and Swiss. Jean-Luc has very little spoken English but manages very well with lots of sign language and an intuitive understanding of what is required.

Ste. Anne

Extending like a crab's claw from the southeast corner of Martinique is a peninsula which forms one side of the Cul-de-Sac du Marin. Ste. Anne lies on the sheltered west side and is the base for three dive operations. Plongée Caritan **19** gets its name from the Hotel Anse Caritan but the dive store is an independent operation owned and managed by Benoit Grondin. If you dive here you will be in the company of French, Swiss and German guests staying in nearby hotels. About 20 per cent of Benoit's divers are from the Hotel Anse Caritan. One instructor speaks a little English and Benoit knows a few words.

The dive area which Benoit uses is very close to his base so the fast pirogue takes only a few minutes to reach the sites. The boat can take up to 16 divers. When we were on board there were 12 divers and there was ample room to kit up and prepare for the dive. Diving is well organised by this store, which Benoit runs in a professional and friendly manner.

A little further along the bay is Histoires d'Eau **18**. A small friendly operation with a clubby, family ambience is owned by Thierry Theroude and his wife. The store is situated right on the beach. Like all the clubs in this area, they are diving the reef tracing the coastline and entrance to Cul-de-Sac du Marin. They also make excursions to Diamond Rock.

The store's photo album is worth browsing. They have some very good shots of the local marine life although if you want to compete you will need to supply your own camera. Little or no English is spoken but the bonhomie transcends language. We arrived as a celebration was taking place. Two people had successfully reached the next level in their training. Who can refuse a glass of champagne when it is offered?

Finally, Club Med **17** has an operation in Ste. Anne. Not surprisingly, this is a big operation but it is not one of Club Med's dedicated dive resorts so there are a number of rules limiting the use of diving facilities.

You may only dive once per day (no matter whether or not the boat has space for you to do a second dive, it is a policy). Maximum depth is 65 feet, maximum time 40 minutes and you must return with at least 1,000 psi or 70 bar. You must dive with an instructor unless you are CMAS two star; PADI and NAUI do not count. For your non-diving time just about every other water sport you can think of is also available (except jet skis).

Club Med uses a 45-foot motor cruiser to reach six sites all within 10 minutes of the resort. Once a week they go to Diamond Rock where they take advanced divers only.

For non-French speakers, the good news is that everyone is bilingual. About 40 per cent of the guests are American, the remainder are French. Although Club Med is an inclusive resort a small charge is made for diving.

One last operator which is worth mentioning is Christian Botiveau. He does not operate a dive store; instead he runs a mobile diving service called Atout Plongée offering diving from sailing boats. For those who would like to combine a sailing and diving holiday, Christian provides all the equipment and his services on board a yacht of your choice. You decide what type of yacht you want to charter and where you want to go and Christian comes along as your personal dive instructor. He brings a compressor, tanks and equipment.

#	Name	Contact	Phone
1	UCPA	Olivier Leblanc	Tel: (596) 78 21 03 Fax: (596) 78 19 42
2	Bulles Passion	Jacques-Yves Imbert	Tel: (596) 78 26 22 Fax: (596) 78 26 33
3	Tropicasub	Lionel Lafont	Tel: (596) 78 38 03 Fax: (596) 52 46 82
4	Submaroubase	Laurent Teillet	Tel: (596) 78 40 04 Fax: (596) 78 05 65
5	TropicasubAlize	Eric Varlet	Tel: (596) 61 49 49 Fax: (596) 61 70 57
6	Subchandlers	Jean-Jacques Aleci	Tel: (596) 66 11 25 Fax: (596) 66 13 36
7	Planete Bleue	Laurent Quaeybeur	Tel: (596) 66 08 79 Fax: (596) 66 10 01
8	Centre Plongée Meridien	Philippe Negrel	Tel: (596) 66 01 79 Fax: (596) 66 01 79
9	Lycee Plongée	Thierry Poisard	Tel: (596) 66 05 26 Fax: (596) 68 05 26
10	Balaou Club	Philippe Denian	Tel: (596) 66 07 61 Fax: (596) 66 07 61
11	Corail Club Caraibes	Elise Lelouarn	Tel: (596) 68 42 99 Fax: (596) 68 37 65
12	Plongée Passion	Cecile Cavernes	Tel: (596) 68 71 78 Fax: (596) 68 72 52
13	Cap Locations	Renaud Clacecq	Tel: (596) 68 72 19 Fax: (596) 68 74 56
14	Okeanos	Michel Hager	Tel: (596) 76 21 76 Fax: (596) 76 19 28
15	Diamant Caraibes	Joel Espinasse	Tel: (596) 76 46 00 Fax: (596) 76 25 99
16	Sub Diamond Rock	Jean-Luc Cecillon	Tel: (596) 76 10 65 Fax: (596) 76 10 65
17	Club Med	Watersport's Mgr.	Tel: (596) 76 72 72 Fax: (596) 76 72 02
18	Histoires D'Eau	Thierry Theroude	Tel: (596) 76 92 98 Fax: (596) 76 92 98
19	Plongée Caritan	Benoit Grondin	Tel: (596) 76 81 31 Fax: (596) 76 96 18
	Atout Plongée	Christian Botiveau	Tel: (596) 70 29 33 Fax: (596) 61 21 42
	Nautica Antilles		Tel: (596) 51 69 72 Fax: (596) 51 85 56

Contact Information

Martinique
Dive Operators

		1 UCPA	2 Bulles Passion	3 Tropicasub	4 Submaroubase	5 TropicasubAlize	6 Subchandlers	7 Planete Bleue	8 Centre Plongée Meriden	9 Lycee Plongée	10 Balaou Club	11 Corail Club Caraibes	12 Plongée Passion	13 Cap Locations
STAFF	Instructors	6	2	1	2	2	3	7	3	2	4	3	4	2
	Divemasters	0	2	1	1	0	1	1	1	2	2	0	0	0
	Diving Associations	C	CN	C	C	C	CN	CP	CP	CP	CN	C	C	C
	Languages	EFS	EF	EFG	F	F	EF	EFS	EF	EF	EFS	EF	EF	EFI
BOATS	Dive Boats	2	1	1	1	1	1	2	1	1	2	2	2	1
	Shaded Boats	1	0	0	0	0	1	2	1	1	1	1	0	1
	Max. Divers per Boat	20	10	12	16	10	20	20-40	25	12	4-9	8	12	8
	Time to Dive Sites	5-30	5-20	5-20	5-30	5-90	10-60	20-60	10-60	15-60	5-30	10-40	5-20	5-15
	Dives per Day	2	2	2	3	2	3	2	2	2	2	2	2	2
	Pick Up by Boat from		RY	R			C	CR	C	C				
EQUIPMENT	Equipment Sets	60	30	15	20	15	70	70	30	20	16	25	25	12
	Dive Equip. for Sale		1				3			1			1	1
	Dive Equip. for Rent		•	•			•			•	•	•		•
	Photo Equip. for Rent		•	•			•			•	•			•
	Tank Fills		•	•			•	•	•	•		•	•	•
	Equipment Servicing	•	•	•			•	•		•		•		•
	O₂ on Boat	•	•	•	•	•	•	•	•	•	•	•	•	•
	VHF on Boat	•	•	•	•	•	•	•	•	•	•	•	•	•
MISC.	Owned by Resort	•				•	•							
	Other Water Sports					•						•		
	Pers. Liab. Insurance	•	•	•	•	•	•	•	•	•	•	•	•	•

**Martinique
Dive Operators
(Continued)**

		14 Okeanos	15 Diamond Caraibes	16 Sub Diamond Rock	17 Club Med	18 Histoires D'Eau	19 Plongée Caritan
STAFF	Instructors	2	2	2	8	3	3
	Divemasters	1	0	0	0	1	2
	Diving Associations	CP	CNP	C	C	CN	CN
	Languages	EF	EF	F	EF	F	EFGS
BOATS	Dive Boats	1	2	1	1	1	1
	Shaded Boats	0	2	0	1	1	0
	Max. Divers per Boat	10	8-13	10	32	18	16
	Time to Dive Sites	10-20	5-20	5-10	10-60	10-20	5-25
	Dives per Day	2	2	2	2	2	2
	Pick Up by Boat from						
EQUIPMENT	Equipment Sets	15	10	15	50	20	25
	Dive Equip. for Sale						
	Dive Equip. for Rent						
	Photo Equip. for Rent						
	Tank Fills	●	●	●		●	●
	Equipment Servicing			●	●	●	
	O$_2$ on Boat	●	●	●	●	●	●
	VHF on Boat	●	●	●	●	●	●
MISC.	Owned by Resort				●		
	Other Water Sports				●		●
	Pers. Liab. Insurance	●	●	●	●	●	●

Scuba St. Lucia

SCUBA ST. LUCIA is the island's largest, internationally most-renowned and longest-established scuba diving operation. An SSI Platinum, PADI & NAUI facility with a multilingual staff of more than 20. SCUBA ST. LUCIA offers daily scheduled dives and scuba courses for beginners and experienced divers.

SCUBA ST. LUCIA'S location in the heart of St. Lucia's marine reserves allows for easy access to the island's most spectacular dive and snorkel sites, all within view of the majestic Pitons. Dive into a marine reserve just steps from the dive center or boat to our farthest site no more than 15 rninutes away.

The latest diving equipment is available for both rental and retail sale. Our 3 custom-made dive boats are designed for your diving comfort. Underwater camera rental and personalized videos are also available.

Associations: SSI, PADI, NAUI

Associated Resort: Anse Chastanet Hotel

Languages: English, German, French

Number of Instructors: 12

Contact:	**The Manager**
Address:	**Scuba St Lucia**
	Anse Chastanet Hotel
	P.O. Box 7000
	Soufriere
	St. Lucia
Telephone:	**(758) 459-7755/7000**
Fax:	**(758) 459-7700**
US Resevations:	**(888) GO LUCIA**

Scuba St. Lucia

ST. LUCIA

St. Lucia

Only 27 miles long by 10 miles wide, St. Lucia's high mountains and twisty roads make it seem much larger. The Pitons, twin peaks that rise almost vertically from the sea on the southwest coast, are among the most spectacular natural features in the Caribbean.

It takes a whole day to drive round the island at a leisurely pace, and even then you will only see a part. The island's superb natural assets, dramatic mountain scenery, white sand beaches and excellent diving have inspired many visitors to return again and again.

A former British colony, independent since 1979, St. Lucia has worked hard to develop tourism. The effort was helped by the construction of Hewanorra, a large international airport created from a World War II runway built by the Americans. Now there are many fine facilities; not only hotels, but restaurants and marinas as well. Day charter boats and sports fishing trips are easy to arrange.

Most hotels are in a limited area on the island's west coast. As a result you can walk, take a bus, or rent a car and drive, and soon find yourself off the beaten track.

Tropical rainforest covers the steep slopes of the central mountains, while most bananas and other crops are grown on the more gently sloping coastal fringe. Not all food is grown on gently sloping land and you may see banana plants perched precariously on steep hillsides. Planting and harvesting are done by hand and the produce is often bundled up and carried to the nearest road balanced on the farmer's head or strapped to the back of a donkey.

Organised sightseeing and hiking tours are available through most hotels and travel agents. Popular trips include round the island tours, plantation tours where you get to see the backbone of the St. Lucia economy at work, and the rainforest tour, a 7-mile hike across the middle of the island. For those interested in nature, the National Trust offers trips to Frigate Island with its colony of nesting frigate birds, and the Maria Islands, two small islands which are home to both a unique species of snake and lizard.

There are many hotels to choose from. The all-inclusive hotels such as Sandals, Le Sport, and Rendezvous typically include food, diving, tours, and drinks—some even supply cigarettes. Most offer comprehensive entertainment plans. This makes them particularly suitable for groups which include non-divers. On the other hand you will have more flexibility and better opportunities for sampling restaurants and nightlife from a smaller, more traditional hotel.

The best diving lies about halfway down St. Lucia's west coast between Marigot and the Pitons. This is also the area of greatest natural beauty for driving and hiking. However, the hub of social activity and nightlife, and some of the best white sand beaches, are about an hour's drive to the north, in the area between Castries and Cap Estate. While deciding where to stay, keep in mind that dive boats can travel down the coast considerably faster than a car. (See our dive operators matrix for times to the dive sites.)

Castries to Cap Estate

The northern part of St. Lucia, between the capital Castries and Cap Estate, is only moderately hilly. The dreamy white sand beaches backed by palms are home to the majority of resorts, hotels and guest houses. Nearby are dozens of restaurants, as well as the island's biggest supermarkets and shopping malls. By car it is only about 20 minutes from Castries to Cap Estate, so everything is within easy reach. Inexpensive local buses cover this route and they run every few minutes.

The most social area is Rodney Bay Lagoon, a body of water surrounded by bars, pubs and eating houses, ranging from an Art Deco copy of a 1920s speakeasy to an Indian restaurant where the chef comes from Bhutan. The St. Lucian Hotel has evening entertainment and several discos and night-clubs are available. Rodney Bay Marina is here, with charter companies, shops and boutiques.

Gros Ilet lies on the northern side of Rodney Bay. At first glance it is like any other sleepy fishing town. A large church rises above the houses and shops, which for the most part are built of wood. Some houses are humble structures held off the ground by wonky posts or piles of stones. Other are more elaborate with balconies and fancy gingerbread.

Cap Estate is home of the Derek Walcott Theatre. The theatre is right beside The Great House, an elegant restaurant created out of an old estate home.

Pigeon Island is a national park which was joined to the mainland at Gros Ilet by a causeway in 1971. During colonial times, when Pigeon Island was an island, it was the main base for the British navy with a fort, hospital buildings, barracks and storerooms. Now it is conserved by the St. Lucia National Trust. There are shady walks and magnificent views from the hilltops. Near the causeway the old officers' barracks have been rebuilt to house an interpretation centre with natural history, Amerindian, and many other historical exhibits. There is a small entry charge which helps support the National Trust.

Marigot Bay is a hidden lagoon encircled by steep green hills and linked to the sea by a narrow channel. Legend has it that a small English fleet, pursued by a stronger French one, sought refuge here. The English hid by tying palm trees to their rigging and their ships merged with the surrounding land. The French fleet sailed straight by.

Today Marigot is a resort and holiday area with a marina which is a main base for The Moorings charter company. It lies about half way between Rodney Bay and Soufriere, and is about 20 minutes south of Castries by road. This is close enough for an evening visit to town, but far enough to be a deterrent after a sundowner rum punch. Although the area is small it is lively, with about five restaurants which range from gourmet to cheap and cheerful. A couple of the places occasionally stay open till the small hours with enough loud music to satisfy those wanting nightlife.

In Marigot you can rent a little cottage and while away the day lying in a hammock enjoying charming views. There is a beach and you are within swimming distance of some reasonable snorkelling. For those who do not want to go to town, there are a food store and several boutiques.

Marigot Bay

CHRIS DOYLE

St. Lucia's Pitons plummet from 2,500 feet to spine-tingling depths below the sea.

This scenic wonderland will match any in the Caribbean, with steep mountain ridges, incredibly lush valleys, wild flowers along the roadside and spectacular views of the twin towering Pitons, which rise to 2,600 feet. Here too is the drive-in volcano, a sulphur spring where heat from the centre of the earth is constantly hissing and bubbling out.

There is a botanical garden in the rainforest only a few miles away where you can take a bath in water that arrives steaming hot from the volcano. Underwater profiles are equally dramatic, and make for the best diving in St. Lucia.

Soufriere and the Pitons

This area will attract dedicated divers who want to be as close to the best sites as possible. It will also attract those whose love of nature is stronger than their desire for convenience and facilities.

There used to be two major resorts here offering diving but currently only one, Anse Chastanet, is open for business. There are several smaller hotels and guest houses. Those not staying in the resorts can make arrangements with one of the stores. However, check if they have a pick-up service as it can be a long walk.

Soufriere has a more local feel than the cosmopolitan north end of the island. The town has many lovely classic gingerbread buildings and a supermarket and pharmacy. Several pleasant restaurants are dotted around the area including Bang, run by an English lord; Dasheen, which probably has the best view in the Caribbean; and the popular Hummingbird which has a delightful waterfront garden. These are not within easy walking distance of each other, but taxis can be arranged.

Vieux Fort

Vieux Fort is a local town completely untouched by tourism. It lies at the south end of the St. Lucia near Hewanorra, the international airport. The surrounding country is fairly flat, with the exception of Moule a Chique, a headland some 730 feet high offering panoramic views over several miles of photogenic white sand beach facing the Maria Islands and the Atlantic Ocean. It is here that the Club Aquarius is located. It is a self-contained resort, but for those wanting to get out, there are several local restaurants including a first-rate Italian one called Il Pirata.

Language: English and Patois
Currency: Eastern Caribbean Dollar ($I.00 US = $2.67 EC)
Population: About 110,000
Telephone Code: (758)

Après Dive

St. Lucia caters for a wide range of activities enjoyed by tourists. All of the larger hotels offer a variety of water sports and the local cultural events are worth sampling.

Golf

The 9-hole Cap Estate Golf course is set in pleasant scenery. Gear is available for rent and lessions with a pro can be arranged. If you happen to be staying in Sandals La Toc, they have their own golf course.
Cap Estate: (758) 452-8523
Sandals: (758) 452-3081.

Hiking

For a group, the best way to get a good guide to the rainforest is through the Forestry Department. They have knowledgeable rangers and can arrange transport to the rainforest in some cases.

For just one or two people it may be easier to join one of the rainforest walks organised by tour agencies. These are available through the activities desks in most major hotels.

Carib Travel: (758) 452-3176
Forestry Department: (758) 450-2231
Hibiscus Tours: (758) 453-1086
Travel World: (758) 451-7443
Toucan Travel: (758) 452-0896/9963

Whether you fancy a canter along the beach or riding into the hills, there is plenty of opportunity for this sport in St. Lucia.

Horse Riding

Country Saddles: (758) 450-1231
International Riding Stables: (758) 452-8139
North Point Riding Stables: (758) 450-8853
Trim's Riding Stables: (758) 452-8273

Most major hotels have their own courts. However, if your hotel does not have this facility you can rent on an hourly basis:

Tennis

Rex St. Lucian: (758) 452-8351
St. Lucia Racquet Club: (758) 450-0551/0106
Windjammer Landings: (758) 452-0913

St. Lucia is the major yachting centre in the southern Caribbean and every kind of sailing activity is available, from day trips to cruising the coast in a chartered yacht. In addition, in most resorts and on major beaches you will find small craft, from sunfish to catamarans, available for hire by the hour. For sailboard enthusiasts, there is a major centre in Vieux Fort. For a different way to experience undersea life you can try deep-sea fishing.

Water Sports

Cats (day charter): (758) 450-8651
Destination St. Lucia: (758) 452-8531
Sunsail: (758) 452-8848/8648
The Moorings: (758) 451-4357/8
The Reef (sailboards): (758) 454-7400
Deep-Sea Fishing:
Mako Watersports: (758) 452-0412/8415
Reel Affair Charters: (758) 452-6736

The shopping in St. Lucia is varied and excellent. The local craft and food market ranks among the best in the islands. It sprawls on both sides of the road at the head of the harbour in Castries and is a marvel of colour and activity. Vendors will enthusiastically offer you local foods, T-shirts, coal pots, straw work and handicrafts. A ferry links this market to Pointe Seraphine, a duty-free shopping complex with over a dozen pleasantly laid out tourist shops. Though built for cruise ship passengers, anyone can visit. You may need to bring your ticket home to take advantage of the duty-free prices. Bagshaw's clothing factory is a short ride out of town next to Sandals at La Toc.

Shopping

This elegant and spacious establishment is perched on a cliff with a view over the sea. All the fabrics are silk screened on site and fashioned into clothing, cushions, and table mats. Nearly every hotel also has a boutique and there are clusters of tourist shops around Rodney Bay and Marigot Bay.

Nightlife

Night owls will find plenty of entertainment in St. Lucia but these activities are mainly concentrated at the north end of the island. The Captain's Cellar on Pigeon Island has low-key musical entertainment nearly every night, including classical music, jazz, folk music, and poetry readings. Pigeon Island is also the site of St. Lucia's famous jazz festival, held in May.

The Derek Walcott Theatre puts on dance, drama and cultural shows from time to time. In addition, many major hotels have musical and cabaret-style entertainment most nights which are open to everyone.

Derek Walcott Theatre: (758) 450-0451
The Lime: (758) 452-0761
Splash: (758) 452-8351
Indies: (758) 452-0727

Information on Accommodation

Hotel Association: (758) 452-5978
Tourist Board: (758) 452-4049
USA: (212) 867-2950
Canada: (416) 236-0936
UK: (171) 437-7920

Getting There

St. Lucia is well served by international and local airlines. Frequent scheduled and charter flights from the UK and other European cities have kept costs reasonable. Direct flights from the USA and good connections with Puerto Rico make St. Lucia very accessible from almost anywhere in North America.

Beware when making bookings to check which of St. Lucia's airports your flight will arrive at and depart from. All transatlantic flights use Hewanorra in the south but some flights from Puerto Rico and other Caribbean Islands use Vigie, near Castries, in the north. American Airlines uses both airports.

It is approximately a 2-hour drive (cost $80) from Hewanorra to the north of the island where many of the hotels are located. Hotels in the Soufriere area are equi-distant from Vigie and Hewanorra.

St. Lucia's dive sites are impressively colourful, on a world class scale. A range of submerged structures gives variety and encourages a diversity of marine life. Walls, fairy grotto rock formations, pinnacles, surreal arches and exciting trenches are all to be found, encrusted in coral and sponge and supporting a throng of invertebrates and reef fish. For those with patience and sharp eyes, seahorses and frogfish can be found around St. Lucia, but sadly they are becoming as hard to spot as a green flash at sunset.

The Diving

The introduction of FADS (fish attraction devices) will add a further dimension to diving in St. Lucia. Currently there is one experimental FAD off the southern end of the island, with plans in place for several others 5 to 6 miles offshore along the west coast. The FAD is anchored in deep water with the attraction device suspended at around 60 feet. It works like an artificial reef but, being out in the blue, it will attract the larger pelagic fish, creating diving conditions similar to those found on offshore pinnacles and sea mounts.

Though these more recent developments will certainly expand the range of diving in St. Lucia, the high quality of the reefs remains the main attraction. The maturity of the diving business means that the reefs have been heavily dived, but past conservation efforts have preserved most areas. Recently, the formation of a marine park has formalised the role of conservation and overall we were impressed both by the condition of the reefs and the abundance of marine life.

The most frequented dive sites spread from the northern tip all the way down the west coast to the most southern point of St. Lucia, with the best diving concentrated between Marigot Bay (see map) and the Gros Piton. Although there is interesting diving to be encountered in the south and southeast, sea states and currents make these dives highly sensitive to weather conditions. Experienced divers may be able to persuade one of the dive oper-

The colours of St. Lucia's reefs look like someone has been down there with the touch-up paint.

ators to take them there, particularly if you are part of a group, but the reward is probably not worth the effort.

There are four wrecks to explore on the west side of the island; two rarely used, but the *Lesleen M* wreck is one of the most popular sites and we have included a full plan and profile. In December 1996 a new wreck dive site was created just outside Anse Cochon where the *Lesleen M* wreck lies. The wreck is a 300-foot barge that was used to build Vieux Fort harbour. The barge is lying in 60 to 110 feet, stern down. The propeller, engines and deck cranes are still in place and the wreck has been made safe for divers to do a penetration dive.

In the Soufriere Marine Management Area (SMMA), dive sites are close together, effectively running in to one another. Although each has its own name and particular characteristics, the demarcation of the sites is somewhat artificial. This is particularly true around the headland off Anse Chastanet. On an island where there may be as many as a dozen dive boats operating each day, this proximity of sites means that there is no necessity for there to be more than one boat at each site. Further north, the popularity of the *Lesleen M* wreck means that there is sometimes more than one operator using the site at any one time.

Most of the dive sites are not buoyed, and some are exposed to current, so many dives are easy drift dives. There are one or two exceptions where ferocious currents whip you along at a scenery-blurring pace, but the dive operator will undoubtedly introduce you to something gentler for your first dive or two. A few beach dives available off resort beaches are ideal for refresher training and equipment checks. In the case of Anse Chastanet and Jalousie beaches, the dives are good in their own right.

All diving is done with a dive leader and, although not mandatory, a ratio of no more than 8 to 1 is the norm. Almost all of the diving on the west coast is accessible to PADI open water or equivalent level divers. Some wall dives plummet to spine-tingling depths and the dive operator will want to be sure that divers have appropriate buoyancy control before tackling some of the steeper walls.

The Soufriere Marine Management Area (SMMA)

The dramatic beauty of the coast in the Soufriere area continues below water and the region has attracted an increasing number of visitors, often to the consternation of local fishermen. In the past, fishing boats competed for space with anchored yachts and day charter boats; divers wished to preserve the reefs and felt threatened by speeding local boats and yacht dinghies; tempers were raised and permanent damage was inevitable as the marine environment came under increasing pressure from human activities. In 1994 the SMMA was formed to manage and resolve these conflicts.

Nothing could be achieved without co-operation and collaboration and the SMMA sought to bring together all interested parties to develop a long-term policy for the area. At the time of writ-

SMMA RULES

- **Diving in the SMMA controlled areas is allowed only with a dive operator.**
- **The collection of marine organisms, dead or alive, is prohibited and carries a fine of $5,000 EC.**
- **Divers must avoid all physical contact with the reef.**
- **Anchoring is prohibited. Moorings are available for yachts.**

ing, many regulations are in effect, but modifications will be made as the SMMA continues to evolve.

The area has been divided into zones which give priority to fishing, recreation, diving or multi-use. A map showing the distribution of these areas is available from the SMMA office in Soufriere. Plans to increase the area under SMMA control to include the coast north to Marigot Bay are still being considered.

Independent Diving

The regulations restricting independent diving were established to protect St. Lucia's reefs from large numbers of cruise ship passengers being allowed to dive, unsupervised and with no long-term interests in the condition of the reefs. The SMMA was considering introducing measures for divers on yachts who wish to dive independently of dive operators. At the time of writing these measures were still in the formative stage.

There were also plans to extend the boundaries of the marine park to include Anse Cochon which would in effect eliminate independent diving in St. Lucia. At the time of writing, it was still possible to dive independently off this headland and on the *Lesleen M* wreck.

Safety

St. Lucia has a good safety record which everyone is keen to maintain. Our experience of diving here would support the view that operators are diving carefully, well within the safety limits. All of the operators carry oxygen and are trained in its use.

At present St. Lucia does not have a recompression chamber, which is a little surprising considering that over 30,000 visitors dive here each year. Plans to install one have reached a fairly advanced stage. DAN has earmarked a chamber for use by St. Lucia and is currently waiting for St. Lucia to dedicate its share of the funding in regard to the management and medical staffing of the chamber. We were told that the funding is now available and that the chamber would be installed by 1997.

The nearest recompression chamber to St. Lucia is Martinique although, because of language and immigration difficulties, the chamber in Barbados is the preferred option unless the patient is French. Barbados is only a one-hour flight away.

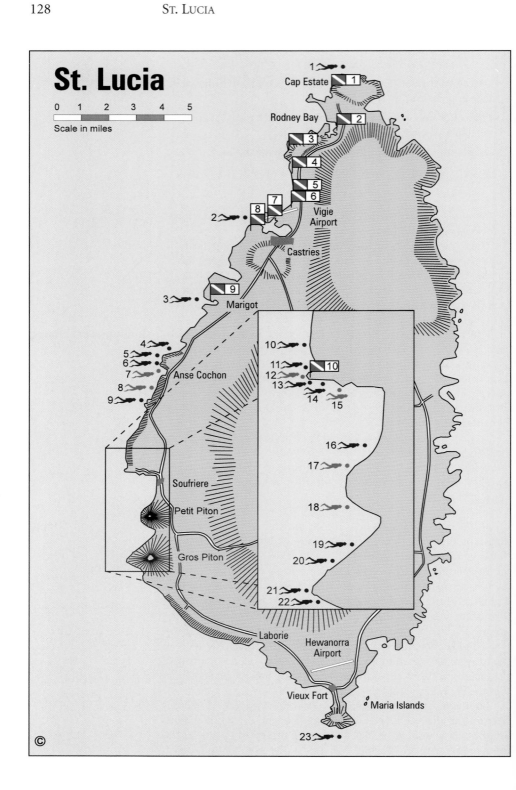

St. Lucia Dive Sites

NO.	SITE NAME	DEPTH IN FEET
1	Pointe Du Cap	20-75
2	Tapion Reef	15-30
3	*Angelina* Wreck	55-75
4	Anse La Raye	40-90
5	Anse Galet	20-90
6	Virgin Point/Cove	30-75
7	*Lesleen M* Wreck	30-65
8	Rosemond's Trench/PetitTrou	20-50
9	Jambette Point	30-50
10	Turtle Reef	40-140
11	Anse Chastanet Reef	25-140
12	Fairyland	40-60
13	Trou Diable	40-60
14	Grand Caille	20-80
15	Pinnacles/Key Hole	20-100
16	Malgre Toute	20-80
17	Superman's Flight	30-80
18	Petit Piton Wall	25-130
19	Jalousie	15-65
20	Coral Gardens	20-70
21	Gros Piton Point	30-100
22	The Blue Hole	90-130
23	*Waiwinette*	90-120

Dive Operators

NO.	OPERATOR	RESORT/HOTEL LOCATION
1	Le Sport*	Le Sport
2	Dolphin Divers	
3	Frogs	Windjammer Landings
4	Dive Fair Helen	Wyndham Morgan Bay
5	Sandals*	Sandals Halcyon
6	Rendezvous*	Rendezvous
7	Buddies	
8	Sandals*	Sandals La Toc
9	Rosemond's Trench Divers	Marigot Beach Club
10	Scuba St. Lucia*	Anse Chastenet

*Owned by Hotel/Resort

1 Pointe Du Cap
20'-75'

This dive site, off Saline Point, is located just off Le Sport Hotel. This shoreline reef with a sandy bottom provides good opportunities to spot sand eels and flounders. The reef is populated by a variety of juvenile fish. Big northerly swells occasionally make conditions unsuitable for diving here.

2 Tapion Reef
15'-30'

Just off Castries, this reef is rarely used by most dive operators but is conveniently close to Sandals at La Toc. It is an attractive and pleasant check-out dive. Nearby, the wreck of the *Volga* lies in 20 feet of water, making it an easy wreck dive.

3 *Angelina* Wreck
55'-75'

Located just outside Marigot Bay, this 45-foot inter-island coaster lies upright on a sandy bottom. It is home to two of the largest French angel fish ever observed in St. Lucia and lies just offshore of an interesting shallow reef. This is an excellent site for seeing antique bottles, as Marigot was once a refuge for English men-of-war.

4 Anse La Raye
40'-90'

This is one of St. Lucia's wall dives, rich in coral and marine life. The shallow areas display brightly coloured fire corals and there is a healthy network of soft corals, best appreciated framed by the sun as you look up toward the surface.

Schools of wrasse linger here and the reef also attracts jacks and Bermuda chub. The intricate pattern of corals creates good shelter in which spotted drums find cover. We found a greater soapfish lying tucked inside a crevice, and a large green moray eel.

Anse La Raye is an excellent example of the colourful reefs of St. Lucia and a good site for underwater photography. It is best dived at around 50 to 60 feet. Surface conditions can be rough, so a quick descent is advisable.

5 Anse Galet
20'-90'

In good visibility this is a lovely dive with interesting coral promontories encouraging exploration of the proliferation of marine life. There are many varieties of tunicates, and crevices contain arrow crabs and cleaner shrimps. Another wall dive, it is well populated with spotlight parrotfish, and schools of sergeant majors gather along the slope.

6 Virgin Point/Cove
30'-75'

This is a semi-circular reef wall with a sandy bottom at around 50 feet at the southern end, dropping to 75 feet at the northern end. Barrel sponges are in good condition at this site and it is home to many needlefish.

In 1986 the St. Lucia Fisheries Department sank a 165-foot long freighter in the entrance to Anse Cochon, to form an artificial reef. It quickly became encrusted in coral, sponges and tunicates. The ship was first made safe for divers and now offers a delightful artificial reef of interest both to those who enjoy wreck diving and those whose interests lie with marine life.

The *Lesleen M* Wreck sits upright on a sandy bottom and it is possible to penetrate the wreck to explore the engine room and hold. Visibility is usually good, though we have dived this site when it has only been moderate. Likewise, it is generally free of current but local operators tell us that currents do sometimes occur here.

Dive operators use this site regularly and it can also be done from a yacht's dinghy, but please do not tie to or anchor on the wreck. Have someone drop you off and pick you up or provide top cover. This is an easy dive, excellent for close-up and macro photography, a good night dive and one of our personal favourites.

Lesleen M [7] Wreck
30'- 65'

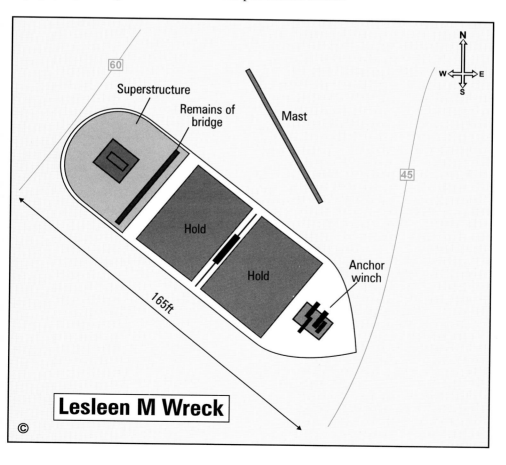

Lesleen M Wreck

Dive Profile

We begin the dive at the stern. This is the deepest part of the wreck, lying in 65 feet of water. The area around the propeller is a tailor-made hiding place for grunts and soldierfish who rest during the day and feed on invertebrates at night.

We are lucky to see an octopus, caught briefly out in the open as it guards a recently caught mollusk for its next meal. There is no point in suggesting that you look out for our many-tentacled friend as by the time this book reaches the shops its life will be over. Octopuses live only long enough to reach maturity and breed, about one year. But, you will not be starved of fish and invertebrates. This wreck is teeming with both large and small fish, and they seem to take little notice of divers.

Swim along the lower edge of the wreck looking underneath and you are sure to be rewarded with some interesting finds, including spotted eels and drums. As you become absorbed in the marine life living on the hull, you might experience the sensation of being watched. Turn to look out at the surrounding sand and you will see hundreds of garden eels, like a field of question marks begging for an answer.

The whole of the hull is thickly upholstered with coral and sponges and living among this rich fabric are tiny yellowline arrow crabs. These delicate spidery creatures look as if they have been fashioned from gold wire and adorned with tiny violet shoes to set off the elegance of their long limbs.

The best coral is on the starboard side of the ship where we discover large areas of white telesto, looking like a mass of ferns after a hard frost and forming a lacy edge to the propeller blades. A huge patch of brown tube sponge adorns the rudder which is also home to a spotted moray when we dive the site. Also along the starboard side you can see star encrusting sponge in shades of blue that a bathroom designer would die for.

Swimming over the bow to the foredeck we find an anchor winch and the remaining stump of the foremast. The rest of the mast lies in the forward hold. Yellow tube sponges have grown on the foredeck and it is a favoured site for sergeant majors to lay their patches of eggs. There is also a resident scorpionfish that you will need keen eyes to spot as its horny ragged appearance blends well with the algae-covered hull.

Light in the hold is inadequate for good coral growth but numerous fish use this area as a daytime retreat. At the aft end of the hold space is a large hole through which the engine was removed before the sinking. Experienced wreck divers can penetrate the wreck here and swim up through the superstructure, exiting through the aft deck. Please do not destroy any coral on the way through. Less experienced divers may like to peer in and see what they can see.

Moving back along the ship, at around 35 feet, is a covered deck that is open at the sides. Large schools of squirrelfish and blackbar soldierfish use this as day time shelter and, if you look inside and up, you will see what appears to be a mirrored ceiling. Air trapped in the wreck has formed a pocket, making silvery patterns in response to water movement.

We finish the dive by swimming over the top of the wreck in 30 feet where delicate spiny sea rods wave in the current, making the top deck look like a roof garden.

Octopus—Not Just a Lot of Legs

The catch which our octopus was guarding would probably have been a crab, the staple diet of this intelligent creature. While they may not immediately strike you as the smartest of creatures, studies show that they are indeed quite intelligent, evinced by their ability to exercise delayed gratification, a trait more usually associated with humans. Our octopus would typically collect half a dozen crabs while out on a hunt-ing trip and then return to its hiding place to enjoy a substantial meal, rather than scurrying back to its den each time it catches one or risking becoming a victim itself by dining al fresco.

Its den is something which the octopus takes pains to prepare and protect. A hole is excavated under a coral head or ledge by squirting water from its funnel. When tucked safely inside, the octopus gives itself added security by collecting rocks which it drags in to cover the entrance. It does not yet seem to have evolved to the point of realising that the little pile of refuse, crab and mollusk shells out-side the entrance is a bit of a give-away.

In general you are more likely to see an octopus at night, but this common octopus can be spotted on the reef during the daytime.

Octopuses are able to conceal themselves even in the open, by the use of colour change. An octopus we surprised in a sandy area between coral heads immediately fled for shelter alongside a vase sponge and within seconds was washed with the same purple hue as the sponge. The octopus is equipped with special cells termed chromatophores which cause colour change by contracting and expanding.

Another characteristic which sets octopuses apart is their care for their young. Unlike almost all other mollusks and fish, the female octopus nurtures her eggs rather as a hen does. She aerates them and fuss-es over them, guarding them for up to 6 weeks. Both she and the male stop feeding once the eggs have been produced and die shortly afterwards. If you see an octopus in the open which makes no attempt to find shelter it is probably close to death from voluntary starvation.

In this part of the Caribbean the most likely sightings will be the Caribbean reef octopus or the com-mon octopus. The former is rarely spotted during daylight, whereas the common octopus can be seen dur-ing the daytime around the rubble at the edge of the reef or on the coral itself.

8 Rosemond's Trench

Petit Trou

20' - 50'

C

Named after the St. Lucian diver who claims to have first found this site, it is an intriguing maze of trenches and tunnels which attracts more than its share of fish, from tiny slender file fish to rotund porcupine fish.

It was the site of our first sighting of a frogfish in the Caribbean, and certainly the largest school of barracuda that we have ever seen. Too numerous to count, they circle divers, perhaps attracted to the bubbles, or maybe just checking out the competition for the abundance of fish inhabiting this area.

This relatively shallow site is often dived as the second dive of the day and it makes a good night dive.

Dive Profile

A dive boat or dinghy can be anchored in the sandy area to the west of this reef in about 15 feet of water. From the boat, swim east until you locate the start of the trench. Swim along the main trench which runs south to north in about 20 feet. The trench narrows for a while and deepens to 25 feet. At the end of the

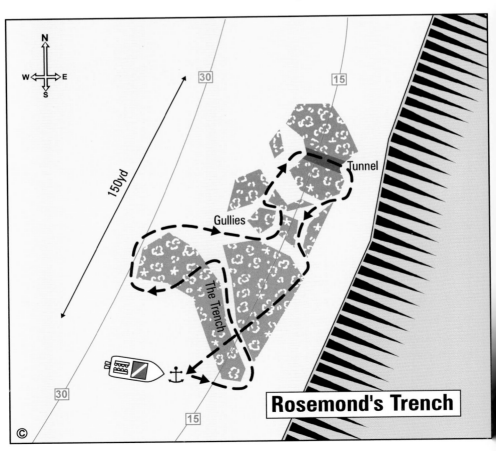

Rosemond's Trench

trench swim over the reef to check around the western end, and then move northeast to an area of gullies and coral heads.

The walls of the trench are covered in sponges including row pore rope sponges of bright purple. Lurking under the overhang at the bottom of the trench, spotted drums weave their way through the structures like waves around a headland.

Check out the giant barrel sponges for a wealth of brittle stars and golden crinoids. Donkey dung sea cucumbers can be seen around the reef, picking a careful and circuitous route through this complex terrain. Large numbers of both yellowhead and bluehead wrasse add colour, and lovely little barred hamlets are plentiful. The sandy bottom attracts Seminole gobies and yellow-head jawfish both of which disappear into the sand and rubble at a moment's notice.

At the time we dive, there are many sergeant majors posses-sively guarding their egg patches. While watching their pugna-cious behaviour, it is easy to identify the male sergeant majors engaged in this activity as they change colour somewhat, becom-ing a dark shade of purple. It is thought that this colour change acts as a warning to other fish to expect hostile behaviour. Individual intruders are easily chased away by the ever vigilant sergeant majors. They are occasionally defeated by a group of fish, usually of mixed species, forming raiding parties. After a brief feeding frenzy the raiding party disperses, its usefulness having ended.

Following the gullies around toward the north, we find a 15 foot long tunnel in 15 feet of water. It is fun to swim through and safe to do so. When we enter the tunnel we can see the exit and, as we emerge from the tunnel, swarms of brown and blue chromis form a welcoming party.

Swimming south now, again through a network of gullies, there are bright fire corals and yellow sponges to light our way. It is here, camouflaged as a sponge, that we find our longlure frog-fish. It sits very still, convinced we can not see it, and succeeds, for a while, in fooling some of our group into thinking that it is just another bit of sponge.

As if the proliferation of sea life has not provided us with suf-ficient entertainment, the big boys drift in. A school of over 60 barracuda begin a slow circumnavigation of the reef, clearly quite aware of our presence. According to local dive operators, it is not uncommon to see these schools in the vicinity of Rosemond's Trench during February and March.

A gentle swim back to the boat over a sandy bottom may afford you a glimpse of a turtle. We see one just as we are enter-ing the water. This is a relaxing, fun dive, suitable for beginners and allowing plenty of time to investigate marine life. And, look out for our frogfish.

Thanks to Rosemond Clery of Rosemond's Trench Divers.

9 Jambette Point
30'-50'

This is the planned site for the sinking of an aircraft to form an artificial reef. Meanwhile, a crescent reef and coral promontories running seawards are home to a variety of juvenile fish. The reef is draped with gorgonians which provide a lace curtain through which you can view schools of squid swimming gently near the surface.

10 Turtle Reef
40'-140'

Named, of course, after the delightful green turtles that occasionally visit this reef, there is much to fascinate divers on this site. There is a plateau at 40 feet which falls off to over 150 feet. Bold pillar coral adorns the shallower part of the reef.

If you are not lucky enough to see a turtle, look out for the flying gurnards instead. Watch quietly as they 'walk' along the bottom foraging for food, and wait to be entertained as they spread their pectoral fins to fly away.

11 Anse Chastanet Reef
25'-140'

This is an extensive reef beginning with a beach entry. The coral is attractive and in good condition, but it is the proliferation of fish that makes this reef special. Many of the photographs in Paul Humann's Reef Fish Identification guide were taken here without ever having to board a boat.

A plateau with depths ranging from 5 to 20 feet swarms with sergeant majors, chromis and wrasse, while cleverly camouflaged frogfish merge into the backdrop of a small cavern guarded by a school of reef squid.

At the edge of the plateau the reef falls away quickly from 20 to 140 feet in a solid wall of mixed corals. Diving at around 50 feet, it is possible to appreciate the life being lived both on and in the crevices made by the coral formations, as well as the schools of grunts passing by this busy reef.

Somewhat deeper, the coral becomes flatter to maximise the capture of light, evinced by a garden of leaf coral that looks like a giant cabbage patch at around 90 feet.

12 Fairyland
40'-60'

 W

Fairyland is named after its appealing grotto-like-underwater structures. Crevices, gullies, large rocks and overhangs are covered in vibrant colourful coral and sponges.

This dive is immediately off a headland and it may be that the presence of a continuous current has kept the coral clean, well fed and in good condition. Despite its popularity as a dive site, the fish seem happy to mingle with divers and are varied and plentiful.

It is a shallow dive, maximum 60 feet, with gin clear visibility. It makes a good second dive for the day and is excellent for macro photography.

Dive Profile

The dive begins near the edge of the Anse Chastanet Reef and is marked by a string of buoys. We drop down to a sand patch at 30 feet and swim southwest through a steep-sided crevice with a sandy bottom. We are struck by the colours on this reef, as if someone has been down there with the touch-up paint.

After emerging from the crevice, we continue round the edge of a large rock that extends to within 15 feet of the surface. This area is covered in orange encrusting sponges, intermingled with an array of gorgonians. The coral is dotted with fan worms and Christmas tree worms and laced with the long tentacles of spaghetti worms. It is good terrain for eels too: we see a goldentail eel, distinguishable from the spotted variety by the flash of yellow on the tip of its tail.

After the rock, we continue across the coral and sand patches. This is an area of large rocks, giant barrel sponges and boulder brain coral, which is home to many types of fish. We see black durgons and a coy balloonfish tucked underneath an overhang. It has such an odd appearance that you would not expect it to

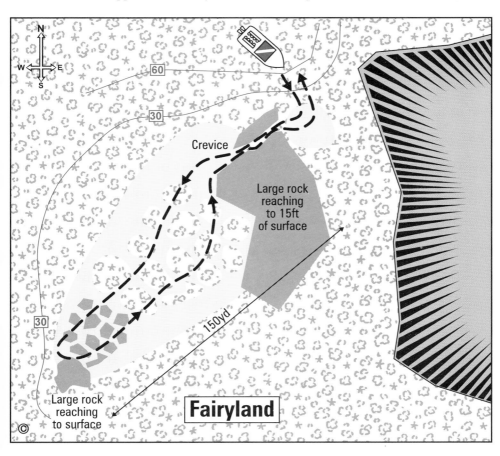

Inflatable Fish—The Pufferfish Family

The Caribbean has a healthy representation of spiny and smooth-skinned puffer and smooth porcupine-fish. At least nine different species put in an appearance. While they all have different markings and colours, the common characteristics make them easy to identify. There are some concerns about their survival if the current practice of selling them dried, inflated and lacquered continues. A creature which is delightful when found shyly hiding beneath an overhang looks grotesque when presented as a lampshade and is an affront to the respect the reef community should command. Please do not further this trade.

The spines of this balloonfish normally lie flat, but become erect when the fish inflates or is alarmed.

The largest species is the porcupinefish, growing up to 3 feet long. We have seen a number at least that length. Despite its size, it has please-don't-hurt-me eyes and a mouth spread in a broad smile. The balloonfish and burrfish, 6 to 12 inches long, have a covering of sharp spines but equally pleading eyes.

These daytime feeders enjoy a meal of invertebrates including snails, urchins and worms. To crush this tough fodder, huge front teeth supported by a potent jaw have evolved . Puffers are confident in their defence mechanism and will bite rather than shy away if you molest them. Admire from a distance.

Apart from eating, the pufferfish use their teeth by grinding them together to make sound. This is interesting when you consider that unlike most other fish, the puffers rely almost exclusively on vision. They have virtually none of the sense of hearing which other fish use both to protect themselves from predators and hunt their own prey.

In many ways the puffer fish is under-endowed to properly protect itself. It is a very poor swimmer, good at direction and hovering but bad at speed. But then, if you only have to catch snails, who needs speed? It is, of course, their unique defence mechanisms that set these fish apart.

By drawing in water, they can double or treble in size causing any predator to bite off literally more than it can chew. The spiny puffers add to the general discomfort of their vastly inflated size by erecting the spines which cover their bodies. But the puffers do not stop there. They are also highly toxic, especially their skin and internal organs. Only the Japanese have acquired a taste for this pernicious food. The resulting dish is called fugu and no doubt everyone hopes the chef is not having an off day when he prepares it. Failure to remove all the noxious sections results in death, as there is no known antidote. And, before you say "well, I'd never eat it," do you know what the secret ingredient in sake is? It is strained puffer testes. Enjoy!

require the added defence of being able to inflate its body. A look inside the fan-shaped vase sponges reveals a mixed community sharing the protection afforded by these structures. In one we find three residents: a large clinging crab, a glasseye snapper and a tiny flamefish.

There is so much good coral that you may find yourself struggling with visual overload. One lovely patch of pillar coral at the base of the largest of the rocks deserves special comment. It looks to us like the landscape of a lunar city, straight out of a Spielberg movie. The polyps are extended during the day giving a soft hazy appearance as though the scene is not really in focus, which adds to the sci-fi effect.

Finally, we arrive at a very large rock that reaches to the surface. We come across large schools of brown and blue chromis here, with individual tangs and surgeon fish darting among them. There are numerous bi-colour damsel fish looking as though they have been caught with their noses in a chocolate vat. Both adults and the more startlingly coloured juvenile yellowtail damselfish are also plentiful.

This is such an easy dive, yet it delivers pleasures that you would normally expect only from a more demanding site.

Thanks to Ponti Francis of Scuba St. Lucia.

Trou Diable 13
40'-60'

The devil's hole holds no horrors, just an intriguing labyrinth of underwater structures through which one can glide effortlessly. The fish seem to find it equally pleasurable, swooping around boulders and canyons as if trying to direct the aimless wandering of divers.

The shallower section, at 20 to 30 feet, is an excellent location for spotting eels including the golden spotted variety. At 40 to 60 feet, a steep slope is decorated with well-developed coral heads and a mosaic of colourful sponges.

Grand Caille 14
20'-80'

Everyone seems to have their own favourite part of this area. Although the name means 'quail' in French, in local patois the name means 'big house' and reflects the interesting underwater architecture of this site, including an arch at 15 feet.

This site was formerly frequented by large fish which sadly have become a rare sight in recent years. We hope the present SMMA policy of restricting fishing to certain areas will reverse this trend. Barracuda are still a common sight, seeming to share our curiosity as they approach divers, and do not swim away unless threatened.

15 Pinnacles
Key Hole
20'-100'

  W

Four substantial pinnacles stand on the edge of a steep slope stretching towards but not quite reaching the surface. As you weave around them you will see a proliferation of sea life. The closest pinnacles are separated by a gap of no more than 4 feet. There is an abundance of coral, including black coral, and as many fish and invertebrates as you have time to see.

There are quite strong currents and a deep drop-off, so buoyancy control is important for safety and to protect the reef from damage. The dive is best done as a drift, as getting back to the entry point against the current is difficult. This is a dive you could do more than once and see something new each time.

Dive Profile

The dive begins between the most westerly yacht mooring and the SMMA buoy. When we do this dive, the top 10 feet of water is very cloudy, but we soon submerge to clear water and can see the first of the pinnacles. Swimming toward it you can see the steep slope of the reef fall away to the south.

An area of broken finger and pencil coral at 20 feet is followed by a huge expanse of live healthy pencil coral, almost as far as the eye can see. It looks like a cultivated meadow ready for harvesting. It is rare to see a predominance of one type of coral covering such a large area.

As you continue around the pinnacle at about 50 feet you will come to a patch of green grape algae which is worth a closer look as it is a favourite haunt of colourful nudibranch. A pile of old tyres here seems a pity but a plan to remove them has been abandoned because they have become part of the reef.

Creole wrasse are here in large numbers. To us they epitomise something of the nature of these Caribbean islands. A strong dark band around the nose reminds us of a shameful past of shackles and slavery; a cobalt blue like the Caribbean sea covers half the body, reflecting the great influence of the sea on these islands; the body then becomes bright yellow like the brilliant sun; and, finally, the tail gives a flash of purple for the spirit of people who know how to party like no one we have ever known.

We continue around the base, and the second pinnacle is alongside the first. The distance between the two is about 4 feet, with a sandy bottom and vertical faces to the two pinnacles. We are swimming against the current which simply means that we travel slowly enough to take in the wonderful display of coral, sponges and black coral which adorn these walls. The feathery black coral found here is not black at all, but a striking fiery orange. This second pinnacle stops 25 feet short of the surface.

Swimming west, the third pinnacle soon emerges and is as much a delight as the first two. It is completely covered in orange and black sea fans with encrusting sponges fighting for an opportunity to be seen; it is a remarkable combination of varied colours and textures. Vase and rope sponges on the face of the pinnacles house enterprising cleaner shrimps. This pinnacle stops 25 feet short of the surface and the entire area is worthy of extended exploration.

We move west again and the fourth pinnacle is found. There is a fissure in the rock here wide enough to enter; its walls are entirely encrusted in sponges. When we enter, we look back to the east and see that the pinnacle, although seeming to be part of the rock wall behind, is in fact separated from it by a foot or so.

Inside the fissure the walls are a mosaic of colour that attract only the brightest fish; perhaps because they are the only ones visible against this psychedelic backdrop. Tiny purple and yellow fairy basslets busy themselves around the walls while rock beauties the colour of buttercups glide elegantly in and out.

The dive ends in an area of sand and coral. You will not be short of things to do on this dive. We could easily have spent the whole time on the first two pinnacles.

Thanks to Victor Antoine of Scuba St. Lucia.

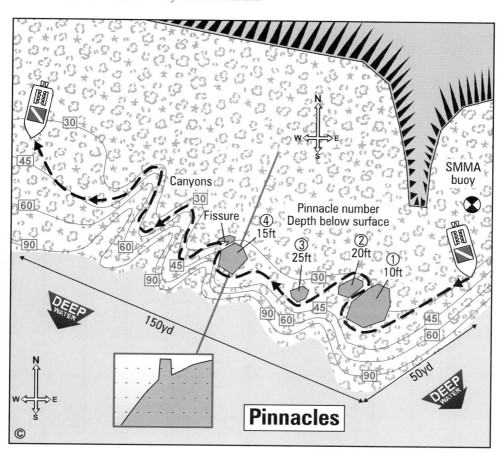

Pinnacles

16 Malgre Toute
20'-80'

This is the first of the dives under the towering Pitons and, following the profile of the land above, the site is a steep slope with rocky outcrops. The reef is lightened with bright yellow tube sponges like patches of sunlight which complement the iridescent purple of the vase sponges.

The profusion of sponges provides a generous selection of homes for basket stars and cleaner crabs living in symbiotic harmony with their hosts.

17 Superman's Flight
30'-80'

 W

Arms spread eagled, cloak flowing as gracefully as a manta in full flight, Superman dived down the steep face of the wall, gliding skilfully across the complex coral formations below him. Deeper and deeper, the deep blue thickening around his accelerating form....

If only we had dived here before we saw the film, but, no matter, we have vivid imaginations and even without the fame this is a spectacular dive. Several days' of filming were reduced to just a few seconds in the final film. However, we reckon even Superman was impressed. Coral as bright as Kryptonite dominates this watery extension to the Petit Piton. The current is generally very fast, enhancing the sensation of gliding along a subterranean flight path.

Dive Profile

There is little to say about navigational guidelines for this dive as the current does all the work for you. The current can move in either direction; when we dive the site it is west to east. Just drop down from the SMMA buoy off the northwest face of the Petit Piton and choose your depth. We find the wall interesting from 75 feet up, with the best light and colours at 55 feet and above.

Initially the wall is a steep slope, with sand and coral heads and

The golden tones of the crinoid's arms almost disguise the golden threads of the tiny arrowcrab's legs.

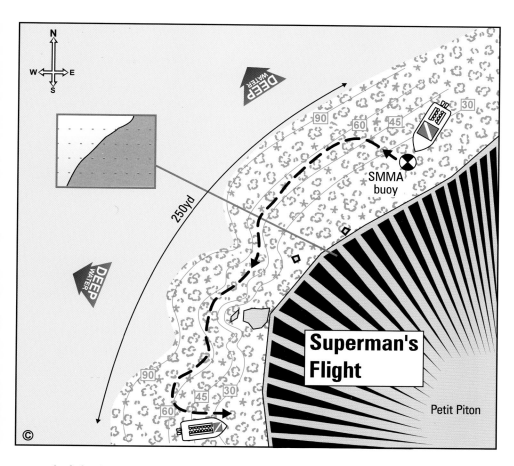

a crowd of glowing purple vase sponges. The reef soon fills in and becomes steeper sided, an almost vertical wall that attracts a great variety of marine life, including bright orange elephant ear sponges.

One interesting find on this dive is the variety of triffid-like crinoids, generally known as feather stars or sometimes sea lilies. These are ancient creatures which once covered the sea bed of the vast warm oceans, covering what is now the land mass of the Americas. In a time of plenty, they were contentedly attached to the mud and silt on the ocean floor. But, as water disappeared and the food became less plentiful in what remained as the Caribbean sea, their only chance of survival was to become mobile. So, that is what they did. They developed the ability to swim a little by waving their arms and uprooted themselves, using their now shrunken roots as stubby legs to manoeuvre over the reef. They have not stopped looking like plants so many people assume that they are permanently fixed in place.

In the Caribbean you will often see the golden crinoid boldly extending its 20 bronzed arms from the security of a vase sponge or crevice. On this dive you will also see the attractive beaded variety. These are more delicate and shyer, so are more securely tucked away, but visible nevertheless. Beaded crinoids are white and the branches appear to be beaded.

Interesting plants to look out for on this dive are mermaid's tea cups which are about 4 inches across and look like a stemmed wine glass. They are pale yellow to green and will be seen in the sand patches between the coral heads.

Coral—Shaping Up to Its Environment

The interesting plate-shaped coral formations on the Petit Piton wall are a helpful clue to identification, but shape alone cannot be used because many species of coral have the ability to modify their shape to suit the environment.

The factors which affect shape include wave action and current, sediment and food supply, the reproductive process, the degree of crowding on the reef and last, but by no means least, sunlight.

Boulder star coral has grown flat to maximise the capture of light at depth.

Shallow water snorkellers, for example, could be excused for thinking that all coral is short and stubby. This shape avoids damage in areas exposed to wave action; coral species which can grow in this way will thrive in these shallow turbulent waters. But these same species in calmer deeper water may develop more delicate structures.

Some species have more flexibility in their shape than others. This may be due to the asexual reproductive process whereby polyps bud or divide to form two polyps, imposing limitations on the shape of the growing coral.

Equally the degree of crowding on the reef can affect shape since a coral that is fighting for space is forced into a compact shape. Obviously to some extent those corals which naturally grow in a compact manner will tend to do best here but that does not stop other, less suitable, varieties from trying to adapt to their circumstances.

Sunlight is another influential factor. Coral needs light to convert food and it does so via zooxanthellae, single-celled algae, which live in the coral and use photosynthesis to convert plankton to energy and oxygen. At shallow depths there is plenty of light but as we go deeper, especially under steep-sided mountains creating shade for a significant portion of the day, we lose light and the coral compensates by creating a broad flat surface designed to capture the maximum amount of light. So obliging is the coral that its polyps are in fact transparent to allow light to reach the zooxanthellae, which is the algae that gives the coral its colour.

When you are not looking at plants you will see big schools of fish at all depths along the wall. A curious Spanish mackerel follows us for the whole dive, and looking out to the blue there are always large fish, usually jacks, patrolling the edge of the reef.

Toward the end of the dive you will find a plateau at the top of the wall at about 30 feet. There are a large number of fish traps here; we count ten. There were also a lovely pair of French angel fish and many banded butterflyfish.

The only disappointment with this dive is that it is finished long before you feel tired as you do not need to waste energy finning. Unfortunately, unlike Superman, we need to get our tanks filled.

With thanks to Scuba St. Lucia.

Petit Piton 18
Wall
25'-130'

 W

Dive Profile

As the name suggests, this is a wall dive which matches the startling topography of the Petit Piton. With little current, it offers ample opportunity to study the proliferation of marine life. The scroll coral here is extensive. It provides a mass of small overhangs which give protection to tiny fish and invertebrates, like flower petals playing host to insects. At intervals huge gorgonians protrude creating lacy frills to decorate this grandly enrobed slope.

The dive is marked with a buoy put in place by the SMMA. Descending close to the buoy line, a steep slope falls away to the south. After descending to the desired depth we proceed along the slope heading west toward the headland.

The lower (below 80 feet) portion of the wall is smothered in overlapping scroll coral like sliced mushrooms prepared for a giant oceanic risotto. As you move along the slope, large gorgonians begin to appear initially in isolated displays and later in groups, a trap for reckless plankton that drift too close to the slope.

As the slope becomes more uneven and punctuated by sandy canyons, the reef offers protective quarters to larger fish, like the pair of French angelfish we observe in their quietly paced inspection of the reef. Nearby is a juvenile example of this rather elegant member of the angelfish family. It is much bolder than the adult version, sporting striking black and yellow stripes contrasting with bright blue tips to its ventral and tail fins. Although it might make an attractive story, this juvenile will not be part of a family grouping with the adult pair as very few species of fish care for their young. The eggs are generally cast into the current, like seeds into the wind, and left to fend for themselves.

Although the slope dominates one's interest, it is worth investing in a look out to the blue where larger fishes, especially black jacks, patrol on the lookout for a tasty snack. The visibility here is generally good so it is possible to catch sight of some of the shyer fish which frequent the reef, such as the mackerel scad we spot.

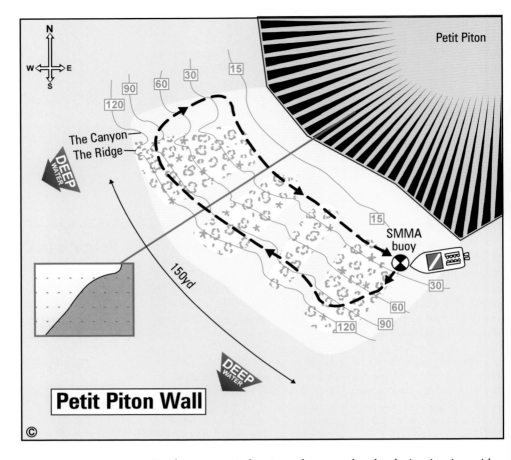

Look up, too, at the steep slope overhead culminating in a ridge silhouetted by the sun above.

As we move along the slope, we see isolated giant barrel sponges which have grown to impressive sizes in the clear water here. The steepness and depth of the slope protect them from the silting which a sandy bottom can cause, especially during serious summer storms. Along the slope, sea whips wave in the current like uncoiled springs having a relaxing day off.

The current increases as we move toward the headland and after 150 yards a sandy canyon littered with large boulders marks the turning point of the dive. Swimming back along the reef, at 35 to 45 feet, we pass over a crowded field of finger coral decorated with golden crinoids (feather stars) competing enthusiastically with the gorgonians for current-borne plankton. We even surprise a golden-tail moray making a panicked dash for cover, no doubt regretting having been born with an excessively adventurous nature.

The return to the buoy is into the current, so most operators will do it as a gentle drift. If you are returning to the buoy, save a few psi for a safety stop alongside the buoy line which is alive with numerous types of marine creatures, including overgrowing tunicates and goose neck barnacles. As you slip back up through the surface of the water, the magnificent Petit Piton stretches skywards like the top of a tropical iceberg.

Jalousie 19
15'-65'

Jalousie is one of the sites at the base of the big sister of the Pitons, Gros Piton. It is another wall dive, but with its many overhangs is an excellent location for critter spotting. Lobsters, moray eels and crabs can all be identified hiding among the coral.

The dives at the base of the Gros Piton generally offer a wide diversity of coral and sponge as well as attracting some of the larger fish, including schools of southern sennet.

Coral Gardens 20
20'-70'

The contours of the Gros Piton continue downwards in a wall for hundreds of feet. A variety of coral is kept in good condition by the current, and barrel sponges have grown large from the ample supply of food which the currents bring.

In the deeper part of the reef the observant diver may see the pretty and unusual sargassum triggerfish, easily identified by three dark lines on the cheek like scars from a sword fight.

Gros Piton Point 21
30'-100'

Sometimes referred to as the Gros Piton Terrace, this steep slope descends in a series of colourful sponge covered steps, giving the impression of terraced gardens.

It is quite an exposed site with moderate to strong currents. Divers are rewarded with large schools of fish hanging effortlessly in the current.

The Blue Hole 22
90'-130'

What a fascinating underwater structure this is. A sandy slide rushes down to 130 feet and is met by a cliff face. The marine life appears to find it interesting, too, and there are often large reef fish here: parrotfish, triggerfish, and angelfish.

Unfortunately, freshwater run-off from a nearby river often reduces visibility to unacceptable levels.

Waiwinette 23
90'-120'

This is another of the artificial reefs put in place by the Department of Fisheries. The *Waiwinette* is a 275-foot freighter which is potentially an interesting dive, but its position off the southern tip of St. Lucia means it is exposed to strong currents. Dive operators will take only experienced divers who can enter the water and descend immediately. There has been little coral growth and so it is of interest only as a wreck dive.

St. Lucia Diving Facilities

St. Lucia's good diving has attracted enthusiastic dive operators and the variety and style of their operations will make it easy to find one that suits you. There are ten dive operators on the island, with more rumoured to be opening their doors any day. Several new operators are local divers who have come to recognise the valuable asset which the island has around its shores.

Operators belong to the St. Lucia Diving Association which ensures that diving has a voice with those responsible for policy making and regulating the diving industry.

All the diving operations are on the west coast of St. Lucia with the exception of Club Aquarius which is located in the southeast corner near to Hewanorra airport. As well as offering the best diving, the west coast is where the main towns and beaches are. Most operators reach the dive sites within 10 to 45 minutes.

Equipment

The standard of diving operations in St. Lucia is high, with well-equipped stores and safe efficient boats. Dive boats are licensed by the local Fisheries Department, ensuring some degree of quality control. Instructors are generally PADI, NAUI, or SSI trained.

Import duties are high in St. Lucia so you should not plan to buy equipment on the island. Some of the operators carry a small stock of spares and less expensive items such as masks and fins. The operators do generally have good quality equipment for rent including, in some cases, underwater cameras. Because of the SMMA requirement to dive only with a licensed operator, few of the dive shops will rent equipment to divers not diving with them, so check the information matrix if you wish to rent equipment to use outside St. Lucia's waters.

Perhaps because of the compactness of St. Lucia's diving area, there are no liveaboards operating out of the island, although there are rumours that someone is considering this. The main benefit would be to allow divers to sample diving on at least one other island but this would involve a fairly long passage in open seas.

Cost

The cost of diving in St. Lucia is about average for the Caribbean, with a single-tank dive costing between $35 and $55. All operators offer packages, the most common being a 6-tank package for $165-200 depending on whether or not you have your own equipment. Training courses are given by all of the operators, with many able to teach the most commonly requested speciality courses. A PADI open water course costs between $350 and $450 with a rate of around $200 being the norm for a referral.

St. Lucia has two large operations, Scuba St. Lucia which is part of the Anse Chastanet resort, and Sandals. Some of the smaller operators are attached to a resort or hotel complex while others are independent. Some of the resort-based dive operations only offer diving to their guests whereas others offer diving to anyone, either on a cost-per-dive or a day pass basis. Check the information matrix for more details.

The day pass system may seem prohibitively expensive but is worth looking into if you want just one or two day's diving during your stay. Keep in mind that it offers you free use of all facilities including diving (excluding courses), and meals and drinks for the day. A Sandals day pass at $135 includes three boat dives a day and is good value for money.

Founded in 1981, Scuba St. Lucia **10** is the oldest and arguably the most well established of the diving concerns on the island. Being located within the SMMA it benefits from an excellent position in the heart of the best diving area. It is possible to dive straight from their beach onto a reef which is teeming with fish. The dive store is owned by the Anse Chastanet resort although non-residents are also catered for and Scuba St. Lucia boats pick up from various resorts on the island. Anse Chastanet is a luxury resort with 7 night/12 dive packages starting at $3,000 for a double room, including dinner. Prices rise in the high season.

They are naturally protective of their locale and have succeeded in preserving the Anse Chastanet reef despite the volume of divers. Mike Allard, the manager of the dive operation, believes in firmly administering reef protection rules and will go so far as to refuse to rent cameras to those who have been seen to damage the reef while using the equipment.

Mike and his co-manager wife Karyn claim an excellent safety record supported by the requirement that all instructors be trained as not just providers but instructors in the provision of oxygen for dive-related injuries. Scuba St. Lucia is a DAN Instructor training facility.

Large purpose-built dive boats make entry and exit procedures very safe and easy. A flat platform on the back of the boat enables entry by a giant stride as an alternative to a back roll. The store has ample space for putting equipment together and rinsing gear. This is a well-run and well-equipped operation in the heart of St. Lucia's finest diving.

Sandals **5** and **8** is approximately the same size as Scuba St. Lucia although it is spread over two sites, Halcyon and La Toc. Sandals, a fully-inclusive resort for couples only, offers a wide variety of water sports. Sandals has a policy of recruiting and training local instructors and dive masters under the overall supervision of Donovan Brown, the water sports training manager.

Situated further north than Anse Chastanet, Sandals is still within easy reach of the SMMA and very close to the more northern sites such as the *Lesleen M* wreck in Anse Cochon. However, with three fast boats operating from each resort, the coverage of St. Lucia's dive sites is comprehensive. When sea conditions are suitable, it is also possible to dive directly from the beach at La Toc onto a small reef.

Although those who are not staying at Sandals can dive with them, it is only by way of a day pass to the resort and there is no pick-up service from other resorts or cruise ships. For guests of Sandals, the resort offers a way of doing a lot of diving without having to count the cost of each dive. Dive boats leave several times a day, allowing you to choose when and how often to dive. Diving is considered an important part of the Sandals' offer so considerable resource is devoted to it.

Other operators who are based in resorts include Frogs at Windjammer Landings, Le Sport, and Rendezvous. There was once a store in the resort called Jalousie cradled in the bay between the Pitons with excellent access to diving in the SMMA. Like Anse Chastanet, there is a good dive straight off the beach. At the time of writing the resort and dive store had closed down. Undoubtedly someone will take over this establishment and re-open it. It is so well located near the good diving that if a dive operation is re-established here it will be worth investigating.

Le Sport **1** and Rendezvous **6** are inclusive resorts owned by the same company but operated separately. These are sister hotels to LaSource in Grenada, but diving is on a much smaller scale than at LaSource. Le Sport currently only offers beach diving although a boat is planned. Diving is also inclusive at Rendezvous resort and Frank Wasson, the resident instructor, offers resort and certification courses as well as daily boat dives for certified divers.

The other dive operators are either completely independent or more loosely associated with an hotel. Frogs **3** at Windjammer Landings is an independent operation within the Windjammer apartment complex. Tom deNobrega, the proprietor, is a well-respected St. Lucian diver whose store is decorated with some excellent frogfish and seahorse photographs. Tom is an ex-commercial and military diver who is keen to see that St. Lucia maintains a good safety record for diving.

Although only a small operation with smaller boats than others, Tom offers interesting diving and the personal service that comes from having fewer divers at a time. He is well informed about the St. Lucia marine environment and is a competent informative dive leader.

Dolphin Divers **2** in Rodney Bay Marina was recently taken under the new ownership and management of British diver Chris Jackman, who has plans to develop the business. Chris was a commercial diver who spent one season working on the excavation of the *Mary Rose*, an ancient warship found just outside Portsmouth harbour in England.

Dolphin Divers has two bases in Rodney Bay lagoon; one is in the marina next to the charterboat fleet. The store rents equipment to yachts. The other base is across the lagoon where Dolphin Divers have their teaching facilities including a pool for confined water training. A friendly bar and restaurant are located here and six double rooms are available for rent for $375 per week.

Dolphin Divers' guests are English and American, drawn mainly from the neighbouring hotels. As it is quite a long boat ride from Rodney Bay to the best sites, it is important to know that Dolphin Divers have efficient purpose-built dive boats with ample room to relax, admire the view, have a snack between dives and still have room to organise your equipment and kit up. Morning trips are 2-tank dives.

It is Chris's intention to open up new sites, especially on the north side of St. Lucia. So far they have identified a reef half a mile offshore in 80 feet of water which Chris said was extremely picturesque, on a par with the diving in the SMMA.

Buddies **7** caters to hotel guests in resorts which do not have their own dive operation. Buddies attracts a good proportion of repeat business, always a good sign. Based in Vigie Cove in the main port of Castries, Buddies is in a good position to collect passengers who wish to dive while their cruise ship is visiting St. Lucia. The owner, Ian Drysdale, is English and can provide BSAC training in addition to PADI.

Rosemond's Trench Divers **9** is based in Marigot Bay at the Marigot Bay Beach Club, but Rosemond's Trench Divers is an independent operation. In fact, much of Rosemond's business comes from outside this resort. The bay is a favourite anchorage for yachts, many of whom use Rosemond's services.

Rosemond is a welterweight boxing champion turned dive operator, and one of the growing number of St. Lucians offering diving on the island. His divemaster, Francis, used to be his trainer. This is a relatively small operation and Rosemond and Francis offer a friendly service. They operate with a small but fast boat.

One of St. Lucia's interesting dive sites, Rosemond's Trench, is named after Rosemond.

Andre St. Omer, the St. Lucian owner of Dive Fair Helen **4** has a base in Vigie Cove with an additional shop in the Wyndham Morgan Bay Hotel and a further store planned in Harmony Suites, Rodney Bay. He is a relatively new dive operator in St. Lucia but is not at all new to diving the island. Andre was previously with the St. Lucia Department of Fisheries and was party to the establishment of the SMMA and the Fisheries' policy on scuba diving.

A new hotel, Aquarius, was opened recently at the southern tip of the island in what used to be Club Med. We understand that it is their intention to offer diving.

Contact Information

1 Le Sport   Martin Dariah   Tel: (758) 450-8551
                                                             Fax: (758) 450-0368

2 Dolphin Divers   Chris Jackman   Tel: (758) 452-9485
                                                             Fax: (758) 452-0802

3 Frogs   Tom deNobrega   Tel: (758) 452-0913
                                                             Fax: (758) 452-1494

4 Dive Fair Helen   Andre St. Omer   Tel: (758) 450-1640
                                                             Fax: (758) 453-6513

5 Sandals   Donovan Brown   Tel: (758) 452-3081
                                                             Fax: (758) 452-1012

6 Rendezvous   Frank Wasson   Tel: (758) 452-4211
                                                             Fax: (758) 452-7419

7 Buddies   Ian Drysdale   Tel: (758) 452-5288
                                                             Fax: (758) 452-0185

8 Sandals   See 5 above

9 Rosemond's Trench Divers   Rosemond Clery   Tel: (758) 451-4761
                                                             Fax: (758) 453-7605

10 Scuba St. Lucia   Michael Allard   Tel: (758) 459-7000
                                                             Fax: (758) 459-7700

St. Lucia Dive Operators

		1 Le Sport	2 Dolphin Divers	3 Frogs	4 Rendezvous	5 Sandals Halcyon	6 Dive Fair Helen	7 Buddies	8 Sandals La Toc	9 Rosemond's Trench Divers	10 Scuba St. Lucia
STAFF	Instructors	2	2	2	1	4	1	1	5	2	9
	Divemasters	1	2	1	1	6	1	2	5	1	3
	Diving Associations	P	CPS	P	P	NP	P	P	NP	P	NPS
	Languages	E	EFGS	EF	E	EF GIS	E	E	EF GIS	EF	EFGS
BOATS	Dive Boats	0	2	2	1	3	1	2	3	1	3
	Shaded Boats	0	2	1	0	1	0	2	1	1	3
	Max. Divers per Boat	N/A	10-50	10-15	8	28-42	10	8-10	28-42	12	12-30
	Time to Dive Sites	5	10-45	5-40	20-35	5-35	20-35	20-35	5-35	10-25	5-15
	Dives per Day	N/A	2	3	2	3	1	1	3	2	6
	Pick Up by Boat from		CRY	R			CRY	CRY		CRY	CR
EQUIPMENT	Equipment Sets	10	12	15	15	43	25	12	54	15	70
	Dive Equip. for Sale		2	1							3
	Dive Equip. for Rent		•	•			•			•	
	Photo Equip. for Rent		•	•			•				•
	Tank Fills		•	•	•		•	•		•	
	Equipment Servicing	•	•	•		•	•	•	•	•	•
	O₂ on Boat	N/A	•	•	•	•	•	•	•		•
	VHF on Boat	N/A	•	•		•	•	•	•	•	
MISC.	Owned by Resort	•			•	•			•		•
	Other Water Sports	•	•	•	•	•	•		•	•	•
	Pers. Liab. Insurance		•	•							•

St. Vincent and the Grenadines

For the adventurous traveller, a nation made up of an archipelago of tropical islands has an almost irresistible allure. The mountainous island of St. Vincent, together with many smaller islands that are called the Grenadines, makes up just such a country and few visitors will be disappointed. St. Vincent's steep valleys and rugged contours culminate in a 3,000-foot active volcano at the island's northern end. St. Vincent's shoreline has rugged rocks and steep slopes, interrupted by beaches of black sand. It lacks both the expanses of white shoreline that decorate many tourist brochures, and the tourists themselves.

The Grenadines, though part of the same country, are in sharp contrast, with hills less than 1,000 feet, spectacular beaches and brilliant turquoise water. Not surprisingly, it is here that you find most of the nation's resorts. The Grenadines are linked to their mother island by plane and ferry.

The Diving

It is impossible to generalise about the diving environment of St. Vincent and the Grenadines, as it covers an area as diverse below the sea as it is on land. Instead, we have described the particular assets of each island's marine life in the section preceding the description of the dives.

Suffice it to say that there is good diving to be had throughout the country. The Grenadines are known for their shark population, both nurse sharks and reef sharks. The sites around Bequia and Mustique have impressively large schools of big fish, whereas St. Vincent has calm waters and genuinely unsullied reefs. The finest black coral we have seen hangs from vertical walls around St. Vincent's coast. The Tobago Cays offer a desert island environment with excellent snorkelling and diving on offshore reefs.

A combination of the type of shoreside holiday you want plus the type of diving which appeals to you should make for an idyllic dive holiday in this area. And, think about trying more than one location. From St. Vincent, a day trip by ferry to Bequia to dive is easy to arrange. Many people charter a yacht, either crewed or bareboat, as a way of diving all the islands. Some of the operators offer a special deal allowing you to buy a 10-dive package that you can use with a

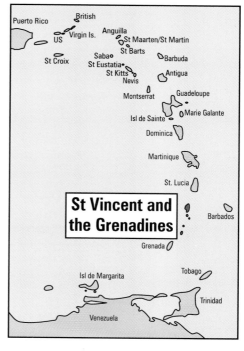

number of operators between St. Vincent and Union Island.

If you are able to travel around the Grenadines to dive, remember that Carriacou is only 5 miles south of Union Island. It has some very good diving, but the Grenadines operators do not go there. Two pleasant and efficient dive stores operate out of Carriacou, visiting all the sites around that island and to the south. (See next chapter—Grenada and Carriacou)

Rules and Regulations

There is no requirement for dive stores to be registered with any government department. The Fisheries Department is relying upon the good sense of the dive operators to act in a responsible manner to preserve the reefs for their own benefit. With regard to the local stores, this has not worked out too badly. In Bequia in particular, the dive stores have put down moorings on most dive sites. Nearly all the dive operators work responsibly and have above average concern for the environment.

The government of St. Vincent and the Grenadines has taken an active role in trying to protect their marine environment, with somewhat mixed results. One of their major successes has been the banning of jetskis and their kin.

Coral is protected; no visitor is allowed to spearfish. Local people and residents can still do so with a permit. This regulation has largely worked as far as visitors are concerned. Arriving yachts have to declare spearguns and are made aware of the regulations. While one or two unscrupulous people sneak out when no one is looking, the wholesale slaughter of fish by visitors, which was very much in evidence 10 years ago, has stopped.

Many of the main areas visited by yachts and visitors are in protected marine zones where no fishing is allowed. These include the northeast coast and Devil's Table in Bequia, Isle de Quatre, all of Mustique, the eastern coast of Canouan, all of Mayreau and the Tobago Cays, the whole of Palm Island, PSV and surrounding reefs.

While this regulation is good in intention, there has been very little monitoring of this or of the use of spearguns. As a result, some of these protected areas are still getting over fished and damaged.

A serious attempt is made to enforce the lobster season. Hotel inspections are made and any hotel found with lobsters in the freezer 2 weeks after the season closes is subject to heavy fines. This has effectively cut down on major trafficking in lobsters, even though there are a few fishermen who still hunt them out of season and sell them to passing yachts.

The Tobago Cays are currently described as a marine park. The government did remove some semi-permanent fishing camps from here that were rapidly changing the nature of the area. A Marine Park manager has been appointed and an office set up in Union Island.

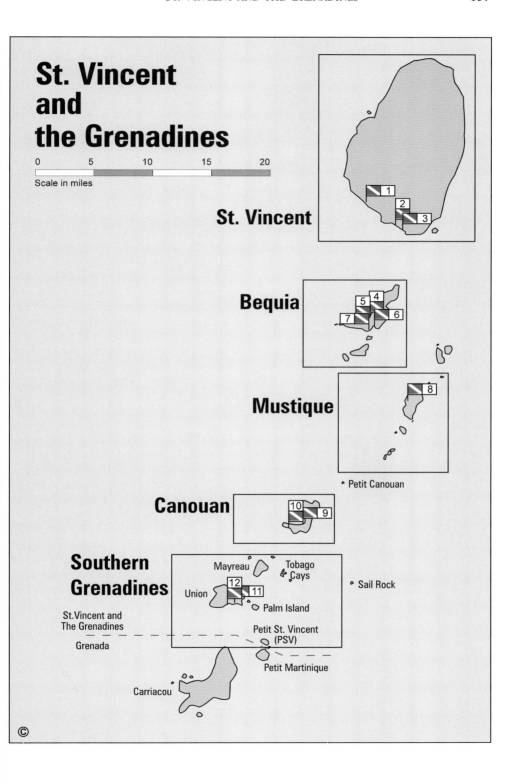

St. Vincent and the Grenadines

0   5   10   15   20
Scale in miles

St. Vincent

1
2
3

Bequia

4
5
6
7

Mustique

8

Petit Canouan

Canouan

10
9

Southern Grenadines

St.Vincent and The Grenadines

Grenada

Mayreau

Union

12
11

Tobago Cays

Palm Island

Sail Rock

Petit St. Vincent (PSV)

Petit Martinique

Carriacou

The major contributing factors affecting the health of the reefs in any given area of the Tobago Cays have been identified. More importantly, rules that most appropriately tackle the specific problems can be drawn up. Yachts can be confined to certain areas to avoid anchor damage and at least contain, if not eliminate, the nitrates problem. None of this has happened yet, but there is always hope.

Visitors need to be made well aware of the rules and regulations and there is a need for officers with a boat and the power of enforcement. If this were financed through user fees, it would be a small price to pay for the preservation of these wonderful reefs.

Independent Diving

Currently, independent diving is permitted, though much of the best diving is not accessible by yacht or dinghy. Even those areas that are sheltered and accessible can elude independent divers. There are some spectacular spots along St. Vincent's west coast but it takes an experienced local operator to know just where to drop you in and which way to turn. It can make the difference between a dull dive over dead and overgrown coral or a colourful parade past black coral trees, open-mouthed vase sponges and the delights of tiny seahorses.

Independent dives that are easily accessible include: the Devil's Table, Bequia; the wreck of the *Puruni*, Mayreau; Peter's Hope near Wallilabou in St. Vincent. (See dive list and site descriptions for more details).

Safety

St. Vincent and the Grenadines has a good safety record, despite the opportunity for some deep diving off St. Vincent and some strong currents around the islands and offshore rocks.

There is no recompression chamber, but the proximity to Barbados and wide availability of small aircraft for charter means that arrangements for the treatment of diving accidents can be easy and fast. Ample opportunity to test these arrangements are supplied by the local fishermen who frequently get bent, diving too deep, for too long and too frequently, in search of lobster and conch. Usually they are diving without any gauges, just a regulator and a tank. They know when to ascend because the air becomes difficult to draw. In effect, they are regularly making out-of-air emergency ascents.

This state of affairs is an embarrassment to the local dive operators, most of whom have offered training and support. But the lure of a lobster sale speaks louder than common sense.

St. Vincent

St. Vincent is about 16 miles long and 8 miles wide. Kingstown, the capital, lies at the south end and is the centre of commercial activity.

Roads zigzag up both sides of St. Vincent, but none crosses the northern central mountain range that is largely inaccessible by car. The agricultural feeder roads that extend from the coasts into the hills are reduced to small footpaths as they near the centre of the island.

The hiking is magnificent. We know of no finer hike in the Caribbean than the one up the volcano, a journey that will take you through farmland, rainforest, cloud forest and finally onto windswept slopes where only small plants can survive. You are often in dense cloud and, if you can wait for a while at the rim, a break may afford spectacular views into the steaming crater and over the whole island.

Other popular destinations in St. Vincent include the Vermont Nature Reserve that has well-maintained trails through lush rainforest. Lookout points may provide a glimpse of the endemic St. Vincent parrot. Several other trails lead to sparkling waterfalls.

Much of the agricultural produce is grown in the north, on both the east and west sides. A good road, with some spectacular scenery, runs two thirds of the way up the western side of the island. A similarly good road runs up the eastern side to Georgetown, St. Vincent's second largest town. After Georgetown, the road to the Rabacca Dry River is in poorer condition. If you make it over this, you can continue on the now rough road to Fancy at the northern tip of the island. At Fancy, you find descendants of the Carib Indians who were in residence when Columbus arrived.

The drive is through lovely scenery, but the part after Georgetown is very slow. The easiest path up the volcano starts just north of Georgetown.

There are tropical delights on land as well as below the water.

**Petit Byahaut/
Wallilabou**

Deciding where to stay in St. Vincent really comes down to two choices: Petit Byahaut or anywhere else. Petit Byahaut is a special case. Set in a lovely little bay with its own pleasant black sand beach and surrounded by peaky hills, the accommodations are in about a dozen elegant tents, on well-made platforms and with proper beds. There is no road into the property and people come and go by boat. This does not mean you cannot get around. Owners Chuck and Sharon arrange hiking trips to all the good destinations, including a volcano trip that begins with a boat trip up the coast.

However, you cannot walk down the road to go pub crawling and eating dinner away calls for advance planning. Petit Byahaut is in the heart of diving country, and they have a dive shop.

We should also just mention a small hotel in Wallilabou Bay set in lovely countryside on the west coast where the diving is good. When they get their planned dive shop going, it will certainly be of interest. In the meantime, it is a little too far away from dive shops for serious divers, except for those diving independently from yachts.

**St. Vincent's
South Coast**

The other visitor accommodations lie along the south coast in the area of Young Island Cut and Blue Lagoon. Two dive shops are here and everything is reasonably close together and well served by buses and taxis.

One resort hotel, Young Island, is an upmarket Robinson Crusoe-like establishment on its own island, just a few hundred yards from the mainland and well connected by small ferries. Otherwise, your choice is among a variety of small family-run hotels, guest houses and rental apartments. This is the most social area of St. Vincent, with pubs and restaurants all along the waterfront, most within easy walking distance.

Language: English
Currency: Eastern Caribbean Dollar ($1.00 US = $2.66 EC)
Population: About 90,000
Telephone Code: Currently (809), changing to (784)

Après Dive

Non-diving activities in St. Vincent are limited to resting, hiking or sailing. It is the undeveloped, unspoilt nature of the island that attracts people, so visitors should not expect much organised entertainment.

Golf

St. Vincent has a 9-hole golf course that has been maintained in varying conditions, ranging from excellent to goat pasture. It is part of a small hotel, casino and restaurant.
Emerald Valley Resort and Casino: (809) 456-7140

You will need a guide to help you scale the Soufriere volcano the first time, otherwise most trails are well marked. It should also be noted that you can look at a good map and find excellent drives and hikes on just about any road that leads into the central mountain range. Buses cover the main roads inexpensively and well, though you need to check on the time of the last returning bus before taking off for the end of the road. Self-drive rental cars are available and any taxi driver will be happy to take you for a tour and arrange guides as needed.

Hiking

Dolphin Tours: (809) 457-4337
HazECO Tours: (809) 457-8634
Sam Taxi Tours: (809) 456-4338

These are available at either the Grand View Club or the Prospect Racquet Club, both on the south coast. In addition, the Prospect Racquet Club and Beachcombers have saunas and health spas.

Tennis and Squash

Beachcombers: (809) 458-4385
Grand View Club: (809) 458-4811
Prospect Racquet Club: (809) 458-4866

St. Vincent and the Grenadines are a popular destination for charter yachts. There are several charter companies and many individual boats available. Bequia, the nearest island, is just 90 minutes away under sail. Day trips, short and long cruises, both bareboat and with a skipper, are available.

Water Sports

Barefoot Yacht Charters: (809) 456-9526
Jubilee Yacht Charters: (809) 457-5237
Lagoon Marina Yacht Charters:(809) 457-4716
Nirvana: (809) 456-9238
TMM: (809) 456-9608

Although not a major shopping destination, there is enough to keep the souvenir hunter happy in a number of small shops and boutiques. Check out Noah's Arkade in Kingstown and the Young Island Dock Shop in Young Island Cut.

Shopping

Since there are not many tourists, nightlife, such as it is, is geared for the local market and gives you a feel of how Vincentians enjoy themselves.

Nightlife

In Kingstown, there is an attractive upstairs bar called the Attic. This most often comes to life on weekends when they have excellent jazz groups. Level Three is a new nightclub and bar aimed at the middle-aged crowd, with 'golden oldies' nights and bands for dancing. The Aquatic Club in Young Island Cut has well-attended discos and live groups, mainly on weekends.

For a quiet spot of gambling in pleasant surroundings, visit the Emerald Island Casino. Make an evening of it and have dinner there as well. It may not be open every night so call in advance.

Aquatic Club: (809) 458-4205
The Attic: (809) 457-2558
Emerald Valley Resort and Casino: (809) 456-7140

Information on Accommodation

Department of Tourism: (809) 457-1502
Hotel Association: (809) 457-1072
USA: (800) 729-1726
Canada: (416) 924-5796
UK: (171) 937-6570

Getting There

St. Vincent and the Grenadines has no airport capable of taking large jets. You will need to take a flight to one of the other islands in the Caribbean and connect with a flight to St. Vincent.

Although this area may not be serviced by longhaul flights, it has a busy efficient network of inter-island flights. St. Vincent and Union Island have small modern airports that act as hubs for private, charter and scheduled services. For about $80 it is possible to fly from St. Vincent or Union Island to St. Lucia, Martinique, Barbados or Grenada. All the small islands in the Grenadines (Bequia, Mustique, Canouan) have airports for small aircraft, making multi-centred holidays easy to arrange.

American Airlines has recently begun a number of American Eagle flights directly to St. Vincent from Puerto Rico and mainland America. Check with your travel agent for the latest situation.

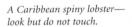

A Caribbean spiny lobster— look but do not touch.

The Diving

Of all the islands covered in this volume, St. Vincent probably has the most pristine reefs. Other islands may have some reefs in good condition while others have been damaged, whereas in St. Vincent there is absolutely no diver or snorkeller damage. The reason is simply diver density. There are relatively few people diving a fairly large area of reefs.

Although dive sites are designated and named by local operators, you could jump in the water off any headland on the west coast and have a great dive. One reason for the good condition of the reefs is that dive boats, cruise ships and yachts cannot anchor on the reefs off headlands because the water is too deep, so there is no anchor damage.

Evidence of the undamaged nature of the reefs is the abundance of black coral at relatively shallow depths. There is also much soft coral and good sponges.

Density of reef fish is high, especially the smaller reef inhabitants. With one or two exceptions, the sites are not notable for larger fish. Sightings of sharks and turtles are not that common. Popular but difficult to find frogfish and seahorses more than make up for the absence of larger pelagics. On a diving holiday in St. Vincent, the operators can pretty much guarantee to find you a seahorse. They even seem to grow to an above average size in St. Vincent's waters. Other more unusual sea life readily shows itself. Cherubfish, tiny angelfish less than 2 inches long, and red banded lobsters are not infrequent finds.

As with all the larger islands to the north of St. Vincent, the dive sites are clustered along the west coast of the island and extend around the south coast. The most regularly dived sites extend only about halfway up the west side. The sheltered west coast creates ideal diving conditions, with little current and benign surface conditions, which is not to say that the diving is not exciting. There are impressive walls and plenty of opportunities for deep diving. Photographers will love the calm conditions.

There is good diving further north but there is no real incentive for dive stores to visit this area, as they are all based at the southern end of St. Vincent where there is plenty of excellent diving. They do dive the northwest area occasionally, combined with a visit to the Falls of Baleine that cannot be reached by road.

We have described the dives currently being used by dive operators but the undeveloped nature of St. Vincent's tourism and diving means that many good diving areas were not being used at the time of writing. Consequently, you may be taken to sites that are not mentioned in this book. There is simply not the number of divers at present to demand the use of more sites. For example, we dived an area called Peter's Hope and found it beautiful, but at the time of writing, none of the dive operators were using it. To be spoilt for choice is a rare experience in the increasingly popular Caribbean; enjoy it while you can.

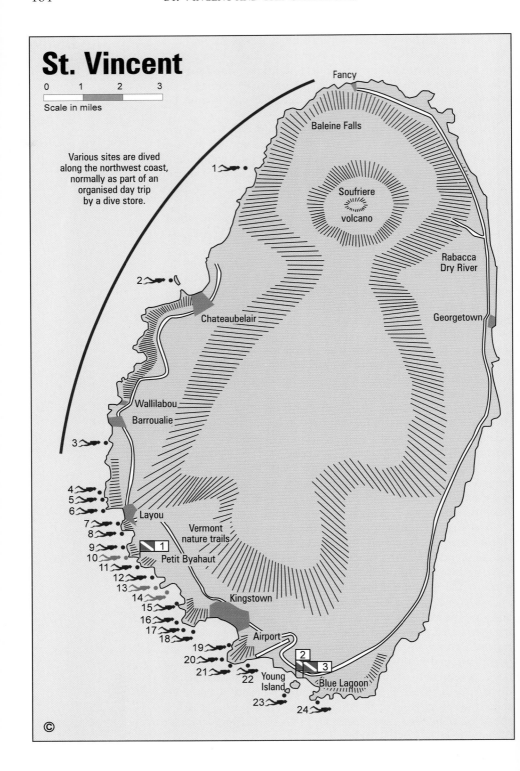

St. Vincent

0   1   2   3
Scale in miles

Various sites are dived along the northwest coast, normally as part of an organised day trip by a dive store.

Fancy

Baleine Falls

Soufriere volcano

Rabacca Dry River

Georgetown

Chateaubelair

Wallilabou
Barroualie

Layou

Vermont nature trails

Petit Byahaut

Kingstown

Airport

Young Island

Blue Lagoon

©

NO.	SITE NAME	DEPTH IN FEET	
1	Mystery Reef	30-80	
2	Chateaubelair/Coral Castle	30-75	
3	Peter's Hope	30-100	
4	Anchor Reef	40-120	
5	Bambaroux	15-120	
6	Emry's Wall	20-140	
7	The Wall (Layou)	20-135	
8	Tarpon Run	40-120	
9	Bat Cave	3-130	
10	Orca Point/Dinosaur's Head	20-90	
11	Pinnacle Rock	15-120	
12	Hans Reef	25-120	
13	New Guinea Reef	20-120	
14	Back Door Reef	25-100	
15	The Garden	40-90	
16	Turtle Bay	40-80	
17	The Steps	30-80	
18	Bottle Reef	30-100	
19	Kingstown Wrecks	40-100	
20	Kingstown South	30-90	
21	Kingstown South South	40-140	
22	The Forest	20-70	
23	Rock Fort	40-90	
24	The Drift	60-90	

St. Vincent Dive Sites

NO.	OPERATOR	LOCATED IN RESORT/HOTEL
1	Petit Byahaut*	Petit Byahaut
2	Dive St. Vincent	
3	St. Vincent Dive Experience	

*Owned by Hotel/Resort

Dive Operators

1 Mystery Reef
30'-80'

An inspiring underwater structure, like a huge Roman amphitheatre, is the pay-off for a trip up to the northwest of the island. The edge of the theatre has a drop-off. The wall below is sculpted with layers of underwater coves. Big crabs inhabit these coves along with a vast array of reef fish.

In the shallow area, nurse sharks sometimes snooze enjoying the warmth of the sun through the clean, clear water.

2 Chateaubelair/
Coral Castle
30'-75'

Different dive operators dive their own preferred part of this small uninhabited island on the west coast of St. Vincent. The area between the island and the mainland is shallow, but on all other sides the island continues its steep descent below the water.

The steep wall has been carved by the sea into a rich pattern of ravines, hollows, and tiny caves that are home to eels, soapfish and other creatures. It is decorated with a variety of black corals including wire coral. Giant grey angelfish often gather over the sand at about 90 feet. There is also a reef 40 feet deep where huge structures, covered with a colourful mixture of corals, rise from the sand like fairy castles.

Pufferfish swim by with big smiles on their faces. Huge schools of tiny silver fish catch the sun in a brilliant display. You will see a good variety of brightly coloured reef fish and creatures such as Christmas tree worms, snake eels and maybe an octopus.

The area known as Coral Castle has huge brain corals, "the size of Volkswagens", according to Bill Tewes, of Dive St. Vincent.

3 Peter's Hope
30'-100'

This site is not currently used by dive operators, but its accessibility to Wallilabou makes it a convenient dive for those who wish to dive independently from a yacht. Local boat boys know which headland marks Peter's Hope and can direct you, but you will need a sufficiently powerful dinghy to travel the 2 to 3 miles south of Wallilabou to reach the site.

A steep slope that is completely covered in coral and sponges runs parallel to the cliffs. The bottom of the slope is at just over 100 feet.

There is an abundance of brittle stars living in the sponges but beware, some of those playing host are touch-me-not sponges which were not given their name arbitrarily. Treat with vinegar if you touch one by accident. As a rule though, you will do more harm to a sponge than it will to you. Where you touch a sponge you will undoubtedly damage that area, leaving it vulnerable to organisms that could, over time, cause the sponge to die.

All the way along this slope you will see big schools of blue and brown chromis as well as small groups of blackbar soldierfish.

There are many juvenile trunkfish no bigger than your thumb nail, so tiny that they appear to be swimming without the encumbrance of fins or a tail.

As the coral on the slope peters out to sand, turn up the slope where there is a huge rocky zone at about 30 feet, offering scope for some fun rummaging in nooks and crannies to finish the dive. Gullies and overhangs provide a perfect environment for long-spined urchins, so watch your buoyancy especially if there is a lot of swell.

Alternatively, you can swim back along the coral at 30 feet where the colours of the reef are soothingly autumnal. Deep orange and brown encrusting sponges create a sensuous glow, as the sun draws out the warmth of their colours, comparable in splendour to any sunset.

Anchor Reef 4
40'-120'

The dive begins in 25 feet of water and drops to 40 feet as you follow the reef out. A wall at 40 feet drops to 120 feet to a sand base. At the top of the drop-off rests an encrusted anchor. There is always a good quantity of reef fish, but the reef is particularly densely populated when the current is running.

There is often current here, though it is still usually possible to do a slow dive by ducking down over the side of the reef.

Barracuda roam along the wall and inquisitive divers can find crabs and invertebrates. Morays grow to a good size and are as interested in divers as divers are in them.

Bambaroux 5
15'-120'

The dive boat anchors in 15 feet on a sandy bottom. The dive route then moves out across the reef to a headland where a small and engaging wall offers a variety of reef life.

Despite being one of the less frequented dives, some local divers rate it as one of the most pleasant. It is an interesting dive, especially for lovers of black coral. Patches of finger coral and gorgonians give contrast during the dive and, although only a small wall, the dive can be quite spectacular.

Emry's Wall 6
20'-140'

Both in the shallows and at depth, large boulders and coral heads provide just the sort of underwater playground that divers love. In the shallow areas, there are boulders to explore in company with parrotfish, damselfish and lovely butterflyfish. Coneys and wrasse are common sights, moving industriously around the reef.

At 140 feet, coral heads appear like islands, surrounded by gorgonians. It is not uncommon for currents to be strong and, as this is a deep dive, it is usually considered to be for experienced divers.

7 The Wall (Layou)
20'-135'

As its name suggests, this site is a wall dive but it also has a glorious coral garden in the shallows, perfect to end the dive. A ledge at 20 feet falls away to form the main part of the wall. A further ledge, at just over 100 feet, gives another drop-off to the deepest part of the dive.

Massive black coral trees sprout from the wall face and, while taking a closer look, you are likely to see the distinctive shape and colour of a spotted drum.

Big black jacks come very close to the wall, and it is always worth sparing a moment to look out into the blue where larger pelagics roam. But it is hard to find a moment to spare as there is so much life on the wall. Five red banded lobsters have even taken up home; clearly no one told them that they are supposed to be rare.

The wall is coral encrusted, including a good deal of fire coral in the shallows, so beware.

8 Tarpon Run
40'-120'

Tarpon seem to be attracted to this small island between Buccament Bay and Layou. Tarpon Run is the most likely place in St. Vincent for finding seahorses. Frogfish also sit on the reef, and the French angelfish are a treat.

For some reason, this reef attracts groupers; some quite sizeable specimens camp out here. Barracuda also make passing visits.

Heavy rains wash land run-off into the sea by way of the Buccament river, making this a dive for dry weather only.

9 Bat Cave
3'-130'

For those looking for a dive with a difference, this could be it. The dive begins in shallow water, about 3 feet deep in the cave, so it can only be tackled when there are no swells. The cave is dark inside, but you will be able to see the many hundreds of bats hanging from the walls. Do not use a flashlight in the cave. You have been warned!

Off to the left, a small patch of light indicates the way out down a long tunnel. It is 30 feet long and only 4 feet wide, so do not attempt it if there is any swell. The tunnel takes you to a fissure in the rocks 30 feet high and 40 feet deep. You swim out through the fissure and can then dive down to two huge rocks, one at 80 feet and one at 130 feet.

The rocks are thickly encrusted with many different sponges and corals and seem to attract a great deal of fish—pretty brave since one of the species of bats in the cave is a fish eater.

The bats are an endangered species and you are asked to pass through the cave quietly without disturbing them.

Sometimes called Dinosaur's Head to reflect the shape of the headland, Orca Point is actually named after Orca Industries who were pioneers in the development of dive computers. Bill Tewes named the site after diving here with their chairman. Bill still uses one of the original Orca dive computers.

This site is a slope off the headland with currents bringing nutrients to the reef, giving it a clean and healthy appearance. All the right ingredients are present to make this an excellent photographic dive so, if you are planning to hire a camera for a dive or two, this would be a good site to choose.

The dive boat mooring is in 30 feet of water. We swim first to the south, carried by a light current. Descending to 100 feet, we find a number of underwater 'islands', large volcanic rocks poised on the coral slope. Coral and sponge have colonised all the available substratum, with lizardfish competing for the odd bit of sand to perch upon.

Orca Point 10
Dinosaur's Head
20'- 90'

  C

Dive Profile

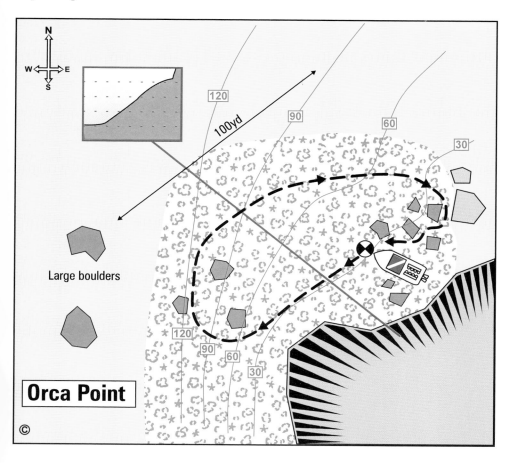

Orca Point

This is a particularly colourful reef, especially on a sunny day. The sun's rays pick out the brassy orange tones of the elephant ear sponges, and the yellow tube sponges reflect back the sun's own colours. The reef looks as if it is on fire. Swimming around the 'islands' reveals any number of interesting finds. We like the feather hydroids, so fine that they seem too flimsy to survive the pressure of four atmospheres.

The current begins to pick up near the headland so we head back, slightly shallower, and take time to explore the reef. Vase sponges are everywhere and most yield some interesting inhabitants. Brittle stars and some of the largest Pederson's shrimps we have seen snuggle confidently inside. Checking under an overhang, an ET-like broad grin and two round soft eyes peer at us from a face considerably larger than mine. A huge porcupine fish has grabbed this secure little spot and is not overly impressed by our excited little faces peering in at him. We beat a respectful retreat.

Across the slope of the reef, row pore sponges stand proud and a myriad of reef fish weave their way around the vases. Look carefully and you will find corkscrew anemones, like curly heads blowing in the wind. A number of black egg-shaped blobs appear to be sponges at first glance, being covered with similar looking excurient openings. The difference is that unlike a sponge which will not react to your presence, the tunicate will close up its pores if you wave your hand close to it.

We are really enjoying this lovely reef but the fun has yet to start. As we head back in toward the bay we are surrounded by massive swarms of fish. The density of the schools is sufficient to darken the water. Everywhere we look the water is speckled with the shapes of brown and blue chromis, Creole wrasse and sergeant majors. Looking up, the surface is masked with the glint of needlefish. We simply hover in mid-water, part of this fluid melee. Though considerably larger than any individual fish, we are dwarfed by this dynamic cloud of marine life.

Below us in 25 feet of water, angular boulders covered in fire coral glow, as if with an inner heat. It looks as if someone has painted the rocks. The smooth covering is occasionally broken by trembling clusters of pink and purple social feather dusters, striking a bold contrast against the harshness of the fire coral.

So often the area below the boat where the safety stop is done offers some of the most interesting features of the dive, and Orca Point is no exception.

Thanks to Bill Tewes of Dive St. Vincent.

Just outside the picturesque bay of Petit Byahaut lies a pinnacle, 60 feet offshore and about 15 feet below the surface. It is possible to spend the whole dive around the pinnacle, admiring the coral and the mass of sea life. There are 7-foot gorgonians and Art Deco azure sponges. Filefish creep by and parrotfish feed, oblivious to your presence.

Large volcanic rocks at 120 feet are also worth investigating and give some clue to the incredible forces that flung these boulders from the erupting volcano.

Pinnacle Rock 11
15'-120'

A diver called Hans Stuber lends his name to this reef. It is another good place to spot frogfish. You drop down onto a garden of gorgonians and swim across patches of brain coral surrounded by sand. At 80 feet a shelf provides a resting place for lobsters.

The dive profile takes you from a coral head out toward the open sea, so sightings of large and pelagic fish are common. There are also some good black corals and colourful sponges. Jacks, mackerel and snappers join divers in their enjoyment of this reef.

Moray eels, scorpionfish and octopus favour the site. With little current, there is always time to explore the area thoroughly. Look out for the luscious anemones, waving their tentacles seductively at passing prey.

Hans Reef 12
25'-120'

The long history of black coral as a semi-precious material in jewellery making has resulted in its increasing rarity on the world's coral reefs. Yet in its natural growing state it projects far more beauty than any polished bangle can convey.

New Guinea Reef has the greatest quantity and range of black coral that we have seen in the Caribbean. And, because the island attracts so few divers, it is in an unsullied condition. The black coral is so impressive that it is easy to ignore the other special qualities of this reef. These include a cave and numerous vertical faces and fissures, painted with an abundance of colourful encrusting corals and sponges like graffiti on a subway wall.

New Guinea 13
Reef
20'-120'

  C

A buoy anchored in 30 feet of water positions the dive boat about 50 feet from a vertical cliff face just inside a quiet bay. While we are preparing our equipment, a great blue heron watches us from the cliff edge wondering, perhaps, whether our activities might distract a few fish that he could take.

We drop down to 45 feet at the edge of the reef and swim along the base out toward the headland. A rolling expanse of finger coral greets us before the wall itself begins to take on a steeper incline. Large sea plumes soften the profile of the reef and numerous juvenile reef fish flitter through their fronds.

Dive Profile

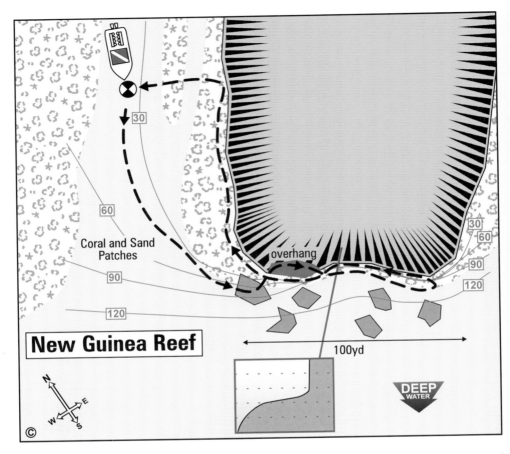

New Guinea Reef

Coral and Sand Patches

overhang

100yd

DEEP WATER

30   60   90   120

N E S W

©

Then the black coral bushes begin. From 40 to 100 feet the reef has an abundance of bushy and feather black coral in several different shades. Unlike the gaudy yellows and purples of the sponges typically found on Caribbean reefs, the effect is altogether more subdued. A combination of soft textures and muted colours creates a tranquil and ephemeral atmosphere. The colours range from soft greens to dusky pinks to rich sienna.

This section of the reef forms a steep uneven slope, so that it appears as a cascading garden of delicate bushes. Wire coral, another type of black coral that thrives here, springs from the substratum like stray unruly hairs. Interestingly, although there are many fish, they are generally young and quite small. We see big schools of tiny chromis, like a junior school outing.

Some large volcanic rocks at the base of the wall, at 100 feet, offer beautifully sponge-encrusted vertical faces. Banded shrimps and arrow crabs snuggle inside sponges, sharing the space with brittle stars.

On the headland, at 100 feet, is an overhang, penetrating into the cliff for about 15 feet. The walls, floor and ceiling are smeared with coral and sponge. As you turn to swim out, there is a lovely vista of sea fans framing the entrance.

Continue around the headland, air and current permitting, and then return along what has now become a completely vertical wall. At 30 feet, there is a feast of invertebrate life for you to browse as you return toward the buoy. Moray eels have plenty of

Red, Green, White—It's All Black Coral

It is called black but it comes in a variety of colours, none of which is black. It looks exactly like a plant, but actually it is an animal. It appears to be and is often described as soft coral, yet its closest relative is hard coral. No wonder myths abound about these beautiful underwater creatures. Lamentably, its preciousness has done little to protect the stocks. The enigmatic black coral of the Caribbean survives in many areas, despite rather than because of its historical attraction to healers and jewellery makers and, latterly, to tourists and divers.

The Latin name for black coral, antipatharian, originates in what was believed to be its medicinal qualities: anti (against), pathes (disease). As with many products with magical properties, black coral was used to fashion ornamental items. Black coral jewellery is still available for sale in the Caribbean. The inevitable over-harvesting that followed meant that it was found only in deeper and deeper water, its rarity adding to its mystical qualities.

Black coral trees—prettier adorning reefs than adorning people.

Unlike soft corals whose polyps have eight tentacles, black coral mirrors hard coral in having six tentacles. The polyps live not inside protective cups like soft and hard coral but on the surface of its shiny black axial skeleton. It is this skeleton which is polished and sculpted into jewellery items. The black skeleton is responsible for the more muted colours of the live black corals. The polyps are translucent with colour pigments of pinks, grey, browns and green which, set against the background of the black axial, transmit subtle shades.

Many varieties of black coral occur on Caribbean reefs: bushy black coral, orange sea fans, and long curly wire coral. A few clues will help determine the difference between soft corals and black coral. Black coral polyp tentacles expand and retract a little, but do not disappear inside protective cups so the appearance of the black coral never changes. By comparison, soft corals have fat bushy branches when the polyps are extended which become smooth and thin when retracted. Black coral bushes are generally finer and more feathery than soft corals.

Please help protect the black coral of the Caribbean by not buying coral jewellery.

places to hide and we see dozens of fireworms crawling over vase sponges or challenging the sea urchins.

New Guinea Reef offers you a rare opportunity to see healthy colonies of black coral in their intended environment.

Thanks to Berris Little of St. Vincent Dive Experience.

14 Back Door Reef

25'-100'

This is our second dive of the day but it is by no means second rate. Even the name of the dive, Back Door Reef, because it is immediately behind the site known as The Garden, implies a poor relation. Yet, we find it an enchanting experience and one which by chance brings us into contact with the many conflicting attitudes to coral reefs.

Back Door Reef is a steep slope with much to see on the shallow plateau at the top of the slope, as well as down to 100 feet. Relatively unusual coral species and interesting algae make this dive different from the norm.

Dive Profile

The site is buoyed in 25 feet of water. Below the buoy, the coral is fairly grey with sand patches. We swim out into deeper water and the scene transforms. Finger coral spreads out before us like the prairies at harvest time. Investigating some bright green patches, we see a patch of green grape alga. This alga grows in abundance among the finger coral. The corn-yellow glow of the coral and the tender green of the grapes makes the reef shine with health like a spring day.

As we swim to the west, the fields of finger coral persist, intermingled with delicate pencil coral. At 45 feet, in a small hollow in the coral, we find a nest of sea pearls: two large pearls and a clutch of the elongated variety. The large pearls were 2 inches in diameter. Sea pearls are single-celled green algae, one of the largest single cells in the plant or animal kingdom. Thankfully, knowledge rarely destroys imagination and it is impossible not to think of these Fabergé egg look-alikes as precious.

Moving along the slope, at 50 feet, the finger and pencil coral are replaced by Graham's sheet coral and what looks like honeycomb plate coral, although this species is not reported in this area. Further investigation is needed. The sheet coral lies in overlapping layers of golden brown shelves, covered in tiny white polyps like stars on a Caribbean night.

As we swim toward the headland, soft corals began to appear. Eventually these will become the predominant growth on the adjacent Garden Reef.

The fish life includes many varieties of reef fish. Stoplight parrotfish in several phases scrape at the coral. Bi-colour damselfish and juvenile jackknife fish flicker among the sea plumes. Swimming back in shallow water, 20 feet, we find two lettuce sea slugs feeding on the algae. Obviously named for the ruffled lettuce leaf-like frills

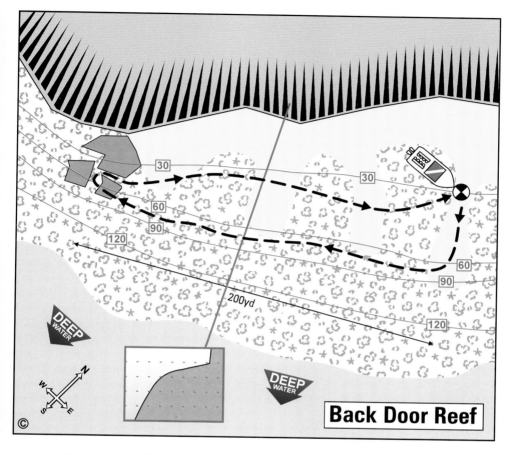

Back Door Reef

running along its back, this little mollusk is considerably prettier than any lettuce we know. Its frills are edged with pink, and shaded from a mint green at the outer edge to a deeper moss green in the centre, no doubt caused by eating all that green algae.

One of our finds is not so enchanting. A 20 foot deep fishing net lies across the reef, from the shallows down the length of the slope, inevitably entangled in the coral. In the surge the net tugs at the coral but the real damage will be done when the net is lifted. A few fish struggle in the net but the catch hardly seems to justify the long-term damage to the habitat. As we examine our find, we hear a "whoosh splat" as a speargun is fired. Fishermen are spearfishing along the reef.

St. Vincent offers divers an undeveloped island and dive industry. We have to accept that the consequences are sometimes shocking. The concept of reef protection is undeveloped and it will take time for a nation that has traditionally fished these reefs to decide where its best long-term interests lie.

Thanks to Bill Tewes of Dive St. Vincent.

15 The Garden
40'-90'

Another sloping reef with volcanic rocks littering the area, The Garden provides numerous hiding places for invertebrates and mollusks. Look out for octopus among the rocks; crabs are also a frequent find. Cherubfish are one of the site's assets. Because they are only tiny, they seem like juveniles, especially as they look as if they are going through a colour change. The daub of yellow around the fish's face is a permanent feature, contrasting forever with the royal blue of the body.

The fish life is very active and in abundance on this reef, giving novices and experienced divers plenty to see. Pretty butterflyfish and harlequin bass make up the population of the reef, along with rock beauties and hamlets. Lurking beneath overhangs, big porcupinefish peek out, ready to make a dash for more secure cover. Divers who try to coax these creatures to puff up have come off the worse for wear after receiving a painful defensive nip from the tough beaked mouth of the porcupinefish.

Because there are rarely currents here, the site makes a suitable dive for beginners or as a check-out dive.

16 Turtle Bay
40'-80'

Sadly this is not named for the profusion of turtles but is a very pleasant dive nevertheless. This is a sloping reef that often reveals a frogfish or two. The reef is good both shallow and deep.

Both adult and juvenile reef fish are plentiful. Sergeant majors guard their eggs unaware that in the eyes of most divers its egg patch does not offer a tasty meal. This is a dive with something for everyone, including a good cross section of eels. Sand eels and snake eels especially are a common sight.

17 The Steps
30'-80'

If you visit Fort Charlotte and look out over the ramparts to the sea below, you will see a staircase carved into the cliff, with a small pool constructed from the rocks at the water's edge. This area was once a leper colony and the steps were used to reach the pool where the lepers bathed. A reef extends out to sea that forms The Steps dive site.

Dive operators dive down this small wall across the reef and over a sandy area before finishing the dive in the shallows. It is an exceptionally colourful site that makes a good night dive. Squid, snails and morays abound at night and the coral polyps bring the reef to life in the beam of the diver's lights.

The appeal of finding ancient rum bottles draws divers to this site, but it is a lovely reef dive in its own right. Being directly below Fort Charlotte it truly is an historic site.

You descend along the foot of the underwater rock headland. To the right is a gentle coral slope, decorated by sponges and small soft corals. On the left, the headland turns into a sheer wall adorned by deepwater sea fans. Small bushes of black coral occur in several colours.

At the bottom of the headland, at 100 feet, you will be ascending through huge schools of grunts. A curious current pattern makes it possible to have the current with you the whole way.

As with many of St. Vincent's dives, there is a great deal of variety because the site includes both a wall and a coral garden. The fish life is tremendous and schools of tarpon, like armour plated warriors, are often seen cruising the reef. These fish are not shy, so if divers move quietly through the school it will not disperse.

Because there have been no rules restricting the removal of ancient bottles, it is becoming harder to find them, particularly at shallow depths.

Bottle Reef 18
30'-100'

There are at least 11 wrecks in Kingstown Harbour but until recently only two were dived. The 120-foot inter-island ferry *Seimstrand* and the freighter *Nomad* collided in the harbour and sank in 1984, creating an unintentional artificial reef for the divers of St. Vincent. The *Nomad* is in relatively shallow water, at 40 feet, whereas the *Seimstrand* sits in 80 feet of water.

While diving these wrecks, local divers had noticed two large old anchors nearby, but not until 1988 when exceptional currents, after an eclipse, swept through the harbour was a third wreck revealed in the same location.

The third wreck was clearly old and little of it was visible. Eight cannons, vases, a stove and big copper cooking pots have been exposed. Preliminary investigations suggest that this is the slave ship *Africa* that sank in 1784. If this identification is confirmed it could be the first intact slave ship to be excavated. All the slaves were safely removed from the ship before it sank, making these men and women the likely ancestors of some of today's St. Vincentians.

Plans to build a cruise ship dock nearby are in an advanced stage. The new dock might require the removal of the *Seimstrand* and the *Nomad,* but moving the *Africa* without time to carry out proper archaeological excavation would mean the loss of valuable historical artefacts.

These conflicting needs are currently being examined and the Kingstown Port Authority has closed the site to divers without special permission. Local operators will be able to give you the status of the site.

Kingstown 19
Wrecks
40'-100'

20 Kingstown South
30'-90'

Named after its location, it might be more appropriately called lobster hotel. The unusual red banded lobster is found here alongside slipper and spiny lobsters. The red banded variety is, not surprisingly, marked in bands and spots of red as well as white and gold. You will need to look carefully as they are only about 6 inches long and tend to be shy of divers. Unlike other Caribbean lobsters, they have claws, though they are tiny.

The dive site is a steep slope covered in coral and sponges. Spotted drums and filefish are plentiful and there is the occasional pelagic fish swimming out in the open sea. Huge plate coral plays home to large numbers of reef fish, including some large angelfish.

21 Kingstown South South
40'-140'

Although this site is adjacent to The Forest, the underwater scenery is markedly different. A sloping reef with a steep drop-off is covered with hard corals and black coral.

Often dived as a drift, if currents are strong you may experience all of the variety that St. Vincent has to offer in one dive. Starting with the hard corals of Kingstown South South, the current may sweep you into the swaying gorgonians of The Forest dive site.

22 The Forest
20'-70'

One of St. Vincent's most interesting dives is known as The Forest because of the mass of gorgonians. Huge sea whips and soft plumes reach up to 10 feet tall and create a curtain of swaying fronds through which you can weave your way in and out. Keep a sharp eye out for various species of nudibranch.

The effect is a fantastical forest where fish replace birds and invertebrates substitute for land-based insects. Tiny reef fish mimic the behaviour of humming birds and brightly coloured angelfish easily compare with St. Vincent's parrots. Jacks swoop in and out of the gorgonians and the reef has a lively playful atmosphere.

23 Rock Fort
40'-90'

Just off Young Island, still on the southern side of St. Vincent, is an interesting slope with an abundance of black coral. A gentle slope slowly gets deeper and is littered with boulders. Numerous fish including big varieties populate the area. Consequently, barracuda find it a productive hunting ground.

24 The Drift
60'-90'

On the southeast corner of St. Vincent, exposed to the Atlantic where currents can be fierce, this dive site is in a good location for seeing the larger pelagic fish and over-sized groupers, stemming the tide. Drifting over large rocks and boulders, you are likely to come across barracuda, nurse sharks, Atlantic spade fish, chub and shy but beautiful eagle rays. Turtles are often seen here, too.

The current is variable and on occasion the whole drift will be over in 15 minutes whereas, at other times, the drift can take a gentle 45 minutes. The underwater scenery is rather like a moonscape offering some limited opportunities to duck out of the current temporarily.

St. Vincent Diving Facilities

When you consider the extent and quality of St. Vincent's diving, it is astonishing that there are only three dive operators. So many relatively popular diving destinations in the Caribbean are described as 'undiscovered', 'unexplored' or 'unspoilt' by the travel magazines, yet no one ever mentions St. Vincent. Why? Because it is genuinely undiscovered. As a consequence, there is barely enough business to keep busy the few operators who do provide diving.

The two main operators are located in the south of the island, in Young Island Cut. This makes the boat ride to the dive sites very comfortable on the way out and sheltered on the way back down the west coast, though the sea can be rough for the last couple of miles heading east to Young Island Cut.

Equipment

The operators are able to purchase diving equipment tax free, so are well equipped to meet the needs of divers who do not have their own equipment. All the operators are using Sherwood equipment. If you need repairs carried out on your equipment while you are in St Vincent, you may be in luck if you have Sherwood, otherwise spares will be a problem.

Equipment is available for rent on a daily basis to those wishing to dive independently.

There is not sufficient demand for the operators to carry much stock for sale, although they do have a few items.

Cost

Single tank dives cost between $40 and $50, with packages available for 6 and 10 tanks. For diving independently, equipment rental will be around $35 per day if you need everything.

Open water certification courses vary depending what is included, i.e. course materials, equipment, etc. Check out what is included. On average you are probably going to pay $375 to $425.

Operators

Bill Tewes, the owner and manager of Dive St. Vincent **2**, is rightly credited with discovering, naming, and subsequently preserving most of St. Vincent's excellent dive sites. Bill is a passionate diver, interested in marine biology. He is an active fighter for the cause of conservation in St. Vincent. All staff, with the exception of Bill, are Vincentians. Diving with Dive St. Vincent, you will notice that all the divemasters carry marine life identification slates which they use underwater to point out and identify the marine life.

Dive St. Vincent's diving procedures are to have one dive leader at the front of a diving group and one at the back, so that divers can pretty much follow their own preferred dive profile. Groups of six or more are given their own boat and divemaster. Three fast dive boats make all the dive sites a short, comfortable ride away. Dive St. Vincent uses steel tanks, so apart from the benefits of a smaller tank, you will need less weight than you are accustomed to with aluminium tanks.

Dive St. Vincent offers an interesting dive package for those who intend to spread their vacation around St. Vincent and the Grenadines. You can buy a 10-dive package which can be used with Dive St. Vincent, Dive Bequia, Dive Canouan, and Grenadines Dive. Or, you can take a training course with these operators as you move around, so that you are not confined to one place while you get your certification.

St. Vincent Dive Experience **3** shown on our tables and locator maps closed as we went to press leaving only two operators in St. Vincent.

For seclusion, there is no beating a resort that you cannot reach by road. Petit Byahaut **1** is just that. Guests have to be collected by boat from the next bay. Only yachts can access Petit Byahaut directly.

Charles and Sharon, the owners and managers of Petit Byahaut, offer diving to guests and other visitors to the island. Charles is a divemaster so can accompany divers but cannot teach. Petit Byahaut also has dinghies and kayaks for rent.

Their small dive boat is able to reach most of the good sites quite quickly, as Petit Byahaut is located right in the centre of the area where most of the dive sites are found. They also have equipment for sale at competitive prices because of the government's waiving of import duty on water sport equipment. The hotel is closed from 1st July to 1st November.

Bequia is a gentle island of rolling hills, gingerbread houses, flowers and many beaches. It has an unhurried atmosphere conducive to easy relaxation.

For a holiday, Bequia is on a perfect scale. You can hike anywhere in an hour or two, yet at 5 miles long and with hills rising to 860 feet, the island has many excellent walks in pleasant scenery. Bequia is small enough that you do not need a car and large enough to offer a variety of areas that feel quite different from one another.

Add to this a charming small town in a picturesque harbour, with enough bars, restaurants and boutiques to keep anyone happy. It has a faithful band of visitors that come back year after year.

Bequia is only 9 miles from St. Vincent and there are several ferries a day, so many who stay in Bequia take a day to go hiking or sightseeing in St. Vincent.

Bequia is an island of fishermen, seatraders and shipwrights whose inhabitants are descended from Scottish farmers, French freebooters, North American whalers and African slaves. Boats are built on the beach and it is here that the largest island schooner was built, the 131-foot *Gloria Colita*, which made many successful voyages. In 1940 she was found drifting and abandoned in the Bermuda Triangle. The crew were never found.

Whaling is an old Bequia tradition, though the whaling crew is getting older and it is doubtful it will go on much longer. Licensed by the International Whaling Commission, they hunt from open sailing boats, using only hand held harpoons, and in a good year may catch a whale.

In keeping with its small size, accommodation is in small hotels (the largest has 27 rooms), guest houses and rental apartments. These are spread around the island. Port Elizabeth, the only town, is a picturesque collection of houses and shops overlooking the beach at the head of the bay. The beach is where

Bequia

CHRIS DOYLE

Life in Bequia is always colourful, above or below the water.

everyone gathers, for here the tall palms and broad almond trees reduce the sun's glare to a dappled shade. You can sit on the wall of a flower bed sandwiched between the two main thoroughfares and watch life go by. Inland lies the road, a casual place dominated by shoppers who stroll along unconcerned by the occasional car or bus that clears a path by honking. On the other side schooners, freighters, ferries and yachts come and go. Dinghies and water taxis pull into the dock and little two-bow sailing dinghies dart around like butterflies.

From here you can walk to the south side of the bay by following a tiny waterfront path that links a series of restaurants, bars, boutiques, hotels, guest houses and apartments. Progress can be slow. You meet old friends, make new ones and stop for an ice-cream or drink. This area is the centre of social activity at night. Mainly people gather to chat and eat out, but most nights one of the bars or hotels will also put on a live band.

Port Elizabeth

Port Elizabeth is the most active area on the island and the first choice of many visitors. There are two small hotels, several guest houses and a number of apartments available for rent. While this is not the best area for swimming, the beautiful Princess Margaret Beach is not far away. You can walk there in 20 minutes by following a path over the headland, or you can hop on a water taxi.

Lower Bay

Lower Bay is just over a mile from Port Elizabeth if you take the well-used foot path that climbs over a couple of headlands and along the beach. The distance on the inland road is longer, but the bay is still close enough to town and has a magnificent beach backed by seagrape and manchineel trees.

Spring

Spring also lies about a mile from Port Elizabeth, but is due east across the island and has a windward beach. There is just one hotel here in a remote location, a converted estate with secluded accommodations and a first-rate restaurant for those who like a real hideaway. It is not too hard to walk to town for the first dive of the day.

Friendship Bay

Friendship Bay is on the south side of Bequia, probably not much over a mile from town but the fairly steep hill that lies between makes it seem like a fair walk. It is a large bay with a long and inviting palm-fringed beach facing south over Isle de Quatre and Petit Nevis.

There are two hotels, including Friendship Bay Hotel, the island's largest. There is also a guest house, and several other houses available for rent. The Friendship Bay Hotel has both a good restaurant and a charming beach bar. The other hotels, including the Bequia Beach Club that has its own dive store, have small restaurants, or you can take a taxi or walk over the hill to town.

Language: English
Currency: Eastern Caribbean Dollar ($1.00 US = $2.66 EC)
Population: About 5000
Telephone Code: Currently (809), changing to (784)

Après Dive

For a small island, Bequia keeps you surprisingly well occupied. The pace of life is so delightful that buying an ice cream can seem like a whole afternoon's entertainment.

Hiking

The hiking is good anywhere on the island. The hills near Mount Pleasant afford wonderful views, and below them on the eastern shore there is a deserted beach at Hope that has breaking waves suitable for body surfing. Another excellent hiking destination is Anse Chemin in the northeastern part of Bequia.

Tennis

Tennis is available through most of the hotels:
Friendship Bay Hotel: (809) 458-3222
Gingerbread: (809) 458-3800
Plantation House: (809) 458-3425
Spring on Bequia: (809) 458-3414

Water Sports

Skippered yachts are available for charter by the day or for a Grenadine cruise. Day-charter boats set out on regular schedules to Mustique and the Tobago Cays.
Frangipani Yacht Services: (809) 458-3244
Windward Islands Charter Yacht Association: (809) 457-3091

Nightlife

Nightlife in Bequia moves round the island on a weekly basis, livening up each area as it goes. The longest-standing event is the Thursday night jump up at the Frangipani. Nearby, the Gingerbread has live un-amplified music about three times a week. Schooners, on the north shore, has live music almost every night. The Friendship Bay Hotel, the Harpoon Saloon and the Plantation House all have live groups once a week and down in Lower Bay there are good late-night parties monthly at De Reef or Coco's Place.

Shopping

The shopping in Bequia is excellent, considering the size of the island. There are many boutiques with locally made handicrafts that you will not find elsewhere. Some local specialities include beautifully made model whale boats, hand painted T-shirts, appliqué wall hangings, silk-screened fabrics, and stained glass.

Information on Accommodation

Department of Tourism: (809) 457-1502
Hotel Association: (809) 457-1072
USA: (800) 729-1726
Canada: (416) 924-5796
UK: (171) 937-6570

The Diving

So near but so different, Bequia offers quite different diving from its parent island of St. Vincent. Where St. Vincent is all steep drop-offs and small fish, Bequia is big fish and gentle slopes or submerged rocks. One of the things we enjoy about Bequia diving is the big schools of fish, especially around Pigeon Island. There are also good examples of octocorals along the north coast of Bequia.

Bequia is fortunate in having a good range of sites to suit different weather conditions. There are sheltered-water sites within Admiralty Bay as well as the more exposed sites to the north and around the offshore islands.

For those diving from a yacht, there are a few sites accessible without an operator. Devil's Table (Site 7) and Northwest Point

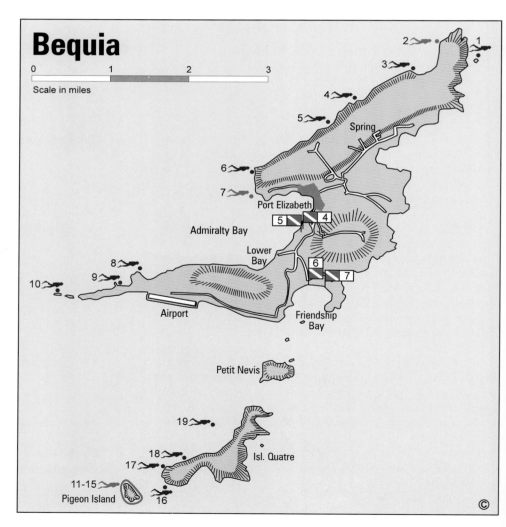

(Site 6) are at the entrance to Admiralty Bay, and can be safe dives to do without an operator. But very strong currents do occur, especially around the time of a full or new moon. Both sites have mooring buoys, so do not anchor your dinghy, and respect that they were placed there by local operators. It is advisable to have someone provide top cover in the dinghy as the current can start while you are underwater. Two divers were fortunate, recently, to be picked up after being unable to reach their dinghy, drifting toward St. Vincent! Some operators would like to see independent diving banned in the Grenadines and this kind of behaviour simply provides ammunition to the cause. The best of Bequia's diving can only be reached by a powerful dive boat and the locations are unsuitable for anchoring a yacht.

Bequia Dive Sites

NO.	SITE NAME	DEPTH IN FEET
1	Bullet Rock	30-90
2	Long Point/Anse Chemin	30-100
3	Flat Rock	20-60
4	Cathedral	30-80
5	Almond Point	30-50
6	Northwest Point	25-100
7	Devil's Table	20-90
8	Boulders	30-90
9	Moonhole	20-80
10	The Wall/West Cay	30-120
11	Swimming Pool (Pigeon Island)	15-100
12	Turtle Bay (Pigeon Island)	30-80
13	Fish Mouth (Pigeon Island)	30-100
14	Ox Head (Pigeon Island)	30-80
15	Coral Gardens (Pigeon Island)	25-70
16	Lagoona	25-60
17	Little Shallow	25-70
18	Herbie's Corner	25-55
19	Wreck of the *Lireco*	50-85

Dive Operators

NO.	OPERATOR	RESORT/HOTEL LOCATION
4	Sunsports	Gingerbread Complex
5	Dive Bequia	Gingerbread Hotel
6	Bequia Dive Resort*	Bequia Beach Club
7	Dive Paradise	Friendship Bay Hotel

*Owned by Hotel/Resort

1 Bullet Rock
30'-90'

Although rarely dived due to currents and surface conditions, this is truly a spectacular dive. It is always a drift dive and only for experienced divers. It is well worth the wait for settled weather.

A couple of hundred feet offshore, Bullet Rock is 150 feet high, with sheer vertical cliff faces that drop below the surface just as steeply. Around the rock is a combination of drop-offs and steep staircases of rock and coral. The bottom, at 90 feet, is interspersed with valleys, plateaux, and pinnacles.

Big snappers pass through, along with jacks and tuna. The parrotfish are huge, up to 4 feet, matching the proportions of the rugged, towering structures that make up this dive. As you might expect, nurse sharks are often seen and the numerous crevices and overhangs virtually guarantee you a glimpse of a lobster or two.

Although the number and size of fish are notable, the covering of sponge and coral is equally impressive. Finishing the dive in 20 to 30 feet of water, a host of cleaner shrimps, gobies, and blennies make a 'how many can you count' game fun. It is best to remain at this depth until it is time to do your safety stop, as the surge can be quite bad above this level.

2 Long Point
Anse Chemin
30'-100'

  W

A brisk northeasterly wind, a full moon the previous evening causing strong currents, and a sudden heavy rain shower conspire to make our boat ride to Long Point, at the northern tip of Bequia, a bumpy spine-jerking ordeal. On arriving at the dive site, the current seems first to run one way, then the other, so we need to re-anchor. Long Point has a reputation for its soft corals but we are beginning to wonder if we are destined to see them.

Long Point is the headland extending north toward St. Vincent. Dive operators use both sides of the point depending upon the currents.

Dive Profile

The dive boat anchors in 40 feet in an area of sand and boulders. The rough conditions at the surface are quickly forgotten as we drop down toward a subtly shifting surface of plump soft tendrils. Sea plumes shiver in the current like nervous dancers. Tall sea rods with extended polyps appear lush against the rocky substratum. A cloud of silversides fill our vision. Like a shower of sparks, they change direction as if an electric current has passed through the water. We have entered another world where fairy tale images replace the tougher reality of surface conditions.

The best part of the dive is northwards from the anchorage and out around the point. If currents prohibit this route, the dive southwards back into the bay is very good with fine examples of soft coral, albeit somewhat shallower.

As you follow the point round, boulders provide a dramatic contrasting backdrop for the forest of gorgonians that crowd this

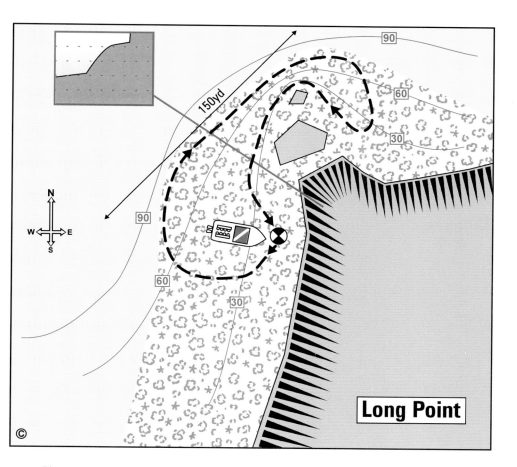

area. Giant vase sponges, normally an impressive sight, have to compete for attention with this heady mix of visual stimuli.

On the headland, prone to currents, the fish life is copious. In the open water, large schools of fish feed, while on the reef saddled blennies, spotfin butterflyfish, and spotted drums all parade their extraordinary colours and shapes.

Those who enjoy a close inspection of the reef will be able to find zoanathids and corkscrew anemones with their attendant cleaner shrimps. Giant and condominium tunicates are present; for a definite identification, remember to test whether the siphons close when you wave your hand near to them.

Long Point is usually a drift dive, so, when you complete your dive you simply surface and the boat will pick you up. We are sorry to leave the calming effect of this soft swaying environment. As if to ease the transition, the sun tears a hole in the clouds, and bathes the soft coral trees in warm yellow light. We slowly ascend and renter the world above sea level.

Thanks to Didi at Dive Bequia.

3 Flat Rock
20'-60'

It is not difficult to see how this site was named. A flat offshore rock provides an underwater playground for rays of all descriptions. Again it is a drift dive, along a slope that ends in a sandy bottom at 60 feet.

The slope has been settled by a colourful combination of soft and hard coral. It provides food and shelter for a healthy mixture of reef fish and other critters. Anemones fare well here as do tube worms; look out for the spindly arrow crabs. But best of all, keep an eye out toward the sand where you are likely to spot stingrays, electric rays and even an occasional eagle ray.

4 Cathedral
30'-80'

This site presents something for everyone. Elaborate stony corals trace a maze of corallites on the face of this sloping reef. Big patches of boulder coral and splodges of colour from sponges create a rich tapestry.

Toward the end of the dive, these are replaced by soft corals and grass beds on a sandy bottom. Nurse sharks are not an infrequent sight as they shelter in the calm of the bay, gaining some respite from this exposed coastline. Divemasters claim they can find seahorses here—keep them to their promise.

5 Almond Point
30'-50'

This lovely secluded bay, lush with almond trees, is as picturesque below the water as above. The headland supplies a dive site rich in soft coral.

Although frogfish might be found almost anywhere around Bequia, this is a particularly favoured hangout. The reef is shared with big green morays and many triggerfish. It seems to be a bay that attracts turtles so you may be lucky and see one of these curious creatures in its natural habitat.

6 Northwest Point
25'-100'

Close to the entrance to Admiralty Bay, where two of the dive stores are located, there is a gentle slope running down from the headland. At 70 feet it turns into sand, although there is an interesting rocky area at about 100 feet. Be mindful of the currents when diving here, as they can be very strong.

We find this a gentle engaging dive, offering countless nooks and crannies to investigate. Inside a vase sponge we see a nimble spray crab. Only an inch across, its golden markings seem to shine, like the metal itself, against the dark background of its shell. Solitary disk corals punctuate the reef like complex buttons, offering access to a secret world.

Looking out across the reef, a large school of boga cruise by. We amuse ourselves swimming with the school and come nose-to-nose with a large cero. We leave it to its patient stalking of the school.

The Devil's Table site, visible from the dive stores in Admiralty Bay, is less than 5 minutes in a dive boat. A reef plateau extends out from the land, marked by a navigation buoy to warn shipping of its presence. It is a popular site with both beginners and experienced divers, though its real value is as a night dive.

With a name like Devil's Table, you might think it a place to be avoided after dark. When the sun makes its silent descent below the watery horizon, the underwater world, freed from the sun's sentinel gaze, bursts into life. The day shift rapidly takes refuge in the nooks and crannies vacated by the night shift. This metamorphosis would seem like the devil's work, if it were not for the ordered beauty and balance of the transformation that takes place each evening at dusk.

The buoy to the east of the navigation mark is above a swaying field of sea plumes and whips. Our dive lights illuminate the fronds, creating eerie shadows as we fin to the trench, 8 feet wide, and run-

Devil's Table 7
20'- 90'

  C

Dive Profile

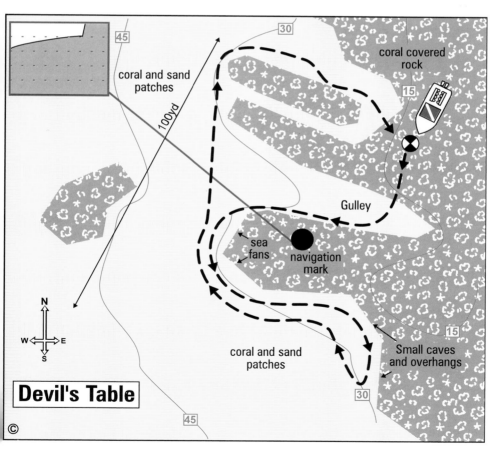

Devil's Table

Sunset on the Reef

Like an efficient factory, the self-contained ecology of the reef is managed 24 hours a day by marine life adapted to either day or night-time conditions.

Schools of cardinal and squirrel fish seen resting in caves and recesses during the daylight hours have large eyes to give them better night vision, and their red colouring makes them difficult to spot in the dark.

Other nocturnal fish, such as grunts, change colour at sunset. Strident stripes become muted blotches as the grunts attempt to melt into the shadows of night. The monochrome colouring of the spotted drums is well suited to darkness.

Most night-time feeders, including coral (they eat zooplankton), are carnivorous, feeding on the many obligingly nocturnal invertebrates which emerge from their burrows in search of their own food. Shrimps, crabs and other mollusks fall prey to eels, rays, drums and squirrel fish.

Under the cover of darkness, a crinoid creeps to the top of the reef.

Crinoids, normally wedged in crevices in daylight, move out and up to position themselves high on the reef, with a good vantage point to catch plankton. They are competing with coral which at night is covered with an army of tiny nocturnal polyps, straining the water for food. The coral polyps can feed in relative safety as their predators, the diurnal parrotfish and butterflyfish, are sound asleep.

The daytime feeders tuck themselves into crevices, generally not much larger than their bodies. Parrotfish sometimes wrap themselves in a mucus sheet. Triggerfish raise their trigger to lock themselves in place. Others rely on being completely concealed, some under the sand. The diurnal fish begin to find security for the night around dusk. It is a dangerous time for them, as the angle of the sun's rays makes it easy for predators from below to see them silhouetted against the surface. They move close to the reef as dusk approaches, tucking into their regular shelter before dark.

For a few minutes, at sunset, the reef goes quiet. We have reached the period when a truce is called. The diurnal herbivores make sure they are safely ensconced before the carnivores set forth. But ever adaptable, a number of fish (jacks, lizardfish and trumpetfish in particular) do not play by the rules and hunt specifically during this transition period. The night feeders, gathering in schools ready to move away from the reef, are vulnerable at this time.

Fifteen minutes after sunset, even the most cautious nocturnals emerge and the transition is complete. The fish do not seem to have an internal clock or moonrise almanac, instead light density is the critical factor. Plan your dive time, taking cloud cover in to account, so that you are underwater before it gets too dark, if you want to witness the changeover.

ning southwest. We are beginning the dive just before sunset, as the daytime feeders are scurrying toward their night-time shelters.

Our light's beams alight on a basket star, 2 feet across. This confused tangle has stretched out its legs and become a huge and efficient feeding machine. As we emerge from the trench, we notice a small piece of coral in a sand patch wink at us! Worth investigating, it is an octopus foraging for mollusks under the sand. It checks out the finger we hold out toward it but quickly decides it is not edible.

We swim to the left as we emerge from the trench where a large rock sprouts a mass of deepwater sea fans. The intricate patterns, like huge spider's webs, are thrown into relief by the glow from our lights. Lobsters play the part of the spiders as they wander freely at night, in search of food. There are Caribbean spiny lobsters and slipper lobsters, too. To accompany them, long-spined sea urchins are emerging from their daytime holes to march across the coral like an army of cleaners, hoovering up anything edible in their path.

Not wanting to venture too far from the boat at night, we return round the rock and back along the trench. We are pleased to spot a decorator crab. Because it is utterly confident in its disguise, we are able to observe it closely. It is completely clothed in encrusting sponges, with just two tiny red claws free of debris peeking out from its shell. This is a symbiotic relationship between crab and sponge; as the crab is given camouflage and the sponge benefits from a mobile feeding area.

Swimming back to the buoy, we notice an electric eel lying quietly on the sand. Our battery powered lights are holding up so we leave this source of power undisturbed and head back to the boat. We have not covered as much terrain as we would during a daylight dive but the Devil's Table at night delivers a feast to satisfy any appetite.

Diving at night requires special training and surface cover techniques. Dive operators will train and brief you on the particular skills needed. Please be especially careful with your buoyancy in order not to damage the reef and beware of blinding fish with your light as they will become disoriented and damage themselves by crashing into the coral.

As a daylight dive, the Devil's Table offers a wreck a few yards off the reef. The wreck is a yacht, in 90 feet of water, and worth devoting 15 minutes or so of your dive time to.

Boulders 8
30'-90'

As well as having some interesting underwater structures, this site is blessed with a panoply of marine life. You descend a gradual slope until you reach the boulders at around 90 feet. These are true boulders, reaching up 20 feet or more from the bottom.

The seascape is like something from a theme park as you

drift effortlessly through tunnels and holes and into caverns. This alone would be fun, but to do so surrounded by a myriad of reef fish is quite a delight. The abundance of fish attracts many predators; barracuda and jacks patrol conscientiously while sennets seem to swoop across the reef, changing direction apparently randomly.

The many hiding holes make it a rewarding dive for those who enjoy finding lobsters, crabs and eels. Nurse sharks and groupers mooch about here, too. The prize of the dive is usually the seahorses which local dive operators can invariably find for you. These coy peculiar creatures are very hard to spot without a practised eye.

9 Moonhole
20'-80'

A little further along the reef from Boulders is a strange collection of buildings designed by Tom Johnson, an American with his own vision of paradise. It is intended to be a place of harmony and peace. The houses appear to grow out of the rocks with no angular lines to disrupt the natural balance of the surroundings.

By comparison with the surreal landscaping above the water, the reef below could seem quite tame. Fortunately the richness of Bequia's reefs still leaves scope for reverence. A sloping reef is smeared with soft coral and patches of finger coral giving a buttery hue to the reef when the sun is high.

Just to the north of the reef is a wreck which can easily be dived as part of this site. The wreck, the *Rick's H*, is a 150 foot freighter that sits upright on the bottom at 100 feet. It is poised just on the edge of a drop-off but is securely held in position as it has sunk about 10 feet into the sand.

10 The Wall/
West Cay
30'-120'

Everyone loves a wall, and Bequia's wall is unlikely to disappoint. As well as the thrill of a sheer drop-off, divers are treated to a cornucopia of marine life hanging in the currents that whisk through the gaps between the cays.

West Cay consists of two large rocks at the westernmost tip of Bequia. Diving around the rocks you are likely to encounter pelagic jacks, big schools of needlefish and sennets. The big draw, though, is black tip or reef sharks, attracted by the strong currents which whip around the headland.

The wall drops to 120 feet on its deepest side and, as you gradually ascend around the rock, you will arrive at a quieter shallow area where bigeyes and squirrelfish shelter from the current. Rays and turtles are also common sightings.

Pigeon Island, locally called Ramier, is a rock 3 miles south of Bequia next to the much larger island of Isle de Quatre. Diving anywhere around this rock is excellent and the operators based in Friendship Bay dive here almost every day. They have designated five separate dive sites, all of which have some special characteristics to commend them.

Pigeon Island

On the west side of Pigeon Island, an arm of rock extending from the cliff face has created a sheltered pool with a sandy bottom at a depth of 15 feet. As you swim out of the pool and around to the left, huge blocks of rock create an intriguing underwater landscape. The quality of the coral is good and there is much variety.

Lovely patches of finger coral draw a mass of tiny reef fish, but look out to the blue as barracuda often cruise by. The huge boulders form gaps and tunnels to explore. You may be surprised to find a 4-foot garden gnome down there, too. This was left behind after a film shoot and put in its current position by one of the local operators.

Despite Pigeon Island's offshore location, this site is a relatively easy dive, although currents can pick up as you reach the corner. If this is the case, you will see big schools of fish enjoying the free ride.

Swimming Pool 11
(Pigeon Island)
15'-100'

This is a sloping stepped reef adorned with brightly coloured sponges and coral. The rock face is fractured with fissures which house lobsters and resting reef fish. Shark lovers will enjoy this dive as nurse sharks hide here.

Turtle Bay 12
(Pigeon Island)
30'-80'

Bobo, our boat driver, picks a careful route through the waves and reefs which ring Friendship Bay. On route to Pigeon Island the boat passes Petit Nevis where one of the last whaling stations in the Caribbean remains. These islands, to the south of Bequia, have stark cliff faces punching up through the sea, topped by thick unruly coverings of scrub.

A quick dash across the open sea between Petit Nevis and Pigeon Island has us in calm water. We see in the cliff above us a deep gaping hole, like a mouth, where the cliff has been undercut by erosion, and realise perhaps why the site is called Fish Mouth. On the stark slopes above the cliff face, century plants make the island look as though the gods have been using it for archery practice.

More impressive than the faceted rock face above the water is the spectacular scenery below. The site has a 50-foot vertical wall, massive boulders and a coral strewn slope. It seems that the fish find it as attractive as divers do; several large schools of fish, including one consisting of a dozen barracuda, swarm about us.

Fish Mouth 13
(Pigeon Island)
30'-100'

  W

Dive Profile

The dive boat buoy is in 45 feet of water above an area of coral, rubble and sand. Immediately as we drop down we see a school of Creole wrasse. We then notice that the school is surrounded by a horde of chromis and tiny silvery specks of silversides.

Initially, we swim toward the wall that is the continuation of the cliff above. A deep fissure scars the wall face, covered in vase sponges and encrusting corals. Our dive guide leads us to deeper water where the slope peters out into sand and huge monolithic boulders sit like ancient monuments to long-forgotten gods.

The first and deepest boulder we explore is dressed in sea fans and soft corals. The top is at 60 feet, and at 90 feet we find that this massive structure has a narrow hole at its base that passes right through it, irresistible to swim through. As though guarding this ancient monument, the school of barracuda describe a slow circumnavigation of the boulder. They appear to be watching us, but I suppose you could say they might be thinking the same thing.

Swimming around the boulder, we are accosted by the sight of

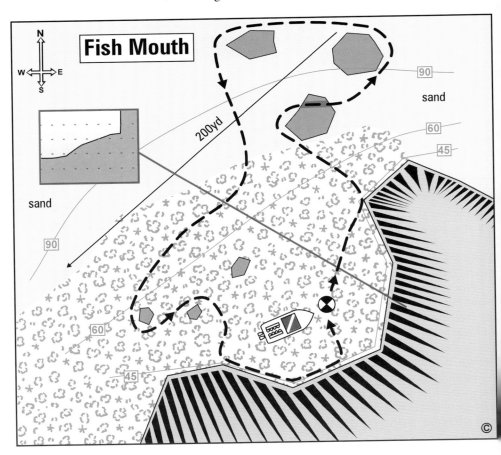

more schools of fish. This time it is bluestriped grunts, distinguishable from French grunts by their black tail and dorsal fin. They bunch together so closely they appear to be touching, making them a difficult target for predators. Above them, cottonmouth jacks hover restlessly. Brown chromis swim in loose formation while tiny blue chromis dash around, as though they have lost something of great value. The sea around us becomes a swirling mass of activity.

Schools Parade

To watch a large group of fish moving seamlessly around the reef, every change of direction executed in unison, it is easy to think of the school as a single entity. Scientists have yet to explain how the message to turn can be communicated and acted upon in what seems like the blink of an eye. Measuring response rates is easier than understanding them; fish in schools can change direction and accelerate to 20 body lengths per second in one fiftieth of a second.

What do we know about how they pull off this feat of synchronised magic? We know their eyes are used to judge distance, whereas their lateral lines (the fishes' version of ears) are used to assess speed. To avoid bruised noses, schooling fish need to swim at the same speed, so they only school with fish of the same size.

So much for how, but why? Watch a school of fish when jacks are around. A loose aggregation will bunch together and

Schooling grunts keep many watchful eyes on a group of patrolling jacks.

move as one, re-forming immediately if the jack swims through the school. They are making a harder target for the predatory jack to attack. If it does attack, the school scatters like chaff to confuse the attacker.

Protection from predators is one of the main functions of schooling. The school is able to keep a watch across a wider area, using hundreds of eyes instead of two. But the predators use schooling, too. A school of jacks can force a school of fish to scatter, making the stragglers vulnerable. And, schools of fish are more successful at attacking algae and egg patches, overwhelming their brave guardians.

Schooling performs a role in the reproductive behaviour of fish. Many reef fish give their offspring the best chance of survival by casting them into the currents at the edge of the reef, but this is potentially dangerous territory. To maximise the chance of success and to protect themselves, fish move in convoy to the edge of the reef to breed. Grunts and squirrelfish, seen in schools under overhangs during the day, move out as a group at dusk before dispersing in search of food when they reach the sea grass beds. They re-form before making the hazardous trip back to the reef and the security of their communal daytime retreats.

As we swim south, the next giant boulder is attired quite differently. The rock is embossed with encrusting sponges and coral. Even rope sponges grow pressed against the surface like a giant network of veins. A careful scan of the surface of the boulder reveals cleaner shrimps and brittle stars. A slight movement at the edge of my vision rewards us with an oversized grouper, trying to creep away quietly before we spot it.

There are many black durgons. They seem such a tastefully coloured fish after the gaudy colours of many reef fish. Delicate white piping highlights their dorsal and anal fins against the dusky blue of their bodies, and the slightest hint of aquamarine eye shadow decorates their plump faces.

Depending upon the current, the dive operator may take you farther around the headland or may follow the coastline south. When you complete the dive, you will find interesting scenery along the wall while you are making your safety stop. But for those for whom the fish offer the most attraction, just hang in the blue and watch the schools shimmy on by

Thanks to Tanya and Wayne at Bequia Beach Club.

14 Ox Head
(Pigeon Island)
30'-80'

Just south of the Swimming Pool is Ox Head. This site is prone to strong currents so local dive stores no longer buoy it. Too many buoys have been lost; it is now done as a drift dive. As with most of the Pigeon Island dive sites, big groupers inhabit this area. These are shy fish but can be approached, taking care not to alarm them. It would be unusual not to see a barracuda or two investigating the area. The terrain is a mixture of boulders and sloping coral covered rock. Two huge boulders form a tunnel that is fun to explore.

15 Coral Gardens
(Pigeon Island)
25'-75'

Strong currents are typical in the area of this site, so it is done as a drift. As always, the currents draw fish and it can be a real fish soup, with hundreds of fish jostling for space in the food-carrying current. Elegant elkhorn coral and a mass of other hard and soft corals decorate the scenery.

16 Lagoona
25'-60'

Lagoona is Bequia's forest. A small wall smothered by huge sea plumes and fans forms a swaying forest of delicate fronds. Trumpetfish love the area because they can lurk among the branches, waiting to pounce on careless prey.

17 Little Shallow
25'-70'

Again this dive has a lovely underwater seascape, typical of so many of Bequia's dives. The coral is in particularly good condition, with nothing broken. It is one of those dives where anything might crop up, from tiny rare marine life to large pelagics.

A relatively shallow dive but again an interesting one. It is typically used for beginners, as a training dive and serves well as a shallow second dive. It is not dived very often, but it can make a change for those mainly diving off the south side of Bequia.

Herbie's Corner 18
25'-55'

Although sunk deliberately to form an artificial reef for divers, this is still an advanced dive due to current and surface conditions. The *Lireco* is a 110-foot freighter sunk in 1986. It sits upright in the sand, with good access to all parts of the ship. The engine room can be penetrated to see some of the original equipment. Even the fuse boxes are still in place.

Whether or not the wreck itself is of interest, the dive offers much to see. The bow area and parts of the stern have become encrusted with coral and sponge. Lobsters and other invertebrates have discovered this unexpected new hotel, making it a great night dive for experienced divers.

Wreck of the 19
Lireco
50'-85'

For such a small island, it is perhaps surprising to find four dive stores, all reasonably large and busy operations; no doubt due in part to the quality of the diving around Bequia's shores. Compared to the other islands in St. Vincent and the Grenadines, Bequia has more hotels and resorts and attracts many sailing boats and the smaller cruise ships.

Bequia Diving Facilities

The quality of equipment used by the dive stores seemed to be very good. The zero import tax on watersports equipment is taken advantage of by the stores to keep their equipment current. Although it also means that retail prices can be kept low, most of the operators do not offer equipment for sale.

Equipment

Despite the competition among four operators, Bequia diving is relatively expensive. If you need to rent equipment, you are unlikely to pay less than $50 for a single-tank dive. Using your own equipment you may get a single-tank dive for $40 to $45. Packages for 10 dives cost between $350 and $400 depending upon whether you need equipment. A PADI open water course or equivalent is around $400.

Cost

In Admiralty Bay, Dive Bequia and SunSports are the two operators. Situated next door to each other and sharing the same jetty, they offer a competitive service. Dive Bequia 5, owned by Bob Sachs, has been operating in Bequia since 1984. If you ask them what kind of divers they attract, they will tell you it is people who like to have fun. They pride themselves on having a relaxed attitude to everything but safety and specialise in giving

Operators

people a good time.

Dive Bequia does quite a lot of teaching and Kristina, Dive Bequia's manager, feels that they do an especially good job with those beginners who are particularly nervous. Their customers come from the USA and Europe. They offer diving to hotel guests, yachts and cruise ships.

Two powerful purpose-built dive boats, each taking up to 15 divers, can not only get you to the Bequia dive sites quickly but can also take you up to St. Vincent to visit the Falls of Baleine and dive on the west coast.

Right next door, SunSports **4**, is another established business having been in Bequia for 9 years. Bob Monnens employs two local dive instructors and is well informed about local marine life.

SunSports offers a high level of customer service; putting your gear together for you, loading it onto the boat and dismantling and rinsing it at the end of the day. It is part of Sunsport's strategy to be in tune with today's divers. They especially like to take out photographers and those interested in the ecology of the reef.

The dive boats are comfortable, with a shaded area, and there is a good training beach right in front of the store. For those interested in doing a rescue course, SunSports can teach medic first aid as they have a resuscitation dummy.

Bequia Dive Resort and Paradise Dive (Karibik Dive Paradise) share Friendship Bay as their location. On the Atlantic side of the island, cool breezes brush the coast making the bay a pleasant location. Bequia Dive Resort **6** is an SSI and CMAS dive centre. They offer a friendly service, primarily to guests of the Bequia Beach Club but also the Blue Tropic and Bay View Apartments. This is a popular area with German visitors, but Bequia Dive Resort is also able to teach in a number of European languages.

Wolfgang Kursch took over the management of the store in 1997. The dive boat has twin 85 hp engines and gives a soft ride. Although exposed to the Atlantic, it is possible to make the boat trip to Pigeon Island almost any day. Bobo, the Bequian boat driver, has a knack for finding a smooth route through the waves.

At the eastern end of Friendship Bay is Dive Paradise **7**. Harald Hess runs a busy operation, mainly servicing German and other European guests who book dive packages through his booking agency in Germany.

Dive Paradise has specialist equipment to fit children and teaches youngsters from the age of eight. This is clearly not a full dive course but, under CMAS rules, children of this age can be given some experience of diving.

DIVE BEQUIA

We are in control, under pressure.

A dedicated and enthusiastic staff, combined with personal service and small informal dive groups are the key to our success.

For those on yachts or anyone taking a multi-centre vacation, we offer discounted dive packages in association with dive shops in St. Vincent and the Grenadines. We offer packages including diving and accomodation with many hotels and apartments.

The best fun in Bequia.

Associations:	PADI, NAUI
Associated Hotels:	Frangipani Hotel Gingerbread Apts. Village Apartments
Languages:	English, Danish
Number of Instructors:	4

Contact:	Bob Sachs
Address:	Dive Bequia PO Box 16 Bequia St. Vincent & the Grenadines West Indies
Telephone	(809) 458-3504
Fax:	(809) 458-3886
US:	(800) 328-2288
E-mail:	bobsax@caribsurf.com
Web Site:	www.empg.com/dive-bequia

Dive Bequia BEQUIA

Mustique

Mustique is the Beverley Hills of the Grenadines; Princess Margaret, Raquel Welch, Mick Jagger and David Bowie have all had houses here. It is a small—2 miles by 1 mile—but beautiful island of rolling hills, set in sparkling water with more than its fair share of lovely beaches. Large areas are still wild and deserted. It is owned and run by the Mustique Company, most of whose shareholders are the island's homeowners.

There is just a small local village, built by the Mustique Company. Its residents tend to the needs of the six dozen fancy homes that are dotted around the island.

Although you can walk around the island, many visitors prefer to putter about on small motor bikes or in open jeeps or golf carts. All are available for rent from the Mustique Company.

The houses vary from the simple and elegantly beautiful to the ornate and fancy, but they all resemble grand residences more closely than the holiday homes which they actually are. Many are available for rent when the owners are not in residence. The prices for a group of six or so can be surprisingly reasonable, and there is not one where you would not feel like a king. In addition, there is a hotel and a guest house.

The hotel and guest house both have small restaurants. Basil's Bar, a beach bar that hangs out over the water on stilts, is very popular especially on Wednesdays when there is a barbecue and jump up.

This island perfectly suits a self-contained group who want somewhere quiet and luxurious, in beautiful surroundings.

Language: English
Currency: Eastern Caribbean Dollar ($1.00 US = $2.66 EC)
Population: About 200
Telephone Code: Currently (809), changing to (784)

Après Dive

Mustique is a tiny island so do not expect a great deal of entertainment, but, what there is, is of excellent quality. Everything is organised either through the Mustique Company or the Cotton House Hotel. See below for contact information.

Horse Riding

Horse riding is available through the Mustique Company
Mustique Company: (809) 458-4621

Tennis

The Cotton House Hotel has a tennis court and some of the rental properties include a tennis court.
Cotton House Hotel: (809) 456-4777

Water Sports

Day-charter yachts are available through the Cotton House Hotel and the Mustique Company

Both Basil's Bar and The Cotton House have live music at least once a week.

Nightlife

There are four boutiques and one general store. Most are close to the landing by Basil's Bar.

Shopping

Mustique Company: (809) 458-4621
Cotton House Hotel: (809) 456-4777

**Information on
Accommodation**

Two things distinguish Mustique's dive sites from those of its sister islands. The reefs are for the most part flat, unlike the steep walls of St. Vincent, for example. In this context, flat does not mean uninteresting. There is an extensive variety of coral and marine life and the reefs follow a range of contours including terraces and boulder strewn areas.

The other noticeable difference is the currents. Most dives are drifts because fighting the Mustique currents is a no-win game. The Mustique Company controls pretty much all of its environment, certainly everything that occurs on the island, but it seems as if the currents are the one rebellious element. No one seems able to predict them.

Mustique has been able to preserve its reefs by careful management and tactful control of its influential guests. Only one blip has meant the loss of a reef in the main harbour, which was damaged repeatedly by yacht anchors. Buoys are now in place although the reef seems gone for good. The lesson was learned, and Mustique's reefs are probably as safe now as they can realistically be. Both Petit Canouan (see Canouan sites) and Pigeon Island (see Bequia sites) are within reach of Mustique.

Consequently, the diving is exciting, fun, sometimes unpredictable and always high quality.

The Diving

House owner's view south over Mustique towards Canouan.

CHRIS DOYLE

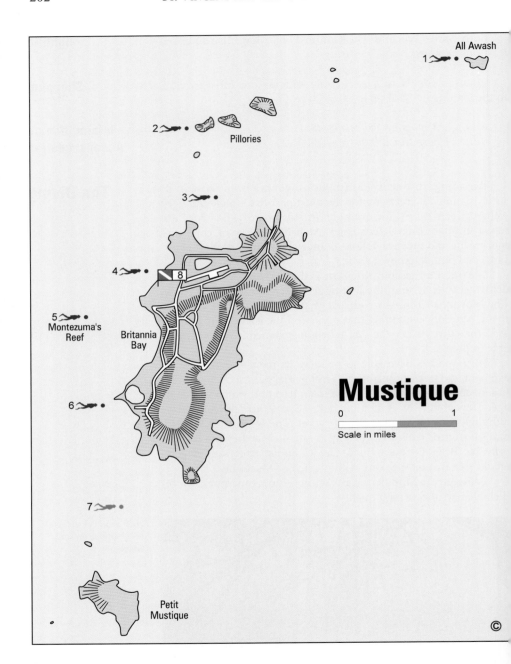

All Awash
1

2
Pillories

3

4 8

5
Montezuma's
Reef

Britannia
Bay

6

Mustique

0 1
Scale in miles

7

Petit
Mustique

©

NO.	SITE NAME	DEPTH IN FEET
1	All Awash	20-130
2	Pillories	15-90
3	Wreck of the *Antilles*	40-120
4	House Dive	Max. 20
5	Wreck of the *Jonas*/Montezuma's Reef	20-40
6	South Britannia	20-60
7	Dry Rock	35-100

Mustique Dive Sites

NO.	OPERATOR	RESORT/HOTEL LOCATION
8		Mustique Watersports

Dive Operators

All Awash 1
20'-130'

This site epitomises the diving in Mustique. A rock in an exposed position to the northwest of Mustique, it is easy prey for the strong currents that sweep up from the South American coast, gaining speed in particular tide and wind conditions. Thus it is not always possible to tackle this site and you should not hold out too much hope. Mustique Watersports makes it out here perhaps once every 6 weeks. They will want to do a check-out dive with you first.

But, like most things that are hard to attain, the rewards are considerable. Most often the south side of the rock is dived, though if currents permit, the east side is dived, too.

From the surface, the reef drops down to 130 feet of spectacular coral, both stony corals and sea whips. A deep valley opens up before the dive continues through an area of encrusted boulders. The reef is exceptionally pretty and the bonus is the volume and variety of fish.

Schools of silvery black jacks, rainbow runners, and snappers waft across the reef while black tip sharks stand off, aloof and secretive. This is the site for big fish and the excitement of a dive out in the open ocean.

Pillories 2
15'-90'

The Pillories are a row of three rocks to the north of Mustique. At the western end of the row is another drift dive, going from west to east as the current winds around the rocks.

The reef slopes at 45 degrees to a sandy bottom at 60 feet. As you move to the northeast, the bottom drops to 90 feet, forming a coral ledge. The slope is covered in sea rods and gorgonians.

Both French and the larger white grunts drift in big schools in the current. And, large means large; schools of 500 to 1,000 are not uncommon. Bermuda chub seem drawn to this area, too.

Toward the end of the dive, a baby reef about 10-foot square has been occupied by lobsters, channel clinging crabs (sometimes called king crab), morays and stingrays.

3 Wreck of the *Antilles* 40'-120'

Before you read about this dive, bear in mind that the dive operator manages to dive it only half a dozen times a year. It is subject to extremely strong currents and is very exposed.

There are two wrecks on the site. One is a 400-foot cruise ship and the other an 80-foot salvage tug. Because of its position, the cruise ship has become flattened, though there are still interesting artefacts to be seen, such as portholes and crockery items. The propellers are still intact and make an interesting sight.

The most impressive effect is the bow with its anchor and chain still in place.

4 House Dive 20' maximum

Mustique Watersports is fortunate in having a shallow but pretty reef, right off their beach. It makes a good check-out dive or night dive.

A patch reef extends out toward the point, frequented by all the usual reef fish.

5 Wreck of the *Jonas/* Montezuma's Reef 20'-40'

The *Jonas* was a 65-foot cement boat deliberately sunk to provide an interesting dive site. Unfortunately, the wreck was dropped on top of the reef instead of beside it, perhaps not surprising with a name like *Jonas*. Since then, wave action in strong swells has caused the wreck to rub back and forth on the reef destroying the coral below it.

Despite its sorry history, the reef and the wreck remain of interest to divers. It is a shallow dive, making it suitable for novices, as a check-out, and as a second dive. It is also accessible by dinghy for those wishing to dive independently, but watch out for currents.

6 South Britannia 20'-60'

The section of this reef which is in Britannia Bay is the area that has been destroyed by yacht anchors. Farther out toward the headland, the reef is still in good condition. Although a buoy is in place, it is still usually done as a drift dive.

Going southwest from the buoy is an area of scattered coral heads and gorgonians. The sand on your right reveals as much interesting marine life as the coral to your left. On a recent dive, nine eagle rays swooped over the sand along with the dive group.

This is generally a fairly sheltered-water site, at least by Mustique standards, so good for windy days and as a second dive. After heavy rain, the visibility can deteriorate a little.

Dry Rock
35'-100'

Many of Mustique's dive sites are around offshore islands and rocks. This particular rock barely qualifies as being above water, as the waves lash the protruding peaks and wash right over them. On a rough day, the wave height is sufficient to shield the rocks so that it feels as if you are being dropped into the open ocean.

Carolin Gatzke, the dive leader, describes the dive for us, in English and German. Her excellent briefing on the boat explains the procedure for a drift dive, describing what the current will do and how to deal with it. We are told that below the surface the rocks form a series of steps like a wedding cake. It sounds as though it will be an exciting dive.

Dive Profile

A backward roll and quick descent has us drifting above a sand and coral bottom at 60 feet. Carolin leads the group in the direction of the reef while Gary, at the rear, tows a surface marker buoy. Almost the first fish we see is a large queen angelfish and we see four more before the dive is finished.

As we approach the first level of the 'cake', there is little to do but ride the fast, but comfortable, current. A school of rainbow runners is doing much the same; the two electric blue stripes on their sides seem to trail in their slip stream. As well as schools, there are many individual fish such as coneys in both the bright yellow and bi-coloured phases. Red hinds, orange filefish, Spanish hogfish, blue tangs and squirrelfish all form part of the moving scenery as we are whisked along the reef.

The lower layer of the 'cake' is at 100 feet, after which there is a sandy bottom harbouring lizardfish and other bottom dwellers.

Stationary lizardfish peer at fast-moving divers being whisked along in the current.

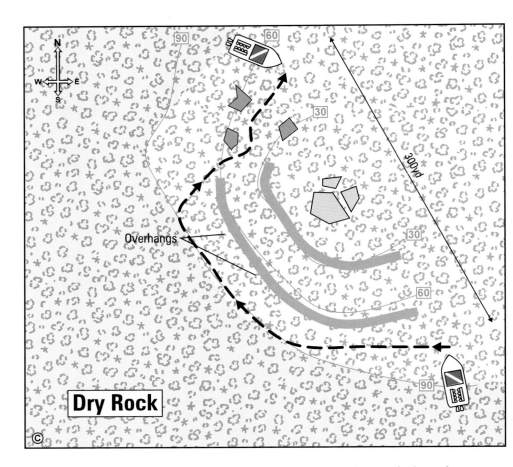

It is at 85 feet, amongst the rocks, that we find two large nurse sharks and one juvenile. Large schools of fish appear all along the reef. A school of Bermuda chub makes a quick pass by then linger a little farther off the group of divers, reluctant perhaps to concede their patch to these interlopers.

The layered effect of this reef makes looking up an attractive vista. Schools of fish, descending the reef, appear like a waterfall flowing over the edge of each layer. Star and boulder coral cover most of the area, but look out for individual disk and mushroom coral, smiling up at you from the slope.

The current carries you in parallel to the reef but when you reach the west corner it can carry you out to sea, so Carolin shepherds the group closer to the reef until the current decreases around the corner. The area around the west corner flattens out and we complete the dive at 45 feet, above an area covered with sea whips and plumes. It is rather like an exposed windswept heathland scene; instead of isolated tall patches of octocorals the surface is almost covered with whips, though none has grown particularly tall.

Patch reefs occur, attracting numerous small reef fish and to our delight a snoozing hawksbill turtle. It appears to be very relaxed about our presence and only when it tires of being gawked at does it make a dignified exit, swimming slowly away.

This is an average day on Dry Rock. Visibility at 75 feet is average. The current can be stronger than today but this is about normal. Average conditions maybe, but definitely an above average dive.

Thanks to Carolin and Gary of Mustique Watersports.

Mustique Dive Operators

There is only one dive operator in Mustique and, as you would expect, it is a class act. A 28-foot diesel custom-built dive boat gives an incredibly soft ride through the choppy waters surrounding Mustique. Each dive is led, with a dive instructor following at the rear of the group.

Carolin Gatzke, Mustique Watersports' **8** manager and one of the two instructors, is an experienced diver. She is knowledgeable and concerned about reef conservation as well as diver safety, in a diving region that typically has serious currents.

Mustique Watersports have access to sufficient sites around Mustique to provide enough variety. In addition, they do occasionally dive Pigeon Island, south of Bequia, and Petit Canouan, north of Canouan.

About 80 percent of Carolin's customers are people staying in Mustique, either the owners or guests of the villas on the island or guests from the Cotton House Hotel. The remainder are short-term visitors, usually on yachts. Windsurfers, sunfish sailing dinghies and kayaks are available to amuse you between dives.

Mustique offers probably about the most expensive diving you will find in the Grenadines but, then, this is Mustique. The level of service is what you would expect, and few divers are likely to feel disappointed in their investment.

Canouan

Set in the middle of the Grenadines, Canouan is a tranquil island of rounded hills. Shaped like an oversized comma some 3 miles long, it is a mere quarter of a mile wide at its narrowest point. The comma curves to form a large bay on the western side.

Much of the vegetation is dry and scrubby, a state attained with help from the island's goats who probably outnumber the two-legged residents. When walking in the hills, it is hard not to be overcome by a deep sense of peace and timelessness. The whole island is surrounded by magnificent beaches, and it is easy to find one to yourself. Large barrier reefs form protected lagoons both on the eastern shore and on the north side of the western end. As the water becomes shallow it turns brilliant turquoise and gold. Looking down from the hillsides on a late afternoon, it is hard not to feel overwhelmed by the stunning colours.

There are two resort-type hotels. The Canouan Beach Hotel lies near the western end of the island and the Tamarind Beach Hotel is just north of the local village. Each is self-contained and both have excellent restaurants. If you feel like a change from being in a resort, there are one or two tiny local restaurants opening up in the village.

The Tamarind Beach Hotel is part of a large development company that has bought the whole northern part of the island, and has plans for building about 120 dream homes for millionaires. They have put in roads and there is wonderful walking throughout the area. The highest hill is part of a conservation area and there is a marked trail to the top. Wherever you walk on the island you are rewarded by breathtaking vistas of the other Grenadines and the sea.

Language: English
Currency: Eastern Caribbean Dollar ($1.00 US = $2.66 EC)
Population: about 400
Telephone code: Currently (809) changing to (784)

Après Dive

For visitors, life in Canouan revolves around the two hotels, both of which offer a variety of activities, primarily water based.

Golf

A new golf course called the Frangipani was nearing completion as we went to press. It is part of the Tamarind Beach Hotel.
Tamarind Beach Hotel: (809) 458-8044

Tennis

Tennis is available at the Canouan Beach Hotel.
Canouan Beach Hotel: (809) 458-8888

Water Sports

Both the Tamarind Beach Hotel and the Canouan Beach Hotel have day-charter boats for visiting the other Grenadines.

Both the Tamarind Beach Hotel and the Canouan Beach Hotel have live musical entertainment from time to time.

Shopping is restricted to the hotel boutiques and a few village stores selling basics.

Department of Tourism: (809) 457-1502
Hotel Association: (809) 457-1072
USA: (800) 729-1726
Canada: (416) 924-5796
UK: (171) 937-6570

*Seen from the air, the reefs
bordering Canouan are visible
through the transparent
turquoise water.*

CHRIS DOYLE

Like Mustique, Canouan has a good range of dives, including offshore rocks and the calmer fringe reef sites. From Canouan, it is a fairly short boat ride to the Tobago Cays and Mayreau. To appreciate the full range of the diving from this island you will also need to read the next section (Southern Grenadines).

Canouan has some good submerged rocks, overgrown with stony corals. Until recently, Canouan has not had any wreck diving, the nearest wreck being off Mayreau. On July 1st, 1996, a 150-foot cargo freighter was sunk 2 miles west of Canouan to create an artificial reef. The ship was called *M/V Shadow* for most of its life although it had recently been renamed the *Bendy K*. It seems likely to revert to its former name, as that is how most local people knew the ship.

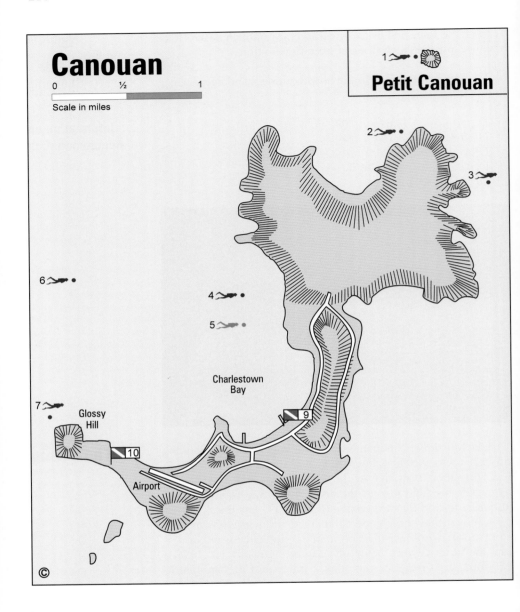

Canouan

0   ½   1

Scale in miles

Petit Canouan

1

2

3

6

4

5

7

Glossy
Hill

Charlestown
Bay

9

10

Airport

NO.	SITE NAME	DEPTH IN FEET	
1	Petit Canouan	20-65	**Canouan**
2	Maho Bay	20-70	**Dive Sites**
3	Billy Hole	25-65	
4	Gabby Stone	35-90	
5	Gibraltar	40-95	
6	Wreck of the *M/V Shadow*	85-100	
7	Glossy Hill	50-60	

NO.	OPERATOR	RESORT/HOTEL LOCATION	
9	Dive Canouan	Tamarind Beach Hotel	**Dive Operators**
10	Glossy Dive Club	Canouan Beach Hotel	

Petit Canouan **1**
20'-65'

This small offshore island can only be reached when the sea state is moderate or calm. Dive Canouan is generally able to make it there two or three times a week. The dive site is on the west side and, due to the presence of currents, is done as a drift. The currents are not particularly strong, giving time to explore the reef and its many inhabitants.

The dive begins with a straight descent to 65 feet where the bottom is covered in coral and boulders. It is a good site to see many types of different hard corals. For those who enjoy the visual effect created by sea fans, this will be an enjoyable dive.

Fish spotters will see schools of yellowtail snappers and many small reef fish. But the prize of the dive tends to be the turtles, barracuda and sharks, which are recurrent visitors to the waters around Petit Canouan.

Maho Bay **2**
20'-70'

To the north of Canouan is a large bay with a fringing reef. Currents sweeping around the headlands provide a reliable source of food which keeps the reef healthy. Sea fans fare well in these conditions.

Also done as a drift dive, the underwater seascape is marked by sizeable boulders. It is perfect nurse shark territory, so check under ledges for the tails of sleeping sharks. If you do not find a shark in one of the many crevices, you will certainly find a lobster or two.

3 Billy Hole
25'-65'

Because this site is on the Atlantic side, conditions can be rough, making it a site for calm days. The bottom, at 65 feet, is strewn with large boulders encrusted in coral and sponge. The sea fans are quite special, large and in good condition. The good flow of water from the currents delivers a constant supply of nutrient material, allowing the fans to develop well.

4 Gabby Stone
35'-90'

Gabby Stone and Gibraltar, two sites close together on the sheltered west side of the island, deliver some lovely calm water diving. Gabby Stone is a little farther along from Gibraltar (see site 5 dive profile). This submerged rock, with a steep slope and many overhangs, creates an interesting underwater profile.

Black coral grows at accessible depths among the star and boulder coral on this site. The reef is alive with invertebrates and the calm conditions allow ample time to observe the busy life being lived on the reef. As in any community, each creature has adapted to a particular niche. Some live off the waste products of others keeping that organism healthy while others are occupied in building the structures that provide shelter to the reef's population.

During the daytime, much of this activity can be observed, but at night the role of the invertebrates becomes more apparent. Dive Canouan uses this site as one of their night dive locations.

5 Gibraltar
40'-95'

  W

The first time we sailed across the Atlantic, we made our landfall in Gibraltar. A towering angular hunk of rock is not by design a welcoming sight, but our circumstances endowed it with so many positive associations; the smells of land, food, people and noise after many days at sea were welcoming indeed.

So, too, does the mass of this submerged offshore rock, parked rudely in the middle of a flat plain of sand, not necessarily lend itself to be described as pleasing, especially as it looms abruptly out of the blue. As we move closer, though, we can see how living coral has transformed this inert chunk of rock into a carrier for some delightful formations.

The rock of Gibraltar is engulfed in hard stony corals, flattened into sheets like layers of lace petticoats, each subsequent layer determined to protrude far enough to be admired.

Dive Profile

The dive boat takes a buoy in 60 feet of water some yards offshore. Under the boat is an expanse of sand. We have been briefed that there will be a 75-yard swim to the rock. Tucking in behind our dive leader's fins, we swim out into the blue. There is nothing to see, just the blue all around us and the sand below. Then, there before us is a cliff face, rising from the sand to within 40 feet of the surface. The base of the cliff is at 70 feet at this point.

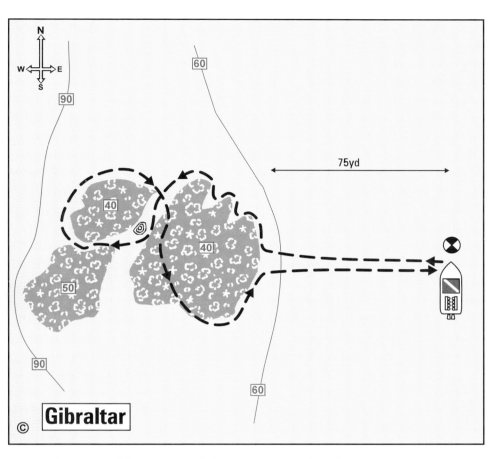

Boulder star coral has smothered almost every available piece of substratum. It has grown in plates rather like an elaborately tiled roof. Occasional patches of Graham's sheet coral occur along with encrusting star coral and cactus coral disks. Here and there, finger coral breaks up the dominance of the sheets of boulder star coral.

Swimming to the right we follow the contour of the rock. A large fissure opens to the left as if someone has taken a giant cutlass to the rock. Once again, following the rock around, we think we have come across another fissure but this turns out to be a steep canyon separating Gibraltar from another smaller rock island to the right. The canyon bottom of bright white sand reflects on the walls that continue to support flowing layers of coral. In the centre of the canyon, a round structure looks like a Modern Art coffee table made from a pile of long-playing records.

Every skirt edge of coral creates accommodation for reef creatures: lobsters visible by their waving tentacles, sleeping nocturnal fish, sheltering groupers, nervous spotted drums and a host of juvenile reef fish. Black and white horizontally striped Princess parrotfish are common, and a school of rainbow runners seems to enjoy racing through the canyon. Emerging from the canyon and turning to the right to round the second rock, we see a large stingray partially buried in the sand. It makes its exit down the canyon, giving us ample time to watch its graceful flight.

The other creature which dominates these rocks is brown variable sponge. The sponges are present in their massive form. They are easy to see as the yellow excurient openings stand proud of the surface, spaced about 6 inches apart.

We finish a trip around the smaller rock and pass again through the canyon, describing a figure of eight. At the end of the canyon, we turn left this time and follow the rock around until it is time to return to the dive boat. Big schools of silversides drift in, keeping a safe distance from the small school of yellowtail snappers that are exploring the area.

A gentle swim back to the boat allows time to absorb and reflect upon the experience of the reef. So often the memories of a lovely dive quickly fade during the business of clambering back on board, tanks hissing as equipment is dismantled, engines fired up and the quiet beauty of the reef is lost.

Thanks to Marcus of Dive Canouan.

---

6 Wreck of M/V Shadow 85'-100'

The *M/V Shadow* is lying on her port side. She was a working vessel until 1994, consequently she is still intact. Prior to sinking, she spent two years stationary on her mooring where the bottom became coral encrusted. She already has an extensive covering, therefore, and this will speed the growth of coral and sponges on the hull. Lobsters have already made the place home, prompting speculation that they, too, moved with the wreck. The open cargo holds could not be better designed to attract marine life which seeks shelter during daylight hours.

The wreck is buoyed, but the exposed position means that it is an appropriate dive for those who have some experience. Dive Canouan will require divers to do a check-out dive first.

---

7 Glossy Hill 50'-60'

The dive boat anchors on sand in 60 feet; from there the dive group swims a few yards to the reef. The dive route takes you around the headland at about 50 feet.

The terrain is a cluster of boulders, furnishing habitat for reef fish hiding under crevices and both stingrays and eagle rays, skimming the sand. Sea fans, gorgonians, sea whips and plumes can be appreciated from afar for their pleasing shapes or close to for the variety of marine life that they shelter.

A shallower but pleasant dive is made along the reef in Glossy Bay, without going around the headland. This can be done as a beach dive from Glossy Dive Club.

There are now two diving operations on Canouan, which for some years had only one operator. A new hotel complex, the Tamarind Beach Hotel, has recently opened in Charleston Bay and Dive Canouan **9** has a smart new store within the complex. Dive Canouan has been based in Canouan for some years, but has only recently moved to this site. The hotel draws guests from the United States and Europe: France, Germany, Italy and the UK. Dive Canouan offers diving to hotel guests, to other visitors on the island and to visiting yachts.

Tony Alongi, the owner and manager, is a commercial diver trained in dive medicine. He used to work for NASA/McDonald Douglas on underwater astronaut training, so we reckoned he was a pretty safe pair of hands for us mere mortals to dive with.

His partner and divemaster, Marcus, is one of the few diver-fishermen to have crossed the line into recreational diving. Having seen the problems which local lobster divers have with repeated decompression sickness, he, too, is a very safety-conscious diver.

Dive Canouan dives the sites around Canouan and makes trips to Mayreau and the Tobago Cays. They have an informal association with other area dive operators offering dive packages throughout the Grenadines. (See entry for Dive St. Vincent for more details.)

As well as the usual range of water sports equipment, the Tamarind Beach Hotel has hydrobikes for use by guests. They look a lot less exhausting than mountain bikes.

Out toward the headland known as Glossy Hill, the Canouan Beach Hotel also has an independent dive operator in its grounds. Glossy Dive Club **10** is owned and managed by Frenchman Oliver Nadal. This is a small operation, offering a personal service to small groups of divers. Oliver takes a maximum of five divers on his boat.

The Canouan Beach Hotel offers a variety of other water sports, including day trips on a sailing catamaran to the Tobago Cays for snorkelling and a picnic on the beach. Divers can take a trip on the catamaran, and Oliver will collect them from the boat so that they can also enjoy a dive in the Cays.

Most of the hotel guests are French, although Americans also stay there. A golfer's target practice range will help you to keep fit between dives.

Canouan Dive Operators

Southern Grenadines

These islands lie huddled together at the southern end of St. Vincent's Grenadines. Each island is surrounded by magnificent beaches and spectacular water colours. About 2 miles to the east of Mayreau are the uninhabited Tobago Cays. Nominally a National Park and definitely an outstanding beauty spot, these four islands lie protected by a vast horseshoe reef, and each island has a tiny beach or two. The Tobago Cays are very popular with yachts, and day trips are made there from all the surrounding islands.

For many, these islands sum up the Caribbean ideal of white powdery beaches and translucent sea. There is good diving and, though the dive boats are based in Union Island, they pick up at all these smaller islands. While transportation between the islands can be arranged, there is no regular ferry service. So, for the visitor staying ashore, each island is a separate destination.

Union Island

Union Island, the busiest island, is the local equivalent of a metropolis, with an airport, a town and a large day-charter industry. At 2 miles long, it is also larger than the other islands and has some good walking. One great hike takes you to the summit of the pinnacle, about 1,000 feet high, with a breathtaking 360 degree view almost straight down. You need a head for heights and the help of a guide. Keep in mind that this is a scramble though prickly plants rather than a relaxed walk.

Accommodations on Union Island are right in Clifton which is very much a local town and far from the usual tourist image of an ideal vacation spot. You do have the advantage of a fair choice of restaurants and bars. Of the available accommodations, the Anchorage Yacht Club is the most sophisticated. Those that like local atmosphere at a good price can choose between the Clifton Beach Hotel, the Sunny Grenadines and Lambi's.

Mayreau

Mayreau's few hundred inhabitants live perched on a rounded hill with a beautiful view of craggy Union Island. Mayreau is just over a mile long and surrounded by pristine beaches, most of which you will have to yourself. Despite its diminutive size, it has no less than four restaurants that cater mainly to visiting yachts. In the north of the island, the Salt Whistle Bay Hotel is hidden in palm trees on a perfect half moon beach that borders a sheltered bay; an idyllic enough location to sit and do very little. Dennis' Hideaway and Guest House, while not right on the beach, has good views and a very peaceful rural setting, making it the most desirable of the budget accommodations available in this area.

Petit St. Vincent (PSV)

PSV is home to a hideaway resort, the most successful, secluded and expensive in St. Vincent and the Grenadines. The resort covers the whole island, which is about half a mile long. Guests stay in substantial stone cottages designed for privacy, with their own patios and hammocks. Each room is equipped with a flagpole, and room service comes by way of a mini-moke in response to flag signals. The island is almost surrounded by a lovely beach. A central hill keeps the terrain interesting, and paths lead to the top.

Palm Island

As you go through the Grenadines, each beach seems more spectacularly perfect than the last. Palm Island's Casuarina Beach is outstanding even in this heady competition: an exquisite expanse of golden sand lined by palm trees and lapped by translucent turquoise water. The urge to jump right in is almost irresistible. Palm Island was created by John Caldwell, an adventurer and author whose book *Desperate Voyage* was once a best seller. The pleasant hotel is set along Casuarina Beach and shares the island with a handful of private houses owned by former hotel guests who wanted a more permanent attachment to this idyllic desert island.

Language: English
Currency: Eastern Caribbean Dollar ($1.00 US = $2.66 EC)
Telephone Codes: Currently (809), changing to (784)

Après Dive

Visitors to these islands have usually come to get away from it all, to lie on the beach, stroll in the early mornings and immerse themselves in the beautiful turquoise sea. Seekers of a full or organised entertainment schedule may want to look elsewhere.

Tennis

Tennis courts are available for guests at PSV and Palm Island.

Water Sports

Day-charter boats visiting the Tobago Cays and other islands are available throughout the area.

Shopping

There are fancy boutiques dotted throughout the Grenadines, mainly as part of hotel facilities.

Nightlife

Union Island, with a large selection of bars, has something going on at least two or three times a week, usually local live groups from neighbouring islands. The Anchorage Hotel has entertainment every Monday, Thursday, Friday and Saturday in the winter season. Lambi's has a band many nights of the week. In the other islands, entertainment is occasional.

Information on Accommodation

Department of Tourism: (809) 457-1502
Hotel Association: (809) 457-1072
USA: (800) 729-1726
Canada: (416) 924-5796
UK: (171) 937-6570

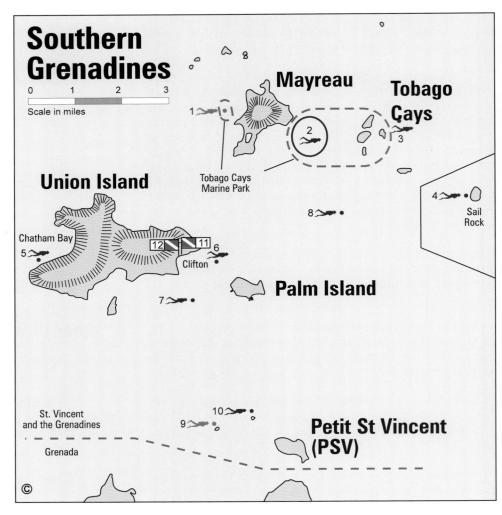

Southern Grenadines

0   1   2   3
Scale in miles

Mayreau

Tobago Cays

Union Island

Tobago Cays
Marine Park

Sail
Rock

Chatham Bay

Clifton

Palm Island

St. Vincent
and the Grenadines

Grenada

**Petit St Vincent
(PSV)**

The Diving

Despite the spread of these islands, we have grouped them together as both of the dive operators who visit these sites are located on Union Island. Guests staying on Palm Island, PSV, and Mayreau are collected from their resorts by the Union Island dive boats. (See also Canouan operators section)

The other common factor uniting the diving is that it is all on submerged offshore reefs, as compared to the fringing reefs around headlands and offshore islands that typify diving in the rest of St. Vincent and the Grenadines. At low water and when the sun is high, these reefs are visible just below the surface from the deck of a boat. At other times, the only clue to their presence is a disturbance on the surface as the waves, brought up short by the face of the reef, break over it.

Looking east from the Tobago Cays where no land stands between you and Africa, a line of frothy white surf breaks the smooth line of sight across the Atlantic. This is the only indication that a reef bars the way to boats arriving from the east.

Another distinguishing feature of this area is that all the reefs are surrounded by brilliant white sand. This reflects the light and gives the underwater world a light, luminous quality all of its own. This is particularly noticeable when the visibility is excellent, which it often is, allowing long-distance views that are probably as delightful as can be found anywhere.

If you ask any diver about the marine life in the Tobago Cays, they will say "sharks". Sharks are, in fact, a common sight throughout the Grenadines, from Bequia south. The vast majority of sightings are of nurse sharks, with reef and black tip sharks making up the balance.

Southern Grenadines Dive Sites

NO.	SITE NAME	DEPTH IN FEET
1	Wreck of the *Puruni*	20-40
2	Mayreau Gardens (Tobago Cays)	30-120
3	Horseshoe Reef (Tobago Cays)	30-65
4	Sail Rock	30-90
5	Chatham Bay	20-40
6	Union Reef/Roundabout	15-75
7	Grand de Coi	20-70
8	Silver Valley	35-65
9	Pinese	15-70
10	Mopion	30-50

Dive Operators

NO.	OPERATOR	RESORT/HOTEL LOCATION
11	Scuba Shack	
12	Grenadines Dive	

Jaws Revisited - Sharks of the Caribbean

In a culture where 'don't worry, be happy' is implicit in the manner and pace of life, it seems entirely appropriate that the nurse shark is the most commonly sighted species of shark in the area. Its round friendly nose, habit of lying ostrich-like with its head under an overhang but 6 feet of tail protruding, and its taste for seafood rather than human flesh makes the nurse shark the perfect shark species to populate reefs frequented by divers.

Though nurse sharks are not known to attack divers, there have been cases where divers have molested a nurse shark and received a bite as just reward for their foolish behaviour. Nurse sharks can be anything up to 15 feet long so will not disappoint those who have not seen a shark before. They have the familiar rigid shark fin and half a dozen visible gill slits. While the nurse shark's skin may look smooth, like all sharks, it is covered with a layer of sharp scales made from the same material as the shark's teeth.

Nurse sharks are the most commonly seen sharks in this area. Though not naturally aggressive toward divers, if you molest one, expect it to defend itself.

Black tip and reef sharks put in regular appearances, too. These are classic pointed-nosed sharks. The mouth, on the underside of the nose, is full of teeth treated rather as disposable cutlery. Teeth fall out on a regular basis and are replaced by the next layer, already grown and ready to take over. Do not be tempted to get too close a look, even with a dead shark, as there is a nerve at the root of the teeth which causes the jaw to close, tightly.

Though different shark species may look somewhat different, the 300 or so species of sharks share a number of distinctive characteristics. Unlike other fish, sharks do not have a swim bladder (like an internal BCD) to enable them to control their buoyancy. Oil is stored in their liver to provide some of this function, though much less effective than an air-filled swim bladder. This partly explains why (conveniently for divers) nurse sharks rest on the sea bed.

Many sharks are night feeders, with eyes adapted to a range of different visibilities. If you catch one at night in the beam of your torch, its eyes will shine like those of a cat caught in a car's headlights. A reflective layer behind the retina maximises the capture of light in dark conditions.

Sharks' senses are extremely well developed. They have three separate means of hearing; their sense of smell is very acute; they even pick up electrical fields, and they not only have good eyesight but many have an eye cover to protect their eyes when they attack their prey.

No wonder we feel in awe when we see these impressive complex creatures, the big game of the ocean. And, a little bit of fear adds a thrill to the experience.

The *Puruni* is a gunboat dating back to the first world war. Locally called the *Purina* (but Lloyds list her as the *Puruni*), she is 150 feet long and, although the deck and hull have collapsed, it is still possible to make out the structure of the ship. Located off the west coast of Mayreau, where there is no dive store, she is dived by the stores in Union Island, Canouan, and Carriacou (see Grenada and Carriacou chapter). The wreck is used as a night dive by the Union Island operators, as a change from Union Reef.

While you can certainly get some elegant views of large schools of fish framed by pieces of wreckage, this dive does not compare in scenic beauty with the reef dives. As the wreck is only 150 feet long, neither is it a dive where you keep moving along looking at the view. The beauty of this dive is that you do not move, you are already there. This is a dive where you stop rushing around and instead get on more intimate terms with the fish and sea creatures, of which there are a great abundance.

Some years ago, a dive operator who is no longer around regularly fed the fish on this wreck with chicken legs and scraps. It changed their behaviour completely and got so out of hand that it became dangerous to descend without an offering, as you were pursued by hungry moray eels aggressively looking for a hand-out. Luckily this has stopped and the moray eels have gone back into holes where they belong; the memory of sergeant majors seems longer.

For those on yachts, this is an easy and safe dive to do from a dinghy. The site has been buoyed by the Tobago Cays Marine Park, but beware of the currents. Anchor in Saline Bay and dinghy out to the navigation mark. The buoy is 100 yards to the west of the mark.

The buoy line leads down directly onto the top of the wreck at 25 feet. The first sight is of honeyed sea rods, stroking the passing current. There are half a dozen thick bushes of these pleasing creatures on the top of the wreck. The buoy line is tied to a winch at the forward end of the boat, which has not deterred four large lobsters from taking up guard duty around the winch.

We are surrounded by fish as we descend, sergeant majors in the majority but with a significant sprinkling of brown chromis and tangs. As we swim around the boat, a school of Bermuda chub arrives and horse eye jacks are always present just off the wreck. Yellowtail snappers and tomate weave their way around the wreck, seeming to be as inquisitive as we are.

On the wreck itself, bright purple and yellow Spanish hogfish disappear into a porthole and reappear moments later through a hatch, as if playing a game of hide-and-seek. The fish are so prolific and lively that it is easy to ignore the wreck, yet it too supports some fascinating life.

Wreck of
the *Puruni*

20'-40'

W

Dive Profile

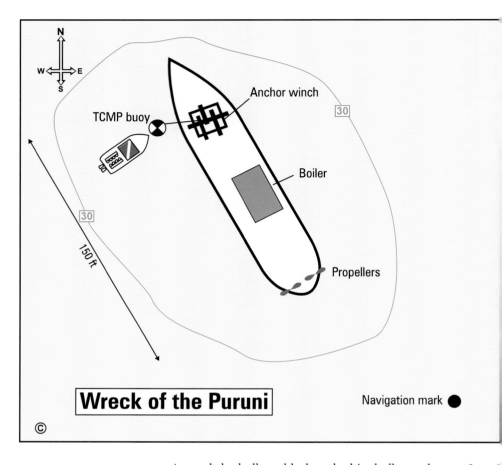

Wreck of the Puruni

Navigation mark ●

Around the hull are black and white bulbous clumps, 3 to 6 inches across, covered in small holes. These are condominium tunicates. Also on the hull are giant tunicates and encrusting varieties. The giant tunicates are up to about 4 inches high and look like rather dull sponges with two openings, often overgrown with algae. They are very sensitive and if you approach too fast they may close down and shrink into a leathery lump. If you manage to creep up on them, you can see that inside their siphons they are a bright yellow or red. The encrusting tunicates look like encrusting sponges with many holes in them, but unlike sponges they will close their siphons instantly if you brush your hand gently close by them. If you wonder why people are so fascinated by these slow responding, sessile creatures, you may be interested to know that scientists think they are probably what we evolved from.

You will find corkscrew anemones and their live-in Pederson cleaner shrimps. There are arrow crabs and small crustaceans; the slower you move the more you will see. All the while you will be distracted and delighted with the fish: Spanish hogfish, sergeant majors, scorpionfish, soapfish, snappers, mackerels, eels, groupers and juvenile angelfish. Some of them will come right up and stare into your mask.

The Wreck of the *Puruni* dive site is in a very active area, and you can be sure of catching something interesting happening just outside the wreck. We have seen a huge permit here, being cleaned by half a dozen gobies. This is an area where large schools of pelagics swim. Turtles are sometimes around and, on the wreck, frogfish have occasionally been found. Around the bottom of the wreck, in 40 feet of water, you may see sand divers lying motionless on the sand.

Those interested in the wreck itself will find the propellers worth investigating and the big boiler is clearly visible. Aft of the bow, toward the winch with the buoy line attached, are four posts. These, like the rest of the hull are encrusted with a mixture of coral, sponges, fire coral and fragile little sprays of Christmas tree hydroids. Unfortunately we see divers hanging on to these posts. Apart from destroying the creatures growing on the posts, it is a good way to get painfully stung.

You will also find dozens of clams attached to the hull. Approach slowly and they will not close up. Slowly is the key with this dive. It is only 150 feet long and shallow so there is plenty of time to make a slow circumnavigation. This boat's days of rushing around are over—enjoy it as a relaxing dive.

Mayreau Gardens 2
(Tobago Cays)
30'-120'

Mayreau Gardens, an area of submerged reefs between the Tobago Cays and Mayreau, includes several dives. Different operators have their own preferences and will take you to their favourite area. Currents will also affect the choice of place of entry.

At slack tide, you can float contentedly along the reef peering at invertebrates under each coral overhang. In times of strong current you get whisked through the gardens like some giant tumbleweed on a wild ride. You see quick flashes of many wonders as you fly by.

There has been some damage to this reef over the last few years, and stronger enforcement of conservation laws would be helpful. The reef is worth protecting. We have dived several parts of the gardens, both deep and shallow, and there is no question that the coral formations are quite beautiful. Bulbous heads of boulder coral, tall pillar coral and rock encrusted star coral decorate the reefs. Shimmering fingers of octocorals contribute to the garden-like scene. Broad sea fans are large enough to hide a diver. In one very deep area, bubbles trickle up from the bottom, signs of local volcanic activity.

We found the volume of fish variable, though you are almost guaranteed a nurse shark or two or three. Big black tip sharks sometimes flash their white bellies at the divers below them.

Schools of chromis are sometimes large, and surround divers as they swim past the coral.

Numerous valleys and canyons allow you to duck in and out of the currents and see what you can find hiding. Look out for spotted drums, trunkfish and porcupinefish; groupers, too, have plenty of places to tuck into.

The dives are always done as a drift; currents can be strong, particularly in the southern area. This makes them difficult to do from a yacht dinghy, partly because top cover and a surface marker buoy are needed. Surface conditions can be very rough, seas picking up quickly as squalls come through or the tide changes, making a small dinghy an unsuitable vehicle. Several divers have come to grief here when attempting to do the dive without local operators and without appropriate top cover.

3 Horseshoe Reef (Tobago Cays) 30'-65'

A semi-circular reef to the east of the Tobago Cays can be dived along its seaward side. The southern end of the reef is dived, as is the area to the north and south of the small boat passage, positioned about halfway along the reef. Buoys have been put in place for yacht dinghies to tie to and, hopefully, the reef will begin to recover from previous anchor damage. These buoys make this a suitable dive to do independently from a dinghy.

The contours of the reef follow the classic shape of the fore reef; a steep slope ending at a sandy bottom. There is exceptionally good visibility here, sometimes up to 120 feet, although we have also dived it when it has been nearer 60 feet.

The currents in this area can be strong and in some conditions this can only be done as a drift dive. This dive is at its best on a sunny day when visibility is excellent. In these conditions, you will remember the dive for its bright light vistas, where 65 feet felt like 30 and everything you saw seemed bright and colourful.

Desert islands ringed by reefs, the Tobago Cays are a delight for snorkellers and divers.

Sadly, among the attractive areas where the coral is bright and colourful there are also some damaged areas, with dead reef and algae blooms that underscore the need for quick action in making this area a protected marine park.

Determined not to be overshadowed by the colours of the reef, the fish community puts forward its strongest contender and populates the reef with parrotfish. In their terminal phase, stoplight parrotfish are decked in iridescent aquamarines, with distinctive yellow patches on their tail fin and gill flap. 'Terminal phase' is the expression used to describe fish who started life as females and then changed into sexually mature males. This most often happens in the absence of enough naturally born males.

They become territorial at this time, and we see some serious-looking muscle flexing as they protect their patch from a wandering competitor. Their aggressive behaviour on occasion results in beak-to-beak contact, an instrument normally reserved for gnawing the coral.

Sail Rock 4
30'- 90'

Why is the best always the most difficult? Perhaps that is part of the reason it is the best. If you set your heart on this dive, make sure you have plenty of time. You cannot do the dive unless the weather is settled so, if the wind is strong, you will have to wait. It is a 2-tank, all-day dive. We were told that a check-out dive is normally done first, but certified divers have been able to dive there without the check-out.

Both dives are done around the rock, with a picnic lunch ashore. Sail Rock has no beach, so you will eat your lunch sitting on the rocks with the waves lapping your feet. It is fun to climb the rock where, depending upon the time of year, you may see baby pelicans stumbling around or nesting birds protecting their eggs. Please do not disturb the birds.

The dive is on the northeast side, down a wall that runs for 150 feet and drops to 90 feet. The wall is smothered in corals and sponges. The many ledges along the wall shield a variety of marine life; the larger overhangs providing cover for sharks and green moray eels.

One of Sail Rock's assets is the abundance and variety of fish, both large and small. The reef supports all the usual reef fish plus the larger pelagics who find it a profitable hunting ground. The visibility is usually excellent.

Chatham Bay 5
20'- 40'

This is the only dive on the west side of Union Island and it seems that it is rarely used by local operators. Poor visibility after heavy rains is one deterrent. In good conditions it is a picturesque dive along a 40-foot wall leading out to the headland.

The wall is a veritable housing development for invertebrates, especially lobsters and shrimps. Turtle sightings are common, so keep a watch out to the blue and along the bottom.

Chatham Bay is frequented by yachts, and this is a dive easily done from a yacht's dinghy.

At the time of writing, the Tobago Cays Marine Park was considering making an artificial reef here from old trucks abandoned around the island.

---

6 Union Reef/ Roundabout 15'-75'

Right outside the entrance to Clifton Harbour in Union Island is a dive along the reef that protects the harbour from the prevailing easterly winds and swells. The dive boat takes a mooring buoy. The dive is generally done at 60 feet going away from the buoy and back at 40 feet.

The covering is about 50 percent coral. Although close to the harbour, fish mill around, including large red snappers and groupers. Rays are also a regular sight.

The dive can be done from a yacht's dinghy but heavy boat traffic requires good top cover and the use of a surface marker buoy.

---

7 Grand De Coi 20'-70'

From Clifton Harbour looking south to PSV there appears to be a clear passage available, yet several reefs lie just below the surface. A navigation mark to the west of Palm Island marks the Grand de Coi reef.

When seas are rough, this is a conveniently close site for those staying in Union Island and Palm Island, avoiding the trip out to the Tobago Cays.

The top of the reef is 5 to 15 feet below the surface. The only indication of its presence is the navigation mark. The reef is circular and the dive route follows the contours of the reef. The covering is a mixture of hard coral and sea whips. The uneven surface creates numerous crevices and holes worthy of investigation. Lobsters are a common find as are crabs and secretive pufferfish. Trumpetfish hang vertically in the sea whips waiting for an opportunity to pounce on preoccupied reef fish.

---

8 Silver Valley 35'-65'

The Grenadines lie on a large shallow bank, much of it only 40 to 120 feet deep. It is strange to think that a mere 11,000 years ago, during the last ice age, this whole bank would have been above water. Today the bank is a mixture of sand and coral. Much of the coral reaches the surface on the offshore reefs around the Tobago Cays and Petit Tabac. But there are other reefs in deeper water, seemingly out in the middle of the sea. Silver Valley is one of these, just visible as a darker patch in the sand between Petit Tabac and Palm Island. It is a vast, gently sloping reef with the top at 35 feet and bottoming out in sand at about 65 feet. The reef has the feeling of being delightfully young and fresh. The individual corals and sea fans are fairly small, but they seem to glow with health, and are well packed together. There is plenty to see, and you will see the most if you move slowly, peeking in sponges and looking among the corals.

Soft corals seem to predominate, with a delightful collection of sea whips, sea rods and sea fans. Between these, you find many brain corals and star corals. The star corals often have their polyps fully extended, and they come in a variety of colours.

Sponges are in the shape of vases, pipes, tubes and fans and they outshine the corals in brilliant reds, blues, yellows, greens and blacks. You can find both golden zoanthids and sponge zoanthids growing on some of the sponges.

Among the corals you will also find mat and encrusting zoanthids, brightly coloured worms, small crabs, crinoids and tunicates. There are plenty of reef fish: blue and brown chromis, parrotfish, wrasses, rock beauties, grunts and angelfish. Out towards the bottom of the reef, where it joins the sand you have an excellent chance of seeing rays and sharks.

Pinese 9
15'-70'

 W

Pinese Reef exposes a tiny patch of yellow sand, determined to be an island, not a wholly submerged reef. It is a short distance from Petit St. Vincent, the beautiful resort island marking the southernmost point in St. Vincent and the Grenadines. It is a dive that can be done from a yacht's dinghy but there can be strong currents, notably around the time of a new or full moon. So, if you do this dive independently, anchor safely (on the sand, not the coral) and preferably have some top cover.

It is slighter deeper than Mopion to the east, which has just about enough sand above the surface to support a small shelter. Pinese is a circular reef with a coral slope dropping to 70 feet on the northern side. It is a classic offshore reef, displaying the typical reef profile of staghorn and broken coral rubble in the shallows and boulder and brain coral deeper down the reef.

Emerging after the dive to the sight of this minute sand island, with PSV in the background, adds to the pleasure of the dive.

Dive Profile

An area of sand, rock and dead coral around the exposed portion of the reef provides a suitable anchorage for the dive boat. There is no current when we start the dive and we swim north over a covering of staghorn and elkhorn coral. These coral types fare well near the surf line, the broken sections forming substratum for other coral, sponge and red algae to take hold and cement the reef.

The coral wall has a covering of hard corals that have sometimes grown in a plate-like formation. Big fish, including barracuda, swim about us, curious to see if we do anything which

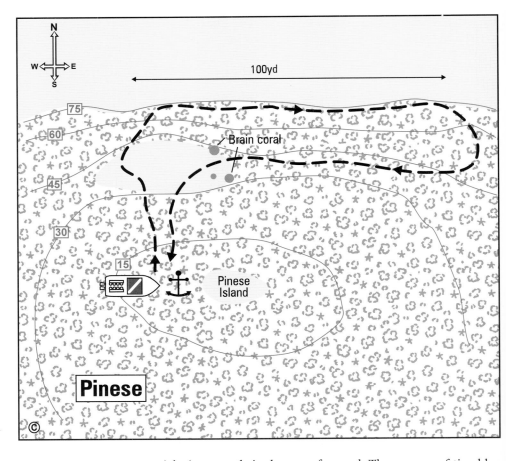

might increase their chances of a meal. The swarms of tiny blue chromis seem the most likely candidates.

An ocean triggerfish, with its peculiar sideways swimming action, appears to be ridiculing our attempts at underwater grace. This is a relatively uncommon triggerfish and one of the least colourful. A large black spot at the base of the pectoral fin on an otherwise grey body distinguishes this fish. If you get a close look you will see a bony dorsal fin that the fish can raise and lock in place. It can be used to secure the triggerfish in a crevice where it can rest safely.

Another interesting find is a scorpionfish. Hard to spot, as they are so well camouflaged, these grumpy-looking creatures lie quietly on the bottom. If disturbed, they extend emerald wings to speed their escape. The sandy bottom at 70 feet is littered with lizardfish, another patient bottom dweller.

After swimming east along the coral slope, we ascend to 40 feet and head back, as a little current has picked up. Large boulder and brain coral heads, 6 to 8 feet across, are little microcosms of reef life. Each has its own community of reef fish and invertebrates.

Visibility is only average as clouds of plankton drift in the current. But, as we surface, the blinding sunlight of a Caribbean afternoon penetrates the water, reflecting on the sand, so that the water seems lit from below.

PSV has two offshore reefs to the north, both of which are attractive dive sites. Mopion is the shallower and the easternmost of the two. Currents necessitate making this a drift dive.

The currents carry you along a steep slope adorned with delightful coral formations. Small caves give some lee from the current and offer an Aladdin's cave of treasures. Fairy basslets and damselfish inject colour and movement around sponges, growing in interesting shapes and colours. Look out for wriggling tentacles poking out from under rocks where spiny lobsters lurk.

For mixed groups of divers and snorkellers or swimmers, Mopion is excellent as it has an almost completely enclosed lagoon, and blinding white sand on which to lie and soak up the sun. It even has a small thatched shelter giving some shade from the sun.

Mopion 10
30'-50'

Two operators use Union Island as a base, primarily for diving the Tobago Cays. Both are long established and run by West Indians. These operators offer equipment rental and tank fills for independent divers, as well as regular boat dives. Prices are average for the area.

Glenroy Adams, originally from Bequia, owns and runs Grenadines Dive **12**. He has been operating in Union Island since 1989. He is part of a network of dive stores in St. Vincent and the Grenadines, offering a dive package for visitors who will be moving about the islands. Typically this will be of benefit to those on charter yachts. Much of Glenroy's business is with yachts, although he also services local hotels and the island resort of Petit St. Vincent. There is a surcharge of $30 for collection and return to PSV.

Glenroy has done much to educate the younger generation in Union Island about the value of the reefs.

Scuba Shack **11** also located in Union Island's Clifton Bay, was previously based on nearby Palm Island. David Allen, a Trinidadian, has been taking people diving in this area for the last 11 years. David is not qualified to teach, acting as a dive guide only.

He prefers small groups of six or less and allows people to make a relaxed dive, at their own pace. The store does not offer night dives and covers only the most local dive sites.

Southern Grenadines Dive Operators

Contact Information

ST. VINCENT

1	Petit Byahaut	Charles Meistrell	Tel: (809) 457-7008 Fax: (809) 457-7008
2	Dive St. Vincent	Bill Tewes	Tel: (809) 457-4714 Fax: (809) 457-4948
3	St. Vincent Dive Experience*	Perry Hughes	Tel: (809) 456-9741 Fax: (809) 457-2768

BEQUIA

4	SunSports	Bob Monnens	Tel: (809) 458-3577 Fax: (809) 457-3031
5	Dive Bequia	Bob Sachs	Tel: (809) 458-3504 Fax: (809) 458-3886
6	Bequia Beach Club	Wolfgang Kursch	Tel: (809) 458-3248 Tel: 07 141 923261
7	Dive Paradise	Harald Hess	Tel: (809) 458-3563 Fax: (809) 457-3115

MUSTIQUE

8	Mustique Watersports	Carolin Gatske	Tel: (809) 456-3486 Fax: (809) 456-4565

CANOUAN

9	Dive Canouan	Tony Alongi	Tel: (809) 458-8044 Fax: (809) 458-8851
10	Glossy Dive Club	Oliver Nadal	Tel: (809) 458-8888 Fax: (809) 458-8875

SOUTHERN GRENADINES

11	Scuba Shack	David Allen	Tel: (809) 458-8824 Fax: (809) 458-8804
12	Grenadines Dive	Glenroy Adams	Tel: (809) 458-8138 Fax: (809) 458-8122

*Closed May 1997

St. Vincent and the Grenadines Dive Operators

		Petit Byahaut	Dive St. Vincent	St. Vincent Dive Experience*	SunSports	Dive Bequia	Bequia Beach Club	Dive Paradise	Mustique Watersports	Dive Canouan	Glossy Dive Club	Scuba Shack	Grenadines Dive
		1	2	3	4	5	6	7	8	9	10	11	12
STAFF	Instructors	0	2	2	4	3	1	3	2	1	1	0	2
	Divemasters	1	2	2	2	2	2	0	0	1	0	0	1
	Diving Associations	P	NP	N	P	NP	CS	CP	P	P	P	P	NP
	Languages	E	E	E	E	DE	EF GI	EG	EG	E	EF	E	E
BOATS	Dive Boats	1	3	2	2	2	1	2	1	2	1	1	2
	Shaded Boats	0	3	2	2	2	0	2	1	2	0	1	1
	Max. Divers per Boat	8	8-14	6-12	10	15	15	8-15	12	6	5	5	8
	Time to Dive Sites	5-60	5-10	5-30	5-15	5-15	5-30	5-40	5-30	5-25	5-30	5-15	5-15
	Dives per Day	OD	2	2	3	2	2	2	3	OD	OD	OD	2
	Pick Up by Boat from	Y	CRY	CRY	CRY	CRY	RY	Y	Y	CRY		CRY	CRY
EQUIPMENT	Equipment Sets	12	17	20	10	15	6	15	12	10	6	8	16
	Dive Equip. for Sale	3	1	1	2	1			1	1		1	2
	Dive Equip. for Rent	•	•	•	•	•	•	•		•		•	•
	Photo Equip. for Rent		•			•	•				•		
	Tank Fills	•	•	•	•	•	•	•	•	•		•	•
	Equipment Servicing	•	•	•	•			•	•			•	•
	O₂ on Boat		•	•	•	•	•	•	•		•		•
	VHF on Boat		•	•	•	•	•	•	•	•		•	•
MISC.	Owned by Resort	•					•		•				
	Other Water Sports	•		•			•	•	•	•	•		
	Pers. Liab. Insurance	•	•	•	•	•	•	•	•	•	•		•

Sanvics Scuba & Watersports Club

Come and enjoy an idyllic summer of watersports action and adventure. Experience the ultimate excitement both underwater and on the water: romantic sunset cruises to secluded bays and hidden beaches, tours to off-shore uninhabited islands where the swimming, SCUBA diving and snorkelling is a vacationer's paradise.

Visit a marine world of colourful parrotfish, barracudas, elegant rays, spotted drums, big groupers and black coral trees with our daily one and two tank dives to coral reefs, walls and wreck sites.

Located in Renaissance Grenada Resort on Grand Anse Beach, we are committed to an international standard of watersports excellence at very affordable rates. The dedication of our staff coupled with ultramodern equipment are the reasons why our professional service is rated number one on the island.

Come, let your temptation get the better of you. We promise you an action-packed watersports adventure you'll never forget.

Associations:	PADI
Associated Resort:	Renaissance Grenada Resort
Languages:	English, French, German Italian
Number of Instructors:	3

Contact:	Sandra Thompson
Address:	SANVICS Renaissance Grenada Resort Grand Anse Grenada
Telephone:	(809) 444-4371
Fax:	(809) 444-5227

Sanvics

GRENADA

Grenada & Carriacou

The country of Grenada comprises the main island of Grenada plus the smaller islands of Carriacou and Petit Martinique to the north. Petit Martinique has no dive facilities so we have not included information about it. Carriacou is a dive holiday destination in its own right, and as it lies to the north of Grenada close to St. Vincent's Southern Grenadines, we have described Carriacou first.

Carriacou

Some 7 miles long, Carriacou is the largest of the Grenadines. A vast barrier reef protects the eastern shore and creates a sheltered lagoon that is over a mile wide in places. Half a dozen uninhabited islands lie close offshore. Along the coasts is an abundance of typically beautiful Grenadine beaches.

Three craggy hilltops approach 1,000 feet, and they add interest to the topography as well as making the island seem even larger. The hikes almost anywhere on the island are wonderful, especially up the hills if you are willing to do some climbing in exchange for panoramic views.

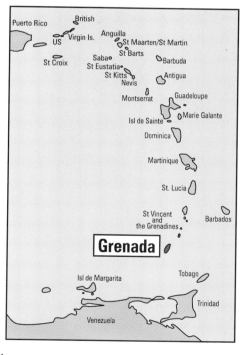

Carriacou is 15 miles north of Grenada and to some extent is out of mind as well as out of sight. The main thrust of tourist development has been in Grenada, and Carriacou residents are known for going their own way.

In the past an active trade in smuggled liquor and cigarettes kept them from wanting too much influence from the main island. As a result Carriacou has been almost forgotten by time. Although there are several hotels and guest houses on the island, they are low-key and relaxed and they hardly disturb the tranquil surroundings.

People live mainly by subsistence farming, fishing and trading, catching a dollar whenever they can. Carriacou has some of the best boat builders in the Windwards and boats are built by eye on the beach. This is one of the last hold-outs of commercial sail, and a small engineless fleet sets out daily to fish or to carry cargo to Grenada. These sloops compete yearly in the Carriacou Regatta which takes place on the weekend before the first Monday in August. This competition has inspired the development of an increasingly fast fleet and new Carriacou sloops can keep up with most modern yachts of the same size.

There are just enough yachtspeople and other visitors to support several pleasant restaurants and you could eat at a different place every night for a week. In addition, there are reputed to be over a hundred rum shops. Nightlife, when it happens, is local.

The only town, Hillsborough, is built on the beach with one main street. It is a sleepy town where flowers pop out between the houses. The essentials are here: food stores, a bank, and basic hardware shops. Apart from that, there are stores crammed full of

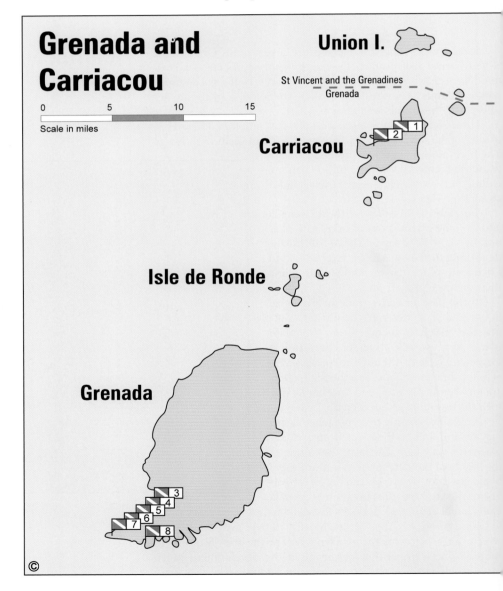

an eclectic collection of goods, from rope and fabric to knitting wool and plastic shoes. Carriacou is ideal for those who like undiscovered islands and who want little more than good diving, quiet beaches and pleasant hiking.

Besides Hillsborough, there is another area of commercial activity a couple of miles away in Tyrrel Bay. This is the most protected anchorage in Carriacou and, consequently, is popular with visiting yachts. Although neither of Carriacou's dive stores are based in Tyrrel Bay, both stores are happy to collect from here as it is only a short boat ride away.

One of Carriacou's two dive shops is in Hillsborough, the other is on L'Esterre Bay which is halfway between Hillsborough and Tyrrel Bay. There are three small hotels, one of which, the Caribbee Inn, a secluded hideaway all on its own, is in the north of the island. It is far enough away that you will probably want a rental car if you plan to dive on a regular basis. All other accommodation is on a bus route or close enough to walk if you have to.

The Silver Beach Hotel is right on the water at the north edge of Hillsborough. The Cassada Bay Hotel is a mile south of Tyrrel Bay on a small hill with a wonderful view over the islands to the south. In addition, there has recently been a proliferation of self-contained rental cottages and apartments, many of which are available at an excellent price.

The Isle de Ronde archipelago lies to the south of Carriacou, roughly halfway between Carriacou and Grenada. Isle de Ronde is a small uninhabited island surrounded by a number of rocks, barely qualifying as islands. This area is visited only by divers and yachts.

Language: English
Currency: Eastern Caribbean Dollar ($1.00 US = $2.66 EC)
Population: About 5,000
Telephone Codes: Currently (809), changing to (473)

Après Dive

The pace of life in Carriacou is conducive to a peaceful holiday, with good diving to fill the days and pleasant evening strolls. For a more lively environment, take a trip down to Grenada which is only a short flight away.

Hiking

There is great hiking, strictly of the do-it-yourself kind. Do not be afraid to ask for directions if you need them.

Tennis

A tennis court has been built at the new Alexis Guest House in Tyrrel Bay. It seems that the designers were a little confused by the game for they built the fence along the outer boundary. They may have created the world's first mini-tennis court.

Signs of tourism are thin on the ground in Carriacou, but people and charm remain in abundance.

Water Sports

Day sailing trips and longer charters with a skipper are available, some include fishing. Carriacou is close enough to the Grenadines to make day trips by yacht a pleasant day out.

Carriacou Islander: (809) 443-8238
Kontiki Expeditions: (809) 443-7404
Romany: (809) 444-3167
Silver Beach Hotel: (809) 443-7337

Nightlife

After Our's, a combination supermarket, restaurant and nightclub, has just opened in Tyrrel Bay.

Shopping

Shopping is basic, with two gift shops in Tyrrel Bay: the Unique Boutique in the After Our's complex, and Scraper's.

Information on Accommodation

Grenada Hotel Association: (809) 444-4847
Grenada Board of Tourism: (809) 440-484
USA: (800) 972-9554
Canada: (416) 595-8278
UK: (171) 370-5164/5

Getting There

Carriacou has a small airport with the added interest that the runway crosses one of the island's main roads. Inexpensive flights to Grenada operate several times a day. In addition a high speed ferry goes between Carriacou and Grenada every day.

See the following section on Grenada in this chapter for information on international connections.

With one exception, every Carriacou dive site is located around an offshore rock or uninhabited island. Even so, under the water there is a range of diving from vertical walls and undulating slopes to table reefs. Carriacou is fortunate that four of its satellite islands are off the sheltered west coast, generally having calm waters. As if to pay for this convenient asset, the remaining rocks are exposed and distant. It can add to the excitement of a dive to make an offshore trip in the dive boat, but one has to accept the limitations imposed by the weather.

Fortunately, on windy days the sheltered rocks offer some fine diving, and the offshore rocks are enjoyed all the more for having to wait a day or two. The farthest diving, around Isle de Ronde, is 15 miles away and the boat trip can be rough, especially on the way back.

Do not be deterred, though. If you have the chance to make an expedition to this area, take it. The dive stores ensure it is a fun day, providing a satisfying lunch to enjoy while anchored in the lee of Isle de Ronde. Surrounded by inviting cerulean water, you might wonder if you have found paradise at last.

Carriacou is also only a short distance from the dive sites of the Southern Grenadines (see previous chapter). Both of the Carriacou dive operators dive the wreck of the *Puruni* off Mayreau, the reefs off Petit St. Vincent and the Tobago Cays.

The marine life on Carriacou's reefs is rich and varied. We were very impressed with the diving. Though less talked about than the Grenadines just a few miles to the north, Carriacou has comparable coral formations and an abundance of octocorals. We found the sheltered dive sites had a great deal of charm and the drama of the offshore reefs made a good contrast. And, the pleasant efficient dive operators enhance the diving experience around this small island.

For information on rules, regulations and safety, see the Grenada section later in this chapter.

The Diving

Independent Diving

Independent diving is permitted, although the diving environment does not make it easy. Because much of Carriacou's diving is around offshore rocks, many of the sites are out of range for a small dinghy and unsuitable as a yacht anchorage. Yachts anchored in Tyrrel Bay are in reach of Cistern Point (Site 5) and Sandy Island (Site 2) is a popular lunch time anchorage, allowing divers to dive the reef to the north of the island. See our detailed dive profile and site map. Please note that Sandy Island is under threat from erosion and is a conservation area. The island is getting smaller, and without the reef to the north to protect it, it would have disappeared by now. So, please do not add to the problems. Do not anchor on the reef and do not attempt a beach entry; it is dangerous and very damaging for the reef.

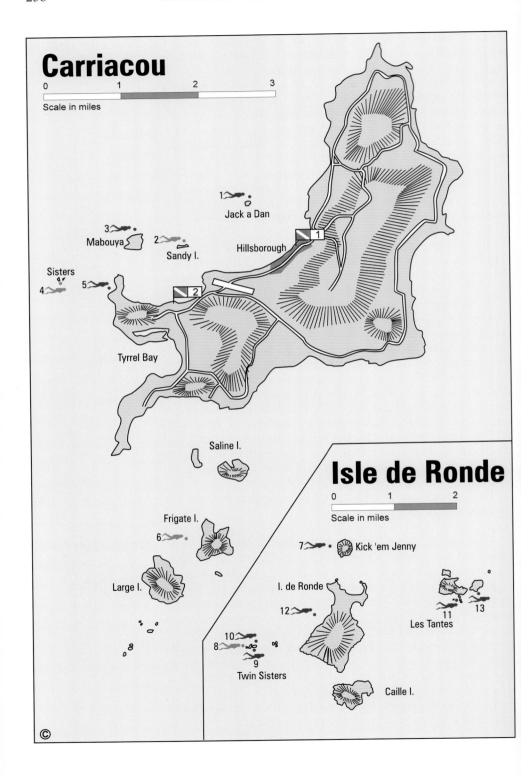

Carriacou

0   1   2   3
Scale in miles

1 Jack a Dan

3 Mabouya
2 Sandy I.
Hillsborough   1

Sisters
4   5   2

Tyrrel Bay

Saline I.

Isle de Ronde

0   1   2
Scale in miles

Frigate I.
6   7   Kick 'em Jenny

Large I.   I. de Ronde
12   11   13
Les Tantes

10
8
9
Twin Sisters   Caille I.

©

NO.	SITE NAME	DEPTH IN FEET
1	Jack a Dan	20-60
2	Sandy Island	20-60
3	Mabouya	30-70
4	Sisters	20-100
5	Cistern Point	15-60
6	Frigate Island	30-70
	ISLE DE RONDE	
7	Diamond Rock/Kick 'em Jenny	20-120
8	Big Blue (Twin Sisters)	25-140
9	Turtle Head Bay (Twin Sisters)	20-130
10	Kitzbuhl (Twin Sisters)	15-50
11	Lee Rocks	25-80
12	Isle de Ronde Reef	40-80
13	Les Tantes Rocks	30-120

For Isle de Ronde sites also see Grenada operators.

Carriacou Dive Sites

NO.	OPERATOR	RESORT/HOTEL LOCATION
1	Carriacou Silver Diving	
2	Tanki's Watersports*	Paradise Inn

*Owned by Hotel/Resort

Dive Operators

Jack a Dan **1**
20'-60'

This shallow reef makes an excellent training dive site and has enough interesting marine life for it to be a good check-out dive. The top of the reef is at 20 feet and conditions are nearly always calm.

There is a good variety of coral, both hard and soft, which attracts large numbers of reef fish. The reef follows a gentle slope down to 60 feet and an area of sand and large blocks gives interest to the terrain.

Sandy Island **2**
20'-60'

  W

In contrast to the dramatic coral formations of the Tobago Cays reefs, Sandy Island delivers a meadow of swaying soft corals, reminiscent of a stroll through a heathland, thick with ferns and mountain flowers. The entire reef seems to float with the gentle movement of this forest of bushy sea whips and feathery sea plumes, while big schools of chromis and wrasse flitter between the fronds like butterflies on a spring morning. It really is a delightful dive and the imperilled state of Sandy Island itself sharpens the diving experience, making it seem even more special.

Sandy Island is pretty much anyone's idea of a desert island. It is an acre strip of sand anchored at one end by a copse of palm trees. A walk around the perimeter will take you no more than 5 minutes, except that the sand is so toe-wigglingly good that it is easy to find excuses to retrace one's steps and investigate the shore's flotsam. After a dive it provides a delightful venue to relax and enjoy the sunshine. Sadly, though, the island is being eroded and even by the time this book is published it may have split in two with little hope that the eastern section will survive, as no vegetation remains.

A belated conservation policy has recently been developed. One consequence is to ban cruise ships from disgorging their passengers on mass onto the island. As a cruise ship passenger, the only way to experience the island is to dive its reef. Yachts are currently permitted to anchor off the island and it remains a popular lunchtime spot. The site is within easy access of the two Carriacou dive operators, both of whom use the site for night dives in addition to the regular daytime dives.

Dive Profile

A navigation mark in 15 feet of water, indicating the eastern end of the reef, serves as a tying post for the dive boat and makes this an easy dive to do either with a local dive operator or from a yacht's dinghy. The best part of the reef lies a little way to the northwest so local operators have placed two buoys along the reef edge. If you begin at the navigation mark, either conserve air with a surface swim until you can see the edge of the slope or drop down and follow the reef out. People have been seen making a beach entry which, apart from being dangerous due to the rocks and surf, causes significant damage to the reef.

The reef falls away in a steep slope to a sparkling white sandy bottom at 60 feet. Swim northwest along the slope. The soft coral

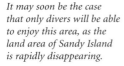

It may soon be the case that only divers will be able to enjoy this area, as the land area of Sandy Island is rapidly disappearing.

crowds the slope stretching to 6 feet or more in height. Trumpet fish hang vertically playing hide and seek among the branches in the hope of fooling both prey and predators. Their ability to change colour to camouflage their presence in this dense covering of soft corals can make them difficult to spot but, once your eye has tuned in to one, you will see them everywhere.

At this lower portion of the reef wall, you will also find hard corals. Boulder and star coral predominate but do not confuse the star coral with the mat zoanthids which can be seen nestling in crevices. Approach slowly and you will see the rows of dwarf tentacles which will retract, if your presence is detected, giving the appearance of hard coral.

Visibility can deteriorate as you make progress along the wall and we find ourselves quickly immersed in a soup of plankton. The compensation is the schools of fish which materialise from nowhere to feast on this passing meal. There are schools of chromis, surgeonfish and sergeant majors as well as barracuda, awaiting their turn in the food chain.

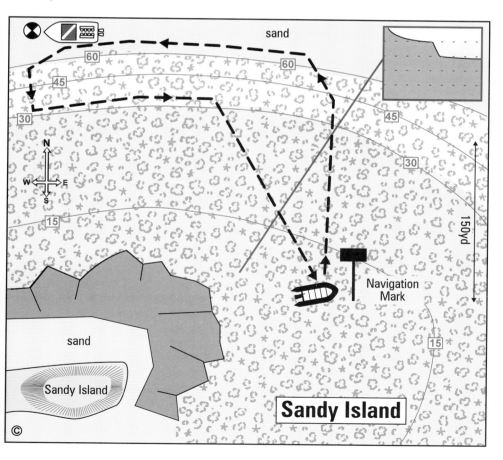

To complete the dive, save enough air for what can be a rigorous swim back along the top of the reef to the buoy. Ascend the slope and swim diagonally across the reef in 15 feet of water. As you look down on to the reef you can see damselfish guarding their carefully manicured algae patches, courageous enough to chase away even a diver should you venture too close. If only these industrious little farmers could be put to work ashore, then the future for Sandy Island would not be so bleak.

Trumpetfish—Masters of Disguise

Trumpetfish are some of the sneakiest fish which hunt on the reef. Their long thin shape enables them almost to disappear from view among gorgonians. They very intelligently orient themselves vertically so that they can hang among the branches of the sea whips, unobserved by their prey.

When the trumpetfish is not hanging vertically in the sea whips, it reverts to a horizontal position, but

will use another fish as camouflage. We have seen them shadowing groupers and parrotfish, swimming so close that they almost touch.

These sly creatures also have the ability to change colour. Trumpetfish have cells called chromatophores which contain different colour pigments and, by contracting and expanding them differentially, the fish can change colour. Observe a trumpetfish hanging near a row pore sponge and you will find a purple fish. See the same fish later hanging among the sea whips and you will find a brown fish, probably with paler horizontal stripes.

Disguise is one thing but the fish still has to attract and capture its prey. Barbels hanging from the trumpetfish's mouth tempt curious fish to investigate. But any fish investigating the mouth of this camouflaged creature may not live to regret it. The

Now you see me, now you don't—a trumpetfish doing a good job of imitating a sea rod.

mouth, though long and thin, is capable of sucking in a fish of considerable proportions.

Trumpetfish understand the importance of timing. Not only will they wait patiently until their prey is close enough to be inhaled, but they have also recognised that time of day is important. Unlike most fish, which are either diurnal or nocturnal, trumpetfish hunt in the twilight zone. They snatch unwary diurnal fish as they head for the shelter of the reef at sunset. Night time feeders, emerging from their daytime holes also fall prey to the ever watchful trumpetfish.

One of Carriacou's shallow wall dives, Mabouya is a popular dive seeming to be able to satisfy a wide range of preferences. Each level of the dive is quite different.

The wall drops to 35 feet before turning into a slope to 70 feet. Big rocks and caves appear near the bottom of the reef. On the slope, sea whips and fans furnish the reef with a soft moving carpet of marine life. Hard star and boulder coral create nooks and crannies housing any number of fish and invertebrates.

Mabouya ⬛3
30'-70'

There are two rocks called Sisters, but also known by locals as the Brothers, not to be confused with Twin Sisters to the south of Carriacou! By now we had lost the plot. Fortunately, Max, driving the dive boat, has a good grasp of the story and whisked us out to the dive site.

We had been warned that the currents here were unpredictable and despite checking before we entered the water, we still dive in the opposite way to what we had expected. But it does not really matter which way round or how much of this site you dive, it has plenty to entertain and amuse right around the circumference of the two rocks.

Sisters ⬛4
20'-100'

  W

We drop down below the dive boat to the bottom of the reef slope at 60 feet. The reef starts with a plateau at 30 feet before descending in a steepish and uneven slope. The first impression is of a swaying forest of a mixture of types of gorgonians. This impression becomes even more focused as the current pulls us south, above an ever thickening forest of giant slit-pore and porous sea rods and sea plumes.

The sensation when diving is about as close as any of us get to the feeling of flying, particularly on a gentle drift dive. Drifting above this dense carpet of coral trees must be how it feels to be a butterfly skimming the surface of a field of corn or a bird flying across the tree tops. An occasional boulder looms up like a mountain peak protruding above the height of the forest. These boulders have a thick cover of deepwater sea fans, breaking up the dominance of the tanned hues of the sea rods.

Whisked past the channel between Sisters, we continue south and then west around the second rock. It is a little shallower here and, briefly, we are out of the current. There is more time now to watch the little bi-coloured damselfish going about their business. A school of grey snappers move across the reef and numerous rock beauties check out the food situation.

The slope of the reef is still sprouting a luxuriant cover of octocorals but at 40 feet where the reef flattens to an area of sand, luminescent azure vase sponges have found space to grow. Higher on the reef, stove-pipe sponges have grabbed a bit of available

Dive Profile

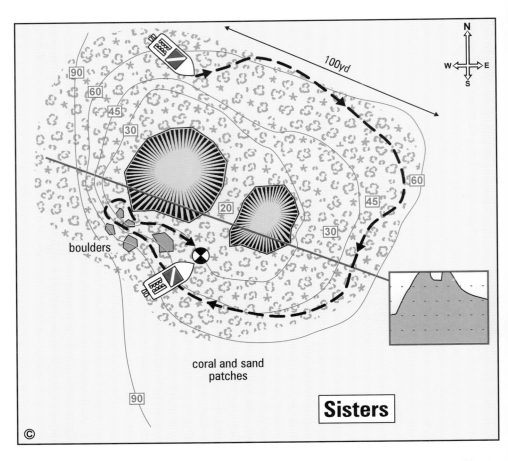

Sisters

space and added variety to the reef life. Sporadic heads of brain coral like full stops appear here and there.

Out in the blue, a group of barracuda make sequential passes to get a better look at us. There is a good variety of fish among the coral, including two large boxfish. They are strange looking creatures with their peculiarly triangular body shape which is formed from a bony box, hence the family name boxfish. This 'box' seems to be moved around the reef more by will power than any swimming prowess. Like a huge bumble bee, frantic flapping of the pectoral fins can barely be seen in the blur of movement. Yet if frightened they can show a respectable turn of speed.

Paddy, our dive guide, skilfully leads us round to a buoy line where the dive boat is now waiting. When the currents allow it, the dive begins at this buoy. You then pass through the channel between the two rocks in 20 feet of water. This is a pretty canyon, though the current may sweep you through too quickly to make a detailed evaluation. If the current is such that you dive along the west side of the largest rock, you will find black coral bushes and a greater propor-

Like a huge bumble bee, the trunkfish's frantic flapping of its pectoral fins can barely be seen in a blur of movement. Unlike the bumble bee, the trunkfish has a hard, bony, box-like skeleton.

tion of hard corals. This area is a little deeper—100 feet or so.

Brothers, Sisters or just good friends, under the water these rocks join in creating an overwhelming display of coral and attendant marine life.

Thanks to Max and Paddy at Carriacou Silver Diving.

This is another easy site, good for training, check-out and night dives. It is not short of life, though, and it may provide your best chance of seeing a nurse shark. An arch seems a popular place for them to rest. Being off a headland, schools of fish often pass by including recently a school of shiny metallic tarpon.

Cistern Point 5
15'-60'

When we did this dive, it was at the end of a couple of weeks of fairly intensive diving; it was becoming more difficult to impress us. The previous day we had been seduced by the luscious forest of Sisters submarine gardens.

Frigate Island showed us a very different sort of underwater seascape and a completely different range of marine life. The hard corals here span a fascinating range of species. The varying morphological developments have created an intricate profile for the reef and a delightful tapestry of colours and textures. Neither over-dived, nor over-fished, the coral is in perfect condition, a terrific example of the beauty of a healthy reef.

We drop down the anchor line in 50 feet and receive our first treat of the dive. Scattered about the sand are numerous conch, their weaving trails traced in the sand like the tracks of lost travellers in the desert, searching for an oasis.

From the anchor, the reef is visible in front of us and we turn to the right. Swimming at the base of the reef where it joins a

Frigate 6
Island
30'-70'

  C

Dive Profile

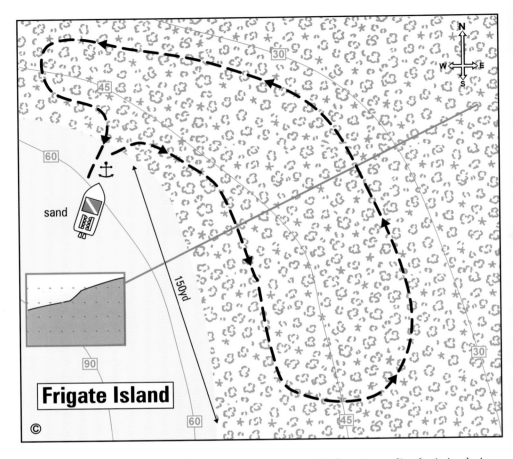

Frigate Island

sandy bottom, we are now at 65 feet. Immediately, it is obvious that the reef is quite exceptional. There are several shades of boulder star coral and great star coral. Rich moss greens sit alongside dusky pastel yellows and browns.

Taking a moment to look out across the reef, the scene resembles a field of gigantic mole hills. Closer inspection shows each mound to be crusted with plates of stony corals, their soft colours belying their hard texture. Some mounds prove to be brain coral, many others have been populated by star coral. These two corals are easy to distinguish as they have a markedly different appearance. Deep valleys and hills carve a winding path across the surface of brain coral. By comparison, boulder star coral is covered in small round crater-like protrusions. You would think it had rained just after Neptune had finished painting them.

On closer inspection you can see smears of reddish purple coralline algae holding the reef together where organisms have undermined the coral heads. It is in these areas that we see many longsnout butterflyfish, only a couple of inches long and most of that nose. All the better to delve into coral heads to extract a little morsel of something tasty.

We continue to move south at around 50 feet and along the way find lettuce coral, Graham's sheet coral, patches of cactus coral and smooth flower coral. The latter is quite different from all the other varieties. Look for something similar in appearance to a sculpture of a bunch of flowers. Each polyp stands separately on a long stalk with a round corallite opening. These coral varieties live in apparent harmony, side by side on the reef, yet there is a definite pecking order and fierce competition for space, light and food.

The Pecking Order of Coral

Because we see no movement among the stony corals on the reef, we tend to think they are inactive motionless lumps of rock. Not so. This is a dynamic community engaged in selfish self-preservation. No end of power struggles are taking place in competition for food, light and space.

Healthy coral is constantly growing and growth needs space but if one coral grows in a way which blocks the light from another, the blanketed coral will eventually die as it is unable to process enough food. And, this passive damage is only one way that corals dominate. Some adopt a more aggressive strategy, directing their battery of stinging cells at neighbouring coral polyps.

By killing neighbouring polyps, the coral creates a dead area of substratum on which it can extend its base. The implication is that some coral is more a victim to the nematocysts of aggressors than an aggressor itself. Some sort of pecking order does seem to exist. Flower coral are at the top of the aggressors' pile, followed by brain and cactus coral. Next comes star coral and then boulder coral. At the bottom of the hierarchy is elkhorn and staghorn and, finally, lettuce and other sheet coral.

The less aggressive, or at least less successfully aggressive, corals survive by adapting well to conditions which do not suit other corals. For example,

Flower, great star and sheet coral create a harmonious display, belying aggressive behaviour behind the scenes.

elkhorn coral have a unique ability to thrive at the wave thrashed edge of the reef. Various types of sheet coral, right at the bottom of the dominance scale, can live in much deeper water than most other hard corals. They need less light and can safely occupy deep water where other corals do less well, making them less susceptible to aggressive matches they cannot win.

This specialisation ensures that a range of different species of coral survive and give the reef balance.

At half tank we turn around, returning in slightly shallower water. This healthy reef draws a wide variety of fish, many—such as the common blackbar soldierfish, squirrelfish and glasseye snappers—using the coral overhangs to shelter until nightfall. Lots of black durgons move constantly about the reef, mingling with yellowhead and bluehead wrasse. An abundance of tangs and surgeonfish keep the algae down on the reef, aided and abetted by a number of different types of damselfish. Zooming in on the coral reveals numerous blennies and gobies as well as shrimps and Christmas tree worms.

When we reach the anchor again, we still have some air left and are in no hurry to terminate this dive. As there is no current, we travel a little way in the other direction, to the north. The reef is similar, a little flatter and shallower, with sand patches and more sea rods and whips.

Whether you hone your coral recognition skills before doing this dive or just decide to enjoy the mosaic of colours, shapes and texture comprising the fabric of this area, it is likely to be one of the high points of diving Carriacou.

Thanks to Tanki of Tanki's Watersports.

Isle de Ronde

The remaining sites are dived from both Carriacou and Grenada, as the area is roughly halfway between the two. It is an exceptional diving area with perfect visibility of 100 feet or more. The marine life is not subject to human generated pollution, as the islands have only a handful of inhabitants who camp out for much of the year on the south coast of Isle de Ronde. Isle de Ronde is also occasionally used as an overnight anchorage for yachts, in very calm conditions. Even so, rarely will there be more than one or two yachts there.

Although the area is dived, it is not a regular occurrence due to the distance from both Carriacou and Grenada. Thus, the marine life is pristine; coral is undamaged, sponges are brightly coloured and prolific, and many fish inhabit the area. It is without doubt the area's finest diving and will compensate you for any discomfort on the journey to and from the site.

From both Carriacou and Grenada the boat ride will be an hour or more. From Carriacou the easy part of the trip is usually the journey out, with rougher seas on the way back. The opposite is true for trips from Grenada. All the dive stores organise trips to this area, offering 2 tanks and a picnic lunch for a package price or a small premium on their normal charges. Lunch, either on the boat or on the beach at Isle de Ronde, is a pleasure in itself. The small anchorage is usually quite calm and the water looks good enough to drink.

This is an active volcanic area, sometimes emitting cracking and snapping noises while you are underwater as the rocks expand and shift. An underwater volcano, considered one of the

Caribbean's most active, lies some 2 miles west of Twin Sisters Rocks. On last measure it was around 500 feet deep. It is thought to have shoaled somewhat. We passed over it and could not get a reading on our depth sounder's maximum range of 300 feet.

**Diamond Rock/ 7
Kick 'em Jenny
20'- 120'**

Above the water, Diamond Rock is a craggy pyramidal structure 700 feet high, barren and unwelcoming. The contrast below water is startling. The slope of the rock as it descends into the sea is covered with a mixture of soft oscillating sea rods and colourful stony corals.

There is a gentle shallow dive with little current around the north of the rock, or at least when you feel current you simply turn around and go the other way. It makes a pleasant second dive after diving Twin Sisters.

On the southeast corner, there is a small wall which drops down to 120 feet but the best part of the dive is generally around 35 to 45 feet. Gently swaying sea fans and beautiful undamaged corals decorate the wall. You stand a good chance of seeing nurse sharks and stingrays but keep one eye out into the blue as you never know what you might see there.

Twin Sisters

Twin Sisters rocks are to the west of Isle de Ronde. They have three dive sites around them. Operators will choose a site based on wind, current and sea state.

**Big Blue 8
(Twin Sisters)
25'-140'**

  W

Big Blue is a dive crammed with all the features divers love. A dramatic wall, the bottom much too deep to be in sight; a cave you can penetrate and surface in; a narrow canyon between the rocks and a ton of fish. And, the last time Tanki, our dive leader, did this dive he saw a hammerhead.

If you take a dive holiday in Carriacou or Grenada, this is the dive you must do. But, you will have to wait for the weather. If you are staying a few days, you would be unlucky not to have weather settled enough. Dive operators will ask for a small premium to cover fuel costs; it will probably be the best investment of your holiday and no more than what you will save abstaining from beer for the day. Most stores make a day of it, doing two dives with a picnic lunch between.

Dive Profile

From the dive boat's anchorage in 40 feet of water, there is a short swim across a reef at 35 feet before a breathtaking drop over the edge and down the wall. The isolated position of this site leaves it free from damage by pollution, fishermen and divers. Thus the wall is covered in beautiful marine life, both soft gorgonians and hard corals. As though as a compliment to the colours of the sessile marine life, angelfish both queen and French cruise the wall. Look down into the blue and you can see forever.

Though you could explore the wall for the whole dive, you will be torn by a desire to experience the rest of the site. A slope covered in corals and sea fans leads you to an overhang where a magnificent green moray resides. These large beautiful eels are common on this site, as are the barracuda which maintain a constant swim past routine.

Before reaching the overhang, the dive leader will want to check your air to decide whether to proceed through the channel to the cave or retrace your fin route to the boat. Current can run against you in the channel so it is a sensible safety precaution to check that you have enough air to complete the dive via that route.

Through the channel, at a depth of 30 feet, sea fans spread their complex web across the current. On the right, at 15 feet, a cave opening appears. Slipping in to the darkness of a cave is always thrilling. First descending slightly and then ascending, an internal cavern opens up. Surfacing is safe so long as there is no

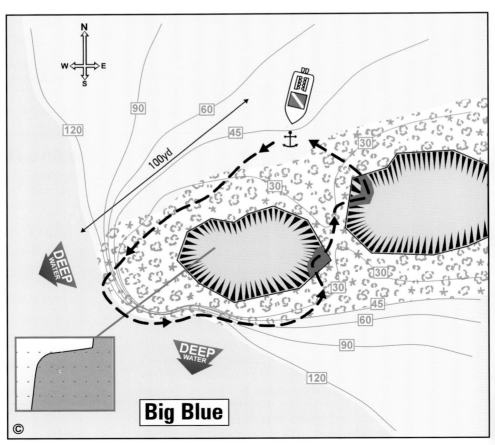

Big Blue

strong swell or surge, as the ceiling is higher than you can reach. (The dive leader will not allow you to enter the cave if surge conditions are inappropriate)

Using a light you can see stalactites hanging from the roof and quartz crystals that make you imagine you have discovered a secret store of precious jewels. The absence of light inhibits growth of coral but it has not stopped lobsters and shrimps from making it home.

A second opening offers an alternative exit, and it is back out into the light again. Schools of jacks and snappers look inquisitively at the emerging divers.

OK, so we still have not seen a hammerhead, but complaining about a dive like this seems a little churlish.

A rock resembling a turtle's head caused this site to be named. The dive is on a big table of coral in absolutely perfect condition. There are numerous species of hard corals, including the elusive black coral, vying for space. The environment is similar to that found off Frigate Island, but wider and deeper.

**Turtle Head Bay 9
(Twin Sisters)
20'-130'**

What a surprise to discover an underwater seascape reminiscent of a ski piste. Angular rocks with stretches of sparkling white sand between will make Franz Klammer fans positively sentimental, though he never had to execute racing turns in blunt-edged fins.

For those not taken with the skiing analogy, there are two anchors worth examination at 25 feet. Generally the marine life here is varied and plentiful. Ocean gars have even been seen milling around.

**Kitzbuhl 10
(Twin Sisters)
15'-50'**

This dive can only be done when the current is not very strong and surface conditions are calm enough to anchor the dive boat on the windward side. The dive starts from the north and goes around the rocks anti-clockwise.

It is done as a drift dive either passing through the gap between the rocks or going right around the edge of the group. The rocks below the water appear in shades of yellow, orange and red from the encrustation of sponges. Divers are attracted by a wide variety of marine life, including sharks, green morays, lobsters, turtles and schools of jacks.

**Lee Rocks 11
25'-80'**

12 Isle de Ronde Reef
40'-80'

Just to the south of Corn Store Bay, the anchorage on Isle de Ronde, is a pleasant reef, perfect for a second dive. It is a small wall and slope, covered in a charming mix of gorgonians and stony corals. Some excellent brain corals have grown, showing how perfectly formed these structures are when they survive undamaged.

Although in the lee of Isle de Ronde, currents are still encountered, causing the site to be dived as a gentle drift.

13 Les Tantes Rocks
30'-120'

Perhaps not given the most attractive of names, the areas around Les Tantes Rocks are another set of spectacular dive sites. Different operators dive their own preferred area. All the sites have interesting underwater seascapes including tunnels and deep crevices.

Some operators dive along a steep slope to 100 feet, known as Diablo's Den or Les Tantes Wall, coated in bright sponges and large brain corals. A rich cover of sea whips and plumes give the slope constant movement. The faceted wall hides a myriad of marine life and one crevice forms a swim through.

Around on the Atlantic side there is a shallower dive with stunning visibility and many reef fish. Big midnight parrotfish, queen angelfish and nurse sharks all patrol the reef. Many rocks, overhangs and holes make this interesting terrain.

A site known locally as 'Face of the Devil' is an area of big volcanic rocks strewn along a gentle slope. The depth is to 100 feet but there is good marine life much shallower, too. The rocks have a brocaded surface created from orange and yellow sponges and star corals. Big fish cruise by and usually you will see barracuda and nurse sharks. Schools of sennets and silversides are common.

Carriacou Diving Facilities

For a small island, Carriacou has good diving facilities. The scale of the facilities is appropriate to the number of divers visiting the island but small does not mean less well equipped or professionally operated.

Equipment

The dive stores use adapted pirogues as dive boats, with powerful engines to cope with the offshore conditions. Typically there will be no more than half a dozen divers or fewer on the boat. Dive equipment is modern and well maintained.

Cost

Prices are average for the area at around $40 per dive. The cost per dive comes down when you buy a dive package.

Two dive stores offer diving from Carriacou. Both are located at the northern end of the island in or near the main town of Hillsborough. Both provide PADI instruction though their owners were originally trained in Germany with CMAS and have logged many thousands of dives around the world.

Carriacou Silver Diving **1** is owned by Max Nagel and Claudia Badziong, a friendly professional couple who have been on the island since 1993. Max worked for the previous owner before buying the operation from him. In 1995 they moved into smart new premises just a few hundred yards along the road leading out of Hillsborough, to the north.

The store is well equipped with powerful compressors, shower and toilet, and a good clear area to put equipment together, run teaching sessions, etc. There is a short walk across the road and down to the beach to the dive boats. Two pirogues, one 20 feet and one 30 feet speed you to the dive sites.

A portable compressor (Bauer Capitaine 140 litre per minute) is available for rental to those who will be travelling and diving throughout the region. About one third of Carriacou Silver Diving's business is from yachts, the balance being from hotels, guest houses and day visitors to the island, usually from Grenada.

The store also works with two local yachts offering sail/dive daily excursions and longer charters. *Posh Ratz* a 50-foot Gulfstar taking up to four guests is available for charter cruises while *Suvetar* offers short sail/dive charters to the Grenadines.

To the south of Hillsborough in L'Esterre bay, opposite Sandy Island, are Paradise Inn and Tanki's Watersports **2**. Tanki has been in Carriacou since 1989 and is now married to the daughter of well-known local artist, Canute Caliste. Tanki's wife is the manager of the Paradise Inn guest house while Tanki supplies diving to guests of the Inn and other divers.

They offer an interesting package of a combined holiday diving from the guest house and from the yacht *Romany*. Guests spend two or three days in the guest house before sailing on Romany to spend the night at Isle de Ronde, with Tanki providing rendezvous diving on Twin Sisters and Diamond Rock. The next week a similar trip, but slightly longer, is organised to the Grenadines. Where distances make it impractical for Tanki to provide rendezvous diving, he has arrangements with local dive operators.

Tanki, like Max, is determined to preserve the quality of Carriacou's reefs and in the absence of government policy or support he maintains a *no touching, no spearfishing* rule with his divers. His interest in the marine life is sincere and comes across to those who dive with him.

Operators

Grenada

Grenada is the most photogenic of the Windward Islands, with rounded green mountains, sparkling waterfalls, golden beaches and the picture perfect capital of St. George's. It is hard to take a bad photograph of this small city built on a hill between two waterfronts. On the western side lies the Caribbean Sea and to the east is the Carenage, a protected basin that was once a volcanic crater. St. George's starts at the summit of the hill and spills down both sides to the water's edge.

St. George's was built in the days when ships made most profit outward bound, laden with spices and rum. They would return with a ballast load of bricks and tiles and many buildings of this era survive, their brick walls and roofs made from 'fish scale' tiles which have been mellowed by age into dark shades of red. Flowers grow around the houses, and shops are linked by breadfruit, mango and banana trees, with the whole picture framed in blue by the Caribbean Sea.

Grenada's Carnival is celebrated in August each year.

Grenada is about 15 miles long by 10 wide, but as with the other islands, the twisty roads and mountains make it seem larger; a leisurely tour will take a whole day and even then there will be much you have missed.

Geologically, Grenada is a little older than St. Vincent and Dominica and its rough edges have been rounded off by time. The mountains reach 2,500 feet and are not quite so dramatic as those of the islands just to the north, but they are accessible and easier to explore. Along the roads are pretty wooden houses surrounded by small colourful gardens. Grenada's main crops, nutmeg and cocoa, are so decorative that, as you take a winding path through them to reach a hidden waterfall, you may find yourself reminded of the Garden of Eden.

With assets so fair, it is not surprising that Grenada has attracted quite a few visitors, but tourism has not developed as rapidly as in some other islands because of the island's rather turbulent recent political history. Many people heard of Grenada for the first time when the Americans launched their 'rescue' mission in early 1983. But this was just one phase of a period of political experimentation that started with independence from Britain in 1974.

Grenada was ruled at the time by Eric Gairy, a colourful leader whose politics were divisive. When England thrust independence on Grenada, most of the people responded by going on strike in protest. This was followed by an initially peaceful revolution led by Maurice Bishop, a charismatic lawyer. The revolution got bogged down in its own dogma and proved incapable of dealing democratically with dissent. Finally the hard-liners shot Bishop and half his cabinet and the stage was set for the United States' intervention, which was locally very popular.

Grenada has always been pleasant to visit, even through all the strife, and the people liked visitors even during the communist years. Now life on the island is more settled and Grenada has the added advantage of an international airport—a gift from the Cuban people who came and built it. Two new hotels have been built recently, and a continued gradual expansion of tourism is to be expected.

Visitor accommodation is nearly all to be found in the southwest corner of the island, between St. George's and Mount Hartman Bay, and dive shops are scattered throughout this area. Visitor facilities are concentrated in this small section which means they are easy to get to. Another plus is that the rest of the island is unspoiled and unaffected.

Grand Anse

The centre of tourism is at Grand Anse, where a perfect beach stretches for a mile and a half. The beach has remained pleasant because building restrictions have kept newer hotels from being built too close to one another, and everything is kept below the level of the highest coconut tree. The majority of hotels lie behind this beach. Some, like Spice Island Inn and the Flamboyant, date back to the early days of tourism in the island.

This bay is also the home of the Renaissance Grenadian which has 186 rooms, making it a large hotel by Grenada's standards. Many smaller hotels, some with only ten or twenty rooms, can be found here. Those that are behind the beach are considerably less expensive.

Point Saline

Two of the newer hotels, LaSource and the Rex Grenadian, have been built out towards Point Saline to the west, where rocky hills are interspersed with gorgeous beaches. These hotels are self-contained and have their own dive shops but they are a fair way from the rest of the activity. With a couple of hundred rooms, the Rex Grenadian is a largish hotel, while LaSource at half that size is Grenada's classiest all-inclusive resort.

True Blue

Other hotels are to be found in True Blue and L'Anse aux Epines, both pleasant residential areas that face part of Grenada's convoluted south coast—an area of hidden bays, beaches and islands. These are generally small, family run establishments, many with fewer than 30 rooms, and they include the Calabash, True Blue Inn, the Horseshoe Bay and Secret Harbour.

Among all these hotels are many rental accommodations in pleasant apartment buildings and cottages. Some, like 12 Degrees North and Coral Cove, are in idyllic waterfront settings. These are both in L'Anse aux Epines and, for the less energetic, a rental car would be essential for getting to the dive shop on time. Many others in Grand Anse are within easy walking distance of the beach and are on a major bus route.

There are one or two hideaways well away from the main drag, including Petit Bacaye and La Sagesse. These have no diving facilities and you would need a car if you wanted to dive.

Organised land tours in Grenada are still in their infancy and are usually arranged for a particular visiting group, rather than done on a regular basis. There are good roads not only around the island, but right through the middle.

Grenville

Grenada's second largest town is Grenville, on the east coast. The main road from town winds its way up through the mountains to Grand Etang, a lake right in the middle of the rainforest, before starting the steep descent to St. George's. This is still one of Grenada's main roads and it goes through spectacular scenery.

Grand Etang

Grenada's Forest Centre and Reserve are at this road's highest point near Grand Etang. The centre is open to the public and contains a wealth of information on the forests. Many maintained trails go into the rainforest and on some you are unlikely to meet another soul. Mount Qua Qua is one destination with a panoramic view over the Grand Etang and the mountains. From here it is easy to see that in this part of the island, civilisation is just a tiny ribbon of road through the forest.

Good hikers can follow a path right across the island to the west coast where it joins the west coast road at Concord Falls. There are shorter paths for the less adventurous.

Grenada has been blessed with more than its fair share of enticing waterfalls that plunge into small tropical pools that could have been designed with swimming in mind. A plunge into one of these leaves you refreshed, and makes your skin and hair feel especially soft. You can easily drive to some, like the Annandale Falls, but you need to hike to the more interesting falls. The prettiest may be Seven Falls, about an hour's hike from the Grand Etang Road. Nowadays you can find quite a few taxi drivers willing and able to take you to these places, but it was not always so. Most taxi drivers used to have a fear of getting their shoes muddy and when an enterprising taxi driver called Henry started to hike off the roads with his customers he was nicknamed 'The Mud Taxi'. Today Henry Safari Tours, which still specialises in off-the-road hikes, is one of the most successful in Grenada.

But you do not need to hike to enjoy Grenada. Just about every road has picture perfect views. There is one agricultural feeder road that is particularly scenic. Called the Clozier Road, it runs between Gouyave and the Grand Etang Road, winding through farms of nutmeg and cocoa with views of the forest in the background.

If you can bear to spend a whole day without diving, there are several estate houses in the country that offer lunch. These include Morne Fendue and Mount Rodney Estate in the north of the island and Rose Mount on the Clozier Road.

One of the advantages of being on an island that has many rental apartments and few all-inclusive hotels is that it has created the right environment for many excellent restaurants. With at least 50 to choose from, there is no need to eat in the same place twice. To take advantage of these you need a car or at least have a taxi driver you can easily call upon. Everything is within a few miles, but the farthest ones will still be too far to walk. There are restaurants in St. George's and scattered right through Grand Anse, True Blue and L'Anse aux Epines. Restaurants like Canboulay and the Red Crab should satisfy the most demanding gourmet. Romantics will love Tabanca and Pirate's Cove, with their perfect views over the sea to the lights of St. George's. You can eat inexpensive Chinese or West Indian food and there is even an American-style steak house. Coyaba Hotel at Grand Anse also has very good food. It is where local people take their families for a special night out.

Language: English
Currency: Eastern Caribbean Dollar ($1.00 US = $2.66 EC)
Population: About 100,000
Telephone Codes: Currently (809), changing to (473)

Après Dive

Grenada is well set up to cater for the needs of mixed groups of divers and non-divers, as a good range of alternative activities is readily available.

Golf

It is hard to say whether goats or golfers get more pleasure from Grenada's 9-hole golf course. It has undergone some renovation recently and hosted a Caribbean tournament. It is open to visitors.
Grenada Golf and Country Club: (809) 444-4128

Hiking

Grenada was custom built for hiking and walking. Everyone should drive around the island and visit at least one waterfall.
Funseeker Tours: (809) 444-1342/441-9443
Henry Safari Tours: (809) 444-5313
K&J Tours: (809) 440-4227/441-9621
Leroy's Tropical Tours: (809) 443-1171/444-3640
Rock Taxi: (809) 444-5316
Selwyn Maxwell: (809) 444-1653

Tennis

If you have your own gear there is a public court behind the beach at Grand Anse near Coconut Beach Restaurant, where you just turn up and play. Many hotels and even some rental apartments are equipped with tennis courts. The following are open to non-resident visitors for a fee.

Secret Harbour Hotel: (809) 444-4439/4458
Coyaba Beach Hotel: (809) 444-4129/4612

Water Sports

Grenada is home to The Moorings, a major charter company with both skippered yachts and bareboats. Several smaller companies offer day chartering and deep sea fishing. One of the day-charter companies, Starwind Enterprises, will combine day sails with diving. Water sports, including sailboards, sunfish, paragliding and beach catamarans, can be found along Grand Anse Beach and at the Secret Harbour Hotel.

Yacht Charters:
Spice Island Marine: (809) 444-4257/4342
Starwind Enterprises: (809) 440-3678
The Moorings: (809) 444-4439/4549

Deep Sea Fishing:
Evans Chartering Service: (809) 444-4424/4217

Shopping

Grenada has excellent shops for visitors. Some of the crafts are made locally and some are imported from other Caribbean islands or south and central America. In St. George's, Tikal, Creation and Gifts Remembered should be on any shopper's itinerary. Many more are in Grand Anse. Check out the shopping mall at Foodfair which includes the stylish Imagine gift shop. The major hotels all have at least one boutique and Le Marquis Mall is worth visiting. Arawak Islands products include soaps, perfumes, spices, teas and herbs, all made locally. You can buy them in many stores, but their packing plant and shop in a traditional house on the road from Grand Anse to St. George's makes a delightful change from the more usual shops.

Nightlife

The Marryshow Folk Theatre on Tyrrel Street in St. George's does occasional concerts, plays and cultural events. You can dance the night away in discos which are very local in character. Some of the best entertainment is in the major hotels which have musical and cabaret-style shows most nights, open to the general public. There is an elegant bar called Casablanca which opens from 11 a.m. to 3 a.m. and has sophisticated drinks, pool tables and occasional entertainment.

Casablanca: (809) 444-1631
Island View Nightclub: (809) 443-2054
Le Sucrier: (809) 444-1068
Marryshow House: (809) 440-2451

Hotel Association: (809) 444-1353
Tourist Board: (809) 440-2001/2279
USA: (800) 972-9554, (212) 687-9554
Canada: (416) 595-8278
UK: (171) 244-0177

**Information on
Accommodation**

Grenada has an international airport, handling flights directly from the USA and Europe. Both scheduled and charter flights
are available, offering flexibility in timing and costs. From the
USA many flights connect via Puerto Rico. From Europe there
are both direct flights and connections via Trinidad. Good inter-
island flights via Barbados, St. Lucia and Antigua make the island
very accessible.

Getting There

Onward travel to Carriacou is an exciting light aircraft flight
taking 15 minutes. Alternatively, a new high speed ferry service
can whisk you up to Carriacou for a day's diving and back in
time for dinner.

The diving environment of most islands in this book can be
described as having a particular characteristic: either fringing reefs,
offshore reefs, offshore rocks, or wrecks. Grenada has all of these.
No particular type of dive dominates to the exclusion of all others.

The Diving

The main island of Grenada has five wrecks including the
famous *Bianca C.* They are at varying depths, giving a good range
of diving. A number of other 'wrecks' are still afloat in St.
George's lagoon with plans to have them removed and sunk as
dive sites. Unfortunately, the longer the plans take to bear fruit,
the more expensive the exercise becomes and the plans are once
again shelved.

Along the west coast are several bays with associated fringe reefs
around the headlands and across the entrance to the bays. In the
southern part of the island the sand in these bays is white whereas
further north black volcanic sand predominates. The reefs slope in
varying degrees of incline, creating gentle underwater scenery.

Around the southwest and south of Grenada are a number of
shallows marked on nautical charts but not evident from the deck
of a boat, except for an occasional patch of rough water. Some of
these shallows are coral reefs. Outside the main harbour of St.
George's, stretching for several miles out toward the airport, lie
three offshore reefs.

To the north, the Grenada dive stores share with Carriacou
operators the diving around the offshore rocks of the Isle de
Ronde archipelago. We have described this diving in the
Carriacou section earlier in this chapter.

The marine life in Grenada has much in common with that of
the other islands in the chain, though we noticed fewer sponges
and more hard coral. There are dives where there is good sponge

growth, but overall we would say that the percentage of cover occupied by sponges is less than on islands to the north. As sponges add many of the brighter colours on the reef, the reefs near the mainland of Grenada can seem less colourful.

Turbidity also contributes to a generally more muted appearance. From time to time, in the summer months in particular, the water around Grenada becomes very green and visibility is reduced. It is believed to be the effect of fresh water from the Orinoco which occasionally reaches this far north.

Rain water run-off from the land exacerbates the problem. Run-off encourages algae growth which sometimes blooms, further reducing visibility. Grenada does have its share of clear sparkling water and the periods of reduced visibility generally only last a few days. Usually the water clears considerably when you drop below 10 feet. When we were diving here visibility was poor compared to normal, but still quite acceptable, and it changed from green and a bit murky one day to blue and clear the next.

The most common corals are boulder, star and staghorn with sea rods and plumes present on most sites. We were pleasantly surprised to see black coral at several sites, not huge trees like in St. Vincent but healthy bushy growths in a variety of colours nevertheless. Depressingly, some local dive operators believe the black coral has only survived because people do not know what it is. This level of cynicism is the result of too many years of apathy and inactivity by government departments regarding reef conservation.

Other creatures we noticed in abundance were a variety of anemones. We saw giant, corkscrew, and branching anemones. Conditions here must suit them.

The variety of dive sites means that there is a good range of depth, catering for both beginners and those looking for something more challenging. The fringing reefs tend to be shallow, down to around 60 feet, and the surface conditions are calm. The *Bianca C* on the other hand is at the maximum depth for no decompression diving, some parts of the wreck being deeper than 130 feet. There can be strong currents near the *Bianca C* but just as often they are weak or non existent. (See Site 15)

Hardly any of the dive sites are buoyed and while some sites are dived as drifts, the dive boats are generally anchored. Evidence of anchor damage is apparent on some sites. The other disturbing find was a selection of garbage, plastic bottles, packing boxes and so on. There were not large quantities but on every dive we saw at least one item. We concluded this was because of the proximity of some reefs to the harbour entrance.

Undoubtedly, Grenada's main asset is variety, especially if you make sure you include a trip to Isle de Ronde where the quality of the diving is excellent. It would be well worth spreading your time between Grenada and Carriacou.

This is a short section because Grenada has virtually no rules affecting divers. Divers may not take coral and there is a closed season for taking lobsters from May 30 to August 31, a shorter period than the islands to the north. We only saw lobster on one of the dives we did here. Maybe we were just unlucky, though; we had been tripping over them on the dives we did farther north.

There is a requirement for dive stores to obtain a permit to dive within the boundaries of St. George's harbour. This seems to be largely a formality aimed at controlling the movement of shipping rather than promoting marine conservation.

Although under some pressure to take positive steps to protect the marine environment some years ago, nothing has been achieved. One area was called a marine park but there are no rules designed to protect the area. Local operators claim to have lobbied the Tourist Department and Fisheries, receiving the same response from both. "There is no legislation in place which would allow us to enforce conservation measures."

It would be possible for the dive stores to agree on certain rules and perhaps, by example, persuade the relevant government bodies to take action. But, as the dive stores have no forum to develop policy, that route does not seem promising either.

A large Moorings bareboat fleet at Secret Harbour, on the south of the island, attracts people who like to sail and dive. Although some pause to dive the *Bianca C*, most head north to Carriacou and the Grenadines for diving. The *Bianca C* can only be dived with an operator, but Moliniere Reef (Site 6) and the *Veronica* (Site 8) are accessible dive sites in a yacht's dinghy. If anchoring near Moliniere make sure you find some sand or tie a line to rock on a short scope.

Grenada has no recompression chamber but both Trinidad and Barbados have facilities just a short flight away. With two facilities so near, there is no real demand for a chamber in Grenada, particularly when there are comparatively few divers compared, for example, to Barbados, St. Lucia and Martinique.

The Barbados chamber is a slick operation and is the chamber generally chosen. Immigration procedures are waived, and for non-French speakers procedures are easier than those in Martinique.

Grenada has a good safety record which is particularly commendable in view of the depth of the wreck of the *Bianca C*, especially in comparison with Martinique which also has some very deep wrecks. The dive operators take a very cautious attitude and none of the local stores are currently doing decompression diving. This inevitably has contributed to the good safety record.

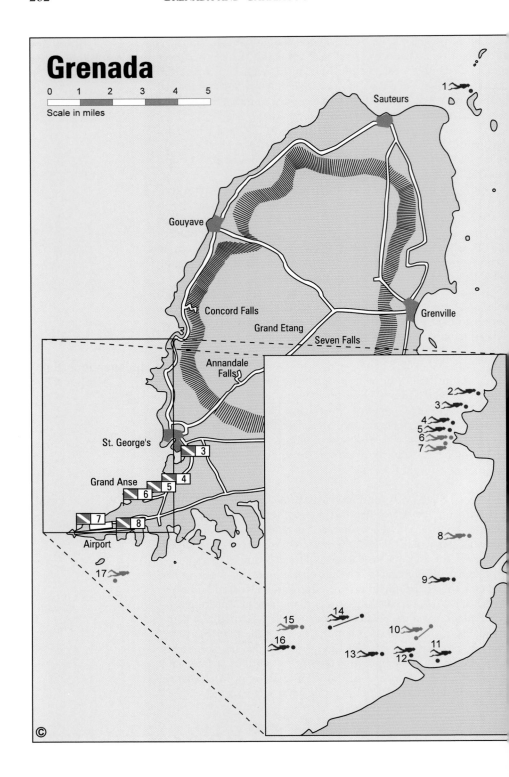

Grenada

0   1   2   3   4   5

Scale in miles

Sauteurs

Gouyave

Concord Falls

Grand Etang

Seven Falls

Grenville

Annandale Falls

St. George's

Grand Anse

Airport

NO.	SITE NAME	DEPTH IN FEET
1	Sandy Island	40-60
2	Flamingo Bay	20-90
3	Happy Valley/Hill	20-90
4	Dragon Bay	25-95
5	Wreck of the *Don Cesard*	90
6	Moliniere Reef	20-60
7	Wreck of the *Buccaneer*	70-90
8	Wreck of the *Veronica*	20-40
9	Red Buoy	20-110
10	Boss Reef	20-80
11	Spice Island Reef	20-30
12	Three Wrecks	40
13	Quarter Wreck	25-35
14	Windmill Shallows/Sammy's Drift	60-130
15	Wreck of the *Bianca C*	90-130+
16	Whibble Reef	60-100
17	Shark Reef	25-65

Grenada Dive Sites

For Isle de Ronde sites see Carriacou section earlier in this chapter.

NO.	OPERATOR	RESORT/HOTEL LOCATION
3	Starwind	
4	Sanvics Watersports	Renaissance Hotel
5	Dive Grenada	
6	Scuba World	Rex Grenadian
7	LaSource*	LaSource
8	Scuba Express	True Blue Inn

Dive Operators

*Owned by Hotel/Resort

Sandy Island **1**
40'-60'

Not to be confused with Carriacou's Sandy Island, this dive site is only visited in calm weather and by special request. Sometimes it is done as a second dive on the return trip from Isle de Ronde. It is located off the northeast corner of Grenada, about an hour's boat ride away from St. George's and Grand Anse.

The dive is onto a fringing reef with a thick covering of staghorn and elkhorn coral. Strong wave action has reduced some sections to rubble. Gorgonians carpet the areas of rubble with soft warm colours. Its location attracts a mass of fish of all types including reef sharks.

2 Flamingo Bay
20'-90'

The reef here is a wall and steep slope down to 90 feet. The slope is encrusted with sea whips and sea fans with sponges adding colour. Fish are attracted to the slope and you will never be short of entertainment.

Schools of Creole wrasse are common along with brown chromis, grunts and jackknife fish. Deeper down the slope, some large groupers hang out and rays and jacks are regular visitors. Rumour has it, and you know what rumours are like, that black seahorses have been spotted. Apparently the trick is not to look for them.

3 Happy Valley/
Happy Hill
20'-90'

Local operators cannot seem to agree whether the site is a hill or a valley. They do agree that it is one of Grenada's prettiest sites. Another steep slope, it shelves down to 90 feet with a good covering of gorgonians. The pillar coral is good, forming towering blocks through which the fish can play hide-and-seek.

The current generally runs south and the dive is done as a drift, often leading right down to the next bay.

4 Dragon Bay
25'-95'

This is a good varied dive with interesting marine life at whichever depth you choose to dive. Sand channels cut into angular volcanic rocks give attractive terrain at shallower depths. As you drift over the top of the slope, the sight of soft fingers of sea rods and sea plumes lull the senses and create a gentle flowing ambience.

Dipping over the reef down the slope, more hard corals emerge and at around 45 feet sprays of black coral add to the scenery. The dark shapes of deep water sea fans create drama and hide lurking groupers. Look carefully and you will see morays heads poking out of small holes in the rock.

Fish life is good, with beautiful angelfish and lots of chromis.

5 Wreck of the
Don Cesard
90'

The *Don Cesard* was a drug runner, caught in active service by the Coastguard and duly confiscated. She was left afloat until she decided if her days were over, so be it, and slowly started to sink. The Coastguard towed the ship to her current position and sank her. A rather exotic history makes this wreck an exciting proposition and it will one day be quite an attraction. Its day has not yet come for those interested in marine life, as it was only sunk in 1995, too recently for reef life to take hold. Fish have recognised its potential, especially as a shelter, and it is likely to become increasingly interesting as time passes.

If you enjoy diving wrecks, then this is quite an interesting one. The superstructure has been removed but everything else is still in place, including the twin diesels in the engine room.

Normally two separate dives, we dive both the reef and the wreck to gain an appreciation of both sites. The proximity of the wreck to the reef allows dive operators to take mixed groups to the site; divers in training explore the relatively shallow reef while others in the group swim out to the wreck.

The *Buccaneer* was deliberately sunk as a dive site and, while the intention was to place it nearer the reef, it is only a short swim away. It makes an attractive dive, especially for photographers. And, if you have never seen black coral, this could be your first.

Moliniere Reef is described as a marine park area, though this is a largely meaningless term in Grenada. Sadly, those who have dived this reef for many years claim that, in the absence of proper conservation measures, it has deteriorated significantly. We found it attractive and absorbing in parts but with clear evidence of damage. There is a substantial amount of algae and anchor damage in the shallows. The site is subject to land water run-off so appears to be being attacked on all sides.

From the anchored dive boat we swim out across the reef in 20 feet. Under the boat are sea plumes and thick sea rods. Two patch reefs appear on either side of us with a sand canyon between them.

The reef then slopes down with a covering of mixed stony and soft corals. Long strands of devil's sea whips sprout from the slope like hairs on a witch's chin. Busy little damselfish harvest the algae. Harlequin bass, the small mottled black and white fish with a yellow underside, eat crustaceans. Feeding on the coral, redband parrotfish are also common on the reef. Apart from the red shading on their dorsal fin, they have a yellow spot on the body side which looks entirely out of place. It is a strange looking fish all round, the orange line extending from its mouth is reminiscent of someone caught eating a colourful ice cream.

Mat zoanthids and corkscrew anemones are worth looking out for, as are fanworms. We have not swum far along the reef when our guide, Wolfgang, indicates it is time to head for the wreck. The Buccaneer is a 42-foot yacht lying on her starboard side in 90 feet of water.

We approach the hull as two very large French angelfish swim past. They are permanent residents according to our dive leader. Consequently, they are not shy of divers and they pose patiently as Brian takes a portrait photograph. Obligingly, they then move to the propeller and pause briefly for a photo shoot before entering the hull. Once inside, they angle themselves so as to be framed inside one of the portholes. Brilliant. You just do not get many photo opportunities like that. And, there has to be a first time for leaving the lens cap on, but why this dive? It is not true what they say—underwater they can hear you scream.

Moliniere 6
Reef
Wreck of the 7
Buccaneer

20'-90'

 W

Dive Profile

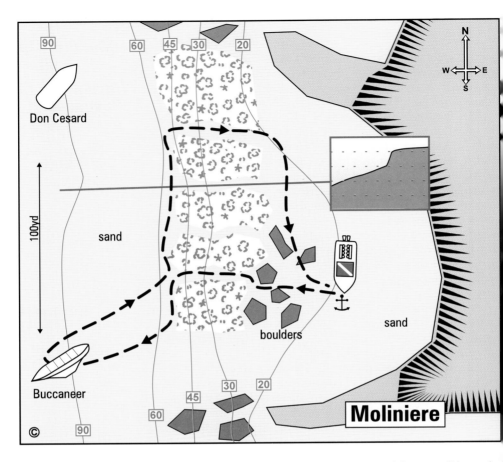

The wreck is only small but houses colourful marine life. Bushy black coral trees grow on the deck and inside the hull: white, orange and green varieties. White telesto adorns much of the superstructure and there are any number of encrusting sponges and tunicates. An Atlantic spadefish comes to check us out and an abundance of shiny blue chromis flitter around our heads.

We turn back for the reef and head north. There are more whips and fans in this area. Some Caesar grunts snuggle into an indentation in the reef and we see several large filefish. As we head into shallower water to end the dive and swim back to the reef, a spread of finger coral carpets our way. Many juvenile fish swim about the reef while yellowheaded jawfish disappear into the sand as our shadow passes over them. Larger lizardfish stand their ground.

Moliniere Reef still has some good interesting marine life, but unless something is done to protect the bay it seems likely that it will become a disposable commodity.

Thanks to Wolfgang of Sanvics Scuba and Watersports (and for noticing the lens cap was still on).

The *Veronica* is a small cargo vessel that sank just outside St. George's. There have been plans to move the wreck to a better site as the current location gets heavily silted from a nearby river. In its favour, the location attracts an extraordinary number of fish. On both the occasions we dived the wreck, there were fish everywhere, big ones, small ones, in schools and solitary.

This is a good dive for photographers as there is very little current to contend with. You can frame schools of fish through sections of the superstructure. Or, if you have a macro lens, a detailed inspection of the hull reveals no end of interesting life, all waiting to be captured on film.

A buoy is attached to the anchor windlass on the bow, creating a rather bizarre reversed image of the ship on the bottom and its anchor on the surface. The top of the bow is at 20 feet. As we drop down through some rather murky water, onto a wreck covered in slimy weed, we wonder whether this is a good idea. The water clears below 10 feet and we realise that part of the sensation of poor visibility is caused by the massed ranks of fish.

Mackerel scads flash by, a blur of silver. Brown chromis and Creole wrasse pour over the wreck, the school of chromis bigger than the wreck. As we begin to swim toward the stern, we become aware of the large numbers of fish on the wreck itself. Sergeant majors, surgeonfish, threespot damselfish, and gaggles of juvenile bluehead wrasse live in apparent harmony on the aft deck of the wreck.

As you pass down the starboard side of the hull, the long arm of a crane extends horizontally for 20 feet. The framework has become encrusted in a variety of sponges. Colourful sea rods grace the edges of the structure making it look as if it has been decorated for Christmas. All it needs is a row of fairy lights.

Wreck of the Veronica

Wreck of the [8] *Veronica*
20'-40'

  C

Dive profile

Colourful sea rods grace the superstructure of the wreck of the Veronica.

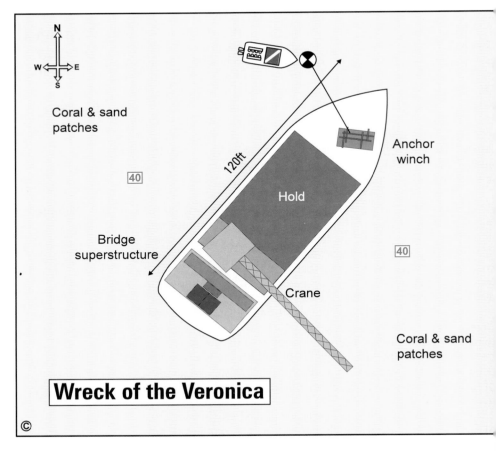

Wreck of the Veronica

We duck down into the hold which has been cleared and is safe to enter. Again, at first it seems as though there is not going to be much to interest us here, when we see some movement toward the aft end. Behind some sections of old machinery, bigeyes and squirrelfish are hiding. We are pleased to have been drawn there as we discover file clams, two Atlantic thorny oysters, several small crabs and a small but thriving black coral bush.

We exit the hold through a smaller opening toward the rear. As we look up, the water above us is saturated with the shapes of fish. Back out on the stern of the *Veronica* there is plenty to occupy us. A West Indian sea egg, like a pin cushion, is making a slow perambulation around the deck gear. The port side of the hull has a thick covering of colourful sea rods. These are brightly coloured branch-like corals whose polyps are a soft snowy white. The effect of the white polyps on the brightly coloured rods is quite delightful. Also along the starboard stern section we find nests of sea pearls attached to the hull.

The very many posts and rails have provided trumpetfish

with endless opportunities to hang motionless, disguised as a stanchion. As you swim along the hull, peer in through the portholes and you may find a bigeye peering back at you. But do not put your nose too close to the hull, there are many fire worms crawling around.

Back to the buoy line for our ascent where a barracuda has taken up station. Curious, he circles us a few times. With such a wealth of fish to choose from, it is not surprising we do not hold his interest for long. But no matter how big the barracuda's appetite, divers can be certain of plenty of fish on every dive on the *Veronica*.

Thanks to Gary at LaSource.

Red Buoy 9
20'-110'

The red buoy referred to in the name of this site is the starboard navigation buoy marking the entrance to St. George's harbour. Unfortunately, things were not so well organised in the 18th century which is probably why a wreck lies close to this spot. The wreck is so old that it is now only visible as clumps of coral shaping an artificial wall.

At 70 feet a number of encrusted Admiralty anchors warrant investigation for interesting critters. Something of an anachronism, a pile of telephones also makes a novel sight. Some pleasing vase sponges decorate the area and are themselves home to a variety of marine life.

Boss Reef 10
20'-80'

  W

An extensive reef runs for 5 miles from the entrance to St. George's harbour out toward Point Saline, near the airport. Three separate dives are done along this reef in depths from 20 to 90 feet. Throughout its length, the reef forms a gentle slope with sand patches and canyons. There are many elements common to all three of the areas dived, for example the profusion of Creole wrasse. There are many differences, too; most noticeably the transition from mainly hard corals at the eastern of the reef to tall fingers of gorgonians at the western end.

Because the top of the reef is 20 feet below the water, there is no surface disturbance to indicate its presence, nor is there a marker buoy. It takes not just a leap into the water but a leap of faith to believe that the dive boat has been carefully positioned above a reef and not just run out of fuel.

Dive Profile

We make our leap and sink down to the top of the reef, dutifully stationed below us. Neil Winsborrow, our dive guide, tows a surface marker buoy, leaving us free to drift as far as our air will allow us.

We slip down the slope of the reef to 50 feet where sand patches push into the reef, making small canyons. The dominant corals

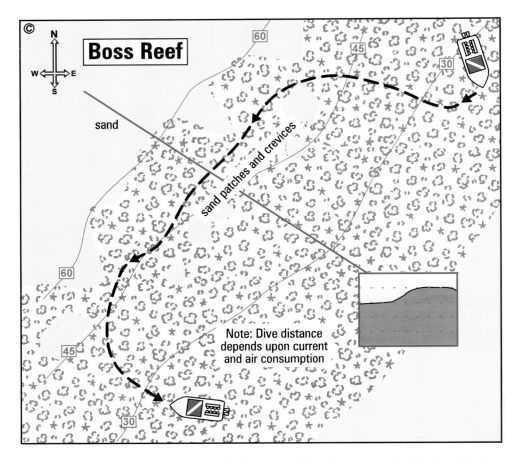

are finger and pillar coral with solitary sea rods, like fox tails, dotted around the stony surface of the reef.

As we drift lazily to the west, the fish make more energetic and purposeful movements around us. Bluehead wrasse and blue chromis stand out against the green of the water. Banded butterflyfish move swiftly in a blur of stripes.

We find several branching anemones tucked into gaps between the rocks. Unlike the giant anemone, the branching variety exposes only short tentacles. It looks rather like a jellified mat with stubby rubber nodules. It is a secretive creature, revealing its long true tentacles only at night. The tentacles you see in daylight are pseudo tentacles. The corkscrew anemones scattered around the reef operate no such dual system. The tentacles, like fine ringlets, are clearly visible.

Other growths which display small tentacles are the encrusting gorgonians inhabiting this reef. Unlike anemones, they grow openly on top of the substratum. Look for patches of growth of short strands almost like a patch of grass, but yellow brown, a few

Personal Valet Service—Cleaning Symbiosis

Within the self-contained ecosystem of the coral reef various other micro-systems are at work, organisms receiving benefit from their association with others. The system of fish cleaning is just such a system. Some small fish and invertebrates live off the damaged tissue, bacteria and parasites present on the skin of other larger marine creatures.

Shrimps are common cleaners, most noticeably Pederson cleaner shrimps and banded coral shrimps. They wave their long antennae to attract the attention of prospective customers. In the Caribbean the main cleaner fish are gobies and juvenile wrasse (especially blueheads whose juveniles are bright yellow like many of the gobies) and butterflyfish. While the gobies remain cleaners all their lives, the wrasse and butterflyfish cease to be cleaners when they mature.

The gobies are well adapted to their specialised life, having long pointed noses and teeth like tweezers able to pick over their customers' scales. Gobies have bright horizontal stripes, almost identical to their counterparts on the Indo-Pacific reefs, the cleaner wrasse. It would seem that this coloration is recognised by fish around the world as belonging to cleaner fish. Recognition and acknowledgement of the cleaner role is vital for the system to work. If fish being cleaned ate the cleaners, relationships would fall apart pretty quickly.

To avoid misunderstandings, ritualised behaviour patterns have evolved. These involve some rather peculiar poses such as the head down position. You will also see fish stationary with their mouth wide open while the cleaners tidy their teeth and gills. It can be a bit alarming coming across such a sight when the fish is a large barracuda.

It would seem that the cleaner fish and shrimps provide a much needed service to the reef

A banded coral shrimp waving its antennae to attract customers to its cleaning station.

fish. A fish with a wound or infestation will visit a cleaning station and will invariably present the damaged area for cleaning. Experiments involving the removal of all cleaner organisms from a reef resulted in the mass evacuation of many reef fish. Only those which were strongly territorial remained, an example of one instinct dominating over another. The remaining fish all showed signs of increased infestations and soon began to look rather ragged.

Cleaning stations are one example of how the reef community works together to support the entire system. Both the cleaners and the cleaned gain from the relationship, so it is called mutualism. Other forms of symbiosis are parasitic, where one creature gains at the other's cost, and commensalism where one gains but the other is left unharmed.

inches to a couple of feet across. If they withdraw their tentacles in response to your presence you will be left with a leathery patch, pock marked where the tentacles once were.

Eager to see as much of the reef as possible, we move further west where the reef begins to show a wider variety of coral. Boulder star and sheet coral occur along with thickets of staghorn coral becoming more common, white tips like a light at the end of each branch. Sea plumes increase in volume, too. Some of the plumes are tall and hide areas of finger and pencil coral.

What looks like a small spinning top is lying on some coral rubble. It proves to be a chocolate-lined top snail. About an inch wide the whorl of the shell is a mix of chocolate brown and cream; it looks almost good enough to eat. The mollusk in the shell grazes on the coral, having a preference for sheet coral.

We see two cleaning stations as we move along the reef. Just before we ascend, our eyes are caught by a flurry of activity as a small school of Creole wrasse completely overwhelms the noble attempts of several cleaner fish to cope with the demand. Half a dozen sharknose gobies are helped by juvenile hogfish as, one after another, the Creole wrasse approach, hang head down or lie on their side, mouth open and wait to be cleaned.

This is a high speed, swim-through fish wash at rush hour. We have every sympathy with the goby we hear mutter "Typical, you hang round all morning doing nothing then they all arrive together."

Thanks to Neil Winsborrow and Dive Grenada.

---

11 Spice Island Reef
20'-30'

We think of this reef as being like the nursery slope in a ski resort. Not only is it ideal for beginners but it is populated by a wide variety of juvenile fish. The small coral heads offer adequate habitat for juveniles without them having to fight for territory with the adult fish population on the larger reefs.

The site is a level sand area edged by a reef of finger coral and brain corals. The relatively shallow water means good light and ample opportunity to make a close observation of the coral. You will be able to see clearly the tiny openings on the coral from which the polyps emerge at night to strain the water for food.

---

12 Three Wrecks
40'

The name is something of a misnomer, being not three wrecks but one very large one cut into four pieces. So, why 'Three Wrecks'? Well, the sinking operation did not go exactly to plan. One of the pieces was accidentally dropped at another site (see Quarter Wreck: site 13) The ship was a large cargo vessel which sank in St. George's harbour and had to be cut up in order to be moved.

This is one of Grenada's sites that is subject to currents and the site is not dived very often, nor by all of the dive stores.

The stern quarter of the wreck lies in shallow water on the edge of Grand Anse reef. This is perhaps the most interesting quarter of the wreck; the propeller, deckhouse and engine room can be explored.

Surrounding the wreck is a pleasant reef with some good coral formations. Sadly, there is evidence of anchor damage and the reef has been heavily fished. The deeper parts of the reef are in best condition with schools of fish taking their chance among the fish pots by swimming along the reef edge.

Quarter Wreck 13
25'-35'

This is a new find which will considerably enhance Grenada's diving. Because it has been dived only recently it is in good condition and with careful management could stay that way.

The reef structure is a narrow ridge 30 feet wide, running from 60 feet at the top to 90 feet on the landward side. On the seaward side, the slope drops to 140 feet before turning into a proper wall descending to considerable depth.

It is a beautiful reef with an abundance of marine life, both fish and coral. Bright sponges and lush gorgonians dress the slope and it has its share of interesting inanimates too. Several encrusted old Admiralty anchors lie on the slope, one with its chain still attached and leading down the slope.

The site is subject to tidal currents bringing bigger fish in to feed and it is not unusual to see rays, turtles, barracuda and even nurse sharks.

Windmill 14
Shallows/
Sammy's Drift
60'-130'

The Grenadians are known for their hospitality but few nations have been called upon to open their homes to hundreds of bedraggled and confused strangers, as was the case on October 22, 1961, the day the 600-foot, 18,000 ton Bianca Costa cruise liner sank in St. George's bay. Any Grenadian over 40 years old remembers the selfless response of the town to the repeated urgent blast of the ship's fog horn as a fire took hold, first in the engine room and subsequently throughout the ship.

The newspaper of the day, the Torchlight, conveys the drama of the event and carries the story of a customs officer who, not content with helping people from the safety of his boat, leapt into the turbulent waters of the bay to assist with securing tow lines to the lifeboats.

There must be many untold tales of bravery that day as a flock of local boats dashed to the aid of the *Bianca C's* 400 passengers and 200 crew. It is not hard to imagine the fear, panic and potential for disaster, yet every person was saved barring two members of crew who were burnt in the initial explosion that led to the fire.

The rescued crew and passengers were cared for by the local

Bianca C 15
90'-140'

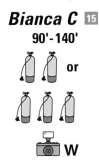

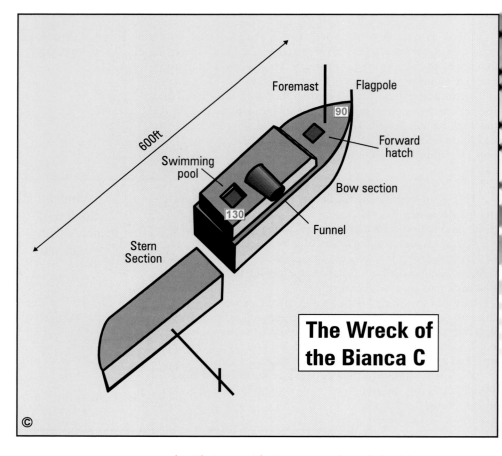

Foremast Flagpole

90

Forward
hatch

600ft

Swimming
pool

Bow section

130

Funnel

Stern
Section

**The Wreck of
the Bianca C**

©

people. Their contribution was acknowledged by the shipping company who erected a statue which stands on the Carenage in St. George's. The other legacy to Grenada is one of the most exciting and sought after dive sites in the Caribbean.

The *Bianca C* lies in 90 to 160 feet of water and it is possible to explore right down to the swimming pool, at 130 feet, as a no decompression dive. Every dive operator does this dive differently, some use a descent line, some do not. Most take a route from the swimming pool area to the bow before either ascending or swimming across to nearby Whibble Reef to complete the dive in shallower water. Bear in mind that you will only get about 10 minutes on the *Bianca C*, because of the depth, so be prepared to dive it more than once to have a good look.

A nitrox course is based on the *Bianca C* each year. These are the only divers penetrating the ship and doing decompression and technical diving on her. (See Contact Information for Mad Dog Expeditions at the end of this chapter.)

We do our dive on the *Bianca C* with Neil Winsborrow of Dive Grenada, the only Grenadian instructor working on the island. His claim that he finds the ship without the use of GPS means he accompanies two highly sceptical divers to the site, over a mile offshore.

We drop into the algae-clouded blue with only the line from Neil's floating buoy to give us any sense of perspective and at 100 feet see only the empty sea bed below us. Undeterred, Neil leads us a short swim until the outline of the powerful bow draws itself in the murk ahead of us. When you know what you are expecting to see you think you will be immunised against its effect, but some spectacles retain their power to 'wow' and *Bianca C* is one of those. Despite its demise, the ship still exudes an elegant dignity, commanding due respect, but in no way dampening our curiosity and we are quickly absorbed in an exploration of her.

The *Bianca C* at 600 feet is the size of two football fields thus, with the limitations of depth, you will not see very much of her on one dive. The ship—strangely we are reluctant to call it a wreck—sits upright, though the stern has broken away and more recently the funnel has fallen on its side. Because of its depth, it is only practical to dive the bow and part of the mid-section as a no decompression dive.

It is a pity that a lot of artefacts have been taken from the *Bianca C*, including the ship's bell. The wheel has been removed and sits in Grenada's museum. Nature has replaced many of these sights by decking the ship with elegant black coral trees, delicate hydroids and sponges, all of which cope well with the depth, as they require little light.

One of the favourite areas for divers is the large deck swimming pool. Recently, one side of the pool has collapsed but you can still swim right into it, as you can the cargo hold. Moving forward, the top of the bow is at 90 feet and the foremast is still

Dive Profile

It is still possible to promenade along the decks of this luxury cruise ship.

The Ship with Nine Lives: The *Bianca C*

The *Bianca C* is a ship which has had many different lives. A potted history shows a raft of different owners and three name changes. And, it is not the first time that she has sat on the bottom of the sea bed, though her current life as an absorbing dive site seems likely to be her last.

Built in the early 1940s, she was an early war victim, being sunk before even being put into service. It seemed as though she was destined not to sail. But, after the war, she was refloated, returned to her original yard, refitted, relaunched as *La Marseilles* and worked as a cruise ship. At that time she carried over 700 passengers in three classes.

By 1957, she was to see another refit by new owners and a new name, the *Arosa Sky*. She became something of a bulk carrier during this period of her life, carrying more than 1,200 passengers. This gives you some indication of her size. Despite the number of fee paying passengers, the owners hit financial troubles and she once again changed hands.

In 1959 the ship was bought by G.Costa du Genoa and renamed after his daughter, Bianca. Another refit, this time to become a luxury liner on a regular route from Naples to Venezuela via Grenada. It was only

2 years later, when anchored in St. George's harbour, that an explosion in the boiler room started the fire to which she finally succumbed.

The British frigate *HMS Londonderry* attempted to tow the *Bianca C* out to sea. Her anchor chains had to be severed by explosive charges in a battle for time to save the harbour from being

The beginning of the end of at least one of the *Bianca C's* lives.

obstructed by the now clearly doomed ship. While being towed to deeper water, a squall swept across the bay and the line parted. As impressive at the end as she had been afloat, the ship determinedly sank below the waves. This time there was no reprieve. As though to underline the finality of her fate, a Trinidadian firm salvaged her mighty brass propellers, for scrap.

Although the ship sank upright on her keel, she has been slowly sinking in on herself. The upper decks have compacted, especially toward the stern. About 3 years ago, the rear third of the ship broke off and fell onto its starboard side. This destroyed one of the swimming pools but left the forward pool intact. The funnel has detached and lies on the sand. The result is that the dive has been getting deeper. Local rumour is that it was once possible to skin dive down onto the funnel, but then we all know things used to be different in the past. Perhaps no one knows that as well as the *Bianca C*.

standing, although now draped with a tapestry of coral and circled by barracuda like art critics at an exhibition. There are plenty of deck features to explore such as the steps to the upper promenade, and one gains a real sense of the ship as it once was.

Meanwhile the *Bianca C* is on its own schedule of deterioration. It is slowly collapsing in on itself as evinced by the recent collapse of the pool. The time might be limited when you can sit on the side of a swimming pool 130 feet under the sea and imagine the chic Italian waiters busily delivering the pre-lunch Pimms while dodging the barracuda.

Thanks to Neil Winsborrow of Dive Grenada.

Generally rated as one of Grenada's better reefs, Whibble Reef is dived as a site in its own right and as a shallower second half of a multilevel dive on the *Bianca C.*

The dive takes you along a sloping sand wall descending sharply to 170 feet. The star boulder and brain coral formations are in good condition, clean and bright, supporting all the normal reef life. The reef has not been over-fished and you will see jacks, groupers, rainbow runners and bluehead and Creole wrasse. Like Windmill/Sammy's Drift, this is a site with a good chance of seeing divers' favourites: turtles, eagle rays, and lobsters.

Whibble Reef 16
60'-100'

As the only site currently being dived on the south of the island, Shark Reef appends another dimension to Grenada's diving. Unlike the sheltered waters of the west coast, the south coast is exposed to the Atlantic, giving rougher sea conditions and strong currents. The result is different sea life.

Scuba Express is the only operator diving this area and their promise of 'guaranteed' sharks was readily fulfilled. We lost count of the sharks and delighted in seeing turtles, too. Visibility is not as good as the west coast but it was adequate.

Always done as a drift dive, the current can nevertheless be variable in strength. For our dive, it takes off the brakes and we have a very fast exciting drift. We drop down the gentle slope to 40 feet. Marvin, our dive leader, tows a surface marker buoy, or, perhaps more accurately, it tows him. At 60 feet the slope flattens to a sandy bottom.

Immediately we become oriented, a big turtle makes a quick pass to investigate us, before swimming away up tide. It clearly knows we have no chance to follow against the current. The rock and sandy bottom is overgrown with sea whips and sea rods, streaming almost horizontally in the current. Many have retracted their polyps, exposing pink fleshy branches. Turtle grass and Y-branched algae cover much of the intervening sand.

Shark Reef 17
25'-65'

  W

Dive Profile

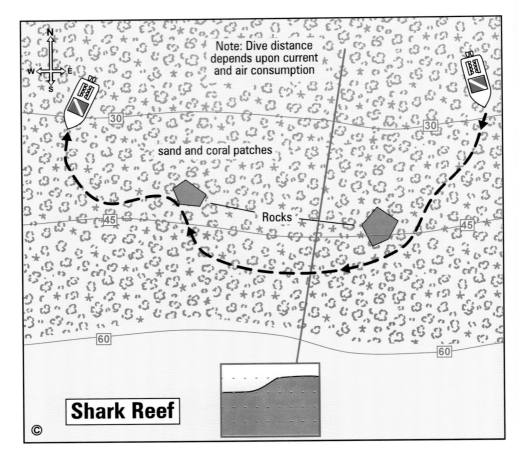

Note: Dive distance depends upon current and air consumption

sand and coral patches

Rocks

Shark Reef

©

While peering into the algae to identify a big shell, a baby shark swims underneath us, between our masks and the substratum we are examining. Determined not to be overlooked, obviously.

Our next find is a cushion sea star. These heavyweights of the sea star family grow up to 15 inches across, with thick short arms. Underneath the sea star are podia enabling them to move and to attach themselves to their prey. The sea star has a sophisticated palate, preferring a diet of clams and oysters. It has a rather strange inside-out method of eating, though. Instead of having to remove the reluctant clam from its shell, it forces its stomach into the clam shell, releasing enzymes to digest the creature. The stomach is then withdrawn, leaving the shell clean.

This is good habitat for lobsters and crabs, too. The big channel clinging crabs and Caribbean spiny lobsters crawl around the rocks. One lobster is so big we are reluctant to get too close.

The full grown and young sharks resting on the bottom are patient enough to let us take photographs, but not so keen on the flash. Small heads of boulder coral play host to a variety of smaller fish although inevitably the speed of the current makes the big game an easier target. Stoplight parrotfish, Spanish hogfish, slippery dicks and foureye butterflyfish all put in an appearance. We also see a very large grouper, possibly a yellowfin grouper. Small schools of grunts and yellowtail snappers ride the current, weaving in and out of the branches of the octocorals.

One large rock covered in pillar coral races towards us like a fairy castle. The down-current side has a deep ledge, a regular shelter for sharks. Moray eels find homes in this terrain and you will see a variety of mollusks, including conch.

The current is not always as strong as it was when we dive this site. More time to explore the terrain would no doubt reveal even more marine life, but for sheer diving pleasure a high speed ride is good fun occasionally. We calculate that we have drifted just over a mile.

Thanks to Marvin at Scuba Express.

Competing with the Caribbean skies, the sea bed has its own stars. This one, a cushion sea star, is at least 12 inches long.

Grenada Diving Facilities

There are seven operators providing diving in Grenada, plus a further two in Carriacou (see Carriacou section earlier in this chapter). We found it surprising that there was no diving association or forum for these operators to work together. On the contrary, there exists a level of friction and animosity among the operators which cannot be good for the future of Grenada's diving. To date, the government has not understood the need to develop a sustainable marine environment policy and the absence of a concerted lobby by the dive operators must only contribute to the lack of positive action.

Every operator is offering something slightly different, described later in this section, though there are a number of similarities. Almost all the dive boats are fast pirogues variously adapted to diving. Only one of the operators has a jetty so most board from the beach and dive entries require the backward roll method.

Only two operations are owned and run by native Grenadians, the others being owned and managed by British or North Americans. Most employ local dive instructors, divemasters or boat captains.

All the operators are diving pretty much the same sites although inevitably individual preferences determine the choice of sites to some extent. Day trips to the sites around Isle de Ronde (see Carriacou section) are organised by all the stores.

Equipment

Grenada tends to attract people who want to do some diving but who also want a variety of other activities, especially where not every member of the party is a diver. Many visitors to Grenada try diving for the first time. As a result, the operators cater for people who do not have any or all of their own equipment and so they carry a relatively high number of sets of equipment.

Grenada has a very high import tax making equipment for sale uncompetitive against US prices. You may find them competitive with European prices, though.

At the time of writing, none of the stores were offering nitrox but a company called Mad Dog Expeditions organises a number of trips each year to dive on the *Bianca C* using nitrox. They provide technical diver training and the opportunity to photograph and document the ship.

Cost

Diving in Grenada is slightly cheaper than the islands to the north. Average single tank dives are between $30-35 without equipment and $40-50 with equipment hire. The presence of several stores creates competition leading to a creative range of package pricing. Most reduce the cost of dives to less than $30 when a package is purchased.

Day trips to Isle de Ronde for two dives and lunch work out at just over $100. Open water certification courses cost between $325 and $375.

All the operators are located on the southwest peninsula of Grenada, close to the main town of St. George's and just a few minutes from the dive sites. All, bar one, are situated on the north-facing coast, on one of the beaches stretching out to Point Saline. Five of the seven operators work on the premises of hotels, although they do offer services to divers not resident in the hotel. If you contact them directly, they can steer you toward a variety of accommodation to suit a range of budgets.

One operator offers a somewhat different service from the others. Mosden Cumberbatch, the owner and manager of Starwind **3**, offers half and full day sail and dive excursions. Two yachts, a Gulfstar 44 and a Morgan 39, make daily sailing trips to Moliniere Point for sailing, swimming, snorkelling and diving for certified divers. Mosden, a Grenadian, is one of the original divers on the island. He has been diving for over 20 years.

Moving west from St. George's harbour along Grand Anse beach, the first dive store you reach is Sanvics Watersports **4**. The store is right on the beach in front of the Renaissance Hotel, a colonial style building offering luxurious accommodation in 2-storey buildings. The hotel offers dive packages for 3, 5 and 7 nights. A 7 night/12 dive package costs from $750-950 depending upon the time of year.

Sanvics is an independent store operating within the hotel and is happy to arrange accommodation in local hotels and guest houses. They even offer a free minibus pick up to get you from your hotel to the dive store. Due to open soon, next door to the Renaissance, is the Riviera which will have self-contained apartments at budget prices.

Sandra and Vic (got it, Sanvics?) took over an existing store on this site in 1994. Vic is a Grenadian come home to retire with his English wife Sandra. Boredom set in quickly and they decided to go back into business with Sanvics Watersports. Sandra runs the store but is not a diver so they employ dive instructors and divemasters.

From their beachfront location, they are also responsible for rental of beach seats and shades and organise deep-sea fishing trips. One fun event they have is a night dive followed by a barbecue on the beach. And, if you are taking a break from diving, try one of their windsurfers, kayaks, sunfish or jet skis, or have a go at water skiing.

Their main dive boat is 32-foot pirogue with two 115 hp engines, and they state that they always take the boat out if they have a booking, even for one. Sandra and Vic's son Jason drives the dive boat. The administration is well looked after by Sandra, leaving the dive instructors and divemasters free to take care of your equipment and diving questions. This is a well-organised operation with a pleasant welcoming approach to divers.

Just a few yards further along the beach a store known as Grand Anse Aquatics operates. Unfortunately, the owner did not make time to see us during the 3 weeks we were in Grenada nor on a subsequent visit, leaving us unable to comment on the operation.

The next operator along the Grand Anse beach is Dive Grenada **5**. Dave Macnaghton is the owner of the store and he is ably supported by Neil Winsborrow, a Grenadian dive instructor. Dave has been on the island for 7 years and has recently been granted Grenadian citizenship. Dave and Neil run an easygoing, informal operation. They think diving should be relaxing and fun.

Dave holds some strong views about reef conservation, however, and has been involved in various plans to buoy the sites in order to eliminate anchor damage. Dave is knowledgeable about marine life and is a good source of information about Grenadian diving.

Dive Grenada is right next door to the medical school and conducts regular training courses for the students. Dive Grenada is also the base for Mad Dog Expeditions when they visit Grenada to dive the *Bianca C.* Mad Dog mix their own gas, using Dive Grenada's compressor.

As one of the longest established divers on the island, it is not surprising that Dave has a wealth of background material on the *Bianca C* and Grenada's other sites, information which he gave freely to us and for which we are grateful.

The remaining operators on this side of the peninsula are in the next bay along. Based on the beach in front of the Rex Grenadian is Scuba World **6**. Owner operator Bob Dunn and his wife Pam run both the scuba and water sports for the hotel. The hotel was opened in 1993 and provides luxury accommodation with a stunning view across the bay. A raised beachfront terrace is absolutely the place you want to watch the sun go down, reminiscing about a day's dive. With a vivid enough imagination you could even see the *Bianca C* motoring slowly over the horizon. We must cut down on the after-dive rum punches.

Scuba World has the only conventional purpose built dive boat on the island. The *Islander*, is a Florida built, 30-foot dive boat with a 200 hp Perkins. It is a little slower than the pirogues but has good shade and shelter from the frequent short but sharp Grenada showers. At the time of writing, a 45-foot catamaran was due to be delivered which will be available for snorkelling and diving trips.

Scuba World offers a range of equipment for sale including Tusa masks with prescription lenses. Equipment is also available for rent to the Moorings fleet based in Secret Harbour. Whether you use your own equipment or rent from Scuba World, everything is carried out to the boat and put together for you.

Bob is very safety conscious and has strictly enforced rules about dive procedures, including rules relating to the *Bianca C.* Scuba World prefer you to do one or two other dives with them before you tackle this dive. They require you to be an advanced diver and to show log book evidence of deep diving experience. A descent line to the wreck is always used.

A local Grenadian, Rafael, drives the boat and helps with dive tours. Pam, Bob's wife, runs the shop, ensuring efficient shore-side service.

Right at the westernmost tip of Point Saline is Grenada's only all-inclusive hotel. LaSource **7** was opened in 1993 to provide a total body and mind holiday. That means many programmes to help you unwind such as Tai Chi, yoga, meditation and a whole host of body treatments from aromatherapy to a salt and oil loofah rub.

Included in the price is all diving except for courses, which are available for an extra charge. Resort courses are included, so if you are travelling with non-divers, this could be a good opportunity to encourage them to give it a go.

The LaSource dive operation is efficiently and professionally managed. The dive store, equipment room, and classroom are all immaculately clean and tidy. Both the store's and customer's own equipment is thoroughly washed each evening in warm water. The BCDs are washed inside and out.

One of the pools at LaSource is used for training, as the beach is subject to quite strong surf. LaSource has not been allowed to build a jetty, leaving the beach clear, though requiring divers to wade out kitted up and then swim to the dive boat.

The dive operation can provide all equipment you need except for wetsuits. The water is warm enough to dive without a suit but if you like to do a long dive, we would suggest that you take your own lycra or wetsuit.

About 25 percent of LaSource guests take advantage of the diving. With 100 rooms that means a booking service for dives is required. LaSource does have two dive boats and organises two dives every day, more when necessary, so getting a space on the boat is not usually a problem. You will have to meet the requirements to dive the *Bianca C,* however. You must be a PADI advanced diver or equivalent, have recent deep dives in your log book, or do a number of dives with the store so that they can assess your skill level.

On the south coast of Grenada is a small bay called True Blue. A dive store called Scuba Express **8** had been open a year when we visited. We met co-owner Marvin Wolf, an American who has given up his previous life as a science teacher to run Scuba Express with Ed Burd, a dive instructor with many years of experience diving around the world.

They are based at the True Blue Inn though the shop is independently owned and managed. Slightly less than half of their divers are from the True Blue Inn. The balance comes from other hotels and through recommendations from tour operators. Working in partnership with True Blue Inn, they offer dive packages starting at just over $500 for 7 nights and ten dives. Rates increase in the high season. The True Blue Inn will suit those looking for a small friendly hotel; the maximum number of guests is 24. Flexible meal plan arrangements enable you to try out local restaurants or cook for yourself in the kitchenette which each of the apartments has.

Scuba Express is the only operator in Grenada to have a jetty, making loading and boarding the boat a very simple process. The dive boat, like most of the other stores, is a pirogue. It has twin 100 hp engines making trips around Point Saline to the main dive sites a comfortable fast ride. Also working from the jetty is an independent operator with a glass bottom boat and a boat used for parasailing.

Adrian, a Grenadian diver, is an assistant instructor with Scuba Express and sometimes assists the Coastguard with diving tasks. He helped in the sinking of the Don Cesard. Either Marvin or Ed leads pretty much every dive, so you can be assured that the quality service that the owners offer is delivered first hand.

Contact Information

CARRIACOU

| 1 | Carriacou Silver Diving | Werner 'Max' Nagel | Tel: (809) 443-7882 Fax: (809) 443-7882 |
| 2 | Tanki's Watersport | Tanki | Tel: (809) 443-8406 Fax: (809) 443-8406 |

GRENADA

3	Starwind	Mosden Cumberbatch	Tel: (809) 440-3678 Fax: (809) 440-3678
4	Sanvic's Watersports	Sandra Thompson	Tel: (809) 444-4371 Fax: (809) 444-5227
5	Dive Grenada	Dave Macnaghton	Tel: (809) 444-1092 Fax: (809) 440-6699
6	Scuba World	Bob Dunn	Tel: (809) 444-3333 Fax: (809) 444-1111
7	LaSource	Gary Fisher	Tel: (809) 444-2556 Fax: (809) 444-2561
8	Scuba Express	Marvin Wolf	Tel: (809) 444-2133 Fax: (809) 444-1247
	Mad Dog Expeditions	Kourosh	Tel: (212) 744-2623 Fax: (212) 744-6568

Grenada and Carriacou Dive Operators

		Carriacou Silver Diving	Tanki's Watersport	Starwind	Sanvic's Watersports	Dive Grenada	Scuba World	LaSource	Scuba Express
		1	2	3	4	5	6	7	8
STAFF	Instructors	2	1	0	3	3	2	3	2
	Divemasters	1	1	1	2	1	1	0	1
	Diving Associations	PS	P	P	P	P	P	P	P
	Languages	EG	EG	E	EF GI	E	EG	E	E
BOATS	Dive Boats	2	1	2	2	1	2	2	1
	Shaded Boats	1	0	2	2	0	2	1	1
	Max. Divers per Boat	4-8	10	8	6-10	10	8-10	10	10
	Time to Dive Sites	5-20	5-35		5-10	10-20	5-35	5-25	10-30
	Dives per Day	2	2	OD	2	2	2	2	2
	Pick Up by Boat from	CRY	CRY		CRY	CRY	RY		CRY
EQUIPMENT	Equipment Sets	10	6	8	25	14	20	20	10
	Dive Equip. for Sale						2		
	Dive Equip. for Rent	•			•		•		•
	Photo Equip. for Rent	•	•				•	•	
	Tank Fills	•	•		•	•	•	•	•
	Equipment Servicing	•	•	•	•	•	•	•	•
	O₂ on Boat	•	•		•	•	•	•	•
	VHF on Boat	•	•	•	•	•	•	•	•
MISC.	Owned by Resort		•					•	
	Other Water Sports	•			•		•	•	
	Pers. Liab. Insurance	•	•	•	•	•	•	•	•

Tobago

Tobago lies northeast of Trinidad. The two islands make up one country, Trinidad and Tobago, but only Tobago is of interest to recreational divers.

Tobago is long and skinny, some 20 miles by 6 miles. Unlike most other Caribbean islands, it is angled more to the east and west than to the north and south. The land is low-lying in the west, rising gradually as you go east. The tallest mountains, reaching to about 1,800 feet, are close to the eastern end of the island. The main road is on the relatively flat coastal plain that edges the southern shore. There is also a good road connecting the north coast, as far as Plymouth, with the rest of the island. This means that it is relatively easy to visit many parts of the island, a great advantage for divers who would like to sample the diving in different areas.

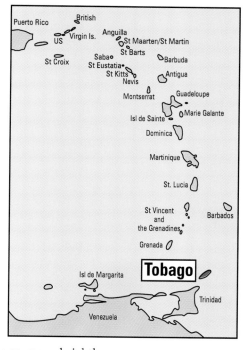

Tobago is wonderfully scenic. It has fine rainforest, several waterfalls and it is ringed with gorgeous pale beaches—beaches where tall palms wave at line upon line of surf, powdery white beaches where the sea turns turquoise and green before washing ashore, and isolated perfect beaches you can have all to yourself.

Tobago has another attraction; it was part of South America a million years ago and is home to a large variety of birds. Over 210 bird species nest in Tobago. These include so many brightly coloured varieties that, if a bird does not have more colours than a paintbox, you hardly bother to look.

Tourism has not developed quite as rapidly as might be expected in an island with so many assets. The reason is partly historical. A few years ago, Trinidad was so rich with oil revenue that it did not really need to look for outside income, and most of Tobago's tourism came from Trinidadians on holiday. With the drop in the price of oil, all this changed and tourism in Tobago is now growing. However, Tobagonians are very protective of their beautiful surroundings and strict regulations keep expansion at a reasonable island pace.

The main town, Scarborough, is on the south coast. The more interesting part of the town lies on a hill that leads up to Fort George, an historic fort surrounded by a lovely park with well-tended grounds. Trinidadians think of Scarborough as a quiet backwater, but for a town of 17,000 it can be pretty lively. If you arrive on a Friday or Saturday, you will be greeted with a whole week's worth of cheerful noise. Every other restaurant blasts music and everyone is out and about, laughing, walking, talking and buying and selling trinkets or food and drinks from tiny stalls.

Those who like to be a little off the beaten track will not find a better endowed island or more kindly and friendly people. In addition, the relatively low level of the Trinidad and Tobago dollar makes Tobago a bargain, a combination of assets that cannot last forever.

The northeastern part of the island is the most dramatic and has the most panoramic views. A road from Bloody Bay on the north coast winds through rainforest to Roxborough on the south coast. Several trails have been cleared. One of the most interesting takes you from high in the mountains to Bloody Bay on the coast. A small information centre on the road has a map of the trails.

The remains of an old road run along the north coast, from Bloody Bay to Charlotteville. This may be passable to the adventurous equipped with four wheel drive, but it makes an even more magnificent hike.

The Argyle Waterfalls behind Roxborough are within a short hike from the road through pleasant forest. Water cascades down three tiers and creates a perfect pool for swimming. There are other waterfalls at Goldsborough and Parlatuvier.

The Hillsborough Dam makes a pleasant destination and wildlife lovers will appreciate the cormorants, anhingas, herons and caimans. Look out, too, for kingfishers and parrots along the road to the dam.

The drive up the east coast from Plymouth to Bloody Bay winds through ever steeper hills with lush verdant scenery and precipitous views. In some places, the insects make such an exotic noise that on two occasions we have stopped our car, mistaking their call for an imminent engine disaster. All along are perfect beaches for a picnic, swimming and snorkelling.

You need to take a boat to get to Little Tobago, an island off Tobago's east coast. It is also known as Bird of Paradise Island because at the beginning of the century its owner, William Ingram, brought 50 of these exotic birds from their native New Guinea. He did it in part to help protect them, as the demand for bright feathers in New Guinea looked as though it would soon exceed those on the available birds. His flock did well until 1963 when it was wiped out by Hurricane Flora. Today, Little Tobago is a national park and has a good example of dry forest that is rare elsewhere in Tobago, as it has nearly all been converted to farmland. Boats are available in Speyside to take you across to the island and there are several naturalist-guided trips each week.

Accommodation in Tobago is well spread out, so you need to decide what suits you best. Store Bay is the major tourism centre at the very western tip of Tobago. This has the most hotels and restaurants, including the fancy new Coco Reef Resort and the more traditional Crown Point Hotel. Store Bay is by the airport, and if you prefer an apartment you will find one not far away.

Western Tobago

The beaches at Store Bay and at Crown Point, a mile away, are some of the island's finest. The dive shops here will not only take you diving locally, but can also organise day trips to other parts of the island. As this is in the flattest part of Tobago, it will suit those for whom facilities and services and easy access to beaches are more important than dramatic scenery and hiking.

Several other hotels are spread along the north coast just a few miles from Store Bay. The larger hotels such as the Grafton Beach Hotel with its sister establishment Le Gran Courlan, or the Turtle Beach Hotel at Plymouth, are self-contained enough that you may be happy without a car, and you can arrange your diving with the hotel. There are magnificent beaches all along this coast, and as you go further, the topography becomes hillier and more interesting. It is along this coast that you will find the Mt. Irvine Hotel with its own golf course.

The road is good, so if you rent a car everything is within easy reach of both Scarborough and Store Bay. A car also makes less well-known accommodation, such as the beautiful Arnos Vale Hotel just north of Plymouth, more accessible. You could also consider less expensive guest houses like the Cocrico Inn.

The other area to stay is in the eastern part of the island, from Charlotteville to Speyside. Here you are in Tobago's most magnificent scenery, with steep hills and dramatic views. This area will appeal to hikers and nature lovers who like to go to bed early and care little for social life. It is very quiet and, even if you rent a car, it is a long drive back from an evening of downtown partying. There are several dive shops both in Charlotteville and Speyside.

Eastern Tobago

Charlotteville is a small town in Man of War Bay, a magnificent bay enclosed by steep convoluted hills. It is scenically unbeatable and, during the dry season, the hillsides become dazzling with bright yellow flowering trees, making it almost impossible to put down your camera. Accommodation can be found in the Man-O-War self-contained cottages or in a few private houses that are available for rent. There is one cute but small restaurant called Sharon and Phoebe's, and two dive shops. It would be good to rent a car, as even the hill over into the next bay is a daunting walk, and Charlotteville is as far away by road from the western part of the island as you can get. There are buses, and with patience you can also get around on them.

Speyside is home to two secluded hotels: the Blue Waters Inn, set in its own perfect bay overlooking the island of Little Tobago, and the new Manta Lodge. There are a few restaurants, including Jemma's, where you dine in a quaint tree house, propped on stilts, round an old almond tree that hangs out over the sea. As befits an excellent diving area, there are several dive shops to choose from.

Language: English
Currency: Trinidad and Tobago Dollar ($1.00 US = $6TT)
Population: About 47,000
Telephone Codes: Currently (809), changing to (868)

Après Dive

Tobago is a peaceful island and you should not expect a busy programme of après dive activities. As well as evening entertainment, the larger hotels provide a selection of sports facilities besides diving. In the smaller accommodation, plan on quiet evenings watching the sun go down, interrupted only by the songs of the treefrogs.

Golf

Tobago has an excellent 18-hole golf course at Mt. Irvine, part of the Mt. Irvine Hotel. This course is in top shape and visitors are welcome.
   Mt. Irvine Golf Club: (809) 639-8871

Hiking

There are a couple of excellent operations that offer hiking in a group, with a guide who is really knowledgeable about the island's plants and animals. These tours usually run on a regular basis, but if you have a large enough group, extra trips can be arranged. Most large hotels can make the arrangements for you, or contact:
   David Rooks: (809) 639-4276
   Pioneer Journeys: (809) 660-4327/5175
   Blue Waters Inn: (809) 660-4327

The offshore rocks and reefs surrounding Speyside offer excellent diving.

Horse Riding

Horse riding is available through Palm Tree Village Beach Resort near Lambeau, just west of Scarborough.
Palm Tree Village Beach Resort: (809) 639-4180

Tennis

Blue Waters Inn, Coco Reef Resort, Palm Tree Village Resort, Le Grand Courlan and Mt. Irvine Bay Hotel have courts, normally just for their own guests, but you may be able to come to a private arrangement. In addition, you can play at public courts at Shaw Park off the Claude Noel Highway near Scarborough.

Water Sports

Day and term yacht charters are available from Kalina Cats in Scarborough. Boat trips run daily from Store Bay for snorkelling on Buccoo Reef. If you visit the village of Buccoo, several families there make a living taking people to Buccoo Reef and to the lovely beach at No Man's Land for a picnic.
Kalina Cats: (809) 639-6304

Shopping

There are just a few surprisingly good shops in Tobago, but they are scattered far and wide. The airport is a good place to start, as are all the shops in the larger hotels. If you are driving near Mt. Irvine Estate, drop by Marie's Place on the road to Plymouth. She has some good souvenir items and local books. You can watch batik and tie-dye fabrics being produced at the Cotton House on the outskirts of Scarborough. A few handicrafts are offered in stalls at Pigeon Point.

Nightlife

The biggest regular event is 'Sunday School' at Buccoo village, starting around 10 p.m. on Sunday evening and continuing through the night. All the larger resorts have their own entertainment programs that are open to all visitors for an entrance charge.

Information on Accommodation

T&T Industrial Development Corp. (TIDCO): (809) 623-1932
USA: (201) 662-3403
Canada: (416) 485-8724
UK: (181) 367-3752

Getting There

Tobago has an airport capable of taking large longhaul jets, and receives regular charter flights from the UK by Caledonian Airways. A Condor flight from Germany was planned at the time of writing.

Strangely, the island does not seem well served by its national airline BWIA, which has no direct flights from the USA. At present, from the USA and other non-European destinations, you will need to fly by way of Trinidad. There are regular flights and ferry services between Trinidad and Tobago.

Just as we went to press, American Airways announced the beginning of regular American Eagle flights directly to Tobago. Check with your travel agent.

The Diving

Coral reef development around Tobago is a fundamental component in the topography of the island. Reef-growing corals have been present for tens of thousands of years and the western end of the island, known as the lowlands, is a limestone platform formed from ancient corals. Buccoo Reef is the submerged extension of this platform and covers 30 acres. Although Buccoo Reef is too shallow for diving, there are many other reef developments around the island, providing good reef slopes and exciting diving. Some of the reefs are fringing reefs; others are fully submerged offshore, having developed on volcanic rocks to the southwest of the island.

Although all the common stony corals found in the Caribbean are present, brain corals have developed particularly strongly in Tobago. The world's second largest and the Caribbean's largest brain coral is found here. There must be something in the water. There is: the Orinoco River.

This massive river, similar in scale to the Amazon, floods out of Venezuela into the Gulf of Paria, is picked up by the Guyana current and carried north to Trinidad and Tobago. This renders Trinidad's water green and virtually fresh at some times of the year. Tobago is far enough away to avoid most of its influence, except in the rainy season (July to November). Water temperature, salinity and turbidity are all affected by this rush of fresh water. The most noticeable effect is the colour. The glamorous turquoise of the winter months is replaced with a more prosaic khaki. Sometimes it can turn quite a lurid green and at others a glowing yellow, creating an unusual golden light under water.

The influx of warm water from the Orinoco River results in water temperatures being higher in the summer months, promoting growth of algae. The turbidity of the sea is caused by algae particles suspended in the water, but remember that this attracts large numbers of fish so what may seem to be a negative can have a positive benefit. Visibility of 50 to 80 feet in the winter months is generally reduced to 30 feet in the summer. It is often the case that the visibility is only poor at the surface, clearing as soon as you drop below 15 feet.

Not all of Tobago's diving is on coral reefs. Many dives, including some of the best in our opinion, are around rocks that have become partly or wholly encrusted with sponge and coral. Some of these sites are predominantly sponge. Huge barrel and vase sponges, long trailing pore rope sponges, brightly coloured encrusting varieties and boring sponges, too, make for colour and textural variety on a par with any classic stony coral reef. And, as sponges attract angelfish, you will not see as many angelfish anywhere in the Caribbean as you see in Tobago.

If you are wondering why we have not mentioned the mantas, it is because they are only one of Tobago's assets and not a very reliable one at that. If you book a dive trip to Tobago convinced you will have the opportunity to cavort with large schools of mantas on a daily basis, you could well be disappointed. A school of about a dozen mantas does live around Tobago's shores but they do not always choose to spend their time around dive sites. Sometimes they will come right into Speyside and you can watch them from the beach. At other times they will not be seen for a week or more, and when you do see one it could be a vague shadowy shape at the edge of your vision.

We spoke to people who had been on holiday for 2 weeks and had not seen one. Of course, the lucky divers who do see them while diving, especially when the mantas are not feeding and are in a playful mood, will take back memories to last them a lifetime. Our advice is to choose Tobago for its varied and colourful diving, and treat the mantas as a bonus, not to be expected but to be enjoyed gratefully if they put in an appearance.

Tobago has a great deal of variety but until recently it did not have a wreck dive. This was rectified in April 1997 by the sinking of the *Maverick*, an old Trinidad to Tobago ferry. The ferry is 350 feet long and has been sunk in 100 feet just off Rocky Point, Mt. Irvine. The top of the wreck is at 50 feet. The sinking took place after our visit to Tobago, so we are unable to describe the dive.

She has been made safe for diving, though she has been left as intact as possible, to make for an interesting dive. Her engines are still in place and divers will be able to penetrate the hold, emerging through the bridge.

Tobago's diving divides into four areas. Each offers different kinds of underwater terrain and sea conditions. If you plan to spend your entire stay in one place, talk to the dive store you are diving with about trips to other parts of the island for diving. Most of them arrange weekly or on-demand trips either by boat or car, or a combination of the two.

Speyside

This is Tobago's famous dive area, home of the elusive mantas and the large brain coral. Other points of interest in this area are the tarpon and dramatic underwater structures. The diving in Speyside is around the coral reefs fringing Goat Island and Little Tobago and the reef within Anse Bateau. Additional dive sites around these two main islands and a number of other rocks are along coral and sponge encrusted rock.

Speyside experiences strong currents running from west to east, called the African Express by locals. Because of the numerous rocks and islands, the currents are constantly forced to bend around, causing strange eddies and counter-currents. One area known as the 'washing machine' results from converging currents. Some of the sites are located in areas of rough water, although Speyside also has many sheltered sites.

Charlotteville

Although some fringing reefs occur in and around Man of War Bay, most of the good diving is around offshore rocks, notably the Sisters and St. Giles. Currents need to be taken into account, but sea state is an equally important factor for diving this area. Around St. Giles, the waves can be very large making re-entry to the boat difficult and placing tough demands on the driver who has to manoeuvre the boat close to rocks. It is well worth diving this area, and waiting a few days for calm weather is a small price to pay.

On rougher days, Sisters, Brothers, and Cardinal Rocks can be dived in almost any conditions. The underwater terrain is predominantly volcanic rock encrusted with sponges and coral.

North Coast

Currently this is Tobago's unknown. Historically, dive stores have done very little diving here but new operations along the north coast are changing this. The north coast is scalloped, forming a series of bays with sandy beaches, steep-sided headlands and some ancient reefs.

From Bloody Bay to Arnos Vale are numerous sites, just now being explored. On one dive our divemaster discovered an old anchor that he had not found before. More treasures are undoubtedly going to be identified in the years to come.

West Coast

Known for Buccoo Reef, the area has a number of different types of dive sites. Submerged offshore reefs to the southwest produce some fast drifts, while the reefs in Milford Bay and Mt. Irvine are sheltered sites, ideal for quiet exploration of marine life.

Rules and Regulations

Tobago is in a formative state with regard to diving regulations. The recent formation of a diving association is the first step in the development of a policy for the management of diving in the area. And, a policy is clearly required if the development of diving-based tourism is going to avoid killing the goose that lays the golden egg.

At present, activities such as spearfishing, catching lobster year round and anchoring on reefs threaten the future of the diving environment. Reef protection schemes need to be put on a proper legal footing, so that the reefs can be protected for everyone.

Buccoo Reef has been declared a restricted area which means that only authorised craft are permitted to enter. Fishing is prohibited there and you are not allowed to remove anything, living or dead. While this is a good reef for snorkellers and glass bottomed boats, it is not generally used for diving.

Because of the strong currents, all dives are done as drifts. **Independent Diving**
Consequently, almost no sites are buoyed. Independent diving is
discouraged because of the problems of divers becoming separated from small dinghies. Some of the sites along the north coast
have less current and are suitable for independent diving, but
make sure you do not anchor your dinghy on coral, and please
refrain from spearfishing as this antagonises both local fishermen
and dive stores.

Many stores will not fill tanks for independent divers whom
they know are spearfishing on the reefs. Spearfishing by independent divers could well result in a call for independent diving to be
banned. This would be a pity for those who enjoy the freedom of
independent diving in this relaxed and friendly island.

Perhaps by the time you read this book Tobago will have its **Safety**
own recompression chamber. There had been a plan to have one
in place by September 1996 but various hitches meant that there
was still no definite date at the time of printing.

In the meantime, there are two options in the case of diving
accidents, Trinidad and Barbados. Trinidad has a number of
chambers because of the country's offshore oil rig platforms and
the associated commercial diving that is taking place.

The main chamber, and the one used by Tobago's dive operators, is at Mount Hope hospital, conveniently located near the
airport. Some operators expressed a preference for the Barbados
chamber because its staff is more familiar with recreational,
rather than commercial, diving accidents. Because Barbados services all the islands in this volume, (except for Martinique that
has its own chamber) there is a well tried and tested evacuation
and treatment procedure.

Tobago has had few DCS type diving accidents. When there
have been accidents, it has usually been related to boat handling
problems such as divers becoming separated from the surface
marker buoy or injuries from propellers as the boat manoeuvres in
difficult conditions. We felt that having well trained and briefed,
competent boat handlers was the single most important factor
affecting diver safety in Tobago's sometimes turbulent waters.

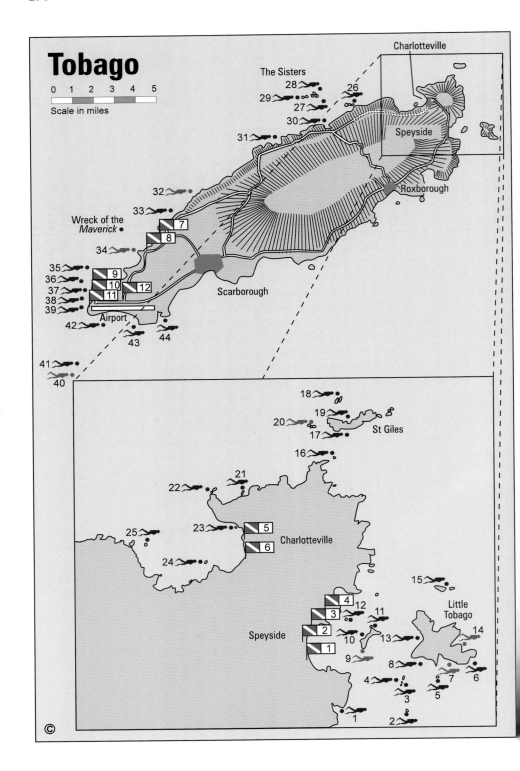

Tobago Dive Sites

NO.	SITE NAME	DEPTH IN FEET
	SPEYSIDE	
1	Inner Space	25-75
2	Shark Bank	50-130
3	Bookends/Paradise	25-75
4	Alps	10-70
5	Special/Isme	30-100
6	Picker	25-140
7	Black Jack Hole	30-90
8	Kelliston Drain/Coral Gardens	30-65
9	Japanese Gardens	35-70
10	Angel Reef	8-120
11	Back Garden	20-50
12	Aquamarine/Bateau Reef	10-70
13	Cathedral	20-100
14	Grand Canyon	50-110
15	Sleeper	30-110
16	Sail Rock	25-70
	ST.GILES	
17	South St. Giles	40-100
18	Marble Island	30-140
19	Washer Roo	30-70
20	London Bridge	30-100
	CHARLOTTEVILLE	
21	Sunker Rock	30-120
22	Long Rock	25-70
23	Pirate's Reef	20-40
24	Booby Island	10-35
25	Cardinal Rock	30-100
26	Brothers	30-70
	SISTERS	
27	The Quarry	25-120
28	East Sisters	35-70
29	West Sisters	50-120
	NORTH COAST	
30	Bloody Bay	30-40
31	Englishman's Bay	30-80
32	Culloden Bay	25-75
33	Arnos Vale	20-45
34	Mount Irvine Wall	20-60

Tobago Dive Sites (Continued)

NO.	SITE NAME	DEPTH IN FEET
	WEST COAST	
35	Buccoo Reef Channel	20-30
36	Ketchup Reef	10-30
37	Kariwak Reef	15-45
38	Dream	30-60
39	Bopez	Max 40
40	Diver's Dream	20-50
41	Diver's Thirst	30-120
42	Flying Reef	25-50
43	Cove Reef	30-90
44	Petit Trou	30-100

Dive Operators

NO.	OPERATOR	RESORT/HOTEL LOCATION
1	Tobago Dive Masters	
2	M-Dive Redman	
3	Tobago Dive Experience*(M)	Manta Lodge
4	Aquamarine Dive (M)	Blue Waters Inn
5	Ron's Watersports	
6	Man Friday Diving (M)	
7	Tobago Dive Experience (M)	Rex Turtle Beach
8	Diamond Divers*(M)	Grafton Beach Resort
9	Wild Turtle Dive Safaris	
10	Viking Dive	
11	Dive Tobago (M)	
12	R&C Diver's Den (M)	

*Owned by Hotel/Resort   (M) Member of Dive Association

Speyside

Speyside has more dive sites in a small area than any other part of Tobago. It is also the home of the elusive mantas.

1 Inner Space
25'-75'

A little further south than most of Speyside's sites, Inner Space is dived only infrequently. It is an interesting dive, nevertheless. Dropping down a steep slope that ends in sand at 150 feet, the tops of underwater pinnacles appear at 75 feet like the peaks of mountains.

The dive is around these mountains. Many fish, including large species such as tarpon, cruise around you. The pinnacles are covered in good sponge and coral growth.

This dive is rarely affected by current, but it is exposed to wind and swell, making the surface conditions rough. Surge can also be a problem. The dive boat stays in the shelter of the bay while the divers don their gear, before moving to the entry point. Divers need to be able to enter the water and descend quickly.

Shark Bank 2
50'-130'

A dive around this isolated rock can be very attractive and enjoyable. It is a small rock with a pleasant reef on the sheltered side. It is dived infrequently because the currents sweep past the rock, requiring too much swimming into the current. This is one of the attractions of the site for some divers. Strange currents can herald unusual marine life and, at the least, guarantee an abundance of fish along the wall face.

Bookends/ 3
Paradise
25'-75'

The old name for this site was Paradise but the visual impact of two rocks separated by a small gap and presenting vertical faces to each other was just too powerful for anyone to resist renaming.

The rocks are in an exposed position, making for a rough water entry. Thus, although this is not a difficult dive, it is classed as an intermediate dive site. Most people are prepared to cope with the conditions to experience this quite extraordinary dive.

To start the dive you pass through the gap then descend into a bowl like an amphitheatre. It is 35 feet deep, quite large; you can fit ten divers in it. The bowl itself has no life but, as you look up to the surface, you see the astonishing sight of the waves breaking and rolling over the bowl. They look like big clouds scurrying across the sky. And, just when you think you have let your imagination run riot, a big shiny aircraft shoots across the sky between the clouds. Or, in reality, a tarpon has just crossed over the bowl. A school of tarpon seems to live permanently at this site, presumably venturing further afield at night to feed.

While you recover your senses, you drift around the rest of the site at 50 feet, taking in the life on the reef that surrounds these two rocks.

Alps 4
10'-70'

On the other side of Bookends is a site known as Alps. This dive also begins with a swim through a cut that gives the site its name. The sides of the cut are like mountains and the passage like an Alpine valley. Unlike an Alpine valley, sharks sometimes hover here. The tarpon occasionally move across to this side and turtles come in to feed and rest.

The reef is in good condition, attracting many reef fish and invertebrates. You will see tangs and parrotfish as well as many grey and French angelfish.

Manta Rays—The Gentle Giants

When you consider that a manta ray can measure up to 20 feet across and weigh up to 3,500 pounds, it is a little surprising that we do not know more about them. Imagine ignoring the existence of wild elephants. But other than an occasional photographic feature, there is very little published about their behaviour.

In the absence of hard data, suspicion and myth have grown which has resulted in the fish being known as a 'devil ray' among many local people. The name is derived from the two horn-like projections called cephalic fins which extend forward at either side of its mouth. These fins are used to funnel plankton into the mouth. The more attractive name of manta derives from the Spanish word for cloak.

There is some evidence to suggest that the cephalic fins will close around anything that touches the mouth. The grip is not strong and some scientists believe that the manta does this to rub against things in order to rid itself of parasites to which it is particularly prone. Their habit of leaping several feet out of the water, before belly flopping back with a bang like a cannon shot, could also be a way of cleaning themselves. This problem with parasites may explain why they seem to enjoy being stroked and the apparent attraction afforded by scuba diver's bubbles. Interestingly, mantas can tell the difference between a bare and gloved hand, the latter being instantly rejected.

MICHAEL LAWRENCE

A manta ray—graceful, unhurried, non-destructive; a perfect role model for divers.

Mantas are graceful movers, using their wings to fly through the water. They are related to sharks so have no swim bladder with which to control their buoyancy. Their close cousins, stingrays and electric rays, have dealt with the problem by learning to live on the bottom. Eagle and manta rays have developed large efficient wings, making flight and gliding a means of staying afloat. The efficiency of this method is proven by the fact that mantas spend most of their time feeding on or near the surface, where much of the plankton is to be found.

Mantas give birth to live young. It is thought that the female manta carries only one embryo. It is born tail first, rolled up like a cardboard tube, a fact for which the female manta is no doubt very grateful, as one reported birth produced a manta 4 feet wide and weighing around 25 pounds.

Mantas are described as pelagic fish, probably migratory, yet the population around Tobago seems stable. Local divers claim that young mantas are often seen in one bay, leading to the belief that they go there to breed. At certain times of the year other mantas, apparently passing through, swell their numbers.

We may know little about the manta's life, but that does nothing to dampen the spiritual lift divers experience when in close proximity to these gentle giants.

South of Little Tobago Island is a small rock that offers some interesting underwater rock formations and much fish life. It is predominantly a rocky slope with a variety of intriguing contours. Beautiful fans adorn the surface along with bushes of black coral.

Numerous bluehead wrasse can be seen on the reef. Rainbow runners pass by as well as the rather strange looking African pompanos. They seem to be attracted to diver's bubbles and will often come very close.

Special/Isme 5
30'-100'

This is a favourite site with local divemasters, but they will only take guests when weather conditions are settled or they are satisfied that they have calm, experienced divers. It is on the exposed side of Little Tobago so the surface conditions can be rough and when the current kicks in, you know about it.

The dive is along a slope with a rocky bottom and plenty of hard corals along the incline. Divers often report seeing large pelagic fish and nurse sharks. Barracuda, black and crevalle jacks, tarpon, mackerel, morays, lobsters and mantas make up the list of frequent sightings. Even on a bad day there is an abundance of fish.

Picker 6
25'-140'

Another boisterous day in Speyside means we have to abandon our planned dive to Bookends and head instead for the relative calm of the south side of Little Tobago. Black Jack Hole is a sloping reef that runs along from the southeast corner of Little Tobago to where Kelliston Reef begins. This is another drift dive, normally taking you as far as the next headland.

At the risk of stating the obvious, it is named because at certain times of the year massive schools of black jacks pass by. It is also known as a reef where the mantas are sometimes seen. We forbid Leon, our dive leader, to mention this fact, as it will guarantee we will not see one. But, sadly, he forgets and drops it into his dive briefing. So, no, we do not see any.

Under the dive boat, the bottom, at 40 feet, has a thick covering of finger and pencil coral. Reef and longsnout butterflyfish root among the coral, and schools of chromis buzz about. As we begin to drift, a barracuda checks us out. We drop to 65 feet and idle in the mild current.

The slope is a montage of corals, sponges and a host of tiny reef creatures. Scattered pore rope sponges wave their branches in competition with sea whips and rods. Finger coral gives way to patches of star coral and boulder star, flattened into plate-like structures. Big brain corals increase in number as we move west.

This variety of sessile life attracts many fish, as many as we saw on any other dive in Tobago. The prize of the dive was a 3-foot

Black Jack 7
Hole
30'-90'

 W

Dive Profile

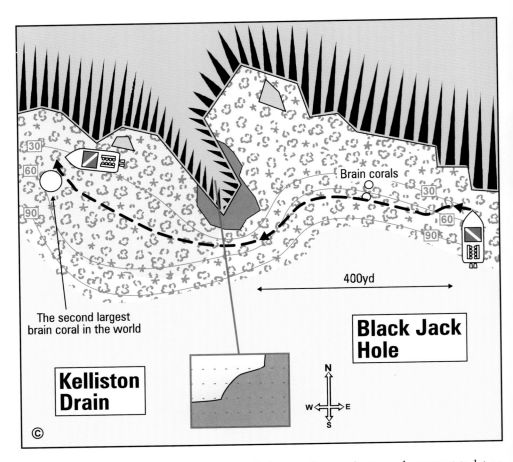

The second largest
brain coral in the world

Brain corals

Kelliston Drain

Black Jack Hole

400yd

N
W — E
S

Nassau grouper quietly snuggling against a rock, content to let us watch from a distance. Unfortunately, the natural defensive action of groupers is to try to blend in with the background, hence their blotchy markings. It probably works well against fish predators, such as sharks, but it fails totally as a defence against spearfishing. They simply position themselves for a perfect shot. Toward the end of the dive, we see someone spearfishing on the reef. We hope they did not catch our grouper, after it has given us so much pleasure. The number of sightings of large, mature groupers seem so low on the Caribbean reefs generally, that we fear for their survival.

Black Jack Hole does not deliver black jacks today, but it does display a bevy of black durgons, various parrotfish, scrawled file-fish and spotted filefish. A school of boga is with us the entire dive and a school of spotted goat fish amuses us for a while. They approach an area of reef, then swarm upon it, twitching their bar-bels as if polishing and tidying the place. When satisfied that things are looking as they should, they move off to another area.

The abundance of fish makes this a good dive to watch fish

behaviour. You can witness parrotfish defending their territories, hackles raised in displays of aggression. Black durgons dart into crevices, raising their trigger to lock themselves in place if alarmed by your presence. Sergeant majors guard their egg patches and show no failing in courage at the size of a diver. They rush toward you and, if you persist, they will nip your fins or hair. They cannot be persuaded that your idea of a wholesome meal is not a patch of purple mush attached to a rock.

About three quarters of the way through the dive, we reach the headland. The corner is steep-sided and overgrown with big vase sponges and fans, undulating in the current. At the bottom of the wall, encrusting gorgonians cover the substratum like a grassy slope leading to a cliff face, more reminiscent of an Alpine scene than an underwater scene.

Past the corner we drift over a plateau at 35 feet, cutting across the corner that forms part of Kelliston Drain dive site. We are on a mission to see the second biggest brain coral in the world. Across the plateau sea plumes and whips rock gently back and forth. We imagine they are working in concert to heave the body of water across the plateau. Pull, relax, pull, relax, a never-ending task.

As we reach the end of the plateau and close to the end of our air, a huge globe takes form in front of us. It stands almost alone on a sandy bottom, as if some lunar space craft parked on the sea bed. Over 20 feet across and 12 feet high, it is hard to think of it as a living animal. It is docile at least; thank goodness the sergeant majors do not grow to this size.

Thanks to Leon of Redman M-Dive.

Kelliston Drain/ Coral Gardens
30'-65'

The dive starts over a flat portion of Little Tobago reef. At 35 feet you reach the reef edge that slopes gently away. The reef has both hard and soft corals, the latter predominantly. Barracuda swim by, checking out the action, and trunkfish fuss around the coral.

The major attraction of this dive is, of course, the massive brain coral, putatively the second largest in the world. It certainly is a whopper. The dome has very few signs of damage and will no doubt continue to expand. It has little competition nearby and divers are sufficiently in awe to avoid touching.

Japanese Gardens
35'-70'

  W

This dive, around Goat Island, is acknowledged as a reef of exceptional beauty and we are not disappointed. Currents are extremely variable, from nothing to the fast steady flow that we experience. It is good to do it slowly, as there is so much to see, but a fast ride along the reef and through a narrow cut brings its own thrills. If you were to dive this site more than once, you would not tire of the experience.

Dives are often given rather fanciful names for which it is

hard to see the basis. But this dive name is descriptive of the cascading garden of hard and soft corals. Sea whips, like bonsai trees, and stony corals, arranged like carefully planned rock gardens, inspire the imagination and the image of an oriental garden is not hard to grasp.

Dive Profile

The drop-off point is close to a row of tooth-like rocks, off the southeast headland of Goat Island. The depth below the boat is 30 feet, on a base of coral heads and big vase sponges. It is evident that there is a great deal of current and some of us drop down the slope to 50 feet to try to get below it. We stay close to the reef while the other divers gather.

Deeper, the current is no weaker and the dilemma of whether to fin hard and use air, or hang on to the marine life is quickly resolved for some. When the group is together we set off at a fast pace, whizzing over a carpet of sponges, black coral and fans. The abundance of current-borne food has given rise to large vases and fat sea rods, locally called sausage corals.

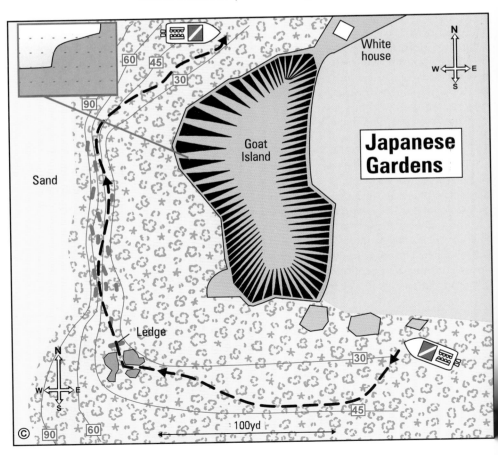

After 150 yards or so we reach the first corner. We have been briefed to stay close to the reef at this point, as we need to negotiate a 90-degree right hand turn through a crevice leading us to the west side of the island. The crevice is 6 feet wide and about 15 feet deep. Once you have committed to it, you are thrust through and spat out the other side. The trick is to stay low, horizontal and with arms, hoses, cameras, etc. tucked into your side. Immediately through, dip over the ledge and you are out of the worst of the current. Some of our group prefer to spin through, upside down, arms akimbo, with legs splayed like a rag doll tossed from a baby buggy, but seemingly enjoying the ride.

If you do the dive when the current is not throwing a tantrum, take time to examine the walls of the crevice. They are beautifully encrusted with sponges, star coral and hydroids, predominantly orange but with striking splashes of green and purple.

Once through the crevice, you reach the prettiest area of the dive. A steep slope marked with a series of coral ledges is a feast of colour and movement. The current has slackened off, but is still variable in strength. Tiny creatures such as arrow crabs, feather duster worms and sponge brittle stars comprise the insect component of the gardens. Bi-colour damselfish and the larger two-tone Spanish hogfish play the part of butterflies and birds.

We approach a second corner where the current picks up again and the plankton-filled water is as thick as porridge. This causes a feeding frenzy as fish hang in the water column like a swarm of bees. A stream of multi-coloured Creole wrasse, heading for the action, reflects the sunlight, creating an underwater rainbow.

Around the corner the terrain alters. The slope is now white sand from which tall sea plumes grow. Despite the vagaries of the currents, the size of the plumes allows them to retain a quiet understated elegance. They have a calming effect on the dive group; buoyancy is brought under control and the absence of large, apparently robust, lumps of sponge breaks the habit of hanging on to the marine life. Trumpetfish hang vertically among the plumes, perfectly camouflaged. Hamlets, too, blend with the autumnal colours of this portion of the reef.

Just as we are about to ascend, we discover a batwing coral crab hiding in a crevice and we are pleased that the current seems to have dropped enough for us to take time to admire it. When we surface, we can see just how far we have travelled as we are looking at Ian Fleming's House, right around the other side of the island.

Thanks to Tyson of Aquamarine Dive.

🔟 Angel Reef
8'-120'

Just in front of Ian Fleming's white house on Goat Island is a reef used by snorkellers and glass bottomed boats. It serves as a dive site, too. The dive is started on a flat area across the reef, moving on down a continuous slope. Generally the current is light at the beginning of the dive, picking up more as the divers move into the main stream.

The slope has some small canyons and plenty of holes in which you will find fish resting. Tangs, sergeant majors, trumpet-fish and Spanish hogfish provide the marine entertainment.

11 Back Gardens
20'-50'

A pleasant shallow dive at the top end of Goat Island that is not usually subject to ferocious currents makes this a good choice for a second dive. It is a gentle slope, alive with wrasse and rock beauties. There are many goatfish, and stingrays lie half hidden in sand patches.

The reef in this area is mainly hard coral with a covering of colourful sponges.

12 Aquarium/ Bateau Reef
10'-70'

The reef around Anse Bateau is used both as a training dive and a normal dive. For training, the gently sloping area of the reef is used, running from 8 to 70 feet. It is an ideal location for navigation training, as well as making a good night dive.

Further out on the reef, there are two rocks that make an interesting dive. The currents determine the dive path. The dive can be done along the reef slope or among an area of rocky overhangs and ledges.

13 Cathedral
20'-100'

One of Cathedral's claims to fame is the mantas. When they are about, this is one of the reefs they cruise along. It is a gently sloping reef with fairly consistent mild currents, usually flowing north.

This side of Little Tobago has developed a healthy coral reef, with plenty of reef-building stony corals to create a substratum to support marine life. Some days the reef is teeming with fish.

The northernmost end of the reef is sometimes dived as a different site, called Flying Manta, but it is really just a matter of where you enter along this section. Where you enter and what the currents are doing is important, however. An area to the northwest of Little Tobago is known as the 'washing machine' because of a whirlpool caused by swirling currents. It is a dangerous area and dive stores give it a wide berth. You should not consider diving this area without an experienced local dive operator. Local fishermen or boatmen do not necessarily understand how the submarine currents affect divers and cannot be relied upon to make correct decisions about entry and exit points.

We have been promised an exciting dive, on the exposed side of Little Tobago, weather permitting. The dive boat rides the big swells comfortably and is ably handled by Tyson our dive leader. As we round the northern headland of Little Tobago, waves pile up on the rocky coastline turning the water white and frothy.

In the bay where we start the dive, you can see the effect of the wave action on the rocks that, coupled with the name Grand Canyon, promises an interesting underwater seascape.

This area always has rough surface conditions so is generally a site for experienced divers. As it is also a deep dive, it is usually done as the first dive of the day.

The divers kit up quickly, eager to be out of the pitching boat, and we descend immediately to 100 feet. The first thing we notice is the thermocline. From the bath-temperature water at the surface we descend to a chilly 74 degrees Fahrenheit. We drop near a rock wall and, levelling out at 110 feet, we begin to move north

Grand 14
Canyon
50'-110'

  W

Dive Profile

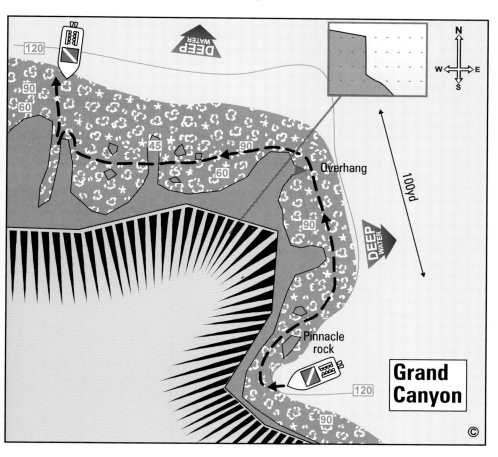

Grand
Canyon

around a huge pinnacle that has been discarded by the cliff above.

The rocks are dusted with purple which on closer inspection reveals itself to be a mixture of crustose coralline algae and encrusting sponges. A few patches of coral have suffered from the changes in temperature and salinity caused by the Orinoco River and are bleached. The resilience of sponges has allowed vase and barrel sponges to thrive in this Orinoco-washed area.

Big fish cruise this coast, and we catch sight of a black tip shark and a school of Bermuda chub. A queen triggerfish, sporting its identifying marks like slashes across its face, attracts our attention and leads us to a scree slope where a dramatic collapse has occurred at some time. Moving on from the wall, we swim across a flat sandy area before the terrain becomes a series of huge canyons carved into the cliff, presumably where the unforgiving sea has found lines of weakness in the rock.

The number of star and brain corals increases, drawing a variety of reef fish. We see porkfish, black durgons, rock beauties and schools of grunts. Spanish hogfish, blue chromis and juvenile bluehead wrasse add to the busyness of the seascape. Some of the rocks are overgrown with fire corals and, as we still feel the surge at 70 feet, good buoyancy control is a benefit. Soapfish do not worry about the surge, they simply lie tucked inside small crevices.

We feel a shadow above us and look up to see the metallic flash of a tarpon. They normally school so we look around for others but this one seems alone. It is around 4 feet long and we see its powerful forked tail.

At the end of the dive, we swim away from the rocks to do our safety stop and prepare to board the boat in these big seas. Strong arms take weight belts and BCDs from us. We are helped to board quickly and safely by an efficient team of boat handlers and divemasters.

Thanks to Tyson and his team from Aquamarine Dive.

---

15 Sleeper
30'-110'

The dive is around the rocks to the north of Little Tobago, along a gentle slope down to 50 feet then a steep drop-off. Strong current washes these rocks, giving rise to hungry marine life such as barracuda, sharks and jacks. There is no reef but the rocks have a healthy coating of various encrusting animals, well fed by the currents.

---

16 Sail Rock
25'-70'

Diving Sail Rock is like diving around a pinnacle. You can circumnavigate the whole rock during the dive, but do not miss the underwater bridge. The dive leader will need to deflate the surface marker buoy to pass through, inflating it when you reach the other side. It is a very pretty dive, with good coral growth and a chance of seeing schools of rainbow runners and horse-eye jacks.

Bleached Coral—Where Has All the Colour Gone?

Imagine if you could only survive in an air-conditioned bubble where the temperature, light, air quality and humidity must be carefully controlled within narrow limits. And then, someone leaves a door open!

The coral reef environment is rather like this protected environment, and hard corals are the most sensitive occupants of the bubble. Under normal circumstances this causes no problems as the reef ecosystem is self-regulatory, creating a very stable environment.

Coral requires a water temperature of between 72 and 85 degrees Fahrenheit. It likes the salinity to be about 35 parts per thousand and can tolerate only 20 parts per million of nitrates. For comparison, fish can tolerate up to 100 ppm. The water must also be clear because the zooxanthellae living within the coral need light and the coral needs the zooxanthellae in order to grow adequately. The manner in which reef creatures hoover up virtually every bit of floating plankton serves to help keep the water clear.

So far so good. But what happens when someone 'leaves the door open,' like man-made pollution running off the land pouring nitrates into the water? Or, in the case of Tobago, how does the coral cope with the Orinoco River bringing fresh water to change the salinity levels, create thermoclines and increase turbidity? Or, during the hurricane season, how do Caribbean reefs react to lower light levels caused by silting?

What seems to happen when faced with a changed environment is that the coral expels its zooxanthellae. No one completely understands why, but the evidence is clear for anyone to see. Because it is the zooxanthellae which give coral its colour

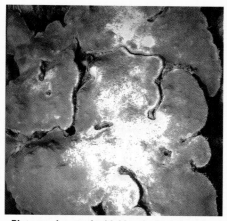

Plate coral spotted with bleached areas where zooxanthellae have moved out or been ejected.

(coral polyps are transparent), coral without any zooxanthellae is white which is the colour of its calcium carbonate skeleton, hence the term 'bleached'. People often think this means the coral is dead, but that is not so. The polyps can survive for a short time but skeletal growth will be very slow, making it highly susceptible to damage because it cannot repair injured tissue before boring and encrusting organisms take hold.

This is because one of the coral animal's waste products is carbon dioxide which when mixed with water becomes carbonic acid, a substance which dissolves calcium. But, because zooxanthellae are plants, they use the carbon dioxide to photosynthesise food, eliminating the production of carbonic acid. In addition, the zooxanthellae significantly increase the amount of food available to the coral, allowing it to grow and repair itself.

If conditions return to acceptable levels, the zooxanthellae will return. Rather as it is for us, a coral's good colour is a sign of good health.

St. Giles

At the easternmost end of Tobago is a cluster of offshore rocks centred on the uninhabited island of St. Giles. Uninhabited, that is, except for large colonies of breeding sea birds: tropic birds, frigates and boobies.

Around these rocks the diving is very exciting and, being further offshore, they attract good marine life. There are more stony corals than sponges, unlike Speyside, and the terrain is rocky with encrustation rather than coral reef.

Like all good things, it comes at a price. It can only be dived when weather conditions are suitable, with experienced divers who do not get seasick. From Charlotteville, the boat trip is relatively sheltered, apart from the last section when approaching the island. From Speyside, the trip is more exposed and longer. Consequently, the Charlotteville operators dive the area more often than Speyside stores, who will usually require a minimum number of divers who want to make the trip.

Competent divemasters are needed to lead these dives. They need to be able to judge the dive from the surface conditions and have the confidence to abort when necessary. Equally important is an experienced pair of hands at the helm of the boat. The boat driver has to take the boat close into the rocks, be able to manoeuvre safely and to follow the surface marker buoy in sometimes difficult conditions. It is not uncommon for surface conditions to change during a dive.

There are five main dive sites around St. Giles; we have described four below. The fifth is on the outside of Melville Island but is so exposed as to be dived very rarely.

---

17 South St. Giles
40'-100'

Some operators dive along the south and west side of the island. This is across rocky terrain encrusted in hard coral and sponges. The dive can take in the rocky bottom joining St. Giles to London Bridge.

The seascape takes the form of rocky outcrops over which schools of fish cruise in the current. Elkhorn coral populates the top of these rocky areas, surviving well in the rough water typical of this area.

---

18 Marble Island
30'-140'

Described as one island, it is actually two rocks that you can pass between when conditions are calm. The dive starts on the outside of the rocks where it is very steep, dropping to 150 feet. Diving at 70 feet, the first 10 minutes of the dive reveals little growth. As the wall flattens out, it becomes more encrusted with stony corals. Reef fish are abundant and, as with all the St. Giles' sites, there is a good chance of seeing interesting pelagic fish. More of a certainty is that you will be rewarded with the sight of big midnight parrotfish.

The name has nothing to do with kangaroos, it is the local name for midnight parrotfish that occur in large numbers here.

This is typical of St. Giles' rocky dive sites, having more than its fair share of holes, overhangs and crevices to explore. These cryptic spots are occupied by lobsters, crabs, moray eels, and resting squirrelfish.

It is a rarely dived site, making it easy to approach the fish, which are more curious than nervous. Although there is current here sometimes, often there is none, allowing plenty of time to mooch in crevices and hover quietly watching the fish in their natural habitat.

Washer Roo 19
30'-70'

Diving the St. Giles area is always weather dependent, so we do not know until we leave Man of War Bay if we will be able to dive these offshore rocks. Not until we arrive at London Bridge will we know whether the waves, surge and current will allow us to dive through the bridge. If there is even the slightest swell, the funnelling effect of the rocks leading to the hole accentuates its effect, making the passage through the hole unsafe. We are lucky, the elements conspire to be kind; we are able to do the dive as we hoped.

From the surface, London Bridge is easily identified; the largest of a group of rocks to the north of St. Giles has a hole right through the middle like a polo mint. Half of the hole is above the surface and the bottom half is submerged. The waves delight in crashing through the hole then rushing back as if they fear what lies on the other side, like children playing chicken. We, on the other hand, are very much looking forward to passing through to the other side.

London Bridge 20
30'-100'

  W

Dexter, the boat driver, manoeuvres the boat carefully in the entrance to the hole. So close are we to the rocks, executing a backward roll seems likely to risk a bang on the head. Of course, we have been positioned safely and we drop into the water to begin our descent to the entrance of the hole. From the northern side, the entrance is wide; the bottom is at 35 feet and about 15 feet across.

The base of the hole is made up of huge slabs of rock like a magnified cobbled street. As we begin to swim through and the hole narrows, we feel the thrust and tug of the water movement. The fish sway back and forth, suspended in space. Tangs, ocean surgeonfish, French angelfish, trunkfish and trumpetfish occupy the channel. The vertical walls are encrusted with yellow and orange sponges and probably a whole lot more, but we are too fascinated by our exciting journey through the passage to take much notice.

Toward the end of the passage, it narrows to around 3 feet. The vertical sides tower above us. At the end of the hole there is

Dive Profile

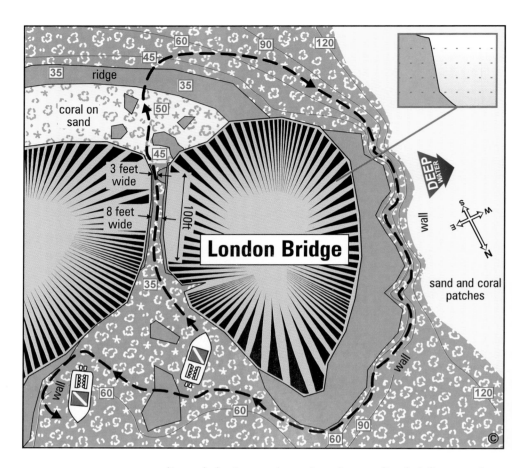

a lip and the instructions given in our dive briefing are clear: swim over and immediately down to get out of the surge and current. We tip over the edge and find ourselves at 45 feet, in an area of sand punctuated with big blocks like giant chess pieces. We are dwarfed by the terrain, as though, like Alice, we are not the right size for the environment.

There is a flat area leading to a ridge that rises to 35 feet. The ridge is covered in vase sponges and a mass of fish and, thinking the excitement is over, we begin to examine the marine life. But, over the ridge we swim a short way before the mild current begins to carry us along a vertical wall, buzzing with life. Exquisite crinoids extend their long arms from vase sponges; green, yellow and amber varieties occur here. We dive the wall at 70 feet but it seems equally lavish deeper and shallower. Deepwater sea fans are prolific at this depth as is wire coral and many hydroids. You will find tiny slate pencil urchins if you look carefully, 1 to 2 inches long, looking like sputniks.

Green finger sponges, dark volcanic sponges, yellow tube

sponges and giant vase sponges oblige many angelfish with a constant supply of food. Rock beauties, French and grey angelfish and a splendid pair of queen angelfish go about their business without any concern for us. Because the area is not over-dived, the fish are not particularly shy and simply ignore divers.

Just as with all Caribbean reefs, there is an abundance of parrotfish. Midnight parrotfish are not a common sight on most reefs, however, but we see many on this site. These big fish are midnight blue with lighter bright markings on the head above the mouth. Smaller reef fish, such as bi-colour damselfish and chromis, create soft clouds across the hard rocky surface.

The current carries us around a corner and we look up at the rugged structures above us. Angular rocks shoulder away the waves as they rush at the cliff face. The wall looks like a series of giant steps, another impression that this terrain is meant for creatures larger than us.

We swim around the western arm of the bridge and pass across the entrance of the hole. A large rock ahead of us has attracted a big school of boga. They swim in a polarised school, their silvery blue bodies forming a streak of sparkling light, an underwater fireworks display. We find a spotted moray protruding from its hole, mouth agape as if pulsating in time with the surge.

Over the rock, another wall awaits our inspection. We spend the remainder of the dive slowly drifting along the wall at 30 feet. We have to swim away from the wall slightly to make our ascent, to give the boat room to manoeuvre. But, as soon as we begin to go up, the current whisks us away. So, we simply hang in it while we do our safety stop.

London Bridge combines an exciting and unusual submarine terrain with colourful interesting marine life. If the weather is right, it is definitely a dive to do.

Thanks to Anne of Man Friday Diving.

The arch of London Bridge provides an exciting underwater tunnel.

Charlotteville

Although sites here are dived more often from Charlotteville, stores along the north coast and those based in Crown Point make trips to some of these sites, as well as those around Sisters.

21 Sunker Rock
30'-120'

Another of Tobago's craggy rocks leads to a steep-sided dive site. You enter very close to the rock, as the drop is sheer. The dive route is from east to west over a relatively short distance. The base of the wall is at 120 feet but, although it can be done as a deep dive, the most attractive area is at 60 feet. The wall has a charming array of marine life at this depth.

22 Long Rock
25'-70'

Just outside Man of War Bay to the east is a dive site around a rock just off the headland. It begins with a wall which then flattens out as you pass around the corner. Although not one of the area's most spectacular dives, it has a reputation for delivering exotics. Whale sharks have been seen there four times (none when we were there, of course). Ocean triggerfish, Atlantic spadefish and eagle rays are more common sightings.

23 Pirate's Reef
20'-40'

Tucked right into the corner of Man of War Bay, this is where you will go if you are learning to dive or doing any underwater navigation training. It is also used as a night dive.

Many small reef fish and juveniles occupy the reef and lobsters are often seen at night.

24 Booby Island
10'-35'

This is used only as a training dive. The reef attracts some fish and marine life, but it does not compare to the other sites around this area in either quality or quantity.

What it does have in its favour is some remarkable black coral around three giant rocks. This is a good site for night dives, when turtles are often spotted.

25 Cardinal Rock
30'-100'

Tucked inside Man of War Bay, this is a well-protected site, offering all the pleasures of diving around a rocky island. A series of big boulders steps down to 140 feet. The seaward side of the rock produces an almost vertical slope. The dive is generally done to 100 feet maximum.

Perhaps the main attractions of the dive are big bushes of black coral, sea fans, and hydroids in deep shades of purple. It is well endowed with larger marine life, too, being a place where turtles are sometimes seen. The shallower part of the dive is in an area of sea rods and fans with a number of hard corals.

Another row of rocks, but this time only a few yards offshore, makes an interesting diving area. Divers enter at the eastern end of the rocks and swim around them anti-clockwise. It is possible to pass between them sometimes, though the gap is narrow and surge can be a problem. There are often strong currents here because the rocks are poised off a prominent headland.

The dive is a mixture of walls and crevices, housing lobsters and eels. There is a good covering of sponges and octocorals, with more whip corals deeper. The rocks go down to 70 feet or so.

Perhaps because of the strength of the current, sharks and tarpons often pay a call, and big schools of fish are common.

Brothers 26
30'-70'

Sisters is a line of five rocks about one and a half miles offshore. Some dive operators dive the two rocks to the west while others prefer the three easternmost rocks.

There is also a dive further to the east around a sunken rock, known as the Quarry.

Sisters

The Quarry is barely awash and, like an iceberg, what you see at the surface is less than half the story. Below this unassuming peak lie complex layers of rock and coral. This multi-storied edifice sits on a sand base at 120 feet. Flakes of rock, piled as high as the surface, create just the sort of terrain divers love.

A tunnel runs for 30 feet, wide enough to pass through but too narrow to turn around in. It has a bend in it, making it quite dark in the areas shielded from the light. It is a favourite place for large green morays to sleep, so if your dive leader's fins start coming back rapidly toward you, it is a fair bet he has met an abruptly awakened moray eel.

The Quarry 27
25'-120'

This is a slow drift along a ledge, in 65 feet. The ledge protrudes from a steep rocky slope, covered in encrusted boulders. The dive route weaves in and out of the boulders. It is possible to pass through the gaps between the Sisters but it is shallow and rocky, making it difficult in the surge, and there is nothing really to see.

There is plenty of marine life, both large and small, around the rest of the site. The many fishing boats along this coast are testimony to the richness of the seas in this area. Expect to see all the usual reef life, living off the nutrient-rich water and finding adequate accommodation in the cryptic terrain.

East Sisters 28
35'-70'

29 West Sisters
50'-120'

The dive begins on the east side of two rocks, going clockwise around to the west side. The dive begins in 50 feet along a rocky slope interspersed with many nooks and crannies that hide lobsters, morays and, occasionally, sleeping turtles.

The slope drops to 120 feet, but the best part of the dive is at 80 feet. There is a good covering of hard and soft corals although the main attraction is big fish. Eagle rays are sometimes seen here but even if they do not put in an appearance for you, the variety of other fish will more than make up for it. At the very least, you are almost guaranteed to see dolphins from the dive boat on the way to and from the dive site. We have seen them every time.

North Coast

The least dived of Tobago's dive sites offer some interesting diving on ancient reefs, with the added bonus of calm water and only mild currents. The diving is perhaps less dramatic than some of Tobago's other dive areas, but the marine life is plentiful and the reefs are in good condition.

30 Bloody Bay
30'-40'

The site is named after the desperate naval battle fought here between the English and the French.

The site is rarely dived at present. Those who have investigated the area report that a number of peculiar looking lumps are the encrusted remains of ships sunk in the battle. The newer stores, along the north coast, plan to dive this area more frequently in the future.

The dive is around encrusted rock and sand patches. There is an abundance of grass that attracts turtles. Turtle grass beds are a rich source of marine life, different from what you would normally find on a reef. Look out for urchins, sea stars, stingrays and sea cucumbers.

One problem can be reduced visibility from river-borne silt, so the site will not be dived after heavy rainfall.

31 Englishman's Bay
30'-80'

The dive starts in the bay and runs out to the point. There is a gentle slope to one side and a steeper slope on the other side. The area is strewn with rocks and boulders that draw crevice-hugging critters such as spiny lobsters. A good many juveniles inhabit the area and, because it is rarely dived, the larger fish are unafraid and inquisitive.

We enjoy this dive for its interesting reef and the sheer quantity of fish. There are hundreds of fish in big schools and more groupers than we have seen on any other reef in the Caribbean.

Though this may be a new reef to divers, it is an ancient reef system. Signs of the reef's history are clear to see. The ancient skeletons of hematypic corals rise like the columns of an ancient Greek temple. Within this honeycomb of stony skeletons lie ancient anchors from ships trapped long ago by the reef.

Our divemaster positions us just west of the collection of rocks on the headland of Culloden Bay. The depth under the boat is 20 feet. The reef here is made up of a mixture of stony corals and sea whips. Big patches of bronze star coral look like crumpled sheets of sandpaper below us. There is a big school of chromis and various wrasse, but nothing compared to what we will see later.

We swim northwest toward the headland, along the base of the reef, at 30 feet. The sand edging the reef shows numerous signs of

Culloden Bay ³²
25'-75'

  W

Dive Profile

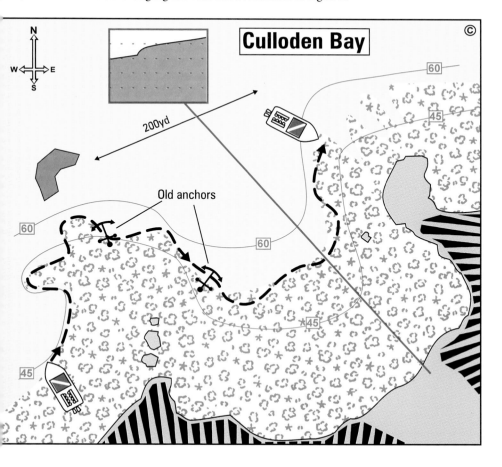

life, currently hidden from view. Burrows and piles of excavated sand litter the area, and we see a perfect print where a ray has been lying. A few yards off the reef, a tall sea plume stands like an oasis in the desert. A school of yellow goatfish dabble in the surrounding sand, drifting from one coral head to another like nomadic camels wandering from one oasis to the next.

This section of the reef becomes a mass of octocorals, taking on the features of a forest with spotted butterflyfish and bi-colour damselfish fluttering among the branches. There is a large kidney-shaped rock a short distance off to the left, which seems to be supporting its own reef ecosystem. We spot the ray whose print we have seen earlier.

The reef edge begins to take a more wiggly line and a small amount of current against us picks up. The visibility deteriorates slightly and there is a pregnant atmosphere. Looking around and ahead to see what is happening, we suddenly enter a cauldron of fish soup. The water turns from green to blue, as every blue fish in the ocean seems to have turned out. Juvenile Creole wrasse, boga and blue chromis form long polarised schools which part just enough to pass around us before re-forming.

We hang in the water, fascinated by this spectacle. We realise that behind us a school of Bermuda chub has also declared meal time. And large groupers, attracted by this fast food opportunity, pop out of holes all over the reef. Comb groupers 2 feet long and tiger groupers, normally slow quiet fish, become positively mer-curial, as they make dashes into the fish soup. A school of mar-gates joins the foray and cottonwicks and grunts hover on the edge of the main action, like spectators at a carnival. A group of black durgons take a more active role in events.

We are reluctant to be drawn away from this entertainment but Rennie, our dive guide, knows that he still has treats in store. Around the next curve in the reef, he points out one of the old ship's anchors. The 6-foot shank suggests that it held a large ship in place. A little farther along, we make out a second anchor. The line of the reef turns seaward and we remain at its edge in 45 feet.

This is now the ancient section of the reef. The skeletons of old corals have formed a complex catacomb structure on which younger corals have grown. There are star corals, boulder star coral, several different types of brain coral and solitary disk corals. These live corals have formed domes that in areas look like a mushroom patch or the tops of people's heads, huddled in conference.

We surface well out to sea. This reef is a horseshoe shape, the ends of which extend seawards and are dissected by sand canyons like tassels on the end of a scarf. The more scientific description is spur and groove formation. Dive operators sometimes start the dive in one of these sand canyons, called a sunk, and then dive over the reef.

Thanks to Rennie and Dolric, our boat driver, of Diamond Divers

This is one of the most frequently dived and attractive sites along the north coast of Tobago. A combination of interesting underwater structures and healthy sea life make it a popular site for operators along this coast. It is just a few minutes from Turtle Beach and Great Courland Bay where two dive stores are based and a new store is due to open in the hotel in the bay.

The dive begins at the edge of a rocky shelf before following a circuitous route around mammoth boulders surrounded by grainy honey-coloured sand that glows in the sun's warmth. The rocks are encrusted in a variety of coral and sponges, producing evocative colours enhanced by the sunlight penetrating the shallow water.

This area has more hard coral than some of the sites to the west. Large brain corals have grown and there is an abundance of star coral. Look out for tube worms embedded in the coral heads.

Perhaps the most attractive feature of this dive is the horde of juvenile fish living on the reef; it is an incredible reef fish nursery.

Arnos Vale `33`
20'- 45'

We have had a couple of days diving on the offshore reefs to the southwest of Tobago before we make this dive. It is a marked contrast to be so close to land and to see the line of the rocky shore that we will be diving along. Although current is often present, it is rarely the rip roaring event of the offshore reefs to the southwest of the island.

This is a gentle dive, allowing time to scrutinise the broad range of reef life present on the wall and in the many crevices and caves along the route. The wall, though small, is quite delightful and for those who like grubbing about in nooks and crannies, it can be an interesting dive.

Mount Irvine `34`
Wall
20'-60'

  C

The dive boat positions us at the beginning of the wall that confronts us immediately we descend. At 20 feet the wall stops abruptly on a base of sand. We swim southwest, except we keep stopping as we see one interesting creature after another on the backdrop of the thickly encrusted wall. It looks like a tapestry, a heavy brocade of rich colours with ribbons of yellow sponge reflecting the sun, like golden threads. The deep pile of the fabric is inhabited by tiny shrimps, gobies and social feather duster worms.

The wall runs between a series of crevices cut into the slope, each worthy of extended exploration. Some of the steep-sided canyons run 20 feet into the cliff face. There is a significant amount of surge as the swell hits the rocky coastline, making it an interesting exercise in buoyancy control. In this area the base of the wall is at 35 feet.

Along the rock face are white blobs, like cotton wool, as though the wall is not very adept at shaving itself. Closer inspection shows the blobs to be white condominium tunicates, dozens of them scat-

Dive Profile

tered about the wall in groups of three or four. Also attached to the rock are large clams. One after another closes up as we approach; we wonder what secret they are conspiring to keep from us.

One of the deeper cuts in the wall forms a steep-sided canyon ending in a cave at 30 feet. Swimming into the cave, we see a hole through the rock, allowing the sun to pour through and illuminate the cave walls. Looking up, sea fans around the top of the hole wave in the breeze, as if people are peering cautiously over the edge. Branching tube sponges have covered the walls of the cave, along with red and orange encrusting sponges.

The dive route then follows the edge of a plateau, thickly overgrown with gorgonians. Look out for interesting mollusks; we see an Atlantic deer cowrie and a clutch of flamingo tongues. The spotted design of this pretty little snail is a mantle covering the shell, which is a much plainer cream or pink. They are barely an inch long and will be found among the gorgonians. Many of the sea rods have been encrusted with strawberry vase sponges; only a few remaining branches protrude from the top of the stem.

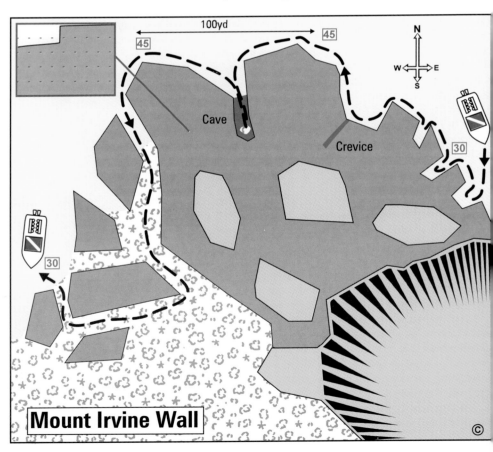

Mount Irvine Wall

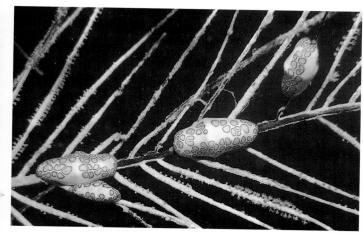

The spotted design of these flamingo tongues is on a mantle, covering their otherwise plain shell.

As we swim over the sand, what appears to be a cauliflower lying on a patch of algae catches our eye. A quick inspection makes it obvious it is an anemone but it is not until later, when we can check it against our field guide, that we discover it is a berried anemone, a creature not known to live in the area. This is turning into not just a visually attractive dive but an interesting one, too.

In these benign conditions your air will last you quite a while and there is more than enough to occupy divers with any kind of interest in marine life.

Thanks to Ashmore 'Fish' James and Andy of Dive Tobago.

West Coast

At the extreme western end of Tobago is a bay known as either Milford or Sandy Bay. The bay covers an area from Pigeon Point to Crown Point. Because this whole area is part of Tobago's lowlands, the bay has a number of shallow reefs. Typically, they are used as training sites. A few of the reefs are no longer used because they have been destroyed (e.g. Grouper Ground), or because local operators do not consider them interesting enough to take their guests, or because local operators want to preserve them. We have described below those which were being dived at the time of writing.

Buccoo Reef 35
Channel
20'-30'

We mention Buccoo Reef not because it is a frequently used dive site but because it is a remarkable reef area, attracting a mass of fish. It is a much better snorkelling site than dive site, although one or two operators occasionally dive in the entrance to the lagoon. Glass bottomed boats tour the area allowing non-divers to enjoy the spectacle of over 70 different species of fish.

The reef has been declared a marine preservation area. Removal of coral or fish is forbidden and entry to the area is restricted.

36 Ketchup Reef
10'-30'

At the opposite end of the bay, running south from Pigeon Point, this site got its name from a wrecked cargo ship carrying—now, what was it? Oh yes, ketchup.

Some say they do not dive it because there are so many other better sites. Others say if you know where to go it is a delight, but one that they want to guard for future generations. The reef has a good cover of gorgonians, especially sea rods and plumes.

37 Kariwak Reef
15'-45'

This reef runs along the southern end of the bay and can be done as either a boat or beach dive. It has a gentle slope with much marine life. Sergeant majors guard their egg patches while hamlets and damselfish graze the reef.

It makes quite a good night dive and is suitable for training.

38 Dream
30'-60'

This is a gently rolling reef right in the middle of the bay. Covered in hard corals, it can be an interesting dive when the tide is rising. Big fish sometimes come into the bay and pause to rest around this reef.

It does seem to suffer from poor visibility, hence the name Dream, reminiscent of the haziness of a dream sequence.

39 Bopez
40' maximum

Bopez, an area of reef plateau with a reasonable covering of coral and sponges is ideal as a check-out dive or for open water training dives. There is little current, giving time to explore the smaller marine life on the reef.

40 Diver's Dream
20'-50'

 W

Diver's Dream, on Drew Shoal that lies 5 miles southwest of Tobago, is in the full stream of the currents that rush up from South America and swirl around the island. At its shallowest, it is 20 feet below the surface, causing some surface waves and distortion of the speed and direction of the current. We dive across the plateau in about 40 feet of water. Other operators prefer to dive to the west of the shoal around the overhang.

It is rated as one of the best dives at the western end of the island, but operators may wish to satisfy themselves, before taking you, that you will be comfortable in the conditions that can be encountered on this exposed reef. As dives go, this can be a race track. It is not a particularly deep dive but you must stay close to the bottom to avoid being affected by a different current from the rest of your group.

While divers may be powerless to fin against the current, fish find conditions ideal, making this a great dive for seeing large pelagic fish and big schools, shimmering in the current. We see our share of sharks on this dive, although we are equally impressed by the interesting terrain and the colours of the encrusting marine life.

Finding Drew Shoal by GPS, our dive leader then assesses the current before deciding where to make the drop. Once positioned, our instructions are to execute a back roll on the count of three, dropping down immediately to regroup at the bottom. At this time of year, September, the top 15 to 20 feet of water is murky. We cannot yet feel the pull of the forceful currents but we assume this is because there is no visual reference in this green soup.

At 25 feet, visibility clears and we drop to 50 feet where we begin to swim toward the plateau of the shoal. Just a minute, we thought this was a fast drift. Well, not today it isn't. Instead we swim a little and then drift slowly, which gives us time to appreciate the interesting life on the plateau. The short distance to the plateau is over sand, with outcrops of sea rods. Normally, you would be whisked over this area, as evinced by the array of barrel

Dive Profile

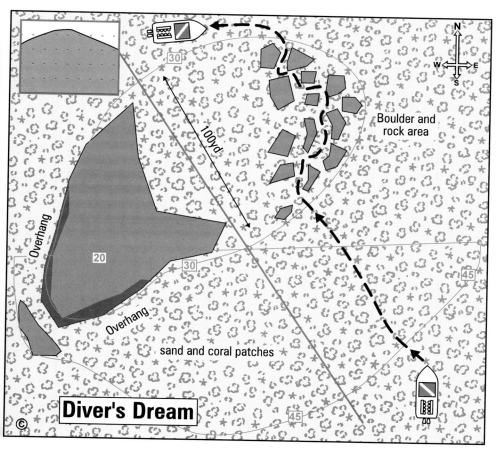

sponges leaning over at 45 degree angles.

Arriving at the edge of the plateau, our welcoming party is a large hogfish. It is unafraid of the divers and pauses from feeding to take a look at us. Its long snout is all the better to sniff out tasty invertebrates, and its crested dorsal fin stands erect, as if the fish is trying to maximise the impression it makes faced with a group of large creatures.

On the plateau, at 35 feet, we find rocks encrusted with orange elephant ear sponges along with feather black coral in matching shades of ochre. The whole area looks as if someone has made a conscious effort to colour co-ordinate the scenery. Thick apricot smudges of encrusting sponges blend with the feathery plumes of the black coral. Even the yellow tube sponges seem tinted with the dominant surrounding orange, as though this watery environment has caused the colours to run. In our imagination, the amorphous lumps of rock appear as parts of a rust-streaked shipwreck.

The surface of the plateau is like a large labyrinth. Rocky outcrops create paths and crevices through which we pass in single file, like ants on a well-trodden route. Where the rocks are undercut, nurse sharks snooze and a substantial green moray catches us unawares, or perhaps it is the other way round. The walls of the crevices are covered in a variety of sponges and where rocks do not create the path, large vase sponges mark the way.

With the predominance of sponges in this area, we are not surprised to see angelfish, though we are astonished by the number. Angelfish eat sponges and they seem to be doing very well on this diet. At least 20 large French and grey angelfish form a loose aggregation around one rock.

Tucked under a rock, a green moray eyes us suspiciously, but is overcome by curiosity. It emerges further and further to get a better look, or perhaps smell, as this is a highly developed sense in eels. In Tobago, you will find many green morays as well as the spotted variety. We saw several eels on every dive we did here.

As we weave around the rocks on the plateau, we are accompanied by big schools of fish: grunts, snappers, bluehead wrasse and longsnout butterflyfish. Numerous bi-colour damsels dash around, ducking behind sea fans and barrel sponges. And in the gaps between the rocks, rays lie partly buried by the sand.

This is an interesting, colourful dive. Some of the divers on the dive boat are diving it, by request, for the third time, as changing currents make it a different experience every time.

Thanks to Viking Dive.

In Defence of the Misunderstood Eel

It is unfortunate for the sensitive moray that its similarity to a snake leads divers to distrust it, there being no shortage of information about how dangerous sea snakes are. One eel, the spotted snake eel, seems positively to go out of its way to deceive. Well, rest assured, there are no sea snakes in the Caribbean.

A moray eel is simply a fish captured in a snake-like body. And there the resemblance ends. A moray does not squirm, it swims. Admittedly, having just one fin, its long dorsal fin, does require it to make long slow undulating movements but it is swimming, nevertheless.

But, morays do themselves no favours as far as putting diver's minds at rest. In order to pass water through their gills they open and close their mouths like a snapping dog. It may appear that they are interested in tasting you, when in fact they are much more interested in smelling you. Do not think that just because you cannot smell underwater that fish cannot. Many fish have a highly developed sense of smell. They can smell things we can only taste.

A fish's sense of smell is considerably more sophisticated than ours and moray eels top the table. Fish give off unique pheromones, a bit like body odour, which a moray eel can use to determine the type and size of another fish. Some scientists speculate that pheromones can also be used to determine emotional states, such as might be given off by an anxious or injured fish.

A spotted moray, more timid than its appearance suggests.

Two nasal canals either side of the head pass water over sensitive cells which detect the presence of a potential meal, allowing the moray to hunt at night without light. Moray eels eat invertebrates, fish and other eels. They can locate sleeping fish tucked into crevices by smell alone, one of the reasons parrotfish wrap themselves into smell-trapping cocoons.

The eel's other secret weapon is its ability to move backwards; few fish can do this. To make reversing possible, eels have very small scales covered in mucus and do not have gill covers, which would snag on objects. This explains how snake eels manage to bury themselves tail first into the sand. Garden eels, too, will disappear tail first into their holes in the sand, in no more than the blink of an eye.

In the Caribbean, you can find nearly 20 different species of eel, more than half of which are moray eels. The largest is the green moray, growing up to 8 feet long and as thick as a weight lifter's thigh. Islands covered in this book all have green morays but the most common types are spotted and goldentail morays, a mere 2 to 4 feet long. Garden eels are part of the conger eel family.

So if you are still not convinced Tobago's big morays are not eyeing you for a meal, make sure you use the deodorant liberally or buy yourself some shark aroma cologne.

41 Diver's Thirst
30'-120'

Generally dived to 80 feet, this wide area is like a submerged fault line. The terrain is composed of a series of ledges. The ledges overlap at obtuse angles, giving endless fascinating shelter for marine life.

It is difficult to find this site and not all dive stores are using it. However, R&C Diver's Den dive the area regularly. Nevertheless, i is a relatively untouched reef with hard and soft corals in excellen condition. As on all the sites in this area, sharks, occasionall including hammerheads, are a common sight.

42 Flying Reef
25'-50'

It is not difficult to see how this reef was named. Lying nearly mile offshore to the south of the airport, it is in its own flight pat as the strong west-going currents push the body of water throug the gap between Trinidad and Tobago into the Caribbean Sea.

The strength of the current will determine how much of th reef you will see. The dive site begins on the slope of the reef. Afte 10 to 15 minutes you can veer off the edge where it flattens out t an open valley of swaying sea fans. As you ascend to 25 feet a ancient anchor encrusted in marine life is worth checking out.

43 Cove Reef
30'-90'

Similar to Flying Reef and just to the north, Cove Reef deliv ers a good variety of marine life. The dive is along a steep re slope speckled with holes in which lobsters, morays and shark take shelter.

The slope is mainly covered with sponges and hard coral This attracts a range of reef fish, including various types of par rotfish, tangs and damselfish. Depending upon the speed of th current you can examine a mass of small reef life or watch th sharks, rays and turtles.

44 Petit Trou
30'-100'

The coral limestone platform that forms the southwest end c Tobago creates some fascinating structures. Petit Trou is part c these lowlands and, apart from providing an interesting bird san tuary, has a lagoon formation which divers can take advantage of.

The dive route takes you through a hole in the reef and on to th fore reef. Currents can be very strong so you will want to have som experience of diving Tobago's fast drifts before visiting this site.

Tobago has a long history of recreational diving; its longest established operator has been in business for 20 years. Yet it is still a nascent industry, experiencing growing pains and struggling to control its own development. Dive stores open and close all the time and there are no conservation laws in force. TIDCO supports the dive operators through marketing activity, but it is beyond its brief to regulate the industry.

The operators have recently formed a diving association that is still finding its way. Some members of the association see improving safety standards as the association's major objective, others feel reef conservation should be its primary role. If the association is to be credible, the priorities and objective membership criteria will need to be agreed upon, and it will have to resolve who will have the power to enforce standards.

Due to Tobago's currents and sometimes rough waters, the boat crew has a highly important role to play in assuring the safety of the divers. Generally, the boat crews we dived with were excellent, but there have been problems with ill-informed or unprofessional top cover. These and other safety issues are being examined by the dive association. It is in all our interests to support their efforts.

At present not all operators are members of the association. We have marked on the list of operators those which are members at the time of writing. Contact TIDCO to confirm the current membership list.

Most diving is from pirogues, and Tobago's surf gives jetties such a short life that all stores, bar one, board from the beach, requiring a short wade or swim to the boat.

Despite high import duties on diving equipment, many stores have invested in their business, resulting in a generally high quality of equipment for rent. Operators do not rent to people not diving with them, as Tobago's currents mean that the uninitiated cannot be depended on to return with the equipment!

If you have Sherwood, Dacor or US Divers equipment, there are a number of stores with personnel trained to carry out repairs.

It is possible to buy dives very cheaply in Tobago, but prices are rising or at least holding at a commercially viable level, as the pressure to meet minimum standards takes effect.

Single-tank dives with your own equipment range between $30 and $35. If you need equipment, you will pay up to $45. Most divers come to Tobago for a 1 or 2 week holiday, making dive packages common. Ten-dive packages work out at under $30 per dive. Expect to pay a premium for night dives, which will not usually include rental of a light. There are also various premiums for distant dive sites, for example Sisters and St. Giles. From the western end, dive stores will offer you a 2-tank package for diving

Tobago Diving Facilities

Equipment

Cost

Speyside, inclusive of transport, for around $100.

Open water certification courses cost between $300 and $400, but check what is included. Make sure videos for teaching are available and whether equipment, training manual, etc. are included.

Operators

For a relatively small island, Tobago has many operators—12 at the time of writing. The stores are spread around the island, covering the four diving areas. At the east end of the island, 4 operators provide diving in the Speyside area and 2 in Charlotteville. Beside their own discrete diving areas, these operators share the St. Giles dive area.

At the western end, four operators are located in and around Milford Bay and Pigeon Point. These stores dive the offshore reefs to the southwest and the northern coast. Usually they dive only up as far as Mount Irvine Wall on the northern side, though they do make trips up to the Sisters. Be prepared for a trip of an hour or more in the boat to the Sisters. Stores in this area transport guests by car to dive in Speyside, a journey of about one and a half hours through some lovely countryside.

Three stores are positioned at resorts in the bays along the northern coast. They are within reach of the dive sites around the numerous headlands along this coast; many of these reefs have had little or no diving to date. These stores are a little closer to the Sisters but a little further from the offshore drifts to the southwest.

Speyside

At the northern end of Speyside, at the end of a long private road, you will find Aquamarine Dive **4**, an independent dive store based at Blue Waters Inn. It is owned and managed by Keith Darwent, a Trinidadian, who has been running dive stores in Tobago for the past 8 years, the last 3 at Blue Waters Inn.

"Divers have to do nothing but breathe", claims Keith, and that was certainly our experience. The only dive store on the island

A converted pirogue, ready for boarding at Tobago's only jetty.

with a jetty, Aquamarine Dive even manages to get you in to the boat without getting wet. Their store is in a new purpose-built building with a pleasant classroom and ample space to sort out equipment, chew the fat and exaggerate about the size of the moray you saw.

The Blue Waters Inn guest book is a catalogue of satisfied customers, both with the hotel and the dive store. The hotel is managed by Reg MacLean, an experienced dive instructor himself who takes an active interest in the dive operation.

Safety is a high priority, manifest in the way the dive is briefed and the boat managed. The dive boats are pirogues with two engines. All dive boat drivers are qualified boat captains. The boat briefing incorporates information about safety equipment, i.e. oxygen, VHF radio, etc., so that all divers are aware of the resources if there is an emergency. All equipment is well maintained and none is more than 4 years old. Keith is a member and supporter of the dive association.

Although Blue Waters Inn attracts many dedicated divers, Aquamarine Dive carries out quite a lot of teaching. Confined water training is carried out in the bay requiring no transition from fresh to salt water.

We found this to be a professional, friendly dive store with the advantage of a beautiful setting in the heart of Tobago's popular diving area.

Situated overlooking Tyrrel's Bay, Speyside, the Manta Lodge is the home of Tobago Dive Experience **3** . Separate companies but with a common owner, the hotel and dive store work together to provide dive holidays. The Manta Lodge has only 22 rooms so the dive store is well able to cope with the diving needs of the guests. Most of those diving with Tobago Dive Experience are guests at the Manta Lodge.

Ray, the dive operation's aptly-named manager, is a commercial diver who still occasionally works on Trinidad's many oil rigs. He is an underwater welder accustomed to working at depths well beyond recreational limits and in zero visibility, making even the toughest of Tobago's dives seem almost straightforward. It is comforting to know that Ray is a qualified dive medicine technician. He will no doubt be recruited to help support the proposed recompression chamber.

Two-tank dives, back-to-back, are the most usual dive combination, although Tobago Dive Experience will meet individual needs and preferences. Most dive sites are no more than 10 minutes away. A trip to St. Giles will take 25 minutes. Teaching of confined water training is carried out in Manta Lodge's pool.

Tobago Dive Experience has Sea and Sea cameras to rent if you want to try your hand at underwater photography but, be warned, taking a camera on a dive is a guaranteed way of ensuring you will not see a manta.

Further along the road in the centre of Speyside, two independent dive operators have their stores. M-Dive Redman **2** is owned by Tobagonian Redman, a popular personality who seems to have nephews all over the island. One runs Redman's store in Speyside, another has recently opened his own operation, called R&C Diver's Den, at the other end of the island.

Redman, who is a divemaster, has no instructor on the staff but can arrange tuition through Diamond Divers. M-Dive Redman works in association with Diamond Divers, taking care of their guests when they want to dive in Speyside.

Diving with Redman and his nephew Leon is always a pleasure. They are friendly, fun and very careful. Redman is well aware of the perils of Tobago's strong currents and organises drift dives with knowledge and professionalism. From his beachfront dive store, Redman squints across the bay to predict the currents and suitability of sites for the day's dive, taking into account the phase of the moon. Currents will always be stronger when the moon is full or new.

Redman knows most of the original names for the reefs, some of which have been changed as Tobago's dive industry has grown. He is generally acknowledged to be the most long-standing reef diver in Speyside, having dived here for 20 years, and is passing his knowledge on to Leon. In particular, it is interesting to talk to him about the mantas.

And, when you finish your dive, Redman has built a restaurant on stilts overlooking the bay where you can enjoy a Caribbean lunch cooked by his wife.

A few yards down the road is Tobago Dive Masters **1** . Ellis the owner manager, is an experienced Speyside diver. He has been working as a divemaster and instructor in Speyside for the past 8 years. Two years ago he began his own dive operation, based in Speyside but drawing guests from the hotels at the west end of the island as well as Speyside hotels.

Talking to Ellis about the local dive sites, it is obvious that he is not only knowledgeable but uses that knowledge to plan dives around the abilities and interests of his divers. He likes to tailor your dive package to suit you.

As well as his store in Speyside, Ellis has plans to open a second base in one of the hotels at the west end of the island.

Charlotteville

Across the hill from Speyside the quiet village of Charlotteville lies tucked into Man of War Bay. Two dive stores operate here Bjarne (pronounced Piarn) and his girlfriend Anne are the Danish owners and managers of Man Friday Diving **6** . They run a professional operation from a pleasant, modern Scandinavian-style building on the waterfront. Kjeld, their pet macaw, entertains divers with his impressively colourful finery, and is occasionally prevailed upon to speak. It helps if you have a peanut in your hand.

Aquamarine Dive

We offer easy access to Tobago's most unique dive adventures. Our finest dive sites are only minutes away. Highly impressive drift dives, curious manta rays, richly overgrown coral reefs, and hordes of friendly fish. The plankton-rich waters make our marine life healthy, diverse and plentiful.

Full tuition is offered by professionally trained staff. We have 3 well equipped dive boats, a fully stocked shop; and we are the only dive hotel operation on Tobago to use a dock for boarding the dive boat.

Blue Waters Inn—A 38 room beachfront resort hotel catering to SCUBA divers, nature lovers, weddings, honeymoons and families. Our rooms consist of 3 bungalows, 4 efficiency apartments and 31 standard rooms. A full service restaurant and bar offering local and international cuisine and cocktails, with breathtaking views across the bay. Kayaking, windsurfing, tennis, hiking, car rentals are also available.

Associations:	**PADI Gold Palm Resort**
Associated Resorts:	**Blue Waters Inn**
Languages:	**English, Spanish**
Number of Instructors:	**2**

Contacts:	**John Keith Darwent (Diving)**
	Reginald MacLean (Hotel)
Address:	**Blue Waters Inn**
	Speyside
	Tobago
Tel/Fax:	**(868) 639-4416 (Diving)**
Tel:	**(868) 660-4341 or 4077 (Hotel)**
Fax:	**(868) 660-5195**
US Agent:	**Into the Blue (800) 6 GET WET**
	Maduro Dive Fanta Seas
	(800) 327-6709
E-mail:	**bwitobago@trinidad.net**
Web Site:	**www.trinidad.net/bwi-tobago/**

Aquamarine Dive

TOBAGO

WILD TURTLE DIVE SAFARI

Wild Turtle Dive Safari is ideally located at Pigeon Point, minutes from many of Tobago's dive sites:

- Experience the thrill of high speed drifts on Diver's Dream and Flying Reef
- Dive the MV Maverick, our new wreck site
- Enjoy the gentle, colourful reefs of the north coast

Wild Turtle Dive is a PADI training facility with caring and professional staff. We love looking after groups.

- Special prices for group packages
- Fully equipped 27 foot dive boat
- Accommodation can be arranged

And while you are diving, non divers in your group can enjoy a day at Pigeon Point. At the heart of the Buccoo Reef National Park, Pigeon Point offers a day out in paradise. Snorkel or swim in the crystal clear water, relax under a palm tree or enjoy a West Indian lunch. A perfect way to relax after a dive.

Associations:	PADI Dive Centre
Associated Resort:	**Sanctuary Resort**
Languages:	**English**
Number of Instructors:	2

Contact:	**Robert de Castro**
Address:	**Wild Turtle Dive Safari** **P.O. Box 154** **Scarborough** **Tobago**
Telephone:	**(809) 639-7936**
Fax	**(809) 639-7232**
E-mail:	**turtle@trinidad.net**

Wild Turtle Dive Safari

TOBAGO

Both Bjarne and Anne are instructors. They are very safety conscious and would like to see the dive association introduce minimum safety standards.

Man Friday Diving prefers to take a maximum of six guests, though they will accommodate groups of up to eight people. As they dive St. Giles frequently, they like to keep numbers small for reasons both of safety and comfort in the boat. They use a 28-foot pirogue with two engines. We received an excellent boat briefing and were pleased to have a competent boat driver to cope with the offshore conditions. The store has two regular boat drivers both of whom have been with Man Friday Diving for 4 years.

About one third of Man Friday Diving's guests are from the USA, the remainder being European, with a good sprinkling of Danes. A few yards from Man Friday Diving are the Man-O-War Bay Cottages, offering accommodation in airy spacious cottages ranging from one to four bedrooms. A double-bedroom cottage for 7 days including a 10-dive package will cost around $800.

As well as diving, Man Friday Diving rent kayaks, both single and double. Bjarne and Anne provide an efficient pleasant service, are well informed about marine life and offer excellent coverage of the dive sites between the sisters and St. Giles, as well as occasional excursions to Speyside.

At the other end of the bay is Ron's Watersports **5**. Ron is a Trinidadian who spends half the year in Tobago and half in Trinidad. He works full-time at his store in Tobago from late November to April. For the rest of the year, he works from his base in Trinidad, offering a full menu of training courses. Many Trinidadians do their confined water training in a pool in Trinidad then complete the course with the open water dives in Tobago. Ron also has equipment for sale and, as an authorised dealer for Sherwood, SeaQuest and Dacor, is able to carry out warranty work.

In Tobago Ron offers diving in the Charlotteville area as well as further afield in Speyside. He takes a maximum of six divers in the boat and prides himself on a personal friendly service. Many of his bookings are groups and he attracts much repeat business. His divers tend to hang out at his store in the evening, and a beach barbecue in front of the store is organised from time to time. He will even join you in a game of cards so you can win back the cost of your dive.

North Coast

Two adjacent bays, Great Courland and Grafton, are the archetypal setting for three Caribbean beach hotels complete with dive stores and a myriad of other water sports. Grafton Beach Resort, a 112-room 4 star hotel, and the Grand Courland Resort and Spa, a 5 star hotel, offering mainly suites, are owned by the same company and share the services of Diamond Divers **8**. The dive operation is owned by the hotels and aims to offer the same high level of service as guests receive in the hotels.

Diamond Divers had only recently opened when we visited Tobago; previously an independent dive operator had been on the site. Barry St. George, the manager and one of Diamond Diver's instructors, has plans to open up many new sites along the north coast, an area dived only infrequently by other stores.

Safety has been given a high priority when equipping Diamond Divers. Besides the store's two dive boats, a 22-foot Carib with two 150 hp engines is planned for a rescue boat, on permanent stand-by in case of emergency. No motorised water sports are permitted off the hotel's beach, making the water of the bay safe for swimmers, snorkellers and divers. Other water sports equipment is available, including stepjets, an aerobic exercise device. All water sports, except diving, are complementary to hotel guests.

Each week, on Monday and Tuesday, trips to dive Speyside are organised. Guests are taken by car to Speyside, make two dives and enjoy a barbecue lunch on the beach.

As befits a store servicing a 4 and 5 star resort, Diamond Divers is a smart operation staffed with conscientious and enthusiastic staff.

In the next bay at the Rex Turtle Beach Hotel, Tobago Dive Experience **7** has their second base, managed by Derek Chung and Carol Peck. This operation services guests of the Rex Turtle hotel primarily, but also attracts divers from other hotels and guest houses.

Just as this book was going to press a new store was due to open at the Arnos Vale Bay Hotel.

Milford Bay and Pigeon Point

The oldest dive store on the island, Dive Tobago **11**, is on the waterfront in Milford Bay. Jimmy, a Trinidadian who has spent almost all his life in Tobago, and his son, dive instructor Jay, run a friendly operation. Dive Tobago is one of the few dive stores to dive the reefs in Milford Bay. Their knowledge of the reefs there is unrivalled. Dive Tobago also dives the reefs to the southwest of the island. Again, they are one of the only stores to dive Petit Trou, on the south side.

Dive Tobago's boat staff are exceptionally well trained and courteous, making the boat end of diving a comfortable experience. Jimmy's wife Cornelia is German and a NAUI instructor, enabling the store to offer instruction in German.

Jimmy is very safety conscious in everything from how he fills his tanks to how his drivers manage the boat. His knowledge of local currents and tides is invaluable when planning dives, and has been called upon to aid in search and rescue operations. Dive Tobago was one of the founder members of the dive association and Jay is currently on the board of directors.

Also available from Dive Tobago are jet skis and water skiing.

Dive Tobago has a pleasant local feel; diving is relaxed and comfortable with this store.

Just along the road is Viking Dive **10**, run by its Viking owner, Goran, a Swede who sailed here some years ago and set up shop. Goran was a commercial diver on North Sea oil rigs before deciding to head for warmer waters. He has been in Tobago for 5 years.

Previously located at Pigeon Point, he now has premises further along the bay on Pigeon Point Road. An after dive barbecue of the day's catch, on the beach in front of the store, is an attraction for some divers. If the dive association's plans to introduce spearfishing rules come to fruition, this may no longer be possible.

As a yachtsman himself, Goran does considerable business with visiting yachts. At his other premises near Crown Point, he offers yacht services such as mail collection.

Currently operating from Pigeon Point is a dive store called Wild Turtle Dive Safaris **9**. This is a new store, opened in January 1997. Aware of the large number of operators already offering diving, Wild Turtle has plans to offer a somewhat different service. They have a 44-foot cruiser called *Bamboo* that they plan to use for dive charters, allowing their divers to experience all of Tobago's dive areas.

The store wants to specialise in night diving and divers will be able to buy a 5-dive package over 2 days, including one overnight on board *Bamboo*. When we were in Tobago, the store had not yet opened its doors but when we checked again before printing they were just opening. It seems to be a friendly, interesting store, offering something a little different.

R&C Diver's Den **12** opened its doors in 1993 as a Tobagonian full-service dive store; Tobagonians consider even Trinidadians foreigners. Ricardo and his partner, Colin, believe that their local knowledge of Tobago's shores puts them in a good position to show divers the best of Tobago's diving.

The store is located a few minutes walk from the beach in Milford Bay, on the premises of Spence's Guest House where many of their customers stay. Transport to the beach to join the dive boat is provided by R&C. Like most of the operators on the island, R&C's dive boats are pirogues. The largest boat has two engines and is used for the offshore dive sites.

From their location in Crown Point, they take divers to the sites to the southwest of the island and along the north coast. Their divers are taken by road to Speyside to do a 2-tank dive, a trip to the bird sanctuary on Little Tobago and a local lunch provided by R&C, served on the beach.

Guests of R&C Divers Den come from hotels in the western end of the island and from local guest houses. A 7-day stay in a guest house, unlimited diving and one day's car rental can be arranged for around $700.

R&C aim to deliver good quality diving, with a commitment to safety and the benefit of local knowledge.

Contact Information

1 Tobago Dive Masters	Ellis John	Tel: (809) 639-4697 Fax: (809) 639-4697
2 M-Dive Redman	Redman	Tel: (809) 660-5464
3 Tobago Dive Experience at Manta Lodge	Carol Peck	Tel: (809) 660-5268 Fax: (809) 660-5030
4 Aquamarine Dive	Keith Darwent	Tel: (809) 660-4341 Fax: (809) 639-4416
5 Ron's Watersports	Ron Tiah	Tel: (809) 673-0549 Fax: (809) 673-0549
6 Man Friday Diving	Bjarne Olesen	Tel: (809) 660-4676 Fax: (809) 660-4676
7 Tobago Dive Experience at Rex Turtle	Carol Peck	Tel: (809) 660-5268 Fax:(809) 660-5030
8 Diamond Divers	Barry St. George	Tel: (809) 639-0191 Fax: (809) 639-0030
9 Wild Turtle Dive Safaris	Robert Decastro	Tel: (809) 639-7936 Fax: (809) 639-7232
10 Viking Dive	Goran Qvarfordt	Tel: (809) 639-9209 Fax: (809) 639-0414
11 Dive Tobago	Jay Young	Tel: (809) 639-0202 Fax: (809) 639-2727
12 R&C Diver's Den	Ricardo Nedd	Tel: (809) 639-8120

Tobago Dive Operators

		Tobago Dive Masters	M-Dive Redman	Tobago Dive Experience at Manta Lodge	Aquamarine Dive	Ron's Watersports	Man Friday Diving	Tobago Dive Experience at Rex Turtle	Diamond Divers	Wild Turtle Dive Safaris	Viking Dive	Dive Tobago	R&C Diver's Den
		1	2	3	4	5	6	7	8	9	10	11	12
STAFF	Instructors	1	0	1	2	2	2	2	2	2	3	2	3
	Divemasters	3	1	1	4	1	1	2	2	2	2	8	2
	Diving Associations	P	P	NP	P	P	CP	P	CNPS	NP	NP	P	P
	Languages	E	E	E	EGS	E	DE	E	EF SG	E	EG	EG	EG
BOATS	Dive Boats	2	1	2	3	1	1	2	3	3	2	4	2
	Shaded Boats	2	1	1	3	1	1	1	2	2	1	2	0
	Max. Divers per Boat	10	14	10	10-14	6	6	10	6	10	10	8	6-14
	Time to Dive Sites	5-25	5-15	5-15	5-20	5-30	5-30	5-60	5-25	5-75	10-20	5-20	10-20
	Dives per Day	2	2	2	2	2	2	2	2	3	3	3	2
	Pick Up by Boat from	CRY	CRY	CRY	CY	CY	CY	CRY	CRY	CY	CRY	CRY	CRY
EQUIPMENT	Equipment Sets	18	10	10	12	6	6	10	34	12	15	12	10
	Dive Equip. for Sale			1	2	3			1	2	2	2	
	Dive Equip. for Rent					•							
	Photo Equip. for Rent				•	•	•		•		•	•	
	Tank Fills	•		•	•	•	•	•	•	•		•	•
	Equipment Servicing	•	•	•	•	•	•	•	•	•	•	•	•
	O₂ on Boat	•		•	•	•		•	•	•	•	•	•
	VHF on Boat	•		•	•	•		•	•	•	•		
MISC.	Owned by Resort				•				•				
	Other Water Sports				•	•		•	•			•	
	Pers. Liab. Insurance				•	•		•	•	•	•		•

[TEEMING WITH LIFE ABOVE AND BELOW THE WATER]

WITH 70 SQUARE MILES OF BLEACHED WHITE SAND EDGING THE COAST OF BARBADOS, IT IS HARD TO SAY WHERE MOST OF OUR TREASURES LIE, ABOVE OR BELOW THE WATER.

THE WATER BELOW THE GENTLY LAPPING WAVES OFFERS DIVERS NINE WRECKS TO EXPLORE, A LUSH BARRIER REEF HALF A MILE OFFSHORE, AND A GENTLY SLOPING COASTAL REEF RICH WITH A VARIETY OF TROPICAL FISH AND SEA LIFE. THE SMILING FACES OF TURTLES GREET YOU ON ALMOST EVERY DIVE.

THE WORLD ABOVE AWAITS, WITH AN ARRAY OF RESTAURANTS TO SATISFY ANY TASTE, TRY LOCAL COU-COU AND JOL BOL, OR SAMPLE THE HIGHEST STANDARD OF INTERNATIONAL CUISINE. VISIT MAGNIFICENT PLANTATION HOUSES AND SEE SUGAR CANE TURNED INTO RUM, OR WATCH A GAME OF POLO, THE SPORT OF KINGS.

WITH A DOZEN DIVE STORES AND ACCOMMODATION FROM LUXURY HOTELS TO BUDGET APARTMENTS, BARBADOS WELCOMES YOU... ABOVE AND BELOW THE WATER.

BARBADOS

JUST BEYOND YOUR IMAGINATION

Barbados

Barbados stands apart from the other islands in this book, geographically as well as culturally. The topography of the island is gentler, reflecting its calmer history. You will not find towering mountains here nor simmering volcanoes, and the museums have no stories of bloody battles between the French, Spanish and English. Barbados was settled by the English in 1627 and has remained in British hands ever since. Even today, when the island has had its independence for over 30 years, the Queen of England is still the Queen of Barbados and the island retains its nickname 'Little England'.

The gently rolling hills of Barbados were an easier environment for agricultural development than the rainforest-covered islands to the west. Sugar cane plantations were highly successful and the island grew prosperous. When tourism as a worldwide industry began to grow, Barbados was well positioned to gain its share of this lucrative market. Long white sandy beaches plus a sophisticated infrastructure of roads, airport, power and water services allowed hotels to be developed along the sheltered west and south coasts. The population of Barbados lives in a virtually unbroken urban continuum from Speightstown in the northwest to St. Philips in the southeast. About one third of the island's population live in Bridgetown.

Thus, holiday makers are well served with accommodation, restaurants and entertainment, all a stone's throw from the beach, leaving the interior of the island unspoilt. For those whose interest in flora and fauna extends above sea level, there are plenty of pleasant walks, beautifully tended gardens and fascinating caves to visit.

Barbados is 21 miles long and 16 miles wide. It was not thrown abruptly into being by violent volcanic activity, but grew as a result of coral reef development. The island is, for the most part, made up of coral limestone which, as well as leaving submerged sections available for exploration by scuba divers, has created interesting structures on land. Underground streams have been carved through the limestone, creating stunning caves dressed with stalactites and stalagmites. In the north of the island somewhat more rugged terrain is the result of clay and sand deposited by the Orinoco River which flowed from South America at a time when South America extended far beyond its current coastline.

Speightstown and the North

Speightstown is the second largest town on the island and marks the end of the heavily populated area. In its heyday, Speightstown was a busy port involved in the export of sugar. Now it has a pleasant easygoing atmosphere, with many colonial buildings, much quieter than busy Bridgetown but offering plenty of local restaurants and nightlife.

The coast from Speightstown around the north of the island is Barbados' most rugged area. For hikers, this territory will lead you along deep ravines and coastal caves. A visit to the Animal Flower Cave at North Point is a chance to see anemones growing in rock pools in the caves. The anemones used to be present in greater numbers, but they are now few and far between. It remains, however, an interesting natural phenomenon.

Further inland is Farley Hill National Park and Grenade Hall Forest and Signal Station. For those who prefer a gentle stroll to a brisk hike, there are plenty of cool shady paths and you will almost certainly see a monkey or two. They usually leave the park in the morning and return around 4 p.m. but one or two seem to hang around all day, probably due to the heaps of fruit left out for them.

Speightstown to Bridgetown

Along the coast between Speightstown and Bridgetown there are numerous hotels, guest houses and apartment hotels. Holetown, about halfway down the coast, was the site of the landing of the first settlers. It is currently the location of the first marine park in Barbados.

Inland from Holetown, in the parish of St. Andrew, is Mount Hillaby, the highest point of Barbados at 1,116 feet. You can take a winding road from the village of Hillaby to reach the summit

Unlike its mountainous neighbours to the west, Barbados has gently rolling countryside perfect for agricultural development.

which commands splendid views of the surrounding countryside. Hikers will enjoy walking down from the summit through the sugar cane estates, which these days supply sugar to Barbados' rum distilleries, and on down to Turner's Hall Woods. Alternatively, you can take a tour on horseback or a tractor-drawn jitney. These walks and tours may not be as dramatic as those on the more volcanic islands, but they offer a wonderful array of wild flowers, ferns and fragrant spice trees.

South of Mount Hillaby is Welchman Hall Gulley and Harrison Cave. Welchman Hall Gulley is a deep wide ravine, full of citrus fruits and spice trees. There is a massive stone pillar, 4 feet in diameter, like a monument from an earlier civilisation. The Gulley was once arranged as a tropical park, then it reverted to its wild state. Although it has once again become a managed nature reserve, it is sensitively managed by the Barbados National Trust. There is still plenty of wildlife and this is another area where you'll see monkeys.

This whole area is riddled with gullies and caves like a massive piece of Gruyère. Harrison Cave is a cave system almost one mile long, and you are taken through aboard a special tram and trailer from which you will see underground springs, waterfalls, stalagmites and stalactites, carefully illuminated to display their colours.

Bridgetown to Christ Church

The commercial and social hub of Barbados is firmly seated in Bridgetown. The town developed because the Constitution River which flows through Bridgetown formed a safe natural harbour. The Harbour is surrounded by an area called the Careenage. Fishing boats tie up here as do a variety of other vessels. Many of the old buildings have been restored, lending a charming character to the area. One of the dive stores has their base on the Careenage.

To the north of the Careenage is Trafalgar Square, with its statue of Nelson, erected 36 years before Nelson's Column was installed in Trafalgar Square in London. Bridgetown has a lively fresh fruit and fish market and many good shops.

Just outside Bridgetown, as you head north, is the Mount Gay Distillery. They offer tours and explain how the rum is made, pressing you to taste a tot or two.

Running south of Bridgetown is Carlisle Bay, protected from the southeast by Needham's Point which houses the military museum. Much of this area is occupied by the Barbados Defence Force, and the recompression chamber is here. The Barbados Museum is also in this area.

Right the way along the coast from Bridgetown to Oistins are many hotels, restaurants and apartments. For those staying in self-catering accommodation, you will never need worry about where or what to eat. There are a wide variety of restaurants, including those offering local Bajan (Barbadian) food, Indian, Chinese, Mexican, seafood and international cuisine. The

Boatyard, just east of Carlisle Bay, has a good restaurant and an entertaining bar, as well as a dive store.

Bird lovers will enjoy visiting Graeme Hall Swamp in Christ Church. This is the biggest expanse of inland water in Barbados and you will find many species of birds among the mangroves. Look out for wintering and migrant waterbirds and shorebirds.

One particularly lively area along the coast is Lawrence Gap. Turning off the main coast road into Lawrence Gap you will find a wide selection of hotels, restaurants and stores. One of the island's largest dive stores is here, too. This is the area which many people head for at night. It has a bright lively atmosphere and is close to the many hotels extending along the coast from Bridgetown.

As you move farther along the coast road, you will come to Oistins. Although of no particular importance today, it was the location of the signing of the Charter of Barbados in 1652. Perhaps it left a few people disgruntled because Chase Vault in the grounds of Christ Church Parish Church has been the centre of sedition ever since. Each time the vault was opened to place in a new coffin, the old coffins were found scattered around the vault. Despite carefully sealing the vault and checking that the seal had not been broken, the next time it was opened the coffins were once again in disarray. Finally the authorities were defeated by the mystery and ordered the coffins to be buried separately in the churchyard.

To the eastern end of Christ Church is Grantley Adams International Airport. A fast freeway links the airport to Bridgetown and then bypasses the town centre on its route north to Speightstown.

Christ Church to Hackleton's Cliff

Right across this southeastern corner are great houses, old colonial plantation houses and mansions. Sam Lord's Castle is perhaps the best known. Dating back to 1820, most of the splendid furnishings have been preserved and it is now under the careful stewardship of Marriott's. Sunbury House in St. Philip's Parish is equally attractive and now doubles as a museum.

If you follow the coast around toward Bathsheba, you come to Hackleton's Cliff, a 1,000-foot cliff overlooking Tent Bay. Andromeda Gardens are just behind the bay and offer a pleasant way to spend an afternoon, amid pools, waterfalls and a mass of tropical flowers. Orchids from the gardens regularly win prizes at the Chelsea Flower Show in London each year.

Getting Around

Barbados does have both public and private bus systems. This works well for getting in and out of Bridgetown but can be a bit longwinded if you want to cross the island. If you want to see a lot of the island or dive with stores in different parts of the island, then renting a car is your best bet. There are over 70 car rental agencies to choose from.

Language: English
Currency: Barbados Dollar ($1.00 US = $1.98 Barbados)
Population: 260,000
Telephone Code: (246)

Après Dive

Barbados has more organised après dive activities than most of the other islands in this book. Sports facilities in particular are generally of a very high standard, as Barbados plays host to many international events.

Golf

Many people go to Barbados for golfing holidays, which seems the best recommendation for the quality of the courses. There are a number of courses, some attached to hotels, but arrangements can usually be made for non-residents to play.

Eighteen-Hole Courses:
Sandy Lane Golf Club, St. James: (246) 432-1145
The Royal Westmoreland Golf Club: (246) 422-4653

Nine-Hole Courses:
Almond Beach Village, St. Peter: (246) 422-4900
Rockley Golf Club, Christ Church: (246) 435-7873

Hiking

Walking could not be easier to arrange than in Barbados. The National Trust organises a 5-mile walk every Sunday, starting at 6 a.m. and 3.30 p.m. If that does not suit your schedule, contact Highland Outdoor Tours who arrange scenic safari hikes to suit your timetable.
Barbados' Nature Conservation Commission has developed a number of nature trails. Those wishing to go it alone should contact them for more information.
Highland Outdoor Tours, St. Thomas: (246) 438-8070
The Barbados National Trust, St. Michael: (246) 436-9033
The National Nature Commission, St. Michael: (246) 425-1200

Horse Riding

Riding is a popular sport in Barbados. As well as recreational riding there is regular horse racing at the Garrison Savannah and a high standard of polo is played in Barbados. From September to March there are polo matches three times a week at the polo club.
For recreational riding, try a ride along the beach with Wilcox or Tony's stables. Or, take a ride through the countryside and stop at a plantation house for lunch.
Caribbean International Riding Centre, St. Joseph: (246) 420-1246
Tony's Riding Stables, St. Peter: (246) 422-1549
Wilcox Riding Stables, Christ Church: (246) 428-3610

Tennis

Many of the larger hotels have tennis courts which can be rented by the hour. Barbados has hosted the Davis Cup on a number of occasions, so you can be sure of good facilities.

There are many courts, so we have mentioned just those where there are also dive facilities.

Barbados Hilton, Needham Point: (246) 426-0200
Glitter Bay, St. James: (246) 422-4111
Sandy Lane, St. James: (246) 432-1311
Southwinds, St. Lawrence: (246) 428-7181

Water Sports

Just as the hotels line the coast from Speightstown to Oistins, so do long sandy beaches and more water sports activities than you will find anywhere else in the Eastern Caribbean. Parasailing, kayaks, water skiing, sailing dinghies and catamarans are all available. It is just a matter of walking along the beach. All of the major hotels offer these facilities and there are no end of freelancers. Some of the dive stores either offer these facilities or are associated with stores that do.

Surfers rate Barbados as one of the Caribbean's hotspots. On the east of the island, the Soup Bowl at Bathsheba is the location for local and international events.

Shopping

Barbados has both sophisticated duty-free shopping and local arts and crafts. The main shopping area is in Bridgetown though you will find local craft shops at many of the tourist centres. A visit to Pelican Village, on the Princess Alice Highway in Bridgetown harbour, is a convenient way of tracking down the full spectrum of Barbados' local wares. You can watch artisans at work before making your choice.

If wood carving is your thing, visit Medford Mahogany Craft Village where you can see huge mahogany tree trunks being skilfully carved into delicate figurines. Or, if pottery is of more interest, Chalky Mountain Potteries in St. Andrews welcomes visitors.

Duty-free shopping transactions can be made over the counter in certain stores by showing your airline ticket or cruise ship boarding pass and passport. On departure from Barbados, just deposit the invoice in the duty-free box located outside the departure hall.

Duty Free Shops:
Cave Shepherd & Co. Ltd.: Bridgetown, airport, and several shopping malls
Harrison's: Bridgetown, airport, and several major hotels

Nightlife

Most of the major hotels provide evening entertainment. If you want to escape the confines of the hotel, there are very many other restaurants and theatres to choose from. The Plantation restaurant and garden theatre in St. Lawrence will transport you to and from your hotel for a buffet dinner and show, with unlimited drinks, all for $44 US. The show includes fire eaters, flaming limbo and a steelband. At the other end of the island, near Speightstown, Mullin's Beach Bar and restaurant is an informal venue with a lively atmosphere which promises to stay open as long as you want it to.

In the centre of Bridgetown on the Careenage, you can sample local specialities such as smoked flying fish or Bol Jol at the Waterfront Café. Some nights they have steel pan music. Or, try The Boatyard just outside Bridgetown which has live entertainment once or twice a week.

Barbados has a well respected jazz festival in January each year which provides both daytime and night entertainment.

Mullin's Beach Bar, Speightstown: (246) 422-1878
The Boatyard, St. Michael: (246) 436-2622
The Plantation, St. Lawrence: (246) 428-5048
Waterfront Café, Bridgetown: (246) 427-0093

Barbados: (246) 427-2623
USA: (800) 221-9831
Canada: (800) 268-9121
UK: (171) 636-9448

Information on Accommodation

Barbados receives flights, chartered and scheduled, from very many destinations in the USA and Europe. Britain's two main carriers, British Airways and Caledonian Airways, both have regular flights to the island. From the US, American carriers have direct flights from New York, Miami, and San Juan. Air Canada has flights from Toronto. At the time of writing, more routes were being opened and it would be worth checking with your travel agent for the current status.

Getting There

Just as the island of Barbados has a very different geographical structure from all the other islands in this book, the diving environment is quite different, too. The two key differences are the presence of a bank or barrier type reef and the presence of several wrecks, acting both as artificial reefs and full wreck penetration dives.

The Diving

Taking the reefs first, Barbados' dive sites include both fringing reefs and barrier or banking reefs, as they are called locally. Remember, though, that the fringing reef does not descend from a steep-sided coastline so there are no plummeting walls and no drops to unknown depths. Instead, the fringing reef slopes gently, usually to no more than 80 feet, before flattening out to sand. These sand areas extend out until the banking reef rises to within 60 feet of the surface.

The Reefs

A Fringe, a Barrier or a Bank?

We have used a number of terms to describe reefs - fringing reef, coral encrusted rock, patch reef - and now in this chapter we refer to a bank or barrier reef.

Although current research is extending our knowledge of coral reefs, the basic theory promulgated by Charles Darwin in 1842 still stands pretty much intact. Darwin described three types of reef, namely fringing, barrier and atoll. There are no atolls in the Caribbean. There is general agreement on how a fringing reef forms, growing initially on the rock along the island's coast. As it develops, dead coral forms its own substratum and the reef grows further out to sea, building a reef flat.

The Red Sea has some of the best examples of fringing reefs, with shallow reef tops, barely deep enough for a diver to pass over, before reaching a wall which plummets down into the blue. The Caribbean islands have much younger, less developed fringing reefs and often a dive near to shore is mainly on coral encrusted rocks. The variety of sessile marine life will be greater here; sponges and non-reef building corals, such as gorgonians, will all take hold on the rocky substratum.

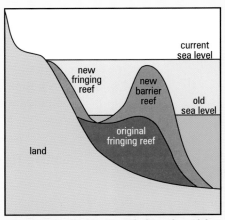

Section through a barrier reef, shows how rising water level caused its formation.

There is more debate about barrier reefs. These are reefs some distance from land, separated by a relatively shallow lagoon. Darwin explained this phenomena as land subsiding, thus leaving the fringing reef some distance from land. Later theories claimed rises in water levels at the end of the ice age submerged coastal areas, but the coral grew fast enough to keep pace i.e. stay at a depth with sufficient light to grow. Reefs believed to have resulted from this process are sometimes referred to as bank reefs.

Then came plate tectonics theory (the process of folding and warping of the earth's surface), which is very relevant to the Caribbean with its recent volcanic roots. Volcanic material squeezed through faults in the sea floor causes ridges which provide rocky substratum and, if near enough the surface, these will be colonised by coral.

The Caribbean is known to have experienced dramatic changes in sea level after the last ice age and it seems likely that its offshore reefs are bank rather than Darwin's barrier reefs, either formed from fringing reefs or folds in the earth's crust.

However they were formed, the process of growth and development is the same. Hematypic corals are needed to create and maintain the foundations and structure of the reef. Gorgonians and sponges cannot build a reef, they can only help support the ecosystem. We risk spending so much time working out how it all happened that we forget to stand back and marvel.

The slopes of the banking reefs are of varying inclines, some sloping very steeply. The reef top is between 50 and 150 feet across, with drops on either side to as much as 200 feet. Most of the banking reef descends to around 140 feet before turning into sand, but on the outside there are drops to 200 feet. The banking reef makes for exciting diving, dropping down through the blue onto the reef below. But, it also necessitates diving square profiles, so it is important to stay close to the dive leaders and never descend below them, or else to dive with a computer. As you will be diving a square profile on the bank reef instead of the more normal multi-level dive (where you spend the latter part of the dive on the shallow part of the reef), it is very important to do a safety stop.

The banking reef has been formed by folds in the earth's crust, as a result of volcanic activity on the nearby island chain. Changing water levels have left the banking reef between a quarter and half a mile offshore. Sufficiently deep to cause no visible disturbance on the surface, it is a matter of pride with the dive operators to be able to drop you right on top of the reef.

Of the two areas of reef, it is not surprising that the banking reef is in the best condition. It is far enough offshore to avoid too much damage from man-made pollution, or storm surges. It has suffered anchor damage in places, although there are a few mooring buoys in place with more planned. We were pleasantly surprised and pleased to see the variety and quality of the coral on a number of the banking reef dives.

The fringing reef is more exposed to coastal pollution and the effects of beach creation schemes. Hotels empty chlorinated water from swimming pools into the sea and many also have inadequate facilities for sewage disposal. Hopefully, this situation will improve in the future as a result of a new sewage disposal system being installed in Carlisle Bay. We found the condition to be variable, though, with some of the fringing reefs in quite good condition. Where hard corals have died, much of the substratum has been taken over by fast growing gorgonians.

The variety of coral is certainly very good. Many sites have numerous types of stony corals, and black coral grows in the open areas of the banking reef, as well as in the deeper, darker areas of the wrecks. There is very little algae and some very healthy sponges; vase and tube sponges seem to grow very large.

Fish life, while not prolific due to over-fishing, is interesting, with some popular species being abundant. Seahorses are seen regularly, especially in Carlisle Bay, and batfish are prolific enough to give you a very good chance of a sighting. We saw one or more turtles on almost every dive we did and they appear quite relaxed about divers, especially if you do not swim towards them.

The Wrecks

Barbados has shown a good deal of foresight in the use of wrecks as dive sites. As long ago as 1978, wrecks were being deliberately sunk. Before diving became a popular sport, a few sank by fair means or foul, and now serve as dive sites. Three wrecks, the *SS Stavronikita*, the *Pamir* and the *Eillion*, are conventional wreck sites, allowing ingress through purpose-made entry holes in the hull. Other wrecks have become artificial reefs, some with a swim-through, and all attracting lots of fish. Typically you will find more fish on the wrecks than the reefs.

Ships are not the only relics on the sea bed. In the seventeenth century and onwards, long before people became conservation conscious, sailors on the ships anchored in and around Carlisle Bay would toss overboard their empty bottles. Rum bottles, medicine bottles and ale bottles all lie on the sea bed. Many of the dive operators have collections of bottles and will take you on a bottle hunt. If you find one, you can keep it.

The dive sites are spread evenly along the west coast and halfway along the south coast. Conditions on the two coasts vary,

WRECKS CURRENTLY BEING DIVED

NAME	DATE SUNK	LENGTH (FEET)	DEPTH (FEET)	CONDITION
Berwind	1919	60	20	artificial reef
Ce-Trek	1985	40	40	artificial reef
Eillion	1996	110	50	penetration
Friar's Craig	1985	160	50	artificial reef
Lord Combermere	1974	60	50	penetration
Lord Willoughby	1976	60	100	artificial reef
Pamir	1985	150	55	penetration
SS Stavronikita	1978	360	135	penetration
Wolf	1955	42	40	keel only

depending upon the weather. The west coast is sheltered from the prevailing easterly winds, making it very calm in the summer months but it can be subject to northerly swells in the winter season, creating surf on the beaches. The south coast is sheltered from the northeasterly winds usually experienced in the winter months, but more exposed to the southeasterlies that blow through most of the summer.

Visibility is generally very good, ranging between 60 and 80 feet. There can be periods of poor visibility during the late summer, when the water turns green and visibility can drop to 30 feet or less. Currents also vary. Although Barbados does not suffer from a prevailing strong current, the sites are not as current free as those on the lee side of the more mountainous islands to the west.

One of the island's most popular sites, the *SS Stavronikita*, is on the west side, but at the southern end, so that it is within reach of all the stores. The diving is slightly different along the west and south coasts. They both have their own particularly good sites and it is worth considering splitting your diving between an operator on the west coast and one on the south coast.

The Barbados diving industry is close to the point of moving from a completely unregulated industry to one which is closely controlled. This change is not surprising when you consider the history of diving in Barbados, where two apparently opposing themes have influenced development.

Barbados has been heavily marketed as a holiday location but has never been portrayed as a dive destination. The Barbados Tourist Authority (BTA) has only recently taken an interest in promoting Barbados' diving, so there has been little weight behind calls to government to provide support for the enforcement of safety standards. No hotel or restaurant can operate without approval from the BTA, but there have been no guidelines for diving—a potentially hazardous activity, at least compared to the risk of staying in a dirty hotel room.

Conversely, Barbados was one of the first islands to have an association devoted to diving safety: ECSDA, the Eastern Caribbean Safe Diving Association. ECSDA was, and remains, responsible for fund-raising for Barbados' recompression chamber.

ECSDA's safety rules are not mandatory, but have recently been adopted and amended by the Barbados Professional Association of Dive Operators (PADO). PADO is trying to persuade government that these safety standards should become mandatory. The standards relate to the carrying of safety and first aid equipment, including oxygen; the training of all personnel in first aid; the training requirements of those who are teaching, leading divers and boat crew; and the requirement to check divers' certification cards.

A similar paradox is found in the development of marine parks. Barbados established a marine park on the west coast, in the Folkstone area, in 1981.

FOLKSTONE PARK RULES PROHIBIT:

- **Destroying or disturbing any plant or animal.**
- **Injuring any bottom growth.**
- **Discharging any waste material.**
- **Damaging any buoy.**
- **Using spearguns, hooks, lines, traps or explosives, or any device to catch fish.**

The park still exists but, without being too uncharitable, it is not of any real significance. The park has a patrol vessel but funds allow its use only between 9 a.m. and 3 p.m., observed by the fishermen while they enjoy a beer in the shade of a palm tree, waiting until after 3 p.m. to enter the park to catch bait fish.

Meanwhile, PADO has its own plans for a marine park in the Carlisle Bay area. It also has a proposal with government for the placing of mooring buoys to eliminate anchoring on the reefs. At the time of writing, PADO was waiting for the go-ahead on both of these plans. To help raise funds for these activities, PADO member stores sell dive tags to divers for $5.

Independent Diving

This is permitted in Barbados, but there is little scope to dive independently. There is almost no shore diving and you would not be able to find the banking reef without a dive operator. The only exceptions are the wrecks in Carlisle Bay which can be reached by swimming out from the shore. There is good deal of boat traffic in this bay, however, and caution needs to be exercised.

Safety

If you consider the remedial aspects of diver safety, then Barbados has a considerable advantage in having a recompression chamber. The Barbados Defence Force owns and manages the chamber, under the superb stewardship of Lieutenant Colonel Florence Gittens and her team. Since its purchase in 1989, 230 divers have been through the chamber, of which about half was recreational divers. The balance was primarily lobster fishermen. The chamber team works closely with DAN, providing statistics and consultancy.

In total, Lieutenant Colonel Gittens has a team of 24 medical personnel to call on, of whom eight are specifically trained in the treatment of diving accidents. There are five doctors trained in hyperbaric medicine available to provide support services to the chamber. The chamber services all the islands in this book, with the exception of Martinique which has its own chamber. Divers are even sent from Tobago, despite Trinidad having a chamber, because of Barbados' reputation for expertise in dealing with recreational diving accidents.

Prevention is to be preferred, and Barbados has a reasonably good safety record. The chamber's statistics do show that in 1995 more of their diver patients came from Barbados than all of the other islands in this book put together. We spent some time trying to establish why this was the case. One theory we have is that because the chamber is near to hand, divers and dive operators in Barbados do not take any chances and send people to the chamber if there is any doubt at all about their symptoms.

Another argument is that the square profiles, typical of much of the diving in Barbados, can cause problems for those not diving with a computer or pushing the limits of their computer. Lt. Col. Gittens believes that diving to the limits of computers and some degree of gung-ho diving are the causes of almost all the recreational diving accidents they treat. Both causes are easily avoidable.

Dry Diving in Barbados

Dry diving is the term used to describe the process of diving in a recompression chamber. The body undergoes all of the physiological processes of a normal underwater dive, the difference is you do not get wet. You still clear your ears, you still perform a slow controlled ascent and you still use diving tables to calculate decompression stops.

Recompression chambers are used to treat divers who have decompression sickness (DCS). This dangerous and potentially fatal injury is caused by nitrogen bubbles forming in the blood. Bubbles can be large enough to cut off blood supply, and therefore oxygen, to the body's limbs and vital organs. Bubbles jam into joints causing pain and the inability to straighten limbs, hence the more common term 'the bends'. More dangerous are bubbles reducing blood flow to the brain. By recompressing in the chamber to the equivalent of 130 feet, the bubble size is halved, reducing or eliminating the symptoms, but not the problem. The patient then needs to spend many hours in the chamber allowing the body to expel the excess nitrogen.

DCS occurs when divers do not allow enough time for their body to expel the excess nitrogen which has accumulated during the dive. Not making a slow enough ascent, or taking an inadequate rest period on the surface

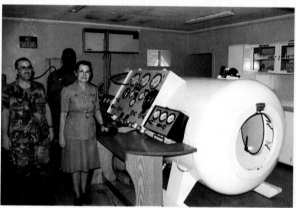

Lieutenant Colonel Gittens and her team manage the BDF's recompression chamber.

before diving again, or boarding an aircraft (the pressure reduction when an aircraft climbs can cause DCS in a diver who would be safe on the surface) are common causes of DCS. Providing divers follow the rules and procedures they are taught when being trained, the chances of DCS are remote.

Despite the excellent services available in Barbados, putting yourself in a position where you require use of the chamber is foolhardy in the extreme. Apart from the hot, noisy and uncomfortable experience, recovery is slow. Treatment can last for several months and still leave victims with severe lower body disabilities. At the very least, victims are not allowed to dive again, even when they have recovered fully. Every treatment also requires BDF staff to accompany their patient and to sit in extremely uncomfortable conditions for several hours. And, if that is not enough, it costs $150 per hour.

The Accident and Emergency Information on the inside back cover shows how to contact the BDF in the event of an emergency. They would rather have a call for a suspected case of DCS, prior to it becoming serious, and are able to give advice. If in doubt, check it out.

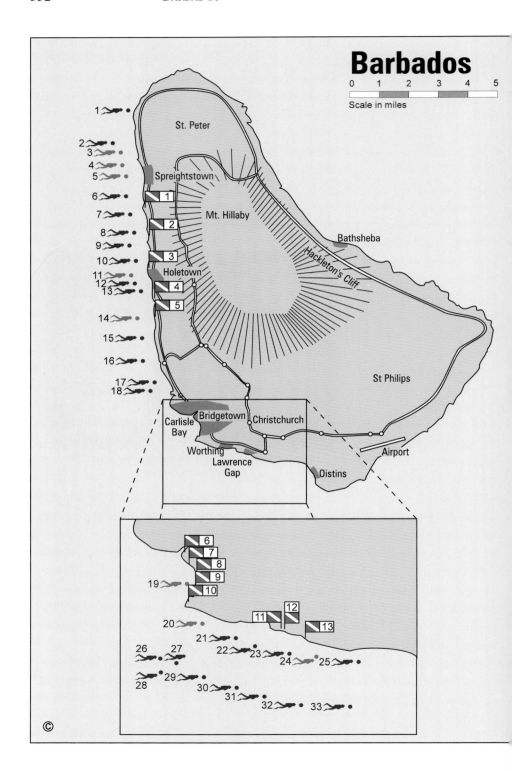

Barbados

0   1   2   3   4   5

Scale in miles

St. Peter

Spreightstown

Mt. Hillaby

Bathsheba

Hackleton's Cliff

Holetown

St Philips

Bridgetown
Carlisle Bay
Christchurch

Worthing
Lawrence Gap
Oistins

Airport

©

NO.	SITE NAME	DEPTH IN FEET
	WEST	
1	North Point Lighthouse	30-100
2	Bonita Bar	50-100
3	Maycock's Reef	60-140
4	Bright Ledge	55-140
5	*Pamir*	30-55
6	Great Ledge	50-80
7	Spawnee	45-80
8	The Farm	55-80
9	Tropicana	60-80
10	Church Point/Fisherman's	40
11	Dottins	45-95
12	Little Sandy Lane	45-80
13	Johnson's	50-85
14	*SS Stavronikita*	20-140
15	*Lord Combermere*	40-60
16	Belle Buoy	20-60
17	Clarke's Bank/Silver Bank	50-140
18	Shark's Bank	60-80
19	Carlisle Bay Wrecks	8-50
	SOUTH COAST FRINGING REEFS	
20	*Friar's Craig* and Asta Reef	30-90
21	Apple Experience	30-80
22	Magic Isle	30-60
23	Pieces of Eight	40-60
24	Southwinds/Close Encounters	30-40
25	Carl's Point	20-60
	SOUTH COAST BANK REEFS	
26	Caribbee	60-130
27	Castle Bank	50-120
28	The Muff	70-130
29	Ernie's Bar	60-135
30	Mount Charlie	75-140
31	Graham Hall Shallows	40-70
32	Little Point	50-130
33	High Wire	65-140

Barbados Dive Sites

Dive Operators

NO.	OPERATOR	RESORT/HOTEL LOCATION
1	Reefers and Wreckers	King's Beach Hotel
2	Blue Reef Water Sports	
3	Carib Ocean Divers	Glitter Bay/Royal Pavillion
4	West Side Scuba Centre (M)	
5	Hightide Watersports (M)	Sandy Lane Hotel
6	Coral Isle Divers (M)	
7	Underwater Barbados (M)	
8	Hightide at the Boatyard (M)	
9	The Dive Shop (M)	
10	Dive Boat Safari (M)	Hilton Hotel
11	Scotch and Soda (M)	
12	Bubbles Galore (M)	Sandy Beach Hotel
13	Exploresub (M)	

(M) Members of PADO.

---

1 North Point Lighthouse
30'-100'

This is not a frequently dived site due to its exposed position, and is accessible only to those stores located at the north end of the west coast.

It benefits from being rarely dived both in the quality of the coral cover and the fish life. In particular the octocorals are abundant. This location is also known for the large schools of barracuda that congregate around the reef.

---

2 Bonita Bar
50'-100'

Although close to Maycock's Reef, the area is hardly ever dived. Fortunately it is not used by fishermen either, so the fish life is prolific. This is one of the sites where you will see snapper, grunts and even groupers. The marine life is very similar to the adjacent Maycock's Reef.

---

3 Maycock's Reef
60'-140'

  W

Maycock's is one of the northernmost reefs dived by the dive stores. Because of its location, it is not dived all that frequently which is perhaps why it is such a colourful reef. The sessile marine life is in very good condition and offers a great variety of species.

The reef is different from all the other reefs around Barbados in that it runs perpendicular to the shore, not parallel. There is a series of reefs, separated by sand valleys roughly 100 feet across. The spurs run seaward for 500 feet and then drop steeply down to 140 feet or more. Across the top of the spurs there is about 40 feet of water and the distance between the spurs is between 50 and 100 feet. Typically you will cover two or three of these reef spurs on one dive.

Dive Profile

From where the boat anchors we drop down on to a sandy bottom and swim towards the first of the spurs. We are struck by the healthiness of the reef in this area. The clues are the brightness of the colours and the density of the cover. But there is life beyond the coral and sponge. While admiring the minutiae of the reef, we almost miss seeing a hawksbill turtle who begins to swim when he sees us, but is curious enough to swim around us rather than away. Before we finish this dive we see two more.

Fish life is good too. Spanish hogfish, numerous French grunts and Bermuda chub lend a cosmopolitan character to the reef. The presence of many wrasse, including juvenile yellowheads and their relatives, the parrotfish, is one of the reasons the reef seems so colourful. We also see ocean surgeonfish and rock beauties. A more unusual sight is Caribbean reef squid, unafraid at first but then, jet propelled, they speed away. There are many crinoids on the reef, as well as corkscrew anemones harbouring tiny shrimps.

This is a dive where you can glide over the top and enjoy the big picture, or get in close and discover a mass of tiny reef crea-

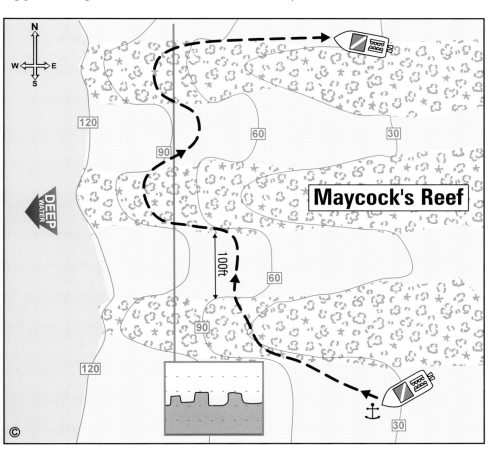

tures forming a fabulous living collage. It is the abundance of coral that creates this rich environment. Apart from the usual boulder, star and brain coral, there is a lot of pillar coral, staghorn, finger and pencil coral and flower coral. You will see bright patches of blue which look like hard coral but are mat zoanthids, a relative of coral.

At 80 feet or more, we notice that more sheet coral grows, creating good shelter for rock hinds and glasseye snappers. Like almost all of the red-coloured large-eyed fish, these shelter during the day and feed at night. Their red colouring makes them almost invisible, but their large eyes maximise their ability to see in the dark.

This site has a great deal of variety to offer and if you are staying in the south it is well worth an excursion to the west coast.

Thanks to Hightide Watersports.

4 Bright Ledge

55'-140'

  W

Located at the northern end of the west coast barrier reef, we are told that Bright Ledge had been given its name because of the quality of the colours on the reef. We certainly have no argument with that; it is one of the brightest, liveliest reefs we dive in Barbados. The reef top is at 50 feet, shelving to 140 feet on the land side and 200 feet on the seaward side. While not actually walls, both slopes are steep, almost vertical in places, and the coral creates a cascading effect as it turns to sheet coral below 90 feet.

The reef is sometimes subject to current, but often there is none at all. When the visibility is very good you can see the reef from the surface, but in poor visibility locating the reef top is an art. Fortunately our boat crew know their stuff and drop anchor exactly in the middle of the reef ridge. We can but hope that PADO will soon have buoys in place.

Dive Profile

There is some current running so we drop down the anchor line in order to keep the group together. The top of the reef, at 60 feet, is a panoply of colour and texture. Big vase sponges, towers of pillar coral, knotted tangles of purple row pore rope sponge, like giant balls of wool, and a carpet of stony corals compete for space and attention.

We are tempted by the drop-off and slip over the edge to 90 feet. The cover is just as dense on the slope as the reef flat and, along with gorgonians, black coral trees are scattered across the reef. Green, amber and white varieties add yet another dimension to the reef colours. Along the edge of the drop-off yellow tube sponges have grown particularly large, as though trying to create a railing to protect against the drop-off.

As on any healthy reef, there are plenty of fish. Damselfish keep the reef's algae in order, Spanish hogfish and princess parrotfish contribute their colours to the scenery. Our eye is caught by a group of strange-looking fish which we later identify as

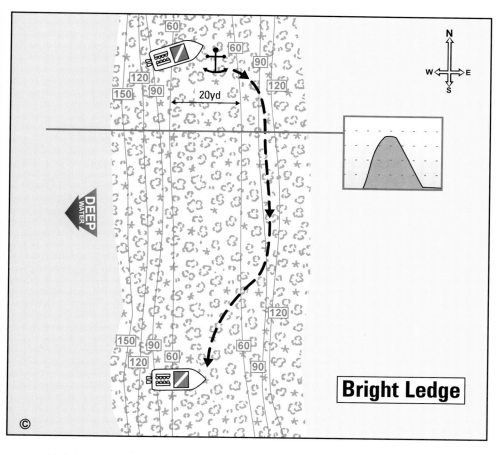

Bright Ledge

orange filefish, strangely named as they are not at all orange. They are silvery, about 15 inches long with peculiar pouting mouths. It is our first sighting of this particular species.

Next, we catch sight of a turtle. Even had we not seen the turtle, we would have been aware of its presence by the bite-shaped holes in many of the sponges. Looking into the sponges, you can see how many creatures call them home. It must be quite disconcerting to have a hawksbill's open beak approaching.

Tube worms and crinoids, too, are a common sight in Barbados and Bright Ledge has its share. There are some big fish to watch if you are not so interested in the sessile life. We see black margates, yellow snappers and rock hinds.

Back on the top of the reef to finish the dive, we enjoy just drifting along above this coral garden.

Thanks to Michael of Reefers and Wreckers.

Turtles—The Caribbean's Only Seawater Reptiles

Surprisingly, for something that looks like a tortoise with flippers, the turtle is a graceful and fast swimmer. In fact turtles seem to swing between the characteristics of a hare and a tortoise.

It takes 5 to 20 years for a turtle to reach maturity and be able to breed. However, once the adult female is ready, the breeding season is a frenzy of activity. She will nest four or five times in one season, producing 130 eggs at a time. And, it is not simply a matter of popping the eggs into a watery nest. She has to crawl up the beach to lay her eggs in the sand. While she may swim with ease, manoeuvring on a sandy beach is a different matter and she barely has enough energy left to crawl back into the sea.

After a breeding season, it takes 2 to 3 years for her to build up her strength and store up sufficient food to make eggs and nest again. Despite her prolific breeding, few of the eggs will survive and many of the hatched turtles will not survive predators once they make it in to the sea.

A hawksbill turtle—efforts are being made to protect its habitat.

Another threat to turtles is man's habit of building hotels on their nesting beaches. Even lights from buildings well back from the beach confuse the young turtles. They instinctively crawl toward the sea, drawn by the reflection of the moon, unless other brighter lights confuse them. Between June and September you can watch the turtles nest but be prepared to sit quietly in the dark until the early hours of the morning.

Turtles are reptiles so breathe air through their lungs. They are able to stay underwater for extended periods, typically 30 to 40 minutes or up to 4 hours if resting on the sea bed. Some species hibernate by burying themselves in the mud and can slow their metabolic rate to be able to stay buried for several months.

In this area, typically, you will see green, loggerhead and hawksbill turtles. Those in Barbados are hawksbills, living on a diet of jellyfish and sponges. The hawksbill's overhanging beak is an aid to identification, and to munching on sponges. Green turtles will be found where you see turtle grass beds as they are vegetarians. They get their name not from their outer colouring but from the green colour of their body fat. Leatherback and loggerhead turtles are also found in the Caribbean. If you have a diet of jellyfish, the similarity between a jellyfish and a plastic bag is a problem. Sadly, turtles often eat plastic bags, which then block their digestive tract and they eventually starve to death.

A large creature protected by a hard shell does not have too many enemies, though unlike tortoises they cannot retract their head and legs, leaving them prey to sharks. But man remains the biggest threat to turtles. Fortunately, in Barbados there is a real effort being made to protect their habitat.

The *Pamir* is a sister ship to the *Friar's Craig* (site 20). She is in very different condition, however. Although sunk in 1985, the ship is still in one piece and can be penetrated in several areas, making it a more conventional wreck dive rather than an artificial reef, like the *Friar's Craig*.

Although not that large, there are many internal areas that can be explored, including the bridge. The ship was modified for diving prior to sinking, by removing all the interior fittings likely to snag divers. Large holes were cut into the hull to assist with the sinking and to give divers a clear trip through the hull spaces.

She is shallow enough to allow a long dive or is often used as the second of a 2-tank dive.

The ship is buoyed and we descend down the line to where the bow still stands proudly erect. Swimming round to the stern and passing the half-buried propeller and rudder, we have time to inspect the encrustation of the hull. Star encrusting sponges make

Pamir 5
30'-55'

W

Dive Profile

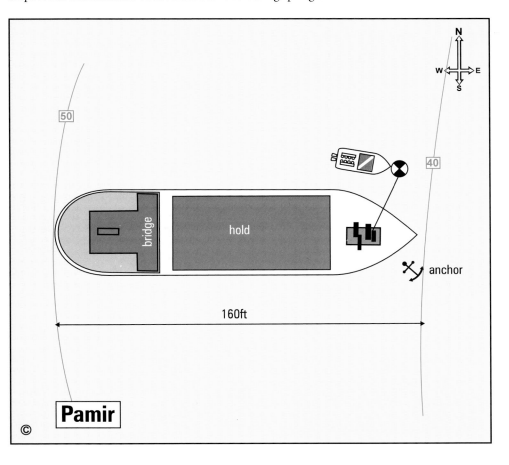

up much of the cover.

We pass the propeller at 50 feet and follow our dive leader, Larry, through a hole on the starboard side, the start of a criss-cross path through the wreck using a number of openings. Although each passage through the hull is not long (unlike the *SS Stavronikita*) some are quite tight, making for some careful finning and buoyancy control to ensure that you do not touch the ship. Although unlikely in most areas to damage marine growth, you are likely to give yourself a grubby coating or damage your wetsuit.

There is plenty of light inside, making a dive light unnecessary. One passage enters through the cargo hold, into the engine room and up a narrow vertical ladder, wide enough for a diver but requiring you to tuck away any spare hoses. At the top of the ladder you execute a challenging 90 degree left turn to exit on to the lower deck.

The large cargo hold has various structures harbouring dozing blackbar soldierfish and grunts. Black coral trees are shades of amber that mimic the rusting ship. On the top deck, we enter the bridge. This structure has survived the damage inevitable when a large ship sinks and provides an area where black coral has grown in abundance. It is fun to stand inside the bridge looking out, quite literally, to sea. Amazingly, one of the windows survived the sinking and divers' trophy cabinets. Larry takes delight in pointing out the toilet compartment, with porcelain still in place, ideal for that classic diver's photograph.

Most of the inside of the ship is too dark to support coral growth. On the hull and superstructure, there are some big anemones, and sponges have taken a good hold. Many sergeant majors live around the wreck; there are dozens of egg patches all guarded by vigilant males. As well as countless small fish, blue and brown chromis especially, there is a large school of Bermuda chub and masses of Creole wrasse.

Swimming over the bow, we sink down onto the anchor. A huge vase sponge has taken it over, forming its own artificial reef. Gobies and sea stars have populated the vase.

For those who are not familiar with wreck diving this is a good warm up before diving the *SS Stavronikita*. As a wreck in its own right, because it is shallow and relatively small, it gives you plenty of time to explore, without fear of getting lost.

Thanks to Larry of Hightide Watersports.

This is another area of banking reef with many similarities to Bright Ledge. The coral cover is very dense, an underwater version of Manhattan. As well as a variety of hard corals, there are lovely fans and sea whips. There is a good chance of finding turtles resting on the reef or grazing on the sponges.

On the outer facing slope you will find a mass of branching sponges, whereas on the inner slope boulder coral has taken a strong hold. Schools of chromis and Atlantic spadefish swell the fish population.

Great Ledge 6
50'-80'

Spawnee is a half mile long area of reef with attractive coral heads in good condition. There is a mooring buoy in place which has protected the reef from anchor damage.

The profusion of sponges attracts angelfish while trumpet fish hang vertically, disguised as sea whips. The terrain makes this good territory for eels and it is one of the sites which barracuda visit.

Spawnee 7
45'-80'

Unusual for Barbados, The Farm is a circular reef, located just off Mullin's Beach Bar. The reef is in good condition, despite its close vicinity to the shore, and the fish and invertebrate life is interesting. You may see lobsters and there are many cowfish. Spanish mackerel sometimes cruise by and there is always the chance of a turtle.

The Farm 8
55'-80'

We did not dive this reef, but it seems to be one of those places that occasionally turn up unusual sea life. We heard that nurse sharks are seen here, a rarity for Barbados. Equally unusual, a divemaster reported seeing a manta. It seems worth a dive just to see if you get lucky. One thing you can be sure of seeing is pretty black coral trees.

The reef is between 50 and 200 feet across the top. The depth shallows to 45 feet going north and becomes deeper going south. The reef has a good density of fish, including green moray eels. Visibility on this reef seems always to be good, even when it is reduced elsewhere.

Tropicana 9
60'-80'

Although this is very close to Dottins, it is very different, being a large flat reef comprised of a mixture of coral heads and sand patches. At its shallowest, it reaches to within 20 feet of the surface; consequently you can encounter surge when there are big swells running.

Large patches of elkhorn are interspersed with a forest of gorgonians, some as high as 8 feet.

Church Point/ 10
Fisherman's
40'

⑪ Dottins

45'- 95'

  W

One of the popular reefs along the west coast, Dottins is part of the outer barrier reef. The reef starts at 30 feet, has a fairly flat top and then falls away to over 100 feet. It can be done as a first dive along the slope or a second dive along the top. For us it is a second dive, having just done a deep dive on the *SS Stavronikita*.

Dottins is known as a good reef for seeing turtles and we hope we will not be disappointed. Even though we have seen turtles on most of the reefs we have dived so far, we can never see too many of these lovely creatures. We are not sure they feel the same way about us.

Dive Profile

The dive boat ties to the buoy marking the reef, but as there is current running we are briefed that the dive will be a drift. As we drop down on the reef and get our bearings, we see a turtle. It is not unduly disturbed by our presence but moves lazily away as if we have spoiled its view. And, a very nice view it is too.

The reef has a covering of about one third octocorals and two

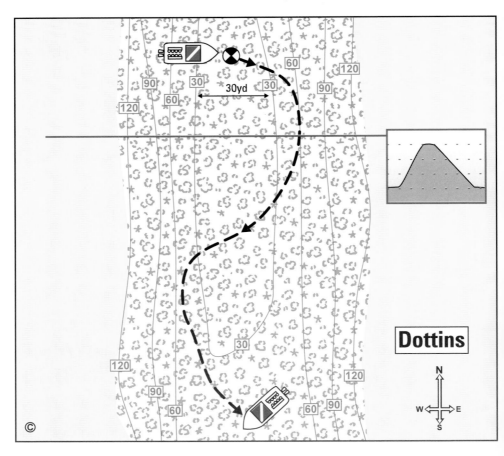

©

thirds stony corals. A wide variety of stony corals seem to find this a lucrative habitat. Most common are boulder star and great star coral and several different types of brain coral. There are some impressive patches of pillar coral; like stalagmites but unlike the hard wet surface of those found in caves, these underwater versions have a soft fuzzy look appropriate to the watery medium. We also find staghorn and finger coral and even an occasional patch of flower coral.

Sponges, too, are prolific. Big branching tube and vase sponges are home to a variety of small marine life and provide food for the many rock beauties we see moving about the reef. Some of the sponge's inhabitants are crinoids. In three colours— bronze, green and white—they wave their long arms at us, catching whatever the current is carrying. The arms have small hooks that attach themselves like Velcro to prey, so very little plankton escapes their grasp. The food is then passed down the arms to the central mouth. Feeding in a similar way are the many worms that dot the reef; both the large magnificent feather dusters and smaller more delicate shy feather dusters display their radioles like a fashion parade.

The fish life on the reef is varied. Hamlets, butterflyfish, stoplight parrotfish and blue chromis abound—and keep an eye open for those turtles.

Thanks to Mary and Stuart of West Side Scuba Centre.

A buoy marks this reef, in 80 feet of water. It makes an interesting multi-level dive, as the reef top rises to 45 feet as you move north. It is an extension of Dottins reef so shares similar coral cover and reef life, including turtles who, even when you do not see them, leave evidence of their presence by the bite marks in the sponges. Although apparently destructive, the ecosystem of the reef requires that a balance of different organisms be maintained. If not kept under control, the sponges would dominate the reef.

**Little Sandy 12
Lane
45'-80'**

It appears that this area is subject to some outside influence, causing a good deal of variability in the marine life. Some days there is an abundance of fish, including big schools. Other days the reef seems bereft of life. There are good coral formations to admire on the not-so-busy days and, when the reef fish are present, so usually are the barracuda.

**Johnson's 13
50'-85'**

14 *SS Stavronikita*

20'-140'

or

W

It is a strange history for a ship to have spent half of its life on the water and half under it. But that is the story of the *SS Stavronikita*, Barbados' premier dive site. The *Stav*, as she is called by those in the know, is quite unexpected in many ways. Despite being a valuable 365-foot freighter only 20 years old, she was sunk deliberately and took only 13 minutes to go down.

In 1976 the *Stav* was carrying a cargo of cement to Barbados when a fire overwhelmed her and she was towed to port where she stayed for 2 years, before being purchased by Barbados to be used as a dive site. But, it is no mean feat sinking a 4,000 ton ship, so explosives experts were brought in from Puerto Rico. It is possible to see the explosion holes where the hull is peeled back like an opened gift. Two hundred pounds of explosives were used, so it is surprising to see her still intact, sitting upright and showing no signs of disintegrating.

As with the *Pamir*, she has been cleared of all fittings likely to trap divers, and the spaces we pass through are clear and open.

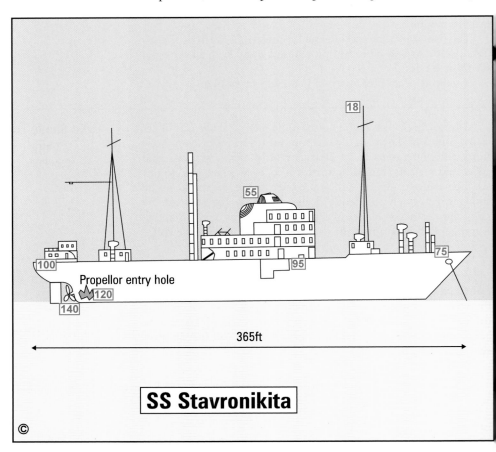

Propellor entry hole

365ft

SS Stavronikita

Colleen emerges from the hold of the SS Stavronikita. Barbados has more wreck dives than any of the other islands covered in this book.

However, as befits the dignity of a large ship, she has to be dived with caution. She is deep and large enough to get lost inside but that, of course, is the thrill of diving her.

Our dive group is split into two: those who will go down to the propeller at 140 feet and penetrate the wreck there (3-tank rating), and those who will dive through the upper deck cabins, maximum depth 100 feet (2-tank rating). This plan enables divers of different experience levels to enjoy the wreck. A spare tank and regulator is suspended at 20 feet in case anyone is short of air for a safety stop.

Dive Profile

The descent down the buoy line takes us to the top of the forward mast at 20 feet. From there we drop quickly down onto the top deck, at 80 feet, passing through a passageway and out toward the aft deck. We tip over the port rail and down to the huge propeller. You can dive underneath the propeller, taking you to a maximum of 140 feet. Our route down is determined by the current flowing across the wreck, the route being designed to keep the party together. It is a couple of minutes longer than a direct drop to the propeller, possible when there is no current. The direct route allows for more bottom time, so our passage through and up the inside of the wreck is accelerated.

The visibility is poor during our dive, perhaps only 30 feet; again, this is not the norm. The main superstructure is hardly visible during the descent via the forward mast, but it looms out of the murk, making an impressive sight. In normal visibility, it is possible to see most of the ship.

We pass to the starboard side of the propeller and enter one of the explosion holes just in front. The prop shaft is clearly visible as we swim inside the ship and up through a series of compartments to enter the cabins. There are numerous cabins linked by a network of corridors. It is possible to go into the engine room but a light is needed. The route we take is dark at times, but never completely black. Escape routes out of the hull are frequently visible.

Our route takes us through the cargo hold and finally up to the bow. In the darker sections of the interior there is no marine growth, but deepwater sea fans make a frilly curtain around many of the entry areas. The dark recesses are tailor-made accommodation for a variety of squirrel fish and black bar soldierfish.

Once out on the deck, sponges occur, some seeming to have taken on the huge proportions of the ship. Tall yellow tube sponges pose like pieces of deck equipment and purple row pore rope sponges give the ship a brighter costume than ever it had afloat. The bow is alive with fish, perhaps admiring the ship's coat of arms still proclaiming her heritage on the side of the bow. A barracuda patrols the foredeck, as if on anchor watch.

It is time to ascend for our safety stop and a last look at the mast as we move up it to the buoy line. The once gleaming mast is now thick with growth, and fish fuss around it like seagulls following a fishing boat.

There is usually little or no current in this area but there are always exceptions to the rule and we are glad of the buoy line to hang on to as the current is strong. From here under normal visibility you can look down on to the *Stav* and see the whole ship, although the fact that it had taken us 20 minutes at a reasonable pace to swim through her is a good indication of her size.

Thanks to William of West Side Scuba Centre.

---

15 *Lord*
Combermere
40'-60'

Sitting in 60 feet of water, the wreck of the *Lord Combermere* is not highly rated by local dive operators, particularly as they have a choice of other good wrecks to dive. The site is rarely dived but, as with most wreck sites, there are a good number of fish and photographers will enjoy the dive.

---

16 **Belle Buoy**
20'-60'

This is an easy, shallow dive on a dome shaped reef. In parts it is a forest of gorgonians. The sides of the dome slope gradually, with hard coral providing an undulating terrain, reminiscent of gently rolling hills. Schooling fish are tame, suggesting they are fed by divers occasionally.

---

17 **Clarke's Bank/**
Silver Bank
50'-140'

A site well worth including in your dive schedule both because it is one of the prettiest reefs and for the unique experience of discovering that your buddy is a submarine. The *Atlantis* submarine visits this reef, which means that no one is allowed to anchor or lay fishing lines or nets. The impact of these rules is manifest in the clean healthy condition of the reef.

If you are travelling with non-divers, think about arranging to dive when your companions are on the submarine. They can see you clearly through the windows, though you will not be able to distinguish their faces. The fish are fed in order to guarantee a good array of sea life for the submarine passengers, so divers benefit from this practice.

The reef slopes gently on one side and steeply on the other. The width of the reef narrows to the northwest, but the sea life is abundant throughout. Both hard and soft corals create an attractive vista of colour and texture.

Although a wreck, the *Lord Willoughby,* lies in sand in about 100 feet of water just off the reef, many operators prefer to spend the time enjoying the reef.

Shark's Bank 18
60'-80'

Pretty much straight off the end of the Careenage in Bridgetown, there is a reef in the shape of a shark. It is a small reef which in February and March plays host to a barracuda convention. Schools of 50 or more mill around as if waiting for something to happen.

Carlisle Bay 19
Wrecks
8'-50'

  C

This is one of the Caribbean's remarkable dive sites. On one dive it is possible to dive three and a half wrecks, sunk between 1917 and 1996. For those interested in marine life, one wreck alone could occupy one dive and the whole site is shallow enough to give you extended bottom time. All this and more. It is a site where seahorses are seen routinely and frogfish and batfish are not uncommon. There are more fish on this site than any other in Barbados. And, you can even reach it by snorkelling from the shore. It is the diver's equivalent of being a child in a sweet shop. The wrecks are:

Berwind: (Sometimes spelt Berwyn but we have it on authority that *Berwind* is the correct spelling.)

A 60-foot French tug boat, scuttled by her crew after being shot by a German U-boat, it is the most encrusted of the wrecks, having been down there for 60 years. She sits upright although listing slightly to port and is pretty much in one piece. Depth range: 8 to 20 feet

Ce-Trek: Ten years ago this 45-foot cement-construction fishing boat was sunk deliberately to make an artificial reef. She lies on her starboard side and has become an underwater aquarium with a host of volunteer inhabitants. Depth range: 20 to 40 feet

Eillion: This 110-foot freighter was sunk in June 1996. She was confiscated for drug trafficking 6 years ago and is now sentenced to spend the rest of her life on the sea bed. The wreck can be penetrated and there is a selection of the ship's equipment scattered around the hull. At the time of writing, we could still see her name across the transom. Depth range: 35 to 55 feet

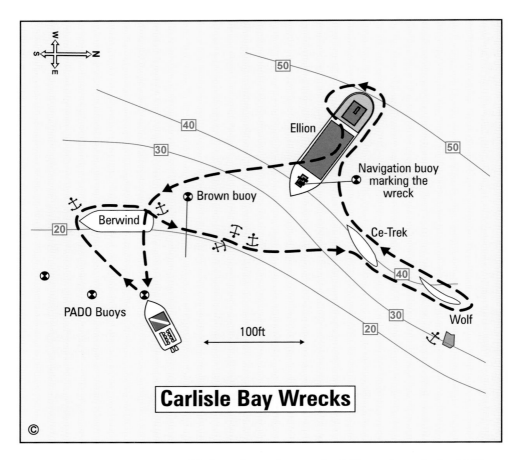

Carlisle Bay Wrecks

Wolf: The only wreck not to be deliberately sunk, the *Wolf* was damaged in a hurricane in 1955 and sank at her anchor. She was a wooden 42-footer and all that remains for divers to see is her keel. Depth range: 35 to 45 feet

Dive Profile

These wrecks are so close together that it does not really matter what order you see them in. The buoys which the dive stores use are close to the *Berwind*. We swim first to the *Ce-Trek*. Under the stern is a deep recess which we feel sure will deliver something interesting. A spotted drum prances back and forth, its tomahawk fin flowing as it turns, like the skirt of a dancer. Tucked behind the drum a dog snapper peers suspiciously at us. Squirrel fish and a rock hind drift in and out.

When I finally drag myself away, I find Brian stroking the throat of a goldentail moray eel. It is not a closely guarded secret that dive stores feed the fish in Carlisle Bay, but it is, after all, an artificial reef, so why not? It certainly results in a mass of fish. Around *Ce-Trek* are schools of tomates, grunts and sergeant majors.

As we swim across to *Eillion*, small patches of coral have their own fish communities. Half a dozen tobacco fish hover above one coral head. Their brown mottled back, in contrast to the white middle section, may be how they attracted the name. Just to remind us of the larger fish life, a sizeable barracuda cruises by.

The *Eillion* has only been down 3 months when we dive this site. We have never seen a new wreck before and it is a strange sight. She is at the stage of still looking like a ship, not a wreck.

It is too early for much encrustation, though on the top deck gorgonians are already 2 or 3 feet high. Flamingo tongues cling to the gorgonians, which is a bit of bad luck for something just getting started because flamingo tongues eat gorgonians. Surgeonfish are also finding a good supply of food, as they eat their way through the algae covering the ship.

The wreck has been made safe for penetration, although we do not go inside. Instead we set off to spend the remainder of our time on the *Berwind*. Having been down the longest, it has the most marine life, inside and out. Peering through a port hole a throng of glassy sweepers stare back at us.

The scorpionfish, beautiful in its own way, but sporting painful stinging barbs along its back.

The outside of the hull is heavily encrusted. Loggerhead sponges grow out from the sides and even anemones cling to the hull. A closer look at the hull reveals gobies and shrimps. Much bigger but easy to miss are several scorpionfish. Heavily disguised, they will remain still unless you molest them which really is not a very good idea.

This area is excellent for macro photography and worth a second visit. It does get busy at certain times of the day and a morning dive is likely to be the least crowded. A number of stores have a daily midday or 2.30 p.m. dive on this site.

Thanks to Michael Young of Underwater Barbados.

20 *Friar's Craig and Asta Reef*

30'-90'

 W

The first dive we do in Barbados, and we are promised two reefs and a wreck which makes us wonder whether none of the three is interesting enough for a dive in its own right. But, on the contrary, this dive is like a taster pack for Barbados. There is a steeply sloping reef to 90 feet, a flat reef in shallower water and a wreck, Barbados diving for the day tripper.

The *Friar's Craig*, a 170-foot freighter, was sunk in 1985. She has been a resident of Barbados for much longer, lying to her anchor in Carlisle Bay since the 1970s. Before sinking, she was cleaned and holes were cut to allow penetration by divers. Her final resting place is a patch of sand 50 feet deep guarded by two reefs, one on either side. When she hit bottom, she was pretty much in one piece but, since then, surge resulting from stormy weather has caused her to twist and break into three, still closely connected, pieces. She now bears little resemblance to her sister ship the *Pamir* (Site 5) which is still in one piece and can be penetrated by divers.

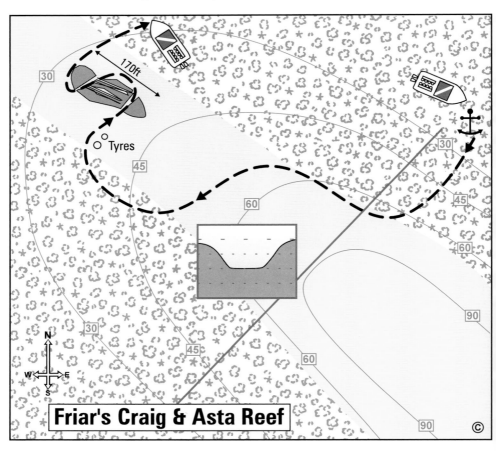

Friar's Craig & Asta Reef

The dive boat positions us off the Asta Hotel, a good clue to the location of the Asta Reef. We descend onto the top of the reef at 30 feet where a mass of sea rods and plumes wave their welcome to Barbados. Common sea fans add their applause. Even at this depth, there is quite a lot of surge.

As we move deeper over the edge of the reef, sponges start to dominate: vase, elephant ear and brown tube sponges. Wayne, our entertaining dive leader, finds a web burrfish, one of the pufferfish family, which decides to inflate just to be on the safe side. Since none of us attempts to take a bite out of it, it no doubt concludes its precautionary strategy has succeeded.

The slope then becomes steep, dropping to a sandy bottom at 90 feet. There is a good covering of hard coral and quite a variety of species. Boulder and great star coral, various brain corals and patches of pillar coral furnish the slope, softened by deepwater sea fans and sea plumes. The guests on the dive boat have set Wayne a mission to find lobster, but instead he finds a number of channel clinging crabs.

We swim west along the reef, for 100 yards, then cross a 200 foot wide sand channel to reach the other reef, called Round Bar Reef. This is shallower and flatter, meeting sand at 35 feet. Sponges, stony corals and octocorals provide a dense under-growth in which many small reef fish forage. Hamlets are common, as are bi-colour damselfish and juvenile trunkfish.

Thirty minutes into the dive we come across several tyres lying in the sand, clearly a sign post to the *Friar's Craig*. This function has not stopped a branching yellow tube sponge from making one of the tyres home, like a plant in an ornamental pot. We turn sharp right and head for the wreck.

The hull of the freighter is heavily encrusted, mainly with sea rods and fans but take a close look and you will find a myriad of marine life: segmented worms, shrimps, tiny gobies and blennies. The wreck acts as a magnet for fish, and we see more here than on the reef. There are hordes of sergeant majors, Spanish hogfish, chromis and grunts. Many trumpetfish use the cover of sea rods to stalk their prey. By Barbados standards, there are big fish here too. Spanish mackerel, black margates and a 3-foot dog snapper flirt with us from the safety of the ship's structures. A small resident turtle normally puts in an appearance, but not today. We have to be satisfied with two big French angelfish.

The bow lies twisted on its starboard side, a crane stretches across the cargo hold, the engine and parts of the ship's machinery sit in the sand to the port side of the aft deck, and the propeller lies half buried in the sand. There is a good swim-through where you will find grunts and squirrel fish sheltering. This is not a wreck for serious wreck divers but we find it harbours a lot of good sea life which provides another dimension to the dive.

Thanks to Wayne of Bubbles Galore.

21 Apple Experience
30'-80'

This is one of the south coast's fringing reefs. On the shallow area of the reef you will find lots of bushy gorgonians, taking on the appearance of a heathland. Deeper down the slope harder coral takes over with some especially pretty areas of finger coral.

22 Magic Isle
30'-60'

This fringing reef runs seawards from the shore for about 100 yards. Elkhorn coral grows on the upper section of the reef, changing to boulder and star coral as it descends. The usual range of reef fish can be found, including grunts, wrasse and squirrelfish.

23 Pieces of Eight
40'-60'

Although a fairly shallow fringe reef, it has quite a good quantity of reef fish. The name comes from the large pieces of coral, rather more than eight, but it gets the general message across. The stony coral tempts parrotfish to make the reef their home. Look out for the small marine life, including shrimps and arrow crabs.

24 Southwinds

Close Encounters
30'-40'

 W

This is a shallow pretty reef, close to the shore, in the shape of a horseshoe. Its main attraction, though, is Sarge the stingray, who likes to be hand-fed flying fish. And, on the rare occasion he does not turn up, the spotted moray eels are eager to entertain for a morsel of squid. Sarge does not like squid, for which Barbados squids are no doubt extremely grateful.

Sarge has been fed since he was young and, although he disappeared for a few months last winter, he came back, but twice the size. He clearly had not been going hungry. He is quite boisterous, like a puppy, and seems to enjoy not just being fed but being stroked, too.

Dive Profile

We are told the dive boat ride will be 40 seconds, we think it was actually 45. The boat anchors on sand and we prepare to enter the water. Our briefing has told us we can feed Sarge and we all hope he will put in an appearance, but you know how reliable fish are.

Eagerly following the anchor line down, we look below us and see only sand. Then swooping in, like a jet fighter hugging the bottom to avoid the radar, comes Sarge. It takes a few minutes for the group to descend and gather and Sarge paces up and down, keen to start lunch. Mike, our dive leader, offers a piece of flying fish and Sarge dashes in, so eager he forgets to put on the brakes and simply piles into Mike. As a thank you, he strokes Mike with his wing before looking to see if any of us happen to have a spare flying fish tucked in our wetsuits.

He takes fish from anyone offering it and always completes the exercise with a stroke of his wing. He appears happy to be handled and although this is somewhat unnatural behaviour, Sarge does

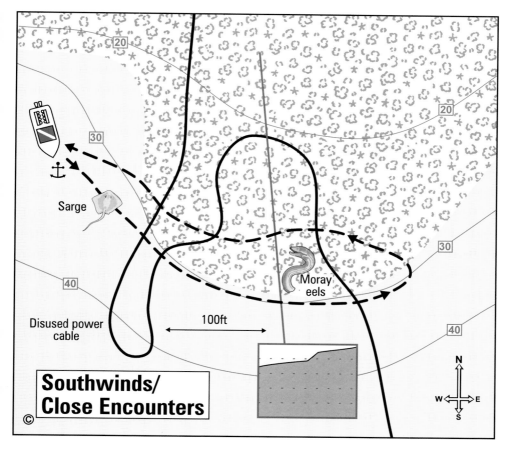

**Southwinds/
Close Encounters**

©

Labels within the map: 20, 20, 30, 30, Sarge, 40, Moray eels, 100ft, Disused power cable, 40, N, W E, S

not seem to be suffering from it. However, divers who have their fingers sucked into Sarge's mouth along with the fish do not necessarily feel the same way.

We drag ourselves off to the reef which starts from a sandy bottom at 40 feet. There is a mixture of coral types. Some of the hard corals are dead but lovely swaying gorgonians have taken their place. These attract trumpetfish, as they provide excellent cover. Large and small trumpetfish blend with the reef, changing colour to suit the background.

The reef is a gentle slope and we swim along it, travelling east. Big patches of pencil coral cover part of the reef, which is well endowed with reef fish. Black durgons, many small yellowtail snappers, grunts and chromis fill your mask with activity. Look into the crevices made by the coral and you will see dusky squirrelfish. They are smaller and shyer than the squirrelfish common on Caribbean reefs. They have the typical large eyes, but are more bronze than red, and their alternating silver stripes reflect the sun, making the fish look as if it has been fashioned from burnished metal.

Mike arrives at an area where a couple of spotted morays live, and lures them out with chopped squid. Normally night feeders, they have no objection to a midday snack. The eel, emboldened by the prospect of food, comes out of his hole and curls and turns around Mike like a whirling dervish.

Time to go back to the boat and another swim across the sand. Your eye may be caught by sudden movement as a sand tilefish disappears into the sand. They will hover, with a quivering movement, just above their burrow in the sand, until they decide you are too close and then they head for cover.

Like the sand tilefish we head for the cover of the boat; feeding Sarge has made us all think of lunch.

Thanks to Mike and his boat captain, Charlie, of Exploresub.

Sarge the stingray performs for the divers in exchange for food.

25 Carl's Point
20'-60'

Although there is a shallower section to this reef, most of the dive is spent at 60 feet. The reef stretches out into a point, where lots of sea fans and gorgonians strain the water for food.

Sumptuous pillar coral is one of the assets of this reef. The range of hard corals creates a terrain which provides hiding holes for spotted moray eels and a crowd of invertebrates.

26 Caribbee
60'-130'

The banking reef is only 30 feet across at Caribbee but that neither narrows the range of marine life on the reef nor the interesting behaviour associated with it. We saw a trumpetfish shadowing a parrotfish like a dive buddy. It was using the parrotfish as camouflage and would pounce from its cover to grab any vulnerable fish. A similar display of aggression was given by a damselfish when a spotted moray had carelessly allowed its tail to rest on the damselfish's algae patch. The territorial damselfish rushed forward and bit the eel's tail, causing it to move off swiftly before the attack was repeated. Puffed by its success, the damselfish returned to its quiet tending of its farm while the eel tried to recover its dignity. Rules are rules on the reef and size does not necessarily enter the argument. But the tables will be turned at night when the damselfish shelters in a crevice and the eel is out hunting, sniffing out its prey as they sleep.

This is the continuation of Caribbee. Steep slopes on either side are smothered in coral and sponges. Nooks and crannies reveal large crabs and sheltering nocturnal fish. When there is no current running, it is a good reef for photography as many small fish inhabit the sponges and corals.

Castle Bank **27**
50'-120'

The Muff is one of Barbados' premier sites. It is a steep-sided ridge no more than 30 feet across, dropping to 130 feet on both sides. The inner slope descends steeply and the outer slope takes a more gentle descent. The top of the ridge is not even, instead it rises and falls like a roller coaster track.

An exciting seascape is not all that makes this a good dive; the marine life is varied and rich. For coral lovers there are pristine coral heads and plenty of black coral. The sponges are jumbo size and extremely colourful. Blobs of startling orange mark the position of elephant ear sponges tucked into gaps between the coral.

The fish, too, seem to appreciate the reef and are always plentiful. In addition to all the usual reef fish, schooling barracuda, including juveniles, are a common sight.

Visibility is generally very good on The Muff, but sea conditions do vary. It can be quite rough when there is a strong southeasterly wind. It is rarely too rough to dive, it simply requires divers to be calm and efficient when on the surface.

The Muff **28**
70'-130'

As an extension of The Muff, it is a very similar dive. The top of the reef is somewhat flatter, but the marine life is every bit as interesting. As well as an impressive selection of hard corals, the sea fans on this reef are the stars of the show. They are large and delicate, a blatant clue to the fact that the site has not been dived for all that long, and there is little or no anchor damage.

Many parrotfish and filefish have made Ernie's Bar their home and hordes of small reef fish get on with their lives uninterrupted by divers.

Ernie's Bar **29**
60'-135'

30 Mount Charlie
75'-140'

You might reasonably expect that the mount in the name described the topography of this reef and you would not be disappointed. To be accurate it is more a mound than a mountain but some poetic licence is to be forgiven.

Mount Charlie is an oval reef, just over 100 feet long and 30 feet wide, which slopes down to 140 feet on each side. The top sits 75 feet below the surface, making a precision drop by the dive boat highly desirable.

The island-type configuration of the reef seems to have resulted in the coral cramming itself onto the reef, as if surrounded by an uninhabitable desert. This has caused some strange morphological developments as sponges bend around to fit the available space. Some very large brain corals have grabbed territory by their sheer bulk. Loggerhead sponges are as common as vase sponges, as if their more solid structure were able to withstand the crush. These sponges are easily distinguished, as the vases have a hollow centre as compared to the honeycomb centre of the loggerheads.

31 Graham Hall
Shallows
40'-70'

Much shallower than the rest of the banking reefs at its top, the ridge is small being only 30 feet high. It does have some charming features though. Some of the very many vase sponges have taken on the shape of giant armchairs, where one side has been broken off or nibbled away to suggest a hollow in which one could sit.

As well as the lovely sponges there is a good variety of coral, even some sheet coral. Soft corals thrive here, too; gorgonians and sea fans add to the attractions of the reef.

32 Little Point
50'-130'

A finger of coral like a pinnacle sticks up from 130 feet making another area of interesting terrain. Dive around the pinnacle and marvel at the volume of marine life supported by this closed community and you will be joined by a procession of fish, probably doing much the same thing.

33 High Wire
65'-140'

An oval 200 feet long and 30 feet wide has a steep side to 120 feet on its landward side and a gentle slope to 140 feet on the seaward side. Stretched across the reef, 20 foot above the bottom, is an old telecommunications cable now totally enrobed in sparkling sponges like a Christmas decoration.

Not to be outdone, sponges on the reef grow like flashy table decorations. You would need a rather large table though, as some of the vase sponges are over 6 feet high.

The reef is half a mile offshore so attracts fish not seen on all of Barbados' reefs. Spanish mackerel, yellowtail and dog snappers and even jacks occasionally put in an appearance.

Because historically Barbados has not been promoted as a dive destination, we were surprised to discover that there were 12 dive operators, one of whom has two bases, and a specialist retail operation. The reason for the large number of stores is in part due to the size of the tourist market in Barbados. So even if, as some recently gathered statistics show, almost 20 percent of visitors do at least one dive, this amounts to a lot of diving. Many of those dives will be resort/discover scuba courses, generating the customers who are helping to keep 12 operators in business.

Operators range from those who have been in business almost as long as there has been recreational diving in Barbados through to recent start-ups. There are both relatively large stores and one-person operations. There are even freelance operators wandering along the beach offering diving. We have not included these vendors as they have no fixed base and simply rent equipment from local operators and hire a local boat for the trip. It is unlikely that they will carry safety equipment, such as VHF radio and oxygen. They do not always know the precise locations of the reefs and, more importantly, they are not always qualified instructors or divemasters, and may not even be certified divers. They may be cheaper but frankly not so much cheaper that they justify the difference in terms of quality, comfort and safety.

There is a dive association called PADO (Professional Association of Dive Operators). The association is relatively new and not all stores have been recruited as members as yet. Its aims are to set minimum safety standards for operators and to preserve and enhance the marine environment.

Overall, we found facilities here pretty good. Most dive stores are running professional operations with decent equipment and good boats, as good as any we have seen in the Caribbean. At the time of writing, several stores were investing in new equipment and attempting to raise the general standard of diving in Barbados.

Unlike on many of the other islands, Sherwood equipment was not so prevalent. Instead, Dacor and US Divers seemed to be the preferred manufacturers. One reason is that Barbados has a specialist diving retailer, Hazell's Waterworld Inc., who also supplies the operators. There are two stores, one in Sandy Bank and one in the Boatyard. Both owned and managed by John Hazell, they are dealers for Dacor, Sports Divers, US Divers, and Apollo. Equipment is duty free and available at US recommended prices. They do not sell wetsuits, as these are subject to very high import taxes. As well as sales, Hazell's offer equipment repair and servicing. Cressi-Sub equipment is also used by one store.

Dive boats are a mixture of purpose-built dive boats, adapted pirogues and in one case a glass bottomed boat. Since all the dive sites are near to land and trips to the sites are in relatively calm water, engine size and speed is not so much of an issue as on some other islands. You may want to choose more on the basis of onboard facilities, shade, number of divers on the boat, and entry and exit methods.

Cost

The Barbados dive industry is quite competitive and dive prices are very similar between stores. The average price for a single tank dive with equipment is $45 and without $35. Packages are available at all stores and these vary rather more. A 10-dive package can cost between $250 and $350 with equipment and $190 to $300 without equipment. Some of the packages are quite creative, so check what is included.

A PADI open water course costs $350, which should include everything: manuals, equipment and certification documents.

Prices are quoted in either Barbados dollars (roughly half the value of a US dollar) or US dollars, so check before you commit to anything. It is worth shopping around to find a store that suits you. The operators with the best boats and service were charging no more than anyone else.

Operators

There are five stores on the west coast. Typically they dive down as far as the SS Stavronikita and sometimes to Carlisle Bay. In and around Bridgetown and Carlisle Bay are a further five stores. They dive the south coast and as far north as the SS Stavronikita. The south coast then has the remaining three stores, all of whom dive as far as the SS Stavronikita and the reefs along the south coast. All operators will arrange transport, free in most cases, by van or car from and to your accommodation, providing you are roughly within their area.

The West

Three of the stores on the west coast are located in hotels, although they are all independent operations. In each case, diving is part of a larger water sports offering to guests of the hotel, but diving is available for non-residents, too.

Hightide Watersports **5**, located in the Sandy Lane Hotel, is the largest of these three operators. The owner-manager Willie Hewitt is a Barbadian, though he grew up in New Zealand where he learned to dive and worked as an instructor for 10 years.

Hightide Watersports' main operation is at the prestigious Sandy Lane Hotel, where they are responsible for all water sports. These are complimentary to hotel guests and divers who book a package with Hightide Watersports. So if you have any energy left after a dive, you can try windsurfing, sailing, kayaking or water skiing. Or for golfing enthusiasts, the Sandy Lane Hotel has its own course.

At the time of writing, less than half of Hightide Watersports' divers were from the hotel, the remainder were from other hotels and apartments, villas, etc. In 1996 Hightide Watersports offered a 7 night/12 dive package at the Woodville Beach Hotel (an apartment style hotel) for $622 per person. We stayed here while conducting our research in Barbados and found it extremely comfortable and flexible with large airy rooms and well fitted-out kitchens.

But back to the diving, Hightide Watersports offers a high level of service including setting up your equipment and dismantling and rinsing it afterwards. They aim to be flexible to cater for different needs. For example, photographers are allocated their own divemaster, so that they do not need to move at the same speed as the rest of the group.

The dive boat is a purpose-built 32-foot dive boat with a 220 hp inboard diesel engine. You enter the water by a giant stride from the back of the boat and re-entry is by a substantial deep ladder. There is a fresh water shower and complimentary refreshments. Dive equipment is Dacor, Sherwood and US Divers. A Nikonos V is available for rent.

Hightide Watersports is a member of PADO, the Barbados dive association, and PIRA (PADI International Resort Association).

The diving area covered by Hightide Watersports at Sandy Lane runs from Maycock's Reef to *Friar's Craig*. Some days 2-tank dives are offered, on other days dives are single tank. The more southern dive sites are covered by Hightide Watersports' other store at the Boatyard **8**, on the south coast. From here you dive from a purpose-built wooden dive boat ably skippered by Victor. By combining diving from these two locations, Hightide Watersports are able to offer dive packages to cover the whole of the island's diving.

Also based in a hotel and managing all of its water sports facilities is a new operation called Carib Ocean Divers **3**. Opened in 1996 by Stuart Kabler, an American, and Wynter Piggot, a Barbadian, the store is positioned on the premises of the Glitter Bay Hotel and the Royal Pavillion. The former is a family apartment style hotel, offering mainly suites, and the Royal Pavillion provides luxury accommodation in all beachfront ocean-facing rooms.

Wynter runs the water sports while Stuart, the erstwhile Caribbean representative for Cressi-Sub, looks after the diving. Stuart claims he started the store because he believed there was demand for a quality operation at that location, and his aim is to provide just that.

The store is equipped with a 32-foot purpose-built dive boat, with small Boston Whalers as back-up. Not surprisingly, the all-new equipment is Cressi-Sub. Carib Ocean Divers has plans to retail a full range of equipment.

The dive range of the store is from Maycock's Reef in the north to Clark's Bank in the south. This store had been open less than six months when we visited, so was still developing its offer. They have not yet joined the dive association but will no doubt be encouraged to do so by the current membership.

Further up the coast at the King's Beach Hotel is Reefers and

Wreckers **1**. Owned and managed by Michael Mahy, a very personable Jamaican/Barbadian, the store operates next to the hotel's water sports facilities but is independent of it.

Michael has been in the water sports business all his life and has been diving for the last 14 years. Although this is the most northern of the dive stores, Michael lives on the south side so can pick up divers who are staying in the south for them to get a taste of the diving along the northwest side. Michael dives the west coast from Maycock's reef to the SS *Stavronikita*.

The dive boat is a pirogue with twin engines, equipped with tank holders. Equipment is mainly Dacor and US Divers. Confined water training is in the King's Beach Hotel pool, and resort courses are conducted on the beach.

Reefers and Wreckers is not currently a member of PADO, Michael preferring to wait until he sees how the association develops. But he is a supporter of the idea of permanent moorings, instead of anchoring on the reef, and has installed some of his own moorings, rather than wait until the association is able to do so.

Michael has a good knowledge of the location of the reefs in his area, having acquired it from local fishermen. He put it to good use when we dived with him, by accurately finding a 30-foot wide reef. Many of the reefs at the northern end of the west coast are less than 5 minutes from his store. This is a small operation; Michael leads every dive, resulting in a personal service tailored to individual needs.

The other two stores along this coast are not located in hotels. West Side Scuba Centre **4** is a beach facility with a bar, and a swimming pool used for confined water training. It is a pleasant place to enjoy a drink after diving and to get a lunchtime snack. Dinner and entertainment are available in the evenings.

Peter Grannum, the owner manager, is a Barbadian who grew up in Trinidad and started this operation in 1993. His experience of diving in Barbados predates the formation of the West Side Scuba Centre, as he was previously a manager for another Barbados store.

West Side Scuba have a 32-foot pirogue with a 225 hp engine, making trips to the dive sites generally less than 15 minutes; this covers a range from Maycock's to Carlisle Bay. The pirogue is fitted with a good alloy boarding ladder.

The normal dive schedule is to do a 2-tank dive in the morning and a single tank in the afternoon. Resort course dives are run over lunch time. Peter believes that many people diving in Barbados are part of a family group, where not everyone is a diver. The 2-tank morning dive has the divers in the party back by lunch time and free to spend their afternoon with their family.

Most of the dives are done as drifts, but for safety reasons the boat is anchored while the divers enter the water. This allows less experienced divers time to adjust their equipment and descend

Many of Barbados' stores have fast, purpose-built boats, providing space to don equipment and offering easy entry and exit procedures.

via the anchor line. West Side Scuba Centre is a member of PADO and sees its main aim to be the establishment of permanent moorings, so that they will no longer need to anchor on the reef.

The only other west side store is Blue Reef Water Sports **2**. This is a beach store operated by Barbadian Alston Fergusson. Alston is an ex-spearfisherman who has been running this operation since 1979. It was previously at the Glitter Bay but was moved to its current location early in 1996 when Carib Ocean Divers took over the site. The dive boat is a glass bottomed boat.

Carlisle Bay and Bridgetown

One store is located on the Careenage in Bridgetown, the others are spread around the edge of the bay.

Coral Island Divers **6** is the only store on the island to operate from a jetty. The Careenage is in the centre of Bridgetown and is used by many tourist-based and other commercial vessels. Coral Island is at the sea end of the Careenage.

The store is a partnership of two instructors, Kip and Sharmain; the store's administration manager, Charlotte; and local investors. Their intention was to cater to cruise ship passengers by providing a dive boat and service able to cope with the particular needs of cruise ships. That meant a big boat, dockside boarding (as opposed to beach boarding), and good safety standards, insurance etc.

In 1993, they opened their doors and have largely achieved their goal. Four times a week they take cruise ship passengers diving in their 40-foot Power Cat equipped with two 240 hp engines, an upstairs seating area and a bathroom. The boat can accommodate up to 25 divers for a 2-tank dive. Coral Island Divers also takes divers other than cruise ship passengers and offers the normal range of 6 and 10-dive packages. At the time of writing, there were plans to acquire an additional boat, a 28-foot cabin cruiser, to take out smaller groups on busy cruise ship days.

Coral Island Divers also has a retail offer, taking advantage of a duty free concession for dive gear. They are a US Divers dealer.

Their other point of difference is that they offer nitrox, training and diving. Both Kip and Sharmain are nitrox instructors. A nitrox introductory course takes 1 to 2 days and costs $150, and a full training course costs $250 and takes 2 to 3 days. A nitrox dive carries a premium of $10 per dive for the gas. They promote nitrox as giving additional safety rather than longer or deeper dives, though they are quick to point out that it doubles your bottom time on the *SS Stavronikita* (at 135 feet).

Coral Island Divers are members of PADO and supportive of its aims to ensure minimum safety standards.

Barbados' oldest dive store is located in Carlisle Bay. The Dive Shop **9** is run by Haroon Degia, whose father opened the dive store in 1966. From The Dive Shop's beach location, the wreck of the *Berwind* is snorkelling distance away.

The Dive Shop uses a 30-foot pirogue, equipped with tank racks and a 225 hp engine. This puts all the sites around the south coast within easy reach, and they dive up the west coast to the *SS Stavronikita*. Boarding is from the beach; the sea comes to within 30 feet of the store so there is an effortless walk to the boat. Carlisle Bay is very sheltered and the beach shelves gradually.

The Dive Shop organises regular bottle hunting dives in Carlisle Bay and, although we are reluctant to make guarantees, the divers on the dive boat with us found a bottle when they did a bottle dive. It was declared a 17th century specimen, but who knows? Our advice to them was to hold the dream and not attempt to get it authenticated, lest it turn out to be a heavily encrusted Coke bottle.

The Dive Shop has Sea and Sea and Nikonos V cameras for rent. Sunfish sailing dinghies and windsurfers are also available for rent.

Many guests come from local hotels and apartments, especially Cacrabank Beach Apartment and the Island Inn Hotel. At Cacrabank, 7 nights including unlimited diving is around $500 per person. Accommodation and unlimited diving at the Island Inn is just under $1,000 for 7 days.

The store is efficiently managed by Haroon who ensures a friendly and informal atmosphere. The dives are lead by his team of divemasters. The Dive Shop is a member of PADO.

Right in the centre of Carlisle Bay is Underwater Barbados **7**, owned and run by Barbadian Michael Young. Michael is a master scuba instructor and an enthusiastic teacher. He has been in business from his beachside store since 1989. He is a member of PADO and believes that one of its key roles should be to educate the local population about the value of the marine environment to Barbados.

Michael uses a 31-foot pirogue with a very good boarding ladder. It has a wide platform as the bottom step, enabling you to gain a secure footing before climbing the rest of the ladder. He also has a 16-foot Boston Whaler which takes small groups, maximum four divers. Boarding is from the beach.

Michael is interested in underwater photography and has both a Nikonos V still camera and a JVC video camera in a housing available for rental. His dive equipment is all Sherwood.

Michael works with many different hotels but he has a booth, run by his nephew, in the Coconut Court Beach Hotel. The hotel's pool is available for confined water training and discover scuba sessions, although the beach in front of the store is calm and shallow enough for training. The Coconut Court Beach Hotel's rates range from $70 to $100 per night per room for one or two people, excluding diving.

You may dive with Michael or one of his team of divemasters. Michael's team works as a close-knit group, providing a personal service which brings back repeat customers from the UK, USA, Germany and Holland.

The other store in Carlisle Bay is Dive Boat Safari **10**, another long established store. It was set up in 1983 by George Hurley, a Barbadian with 20 years experience in the dive industry. His store is immediately opposite the entrance to the Hilton, though he draws divers from much further afield, in particular divers staying at the Oasis, 5 minutes away by car. Double occupancy room rates at the Hilton start at around $150 in the summer, increasing in the winter.

Dive Boat Safari uses a 30-foot pirogue and a 22-footer as dive boats. Boarding is from the beach a few yards from the store. Dive equipment is mainly Sherwood and there is a Nikonos V available for rent.

George leads some dives, carries out training and is assisted by two divemasters. George likes to offer a relaxed diving schedule, bringing divers back to the store between dives. His diving area is from the SS *Stavronikita* on the west side to St. Lawrence Gap on the south side. There is a daily afternoon dive on the Carlisle Bay wrecks, less than a minute's boat ride away. Dive Boat Safari is a member of PADO.

The South

At the easternmost end of the south coast diving area is St. Lawrence Gap where you will find Exploresub **13**. Exploresub is a PADI 5 star centre, offering diving and equipment sales. The owner Mike Seale started work as a commercial diver in 1969 and opened Exploresub in 1988.

The Exploresub dive boat is a purpose-built 33-footer with two 250 hp engines, quite a power pack when you consider they are only seconds away from some of the sites. But they are inside a shallow reef so the boat has to be planing in a very short distance in order to clear the reef. Exciting stuff. A new boat had just been delivered at the time of writing, a 42-foot custom-built twin diesel jet drive. Charlie, the boat captain, has been with the store almost since it opened and it is easy to see how he earned his Barbados Tourist Award for water sports in 1992. He was extremely helpful to divers on the boat.

Exploresub is quite a large operation and prides itself on the friendliness and professionalism of the staff. The dive briefings, given in the store before leaving for the dive site, were very thorough and informative, especially about the marine environment. Despite having several instructors, Mike still leads dives and is an avid underwater photographer. Some of his photographs appear in the Humann Fish Identification Guide. He has five Nikonos Vs available for rent, with any lens you could wish for. He also has an underwater video along with editing and colour enhancing equipment, so you can take away a record of your dive.

Exploresub is a Sherwood dealer, able to undertake warranty work. They also stock Tusa masks and fins.

Customers are drawn from a variety of hotels and cruise ships. The store is located right behind Divi Southwinds where some divers stay, but Exploresub also works with Sand Acres, Bougainvillaea, Little Bay and Yellow Bird. Package rates for hotels are between $80 and $120 per day, including dives, but excluding meals.

Exploresub dives the whole of the south coast and round as far as the SS *Stavronikita* which it can reach in under 20 minutes. On Mondays, Wednesdays and Fridays there are regular lunch time dives to feed Sarge, the hungry stingray, on Close Encounters (Site 24).

Exploresub is an active and enthusiastic member of PADO.

A couple of hundred yards to the west is the Sandy Beach Hotel, home to Bubbles Galore **12** . This is a relatively new operation which started business in The Boatyard in Carlisle Bay before moving to the Sandy Beach Hotel. The store is owned and run by Ravi and Glenn, both Barbadians. Ravi's wife, a divemaster, speaks seven languages so they can probably cope with whatever you speak.

Glenn has always worked in the diving industry but while Ravi has been diving since he was 12 years old, he recently made a career change from accountancy to diving. He finds diving much more fun and that is reflected in the style of the operation. Bubbles Galore like to make diving fun and relaxed. Dive leaders ensure a good atmosphere on the boat and around the store.

Bubbles Galore uses a 31-foot Bertram cabin cruiser as their dive boat, powered by two 140 hp diesel engines. If there is room on the boat, Bubbles are happy for non-diving companions to join the boat trip, to snorkel or just enjoy the sea breezes. From the store adjacent to Bubbles Galore, kayaks, sailing dinghies and windsurfers are available.

About one third of Bubbles Galore's guests are from the Sandy Beach Hotel, the remainder come from a variety of other accommodations. A lot of their business involves teaching, using the hotel's pool or the beach in calm conditions for confined water training. Both Glen and Ravi keep their training skills current, attending instructor training sessions as staff instructors. In 1997 they hosted an IDC (PADI Instructor Development Course) in Barbados.

Bubbles Galore is a member of PADO.

And last but by no means least, Scotch and Soda **11** is based along the south coast in Worthing. Now if the name has not given you enough of a clue about this store, one of the dive boats is called *Hangover*.

Charismatic Ram Edgehill, owner and manager, claims to be the 'oldest living diver' in Barbados but is somewhat more modest about his not inconsiderable talents as a musician. He plays and sings with a band called the Redmen. Ram runs his store from his home, the dive equipment is housed in a building in his garden, and from there it is a short walk down the beach to his dive boats. The larger of the two, *Scotch and Soda*, is a 32-foot sport fishing boat. A 21-foot pirogue, *Hangover*, is his second boat.

Ram has a very impressive collection of ancient bottles and many books on the subject. These are displayed in a variety of cabinets and also set in sand in glass-topped tables in his home.

This is a relaxed diving operation; Ram likes to dive only once a day. Wednesdays and Fridays are party days; he runs family dive cruises to the shallow wreck dives in Carlisle Bay. Non-diving family members and friends are welcome to come along for snorkelling, swimming or just having fun. After the dive, the on-board bar opens. Do not plan anything else for the rest of the day.

Scotch and Soda is a member of PADO.

Questioning our motives or just wondering who on Earth we are? A purple rope sponge demands an answer.

Contact Information

1	Reefers and Wreckers	Michael Mahy	Tel: (246) 422-5450 Fax: (246) 422-5450
2	Blue Reef Water Sports	Alston Fergusson	Tel: (246) 422-3133 Fax: (246) 422-3133
3	Carib Ocean Divers	Stuart Kabler	Tel: (246) 422-4414 Fax: (246) 422-3990
4	West Side Scuba Centre	Peter Grannum	Tel: (246) 432-2558 Fax: (246) 432-2558
5	Hightide Watersports	Willie Hewitt	Tel: (246) 432-0931 Fax: (246) 432-0931
6	Coral Isle Divers	Kip Blumenstein	Tel: (246) 431-9068 Fax: (246) 431-9068
7	Underwater Barbados	Michael Young	Tel: (246) 426-0655 Fax: (246) 426-0655
8	Hightide at The Boatyard	Willie Hewitt	Tel: (246) 432-0931 Fax: (246) 432-0931
9	The Dive Shop	Haroon Degia	Tel: (246) 427-9947 Fax: (246) 426-2031
10	Dive Boat Safari	George Hurley	Tel: (246) 427-4350 Fax: (246) 436-8946
11	Scotch and Soda	Ram Edgehill	Tel: (246) 435-7375
12	Bubbles Galore	Ravi Prathapchandra	Tel: (246) 435-8000
13	Exploresub	Mike Seale	Tel: (246) 435-6542 Fax: (246) 435-8214
	Hazell's Waterworld	John Hazell	Tel: (246) 426-4043 Fax: (246) 435-8063

Barbados Dive Operators

		1 Reefers and Wreckers	2 Blue Reef Water Sports	3 Carib Ocean Divers	4 West Side Scuba Centre	5 Hightide Watersports	6 Coral Isle Divers	7 Underwater Barbados	8 Hightide at The Boatyard	9 The Dive Shop	10 Dive Boat Safari	11 Scotch and Soda	12 Bubbles Galore	13 Exploresub
STAFF	Instructors	1	2	2	2	2	5	2	1	2	1	2	3	4
	Divemasters	0	2	2	2	1	1	2	1	3	2	1	1	0
	Diving Associations	P	PN	PNBC	P	P	PNB	PA	P	PNAC	P	PAC	P	PNB
	Languages	E	E	EG	E	E	E	E	E	E	E	E	EFGIS	EGS
BOATS	Dive Boats	1	1	2	1	2	2	2	1	2	2	2	1	2
	Shaded Boats	0	1	1	1	2	2	0	1	0	0	1	1	2
	Max. Divers per Boat	10	15	12	14	6-12	10-25	4-12	12	16	8-14	4-15	12	14
	Time to Dive Sites	5-25	5-30	5-20	5-15	5-35	5-30	5-40	5-25	5-30	5-20	5-40	5-30	5-30
	Dives per Day	2	2	2	3	2	4	3	2	3	3	1	3	3
	Pick Up by Boat from	C		CR						Y	Y			
EQUIPMENT	Equipment Sets	14	20	18	22	15	20	25	15	20	20	15	20	38
	Dive Equip. for Sale			2		1	3	1	1					3
	Dive Equip. for Rent				•		•	•	•		•			•
	Photo Equip. for Rent	•	•	•	•	•	•			•	•		•	•
	Tank Fills				•	•	•	•		•	•		•	•
	Equipment Servicing		•	•	•	•	•	•		•	•			
	O₂ on Boat	•	•	•	•	•	•	•	•	•	•			
	VHF on Boat	•		•	•	•	•	•	•	•	•			
MISC.	Owned by Resort													
	Other Water Sports	•		•		•			•	•			•	
	Pers. Liab. Insurance	•	•	•	•	•	•	•	•	•				•

Glossary

Algae: These are the plants of the reef. Algae takes many forms such as turtle grass beds, floating sargassum (sometimes called seaweed), pretty flower like-clusters found among the coral and coralline algae which takes the form of calcified encrustations. See sidebar on algae for more information.

Antipatharian: Black corals. A tree-like coral related to stony corals but instead of the polyps living inside corallite cups, the polyps live on the outside of its skeletal framework. This skeleton takes the form of branches. See sidebar on black coral.

Diurnal: Marine life which is active during the daytime and rests at night.

Echinoderms: A group of creatures which includes sea stars, sea cucumbers, crinoids, brittle stars and sea urchins. Their common ancestry is indicated by a five part body system. See sidebar on echinoderms.

Ecosystem: The system by which all the living organisms in an environment interact and contribute to the perpetuation of the environment.

Fusiform: A streamlined or tapered shape which allows a fish to move swiftly through the water. Barracuda are a good example of a fusiform shape.

Gorgonian: A form of coral which lacks the stony structure of hard corals. Gorgonians have a branching structure with apertures from which the polyps protrude. Polyps have eight tentacles (compared to the six tentacles of hard corals). Sea whips, rods plumes and fans are all part of the family of gorgonians.

Habitat: The natural living environment of a creature.

Hard Coral: Sometimes referred to as stony corals, these are the reef builders. Corals which form a hard calcium carbonate structure which houses the soft coral polyps are described as hard corals. These structures grow and thus extend the reef, providing further substratum on which other marine life can grow.

Herbivorous: The vegetarians of the sea. Refers to fish which eat algae. These are generally daytime feeders. These fish are necessary to keep the algae under control so that it does not suffocate the coral.

Hermatypic: These are reef building corals housing zooxanthellae to help the coral process enough food to grow at an adequate rate to build the reef.

Invertebrates: Creatures without a backbone. Generally used to describe any non-sessile marine life which is not a fish.

Mollusk: A creature with no skeleton, many of which have a shell to protect their soft bodies. The shell is formed from calcium carbonate secreted by the creature's mantle, a type of outer skin.

Nematocyst: A stinging mechanism used by many cnidarians (corals, hydroids, jellyfish and anemones) to catch their prey. They can cause anything from a mild irritation to a painful sting on human skin.

Nocturnal: Fish and other creatures which are active at night and rest during the day. Most hard corals, many invertebrates and the various species of big-eyed reddish fish are nocturnal. See sidebar on sunset on the reef.

Octocorals: What are referred to as 'soft' corals in the Caribbean. They are named for the eight (octo-) tentacles of the coral polyp, and in the Caribbean the class comprises mainly gorgonians.

Plankton: Tiny specks of life adrift in the ocean's currents and subject to the voracious appetites of plankton feeders on the reefs and in the open sea.

Pelagic: Open-ocean creatures not usually found on reefs although they occasionally venture inshore.

Podia: Tube-like feet found on echinoderms such as sea cucumbers and sea stars. The podia are controlled by an internal hydraulic system, giving them impressive holding power for very little energy. As well as aiding movement the podia transfer food to the mouth. See sidebar on echinoderms.

Polyp: The coral animal is called a polyp. The large stone-like structures you see on the reef are merely the homes of the coral animals, it is the small many-tentacled polyp that is the living coral. Sea anemones are simply large single polyps without the outer calcium carbonate structure of coral.

Sessile: Creatures that are permanently attached to a substratum and cannot move their location, though they may be able to move parts of their body.

Symbiosis: A way of living in harmony. When two creatures live together in a dependent relationship where both gain, they are said to have a symbiotic relationship.

Substratum: A rock or other hard surface which can be used as a base from which sessile marine life can develop.

Test: A kind of skeleton or shell. For example the hard round 'shells' of sea urchins or sand dollars found lying in the sand are the tests of the creatures. They are not strictly speaking exoskeletons, like a lobster shell for example, because the urchin has a thin layer of skin on the outside.

Zooplankton: Tiny animals which drift in the water column providing food for the many carnivorous filter feeders on the reef, such as coral. They have little chance of escape as they have hardly any ability to direct themselves.

Zooxanthellae: Tiny plants that live in a symbiotic relationship with coral. Using photosynthesis, these plants provide the coral with food and process the coral's waste products. See sidebar on coral bleaching.

Bibliography

The Nature of the Islands, Virginia Barlow
Cruising Guide Publications

Caribbean Reef Invertebrates and Plants, Dr. Patrick I. Colin
TFH Publications Inc., Reigate, UK.

Coral Reefs, Les Holliday
Salamander Books, London

Reef Coral Identification, Paul Humann
New World Publications

Reef Fish Identification, Paul Humann
New World Publications

Reef Creature Identification, Paul Humann
New World Publications

Coral Reefs - Peterson Field Guide, Eugene H. Kaplan
Houghton Mifflin Company, Boston

Southeastern and Caribbean Seashores - Peterson Field Guide
Eugene H. Kaplan
Houghton Mifflin Company, Boston

Coral Reefs of Tobago, Richard S. Laydoo
Institute of Marine Affairs, Trinidad

Marine Plants of the Caribbean, Littler, Littler, Bucher & Norris
Smithsonian Institution Press, Washington D.C.

Ecological Studies in Tropical Fish, R. H. Lowe McDonnell
Communities, Cambridge University Press

The Life of Fishes, N.B. Marshall
Weidenfield and Nicolson, London

Shadows in the Sea, Harold W. McCormick & Tom Allen
Weathervane Books, New York

Marine Biology, James W. Nybakken
Harper Collins

Encyclopaedia of Recreational Diving, PADI

Caribbean Reef Fishes, John E. Randall
TFH Publications, New York

Guide to Marine Life, Marty Snyderman & Clay Wiseman
Caribbean-Bahamas-Florida
Aqua Quest Publications, New York

Reef: A Safari Through the Coral World, Jeremy Stafford-Deitsch
Headline Book Publishing Plc, London

Watching Fishes - Life and Behaviour on Coral Reefs,
Roberta Wilson and James Q. Wilson
Harper & Row, Publishers, New York

Corals of the World, Dr. E. Wood
TFH, Reigate, UK.

Coral Reefs of the World, Volume 1 Atlantic and East Pacific
UNEP and IUCN, Cambridge, UK.

* See following Recommended Reading section.

For the purpose of identifying the life you will see on the reef, the Humann identification guides are excellent. For information about habitat and behaviour in addition to identification, the Kaplan guides are very good but the quality and volume of colour photography is not as high as in the Humann books. Some of the research data quoted is a little out of date and the Guide to Marine Life by Marty Snyderman and Clay Wiseman provides lots of material of this type supplemented by excellent photography.

Watching Fishes is a fascinating and easy read if you would like to understand 'why?' as well as 'what?'. It is sensibly organised into pertinent sections such as feeding behaviour, reproduction etc., answering so many questions about the life of a reef fish.

Index

Page numbers in **bold** indicate sidebars.

Algae, **41**, 97, 174, 388
Anemones, 106, 270
Angelfish, 21
Antipatharian,, 173, 388
Banded coral shrimp, 271
Banking reef, 345
Basket star, 50
Black coral, 171, **173**
Black durgons, 196, 303
Black tip shark, 220
Bleached Coral, **309**
Brain coral, 246
Branching anemones, 270
Cherubfish, 176
Christmas tree worms, **56**
Cleaning stations, 272
Cleaning Symbiosis, **271**
Cnidarians, 63
Conch, 19, 22
Condominium tunicates, 319
Coral, 19, **144**, 171, 173, 246, **247**, **309**, 388
Corallimorph, 62
Corkscrew anemones, 270
Creole wrasse, 140
Crinoids, 104, **105**, 143, 190, 363
Cushion sea star, 278, 279
Damselfish, 242, 374
DCS, **351**
Decompression sickness (DCS), **351**
Decorator crab, 191
Devil's sea whips, 54
Diurnal, 190, 388
Echinoderms, **105**, 143, 278, 388

Eel, 90, 324, **325**
Feather duster worms, **56**
Feather stars, 143
Fireworms, 24, 54
Flamingo tongues, 321
Fringing reef, 345, **346**
Frogfish, 40, **49**, 57, 59
Garden eels, **325**
Giant anemone, 270
Goldentail morays, **325**
Gorgonians, 19, 388
Green moray, 324, **325**
Green turtles, **358**
Grouper, 302, 318
Grunts, 195
Hawksbill turtles, **358**
Jellyfish, 23
Lateral line, 52
Lizardfish, 205
Lobster, 22, 162, 178
Loggerhead, **358**
Manta Rays, 298, **300**
Moray, **325**
Night, **190**, 191
Nocturnal, **190**, 389
Nurse shark, **220**
Ocean triggerfish, 228
Octocoral, 19, 389
Octopus,, 132, **133**
Parrotfish, **88**, 225, 313
Porcupinefish, **138**, 176, 371
Pufferfish, **138**, 176, 371
Ray, 22, 298, **300**, 372
Recompression chamber, 350, **351**
Red algae, **41**

Red banded lobster, 178
Reef shark, 220
Reef, 345, **346**
Sargassum algae, 97
Schooling, **195**
Sea cucumber, **105**
Sea lilies, 143
Sea pearls, 174
Sea star, **105**, 278
Seahorses, 192
Sergeant majors, 135, 303
Sharks, 22, 192, 219, **220**
Snake eels, 90, **325**
Spiny lobsters, 178
Sponges, 20, **21**, 166, 363
Spotted moray, **325**
Star coral, 246
Stingray, 372
Stony coral, 246
Tarpon, 299, 308
Terminal phase, 225
Triggerfish, 196, 228, 303
Trumpetfish, **242**
Trunkfish, 245
Tube worms, **56**
Tunicate, 170, 222, 319
Turtles, 20, **358**
Urchin, **105**
Worms, 23, 54, **56**
Wreck, 51, 90, **91**, 191, 192, 204, 214, 221, 264, 265, 267, 275, **276**, 348, 359, 365, 370
Zoanthids, 106
Zooxanthellae, **41**, 144, **309**, 389